The New American Reality

The New American Reality

Who We Are,
How We Got Here,
Where We Are Going

Reynolds Farley

Russell Sage Foundation
New York

The Russell Sage Foundation

Library of Congress Cataloging-in-Publication Data

Farley, Reynolds, 1938–
    The new American reality : who we are, how we got here, where we are going /
Reynolds Farley.
        p.   cm.
    Includes bibliographical references and index.
    ISBN 0-87154-237-4 (cloth : alk. paper)
    1. United States—Social conditions—1945– 2. United States—Economic conditions—1945– 3. Social indicators—United States. 4. Economic indicators—United States. 5. Social change—United States. 6. Family demography—United States. 7. United States—Census. I. Title.
    HN58.F37   1996
    306'.0973—dc20   96-20404
                                                                                    CIP

Text design by Gene Crofts.

RUSSELL SAGE FOUNDATION
112 East 64th Street, New York, New York 10021
10 9 8 7 6 5 4 3 2

To Gail

For more than three decades of animated support and encouragement, and for lots of patience

Contents

Acknowledgments   ix

Chapter 1   America in Flux: New Evidence About
Our Changing Society   1

Chapter 2   The 1960s: A Turning Point in How We
View Race, Gender, and Sexuality   22

Chapter 3   The 1970s: A Turning Point in the
Nation's Economy and Whom It Rewards   64

Chapter 4   Changes in American Families   108

Chapter 5   New Americans   151

Chapter 6   Racial Issues Thirty Years After the
Civil Rights Decade   208

Chapter 7   Americans on the Move: New Patterns
of Internal Migration   272

Chapter 8   The Evidence About America in
Decline and the Challenges of the 1990s   334

References   357
Index   371

Acknowledgments

For almost a half century, the Russell Sage Foundation has encouraged research on change in the United States, based on information from decennial censuses. Over the past decade or so, they have published seventeen volumes on the census of 1980 and the two-volume *State of the Union: America in the 1990s,* which I edited, on the 1990 census, with more to come.

In working with the eighteen authors of *State of the Union,* it became apparent that two overarching trends have produced a new and different United States. First, because of shifts in family structure involving delayed marriage, more divorce, more childbearing by unmarried women, and more cohabitation, adults spend fewer years as spouses, and children spend less time living with both parents. Second, economic trends since 1973 have greatly benefited persons with technological training and specialized skills but have led to stagnant or declining wages for much of the labor force. Hence, we are in an era of economic polarization.

The 1990 census pointed out several other pervasive trends. Linked to structural shifts in family life and the economy are far-reaching changes in how women spend their adult lives—fewer years married but many more years employed. For the first time, the census reports a diminution of the gender gap in earnings as women increasingly invest in education and obtain more rewarding jobs. The census also describes a fundamental demographic trend unpredicted just a couple of decades ago: a rapid shift in the country's racial composition, attributable to new immigration laws and economic shifts. The latter two forces have encouraged rapid growth among Hispanic and Asian populations, while the white and African American groups continue their slow growth. A related and less positive trend has been the persistent black-white gap, as measured by almost all key indicators. Differences in unemployment, earnings, poverty rates, and college enrollment were as large in the early 1990s as twenty years earlier. Finally, internal migration continues to transfer political power and economic advantage from the Midwest and Northeast to the Gulf Coast states, areas in the Southwest, and the Pacific rim. Within metropolitan areas, the long-run shift of population from older central cities into outlying suburbs continues, with the 1980s being unique in the suburbanization of blacks and the emergence of edge cities.

This work was largely accomplished while I was a visiting scholar at the Russell Sage Foundation. I thank Eric Wanner for strongly encouraging me to summarize what the 1990 census told us about social, economic, and demographic change, thereby maintaining the tradition started by Conrad and Irene Taueber with their comprehensive summaries of the 1950 and 1960 censuses. I also appreciate Eric Wanner's prodding me to think—and then write—about whether this is really a nation in decline, as many authors have recently argued. I conclude that this nation is not in decline but rather is one undergoing rapid social and economic change, changes that benefit many but leave others farther behind. The most important policy questions for the 1990s follow clearly from these trends as illuminated by the census.

Many of the arguments in this book—and some of the figures—are borrowed from the authors who wrote chapters for *State of the Union*. I thank them since their ideas and work are the base from which this project has grown. Numerous colleagues read and commented extensively upon chapters, including William Butz, Nancy Casey, Sheldon Danziger, Peter Gottschalk, and Frank Levy. While at the Russell Sage Foundation, Daphne Spain and Suzanne Bianchi were finishing their book about the changing status of women, *Balancing Act: Motherhood, Marriage, and Employment Among American Women* (RSF 1996), and I appreciate their insights and assistance. My colleagues at the University of Michigan's Population Studies Center, as well as the center's excellent facilities, aided this project. Accessing data from the Public Use Microdata Samples of the decennial censuses and the Current Population Survey was made easy by the Explore and Extract programs developed by Albert Anderson. Lisa Neidert, the director of data archives, often assisted in obtaining and making available the requisite data. I am especially indebted to Judy Mullin—who prepared many drafts of the manuscript and carefully produced the figures, tables, and maps—for her encouragement, especially when I thought the work would never be completed.

Reynolds Farley

Chapter 1

America in Flux: New Evidence About Our Changing Society

Bad news travels faster than good news. It gets repeated more often. For fifteen years, an increasingly popular theme for those who write about current trends is that America is in decline, perhaps in rapid decline. Every year, one or two books receive great attention for a new or variant interpretation describing how social and economic trends are weakening this country.

Censuses are cameras that capture and freeze-frame a history. They were used primarily to calculate how many men could be mobilized for war or how much property a new king might tax. The counting of the Israelites that Moses decreed the second year after the Exodus from Egypt gives us the *Book of Numbers*, and the gospel of Luke informs us that Christ was born in Bethlehem because of Caesar Augustus' decree that all persons be taxed in their home cities. The United States is different. With great ingenuity, the framers of our Constitution decided that population size would determine democratic representation in the United States: Article I mandates that Congress carry out an enumeration every ten years. Thus, we are the only nation in the world with a history of twenty-one consecutive censuses.

The censuses provide us with the basic data we need for our system of representative democracy. But since the early 1800s they have been much more than mere head counts, thanks to Thomas Jefferson's suggestion that censuses be used to gauge the state of our union. They are the primary sources of information about ourselves, our jobs and earnings, our prosperity or poverty, where we live and with whom, what kinds of homes we own or apartments we rent, our skin color, the languages we speak, and our ethnic roots. They reveal social and economic trends in a uniquely rich and detailed manner. The 1990 census and many surveys conducted more recently tell us how people are now adapting—some with great success and others not well at all—to the massive social and economic trends that will make the

1

United States in 2000 extremely different from what it was in generations past. And by informing us about where we as a nation are today and how we got here, censuses supply the crucial information we need if we are to continue our efforts to reduce poverty, to increase the productivity of our work force, to eradicate crime, and to provide equal opportunities for women, for African Americans, and for the Native Americans who were here long before Leif Eriksson, Christopher Columbus, Henry Hudson, and Giovanni Verrazano sailed west from Europe.

Just a little more than a generation ago, in the 1950s, a young white man with a high school education, a strong back, and a dedication to hard work could likely find a good blue-collar job with a prosperous manufacturing firm, a job with comprehensive fringe benefits, including health insurance and a pension program. He knew that if he came to work regularly and pleased his boss, his wages would rise year after year. He most likely had a union to protect his interests, a union strong enough to shut down his plant if wage increases were meager. He could afford to marry while he was in his early twenties and could buy a starter home in the suburbs before he reached thirty. Although some women in the high school graduating classes of the 1950s attended college, most did not. Rather, they married before they were old enough to vote or drink liquor. Divorces occurred, but they were rare, and women expected that their husbands would remain with them and support them while they stayed at home taking care of the three or even four children they had while they were still in their twenties. Many white women held jobs in that brief interval between the completion of school and marriage, but few did so when they were caring for young children. It was unusual for couples to live together before their weddings, and childbearing by single white women was very rare. Some women did get pregnant while single, but most of them married quickly because childbearing by single women was unacceptable, and men knew that if they impregnated a woman, they would be obligated to marry her. Women had few occupational choices, so one aspiring to serve in Congress, become a military officer, a corporate executive, or an advocate for equal rights for women was an oddity.

It is a very different nation in the 1990s. A young man graduating from high school with a dedication to work and a strong back may find an attractive job with good benefits, but the odds are not in his favor. If he is successful in locating work, the job will pay about 25 percent less—adjusted for inflation—than did a similar job twenty years ago, and seldom will there be an effective union demanding annual pay increases. A young woman might marry her high school sweetheart right after graduation but, if she does, she knows that their chances for a home in the suburbs and middle-class prosperity are slim unless both of them work full-time and at least one of them gets specialized training in college. Since more than one-half of recent marriages end in divorce, a realistic young married woman must plan for the possibility that, by her thirties, she will be heading her own family with a child or two.

Young people have adjusted to these pervasive changes. They now stay in school longer, improving their chances for employment, and typically they delay their marriages until they are much older. And a growing proportion apparently will not marry at all. Compared to their peers of a generation ago, young people are having few children. Other changes provide young people with possibilities unknown— almost unthought of—four decades ago. Much progress has been made in expanding opportunities for women. As recently as the 1970s, just a handful of women earned advanced degrees in medicine, law, and business administration. Now, thousands do every year, and not just the top-ranking professions are undergoing this shift. Women are now pursuing many occupations; for example, as telephone linemen, bartenders, or police officers. Many of the barriers facing blacks also have been lowered or eliminated, producing substantial increases in black political power and a modestly growing African American middle class.

New Social Values

During the last third of the twentieth century, our population participated in major changes in social values dating from the 1960s and dramatic economic shifts dating from the 1970s. Why have these changes occurred? Will these trends continue or will there be a shift back to the lifestyles of the post–World War II era? Let's consider the social values first. Three long-term trends culminated in major turning points in the 1960s. First, there was the civil rights revolution. Although many organizations, such as the National Association for the Advancement of Colored People (NAACP), sued for equal opportunities for blacks, the system of racial segregation that evolved from slavery and was ratified by federal courts in the late nineteenth century continued to thrive after World War II. We defended our democracy

and defeated both German and Japanese dictators with strictly segregated, or Jim Crow, armed forces. During and after that war, blacks
migrated to the North where there were no *official* segregation laws
but where there were neighborhood, school, and job segregation patterns akin to those of the South. Jim Crow had moved North just as
rapidly as did African Americans.

This was challenged after World War II. Dr. Martin Luther King
Jr. led an effective movement, capped by the historic March on Wash-
ington in August 1963. The next year, Congress enacted and President
Johnson signed one of the most important laws of this century: the
Civil Rights Act of 1964. Twelve months later, after bloody marches
in Selma, Alabama, caused three deaths, Congress passed the Voting
Rights Act—a law that finally made the Fifteenth Amendment opera-
tive in all fifty states. Following the murder of Dr. King in April 1968,
Congress approved the third major civil rights act of that decade—the
Fair Housing Law, banning racial discrimination in the sale or rental
of housing. White Americans who had accepted a system of racial
stratification based on white dominance and black subordination came
to endorse principles of racial equity and nondiscrimination.

Blacks and whites have not achieved equality of status nor has racial
discrimination disappeared. However, there is no longer social support
for those blatant practices of racial discrimination that kept our sports
teams all white, that kept blacks home on election day, that steered black
women to domestic service and black men to manual labor, and that
kept Rosa Parks in the back of the bus until that fateful December 1,
1955. By 1995, forty African-Americans served in Congress, four were
selected by President Clinton for his cabinet, two have served on the
Supreme Court, and one was appointed the nation's highest military officer. While blacks still have extremely high poverty and unemployment
rates compared to whites, opportunities for recent generations are much
improved and, in all major metropolises, there are now moderate-to-
large middle-class black communities.

The second long-term trend concerns society's views about careers
for women. The employment of mothers has changed dramatically
since the 1960s. When urban jobs replaced farming and when industrial work became the standard for men, our society reached a consensus that the welfare of children was best served if mothers maintained
the home and raised the family while men worked outside the home
for pay. A woman might work before marriage or even before the birth
of her first child, but most employers fired women when they married
or became mothers. No federal law prevented such practices but, more
importantly, few women—or men—challenged this pervasive and

widely enforced norm. Women who invested in higher educations benefited, not so much because their own earnings were great, but rather because they married college-educated men with high earnings. This changed. Women born in the baby boom breached those traditions: they continued their schooling and then began their careers, careers that increasingly resembled those of their brothers and fathers. Betty Friedan, in *The Feminine Mystique* (1963), challenged the traditional values that stressed that men should achieve in their occupational careers while women, even highly educated women, contentedly raised their children, aided their husband's careers, and maintained their homes. And then, in a surprising development, women in the House of Representatives successfully amended Title VII of the Civil Rights Act of 1964 to ban discrimination on the basis of either race or *gender* in the labor market. In important ways, the 1960s were the years when doors began to open, eventually permitting women to pursue occupational achievements in much the same way as men did. Now women benefit more directly from their investments in advanced education.

The third major change in social values dating from the 1960s is the sexual revolution. No accurate survey tells us what sexual practices had been in the past, so it is difficult to measure the extent of the changes. Perhaps the sexual revolution is an overstatement, but there have been great symbolic changes. Historically, many state laws sought to limit sexual activity to married heterosexual adults. Many of these were removed from the law books in the 1960s or 1970s. Sexual practices among consenting adults became a private matter much less subject to state regulation. But changes in laws are not necessarily changes in practices. Attitude studies suggest that there has been no large-scale shift toward approval of either extramarital sex or homosexuality. Current surveys of adults find overwhelming condemnation of such sexual activity. So we did not, in fact, shift from Victorian sexual mores to an era of "free love," as one might have inferred from the Woodstock celebration in 1969.

There have been, however, two areas of major change: premarital sex and divorce. Presumably most of those who married in the years after World War II had sex only after marriage or shortly before. This is much less likely today. The age at marriage has risen, and old laws prohibiting birth control were overturned. In the 1960s oral contraceptives and intrauterine devices gave women more effective control over when they could get pregnant and how often. Many young people are now sexually active long before they marry, often involving several partners. There was basically one template for young people graduating from school in the late 1940s or 1950: marry, settle down with the husband as the earner and the wife as the homemaker, and then raise a family, a large family by today's standards. Now young people have many options. A few still marry early, but increasingly they postpone marriage until their late twenties and then both partners work full-time. In the 1980s, cohabitation—although still not common—occurred frequently as a precursor to marriage: it may, in the 1990s, become something of a substitute for marriage.

Consider, too, how values have changed about our personal freedoms regarding living arrangements. Most parents in the 1940s or 1950s would have been upset to find their daughter living with a man as she completed her education or began her career. Now, such living arrangements are widely accepted, though many parents still object. Undoubtedly, in the past, many school boards would have fired a teacher found to be living with an unmarried partner of the opposite sex or known to be in a homosexual living arrangement. Such teachers would probably not be fired today. Indeed, in most circumstances it is not only inappropriate to ask about an employee's personal life style, it is illegal.

While we really do not know for sure how much sexual practices have changed, we know a great deal about long-term trends in the divorce rate. Divorce was rare among couples marrying in the last century, but it has increased steadily since the early decades of this one. Then, between the 1960s and the 1970s, the divorce rate took a one-time quantum jump and remains at an elevated level to this day. Perhaps there are more "bad marriages" or inappropriate partners now than there used to be, but this seems unlikely. Certainly, people are not "rushing" into early marriages the way they did some years ago. More likely, society's views and norms about the importance of personal fulfillment have changed, offering married couples more options when they are unhappy with their unions. Divorce is a more attractive, feasible, and approved alternative than it was in the post–World War II era, even when children are involved. Consequently, only a minority of children will live with both their parents until they graduate from high school. Most will spend some time with just one parent.

Changes in our Economy

The story of the last few decades would be extremely interesting if the only changes in our values had been about racial discrimination, the appropriateness of mothers working and women pursuing careers, and personal sexuality. But there is more. The 1960s were years of social change; the 1970s were years of economic change. In 1973, finance ministers of the oil-producing countries curtailed the export of their product to the West, greatly increasing prices. Shocked Americans watched the cost of their gasoline soar from less than 30 cents a gallon to a dollar and a quarter. This dramatic and totally unexpected jump in energy costs demarcates two extremely different economic eras.

From the start of the buildup of the nation's defense industry for World War II until the early 1970s, our economy prospered. American manufacturers dominated world markets; economic growth was steady, consistent, and prolonged; rates of inflation were low; interest rates were moderate; and, for the most part, unemployment was low. The result was the burgeoning growth of the modern American middle class. During the Depression era and for decades before, our nation's population was overwhelmingly working class or poor. In 1940 just 12 percent of the nation's population lived in households with incomes more than twice the poverty line. But consistent increases in the wages of men from the 1940s through the 1970s brought a majority of whites, for the first time, into the middle economic classes. By the early 1970s more than 70 percent lived in households with incomes at least twice the poverty line. These economic gains allowed men to marry early and support rather large families on the basis of their own earnings.

Two additional changes expanded the middle class both symbolically and economically. The nation invaded and conquered a crabgrass frontier after World War II. With the help of government loans, millions of lower- and moderate-income families could buy attractive suburban homes—so long as they were white. And the occupational structure shifted first from agricultural to blue collar, and then gradually to white collar. An important component of this process was the ability of our economy to shift millions of unskilled or moderately skilled workers from the agricultural sector to higher paying jobs in manufacturing industries, construction, and transportation.

Economic trends since 1973 are very different and certainly not all bleak. There has been a rise in income and, by almost all indicators, we are now a more prosperous and richer nation working at better jobs. But these new trends differ fundamentally from those of the earlier era. There have been major shifts in who does very well and who just hangs on, and the gap between those at the top and those at the bottom of the economic ladder is much bigger. We have had several recessions and during one of them—that of 1981–82—

the unemployment rate reached a post-Depression peak. Interest rates climbed so high in the late 1970s that new home building and factory construction virtually came to a halt. Foreign producers invaded domestic markets, and our trade balance with the rest of the world, which had been strongly positive, became negative as we bought Japanese cars rather than cars built in Flint or Detroit.

The 1980s saw a thorough restructuring of manufacturing. Inefficient plants were closed, production was shifted to low-wage areas of the United States or abroad, and manufacturing processes were redesigned, eliminating many blue-collar and supervisory jobs. Simultaneously, consumer spending shifted from manufactured goods toward services. A dramatic example of this is the rising share of national income devoted to health care services: in 1960, 8 percent of personal expenditures went to health care; by 1995, they consumed 15 percent. The outcome has been fewer employment opportunities and lower wages for men with less than college educations, somewhat improved employment opportunities and wages for women at most educational levels, no growth of the middle class, and—by almost all economic markers—a widening of the gap between the have's and have not's.

America in Decline

Bad news travels faster than good news and gets repeated more often. For fifteen years an increasingly popular theme for those who write about current trends is that America is in decline, perhaps in rapid decline. Every year one or two books receive great attention for a new or variant interpretation describing how social and economic trends are weakening this country. Authors disagree about what forces are driving the trends or what should be done to correct the problems, but there seems to be a consensus that something is quite wrong now, something that was not so wrong thirty years ago. It is extremely important to get the story correct if we are to understand what has been happening, what is likely to occur in the future, and what we might do to produce favorable outcomes. The census, and similar studies of our population, provide us with the information we require.

Let's review the major themes that come up frequently in the "America in decline" arguments. First, there is the idea that the economy is failing to provide the jobs that sustain the middle class, and that no simple changes will get the economy back on track. Barry Bluestone and Bennett Harrison were among the first to write in this vein in *The Deindustrialization of America,* published in 1982. Using data from the late 1970s and early 1980s, they argued that this nation was losing the good blue-collar jobs that kept the middle classes economically solvent. In dozens of tables and vivid descriptions, they pointed out that manufacturing plants had been closed and jobs eliminated, producing economic havoc for men who had worked diligently for years and for the wives and children they supported. Bluestone and Harrison noted that long-term economic trends, such as emphasis on greater labor productivity, were producing these changes, but they stressed that political and entrepreneurial decisions of the early 1980s hastened this process. Indeed, they laid much of the blame for America's decline on tax policies that allowed owners to close plants or shift production outside the country without providing severance pay or other benefits to their long-term employees who found themselves unemployed. In Bluestone and Harrison's view, policies of the 1980s encouraged rapacious Wall Street speculators to use innovative financial procedures to buy profitable manufacturing firms, loot their net worth, and then let them go out of business, resulting in great gains for speculators, investors, and their lawyers, but unemployment for blue-collar workers.

Six years later, the same authors returned to this subject with a new interpretation in *The Great U-Turn* (1988). They reemphasized many of their earlier themes: the disappearance of many good jobs and the federal government's policies in the 1980s that encouraged modern capitalists to make great profits through paper transactions by buying out firms and then liquidating them. However, their second book was published at the end of the decade, so they had to explain the sustained growth of employment in that decade, a growth of jobs that distinguished the United States from Western European nations where job growth lagged and unemployment soared. They stressed two themes: first, that while numerous jobs were created, many of them were "bad" jobs, paying much less than the desirable manufacturing jobs that disappeared; and second, that as a result of this labor market trend, economic polarization was occurring. The United States, they argued, was dividing into two classes: a prosperous elite and a growing population of employed persons whose modest and uncertain earnings left them just above the poverty line. As they put it, the economic trends of the 1980s produced a great hollowing out of the middle class. A variety of causes were cited, the most important being the economic policies of the Reagan administration.

An updated version of this economic polarization thesis appears in *America: What Went Wrong,* by Donald Bartlett and James Steele (1992). In a colorful and dramatic manner, they argue that the economic policies of the 1980s channeled great wealth to the economic elite while dismantling the middle class. Chapter after chapter reports the story of ambitious and unscrupulous corporate raiders, accompanied by their legions of affluent lawyers, accountants, and financial consultants who acquired prosperous manufacturing firms using leveraged buyouts, junk bonds, and other innovative strategies. Once in control, these raiders restructured the firms' employment and used up their financial reserves. The result was fewer jobs and smaller paychecks for those who remained on the payroll, along with cuts in pensions or health benefits for former employees.

Although the approach and style are entirely different, an equally pessimistic view of recent economic trends was presented by Paul Krugman in his widely read *The Age of Diminished Expectations: U.S. Economic Policy in the 1990s* (1994). Rather than solely blaming greedy capitalists or short-sighted Washington politicians, he stressed long-term changes that made the economy perform differently in the 1980s, including the drive for greater labor productivity, the slow improvement in the quality of the labor force, and the rise of effective international competition. In his view, no single culprit explained the declining performance of our economy, although the deficit spending of the Reagan era hastened the shift from a steady economic growth that provided benefits to many Americans to an economic growth that benefited a smaller share, primarily those toward the top of the income and educational distributions. Pessimistically, Krugman tells us that most proposed changes, such as cutting the trade deficit or reducing unemployment to a low level, will not have the beneficial effects we anticipate. Our hopes for the future should be modest: we live in a time when diminished expectations are realistic.

An even gloomier perspective is offered by Benjamin Friedman (1988) in *Day of Reckoning: The Consequences of American Economic Policy.* The lackluster economic performance of the last fifteen years, in his judgment, results directly from the deficit spending of the Reagan years, spending that created such a tremendous burden that it stunts economic growth now and into the future. It also, he speculates, leads to unfortunate shifts in our social values since individuals seek to maximize their own short-run economic interests instead of considering the well-being of the entire society. Until we make drastic changes, such as greatly reduced government spending or much higher taxes to pay off the huge debts incurred in the 1980s, our economy seems destined to lurch along in a manner quite unlike the sustained growth of the post–World War II era.

Economists in the 1990s continue to offer new perspectives about how present trends are less favorable than those of the past. Robert Frank and Philip Cook (1995) argue that labor markets are now operating differently, perhaps because of a worldwide demand for the most highly skilled talents. They believe we have entered a "winner take all" society in which the most successful end up with great incomes separating them from the many who tried but lost. Jeffery Madrick presents a pessimistic view in *The End of Affluence: The Causes and Consequences of America's Economic Decline* (1995). From the late nineteenth century through the early 1970s, he observes, the American economy grew at an average rate of above 3 percent annually, despite the Great Depression of the 1930s. But the highly favorable domestic and international conditions that produced such steady and rapid economic growth have disappeared. Thus we have, and will continue to have, an economy that grows at a rate closer to 2 percent annually, meaning that fewer will enter the middle class or remain there.

A second theme is that America's political system is no longer capable of solving the nation's problems, hence, America is in decline. Kevin Phillips (1990, 1993) argues that the Republican Party had a golden opportunity to solidify its base because the traditional coalition supporting the Democratic Party fell apart during President Johnson's term. Democrats once capitalized upon the common interests of blue-collar unionized workers; white ethnic groups, many of whom lived in central cities; and racial minorities who fought for civil rights. But this coalition did not survive the 1960s since union strength declined with the upgrading of occupations and since ethnic identity waned as whites moved to the suburbs, intermarried with other ethnicities, and thereby lost their ethnic roots. Controversies over rights for African Americans, particularly busing for school integration, affirmative action in employment, and crackdowns on discrimination in the housing market, made the Democratic Party unattractive to much of the white middle class. For the Republicans to become the dominant party, they needed to expand their base of support to include the middle class—an effort that President Nixon earnestly pursued early in his ill-fated administration. His resignation and macroeconomic trends beyond his control brought this Republican effort to an end.

In the 1980s the Republicans had another golden opportunity but, in Phillips's view, they were again unsuccessful in capturing the alle-

giance of the middle class. Why? Primarily because the economic policies of the 1980s simultaneously produced "billionaires" and the
"homeless." Phillips's books stress the decline of the middle class in
the 1980s, while the upper and lower tails of the income distribution
grew rapidly. The result, he suggests, was not only an uncertain future
for the Republican Party but the disappearance of optimism from our
society. These changes, he contends, gave the nation a dour mood,
maybe even a mean-spirited one, since there seems to be no feasible
strategy to bring back the steady economic growth that created and
sustained the middle class.

This theme is reiterated from a different perspective by Thomas
Edsall (1984) in his *The New Politics of Inequality*. The declining
strength of unions, the breakup of the once formidable coalition of
ethnic whites and racial minorities supporting the Democratic Party,
and rapid growth at the top end of the income distribution imply that
political as well as economic power is increasingly concentrated in the
hands of an economic elite. The power of the working class and the
lower middle class to protect their own interests in the political arena
waned in the 1980s, thereby transferring great political clout to the
economic elite.

Stanley Greenberg (1995), President Clinton's pollster in the 1992
campaign, offers a similar but updated interpretation of events in *Middle Class Dreams: The Politics and Power of the New American Majority*.
Once-stable, middle-class Americans now feel threatened by new economic trends, but find no solutions in the policies of either party. The
Democrats are widely seen as taxing the middle class to provide welfare checks to blacks and "the undeserving poor," while Republican
policies seem to benefit the rich at the expense of the middle class. In
his view, both major parties have "crashed" because they cannot get
the economy back to the type of growth we had for twenty-five years
after World War II. The future appears bleak for them but offers an
opening for third-party candidates who effectively stress that they are
neither Republicans or Democrats.

A third theme in the America in decline literature describes the
personal ennui of many middle-class Americans and those aspiring to
middle-class status. Katherine Newman used the perspectives and
tools of an anthropologist to enumerate some important changes. In
her first book, *Falling from Grace: The Experience of Downward Mobility in the American Middle Class* (1988), she reported that many young
couples who started their adult careers solidly in the middle classes
in the 1970s unexpectedly found themselves slipping lower as they

got older. Men who began as white-collar managers discovered by their late thirties or forties that they lacked the advanced skills or technological training needed to move into the high-paying jobs they anticipated. Firms urged them to leave by making it clear that they had no future there or just fired them. Other highly successful white-collar managers found out that corporate restructuring and leveraged buyouts meant that the firms where they worked for fifteen or twenty years were to be closed or moved to utilize the cheap labor found in the Caribbean or Asia. But these men entered a job market cluttered with other men having similar skills and experiences, so their re-employment prospects were poor.

No longer could these families make the payments on their attractive suburban homes, keep a couple of cars in the driveway, or provide their children with private schools, dance lessons, and all the other benefits they once thought came with hard work in our economy. These white-collar managers lost their jobs, and aspiring younger workers failed to find good first jobs in an era where there was an increasing emphasis upon personal achievement and personal performance. It was, Newman contended, an age stressing meritocratic individualism: the diligent and competent get ahead; the weak, ignorant, and lazy fall behind. Corporate employment practices were seen as equitable since firms handsomely rewarded the most productive but laid off those who could not achieve. If someone fell out of the middle class, society emphasized that the individual could only blame himself. It wasn't like the Depression when the unemployment rate went up to almost 25 percent. Then, a man could blame structural troubles with the economy and government mismanagement for his woes since many of his friends were unemployed. In the 1980s, if he—or she— were out of a job or earned little, it was because of those equitable labor market processes that rewarded the able but not the marginally competent. The ideology of the 1980s did not call for radical change. Exactly the opposite. In Newman's view, it strongly upheld the processes producing economic polarization.

In her subsequent book, *Declining Fortunes: The Withering of the American Dream,* Newman (1993), presented more evidence about America in decline. Persons entering the labor force in the 1980s, she argued, were unique in the country's history since they were the first birth cohorts who would live their lives with a lower standard of living than their parents. Raised in families that prospered throughout the post–World War II economic expansion, baby boomers expected to find a good job if they got some postsecondary education. They thought they would be able to marry at about the same age as their parents and, just as their parents had done, buy a home in the suburbs while they were still in their twenties and keep two cars in the garage. And—very importantly—they believed that an investment in a college education, guaranteed a solid middle-class life style.

Economic restructuring in the 1980s, she argues, was a mean wakeup call for baby boomers. Their hopes were challenged and, in many cases, dashed. The choice of jobs was limited, the pay levels more modest than anticipated, and uncertainty about occupational progress great. The baby boomers made important adjustments. Since good jobs were hard to find, age at marriage rapidly advanced and, for some, cohabitation became the substitute. Then they found that they could not afford to buy a home. A surprisingly large number of young middle-class adults became "boomerang" children, returning to live in their parental homes in their late twenties or even thirties. Eventually, however, most of the baby boomers married. Once again they had to make a radical adjustment, one that distinguished them from their parents' generation. Whether or not they had children, both the husband and wife had to work full-time if they wanted to maintain a middle-class life style. For those who started families, intergenerational conflict was on the horizon. With both parents employed, even young children from middle-class families had to be in childcare programs. This was costly, greatly reducing the net income from the wife's full-time job. Moreover, the parents of the baby boomers, strongly believing that young children benefited from staying home with their mothers, questioned and criticized the childrearing practices of their daughters and daughters-in-law. But there was no alternative for the baby boomers if they wanted to hang onto middle-class status, so our norms evolved into approval of full-time employment for mothers and full-time care outside the home for even the youngest children.

Since both husbands and wives have to spend much more time at work, there is less time left for taking care of the family, the home, or for leisure. Juliet Schor (1991) describes this perspective about "America in decline" in *The Overworked American: The Unexpected Decline of Leisure*. She observes that for the last twenty years, the average amount of time spent on the job by Americans increased by about one day annually. Why did this occur? The culprit is the capitalist process of keeping wages as low as possible, something that occurred with gusto in the 1970s and 1980s as unions lost their clout and governmental regulations and federal court rulings sided more with employers than with workers. As wages stagnated and then declined, Americans had to select one of two choices: accept lower standards of living or increase the amount of time spent in the office or in the shop. For the most part, Americans chose more work. Producers and their advertisers encourage us to consume more, so our expectations go up as we look for bigger homes, additional appliances, recreational vehicles, VCRs, and, more recently, expensive personal computers. But maintaining or increasing a family's income comes at a great personal cost—the loss of the time men and women once spent with their families and the loss of leisure time.

This has important implications for families. Increasingly, husbands and wives work full-time, but the wife continues to do the majority of work maintaining the home and caring for children. And since time constraints produce strains in their own marriages, Arlie Hochschild (1989) links this factor to higher divorce rates. Similarly, children suffer because they have to spend more time alone or in paid childcare while their parents are on the job. After work, the parents lack the time and energy to devote much attention to their children. Presumably this leads to a "parenting deficit," one that Schor links to the rise of social problems among the nation's youth. As Harriet Presser (1989) observes, we now live in an era when middle-class parents no longer have time for their children. The demands of the workplace outweigh the interests of children.

Barbara Ehrenreich (1989) focuses her attention upon the psychological state of middle-class professionals in *Fear of Falling: The Inner Life of the Middle Class*. The themes are familiar even though her arguments apply primarily to those toward the upper reaches of the income distribution. For two and one-half decades after World War II, men who obtained college degrees were pretty much assured prosperous lifestyles. An important gender change occurred in the mid- to late-1960s. Women began to pursue college educations, found occupational opportunities expanding, and started becoming successful middle-class professionals, often married to other middle-class professionals. The ensuing prosperity was accompanied by numerous psychological challenges and a severe shortage of time. However, the expanding economy went through a pervasive structural shift in the 1970s and 1980s. Economic inequality increased: some of the upper-middle-class individuals described by Ehrenreich prospered beyond their most extravagant expectations. But others' holds on middle-class status slipped away. Ehrenreich writes about persons whose investment in education produced doctorates, but who ended up driving taxis or teaching elementary English to immigrants. The prospect of such a plunge—albeit a remote one—was enough to frighten some of the professional middle class, making them uncertain about their status in a manner unknown just a couple of decades earlier.

Other commentators move beyond the economy, politics, and psychological issues to describe an America in decline. *The Bell Curve: Intelligence and Class Structure in American Life,* by Richard Herrnstein and Charles Murray (1994), strongly defends another explanation. Their massive, and often cautious, volume may be interpreted in several ways. They argue that there is a single dimension to human intelligence, that intelligence is genetically determined, and that it is not subject to much change during a person's lifetime. Good schools and specialized training, they suggest, cannot make up the inherited deficits suffered by a child born to parents of low intelligence, and the test scores of late teenagers and young adults that measure intelligence are highly predictive of success in life, including whether or not a woman is likely to bear children before marriage or a man engages in criminal activities. Perhaps the least controversial argument in this book is that our economy increasingly offers the best jobs and richest rewards to those who score highest on intellectual tests and provides few good jobs to those who score poorly.

Fertility patterns, Herrnstein and Murray believe, are destined to drive average intelligence levels lower since those toward the bottom of the intelligence distribution mate with each other and typically bear more children than those toward the top end. They cite evidence of increasing assortive mating by education, leading them to argue that intelligence will be even less equitably distributed in the future. Childbearing by those lacking intelligence, they contend, is encouraged by current welfare programs that provide cash benefits to poor women who become mothers. They strongly recommend a rethinking of all welfare spending—except for the elderly—since many of these programs are trying to improve the lot of those whose lack of intelligence dooms them in our increasingly sophisticated society.

Their most controversial assertions concern group differences in intelligence. Borrowing from the Social Darwinists and eugenicists, they contend that over the centuries distinctive breeding pools produced group differences in intellectual ability; that Eastern Asians—the Japanese and Chinese—are most intelligent; that Ashkenazi Jews from Europe rank higher than other whites; and that the intelligence of African Americans is quite far behind that of whites and Asians. The mean IQ of whites in the United States, they report, is approximately one hundred points; that of blacks, eighty points, a difference they attribute to genetics, not to our social history or to differences in the schools that blacks and whites attend. Since IQ strongly influences social and economic achievement, it is no surprise that Asians and Jews generally do well in the United States, while blacks lag far behind. This leads to their observation that well-intentioned programs to bring about more racial equity—especially affirmative action—will fail because the gaps are rooted in the genes. (For a thorough review and critical evaluation of the arguments of Herrnstein and Murray, see Fraser 1995; Heckman 1995.)

The 1980s were years of steady if modest economic expansion. Thus, it is surprising that the word "underclass" entered our vocabulary for the first time and became a popular term in that decade. Most "America in decline" books describe the unfavorable economic and psychological consequences of recent economic shifts for the middle class, be they the blue-collar workers of midwestern factory towns appearing in the pages of the Bluestone-Harrison books or the professionals living close to Central Park analyzed by Ehrenreich. Fewer authors described those at the bottom of the economic ladder until Ken Auletta (1982) focused attention upon those residents of New York City and Appalachia who seemed unable to enter the lowest ranks of the working class. This sparked a new "America in decline" literature, one that is distinctive for two themes. First is the emphasis upon the spatial concentration of poverty, since these investigators assert that there are now many neighborhoods in our largest cities characterized by very high rates of joblessness, extremely elevated levels of crime, the absence of stable two-parent families, and the lack of opportunities for upward mobility. Second is the consensus that minorities—especially blacks—are greatly overrepresented among the urban underclass.

Shortly after the new underclass was discovered and thoroughly described, analysts offered explanations for the disturbing trends that make many central-city neighborhoods impoverished and dangerous places. In the past, there were urban poor, but many of them were only temporarily impoverished as they developed their skills and found the blue-collar jobs needed to move into the working class or even into the middle class. Quite a few of these urban poor had been internal migrants from farms, who were making the transition to an industrial economy. This favorable process of upward mobility stopped in the 1970s. Charles Murray (1984) laid out one of the most popular and influential explanations in *Losing Ground: American Social Policy: 1950–1980*. He argued that the well-intentioned welfare programs of the War on Poverty, although designed to provide opportunities and lift the unskilled poor above the poverty line, had exactly the opposite effect. They trapped people in poverty. As soon as transfer payments from the state and federal agencies were increased and made more readily available, they became attractive alternatives to work. Instead of taking a job at the lowest occupational rung, but one that might eventually lead to a better and higher-paying position, the poor cashed government checks from expanded unemployment programs, from newly funded general assistance programs for the adult poor, from various job training programs, or from the new Supplemental Security Income (SSI) program if they claimed they were unable to work. Making it easier to obtain Aid to Families with Dependent Children (AFDC) and increasing the amounts of the payments were supposed to help poor mothers and their children, but, instead, they made it possible for women to live on their own and be at least as prosperous as if they had stayed with low-income husbands. Fathers with few job skills could desert their wives and children, knowing that their dependents would be as well or perhaps better off financially, because they received AFDC checks from the government every month. Rapidly enough, unmarried women with limited job skills learned that they, too, could benefit from this generous new welfare system. Realizing that their prospects were slim for marrying high-income men, they bore children on their own and got the state to support them, without working. Thus, in Murray's judgment, the key causal factor explaining the urban underclass was the expansion of transfer payments to the poor.

Lawrence Mead (1986, 1992) elaborated on this perspective by arguing that federal and state payments to the poor weaken and then destroy the incentive to work among those who have limited skills. Once the incentives to work were gone, individuals were unlikely ever to reignite their motivations. Mead assumes that many jobs are available, albeit low-paying positions involving hard work and dingy conditions—the jobs that high school dropouts once filled in great numbers. Some are dead-end positions, but many are not and lead to more secure blue-collar employment. At the very least, working at these jobs teaches a young man habits useful for getting better jobs. With generous welfare payments, today's unskilled workers have no incentives to take such jobs since the government—in his view—provides the attractive alternative of cash support without requiring work. In the long run, avoiding work is extremely costly to the poor, but in the short run, a government check looks more appealing than working for the minimum wage.

A very different explanation for the new urban underclass is offered by John Kasarda and William Julius Wilson. In a series of data-laden papers, Kasarda (1985, 1993, 1995) argues that there was a fundamental employment transformation between the 1960s and the 1980s. It went on throughout the United States, but it occurred most rapidly and dramatically in those older cities that boomed decades ago in the industrial age. The massive employment transformation in these places was not easily visible since total employment often increased and average wages went up, sometimes spectacularly, making economic conditions look quite favorable. What actually happened was that unskilled jobs for blue-collar workers disappeared as some manufacturing firms went out of business, others moved to the outer hinterlands or to the rural South, while still other firms modernized their production by getting rid of thousands of assembly-line workers. The disappearance of manufacturing meant the simultaneous disappearance of thousands of central-city jobs in trucking, warehouses, railroad yards, and construction. Employment rapidly increased for workers who had sophisticated technological skills in healthcare, who were white-collar managers, who could program, sell, or install computers, or who could thrive in the expanding financial services sector. Thus, employment in many cities rose and earnings increased, but by 1990 the mix of jobs was radically different than it had been three decades earlier. It was skewed toward the highly skilled since engineers and MBAs were in demand, while high school dropouts were not. The basic cause of the urban underclass, in Kasarda's view, was not President Johnson's War on Poverty nor a disappearance of the work ethic. Rather, it was the collapse of the job market for unskilled workers and the inability of the inner-city poor to master the skills needed for the new job market.

William Julius Wilson (1978, 1987) focused attention upon the black community of Chicago and provided a similar perspective about the urban underclass in *The Truly Disadvantaged: The Inner City, the Underclass, and Public Policy*. During World War II and for some decades thereafter, unskilled black men came from the rural South to Chicago where they quickly found jobs in factories, trucking firms, or the hundreds of small manufacturing firms located near the south- and westside ghettos. The expansion of American industry provided opportunities for these men to escape the poverty of the rural South and to earn enough money to marry and to rent housing. But between 1970 and the late 1980s these jobs disappeared. The talents needed to work on a Mississippi cotton plantation might be transferred to a Chicago factory, but factory workers did not have the skills to administer X-rays in a hospital, sell pension plans for a bank, or load software onto computers. Importantly, black men could no longer fulfill their obligations as husbands or fathers because they could not get good-paying jobs. This shift in male employment opportunities—much more than the expansion of welfare payments—caused the disruption of family life that is so commonly reported by those who describe the urban underclass. Conditions further deteriorated in underclass neighborhoods, Wilson argues, because the civil rights revolution of the 1960s allowed middle-income blacks to leave the ghetto for more attractive and prosperous neighborhoods, including some where their new neighbors were white. Thus, the concentration of the poor in urban ghettos became more extreme, allowing crime and social problems to fester.

Those describing the urban underclass are careful to stress that blacks are not uniquely prone to crime, family disruption, or unemployment. And blackness is definitely not a factor causing welfare use. Nevertheless, the casual reader of this literature is reminded again and again that a substantial fraction of the neighborhoods in many large cities are impoverished, violent, and troubled places with black residents.

Three ideas pervade this "America in decline" literature. First, economic and employment trends in the recent past are not similar to those of the post–World War II era. Second, that the current trends are very troubling. The middle class is insecure, psychologically and financially, and a surprisingly large number are slipping down rather than moving up. The middle class, as a proportion of total population, is not growing, but an urban underclass may be. Although not reviewed here, there is another robust stream in the "America in decline" literature describing the growth during the 1980s of people whose status is even inferior to that of the urban underclass: namely, the homeless (Burt 1992; Jencks 1994; Rossi 1989). Finally, these writers point out shifts in American families, including the delay of weddings by middle-class people, higher divorce rates, and high rates of childbearing by single underclass women.

Getting the Story Straight

The census of 1990 helps illuminate America's recent past. While there is much to be pessimistic about, the story is not exclusively or primarily bleak. For example, women now have a much wider array of occupational opportunities and higher earnings than ever before. There are jobs in the labor market for millions of women and immigrants. On the racial front, there have been some gains for blacks, and we are gradually assimilating large numbers of immigrants from Asia, Latin America, and Africa. Death rates continue to fall, so life spans are now longer than ever before. School enrollment rates continue to increase, albeit slowly, implying that the future workforce will be more highly trained. Despite considerable sputtering of the economy, at least one major segment of our population is now much better off than ever before—people age sixty-five and over.

Many of those who write about "America in decline" focus on economic trends. Economists pay great attention to indicators of productivity, monetary policy, and national indebtedness, but they do not tell us much about the advance in the age at marriage, the shift into female-headed households, the development of "edge cities," or immigration policy. Nor is much attention devoted to fundamental demographic processes—lower fertility, the aging of the population, and the new internal migration trends. Those who focus on changes in the family do not, for the most part, examine and document the stagnant and falling wage rates of men or the increasing earnings of women. To tell the story correctly, these different perspectives must be brought together. Whether your conclusion is optimistic or pessimistic depends on which indicators you emphasize, so there will always be lively debates about whether the glass is half-full or half-empty. Let me give a striking example. Median household income in the prosperous and full employment span from 1980 through 1993 went up a meager 1 percent, suggesting that it was a decade of stagnation. But per capita income, that is, actual purchasing power of the typical individual, went up a very healthy 15 percent in the same period. The large difference comes about because of demographic shifts in fertility, in household living arrangements, in labor force participation, and changes in the income distribution, all of which will be described in the next chapters.

This story would be much easier to tell if economic changes were the sole cause of changes in our social values or, contrariwise, if changes in our norms directly produced the dramatic changes in employment, earnings, and economic growth occurring in the decades since President Nixon was in the White House. Getting this story straight is much like doing a complicated jigsaw puzzle involving the tessellation of social trends and economic changes. The reward is an improved understanding of what has been happening to our heterogeneous society of 261,000,000, one that will give insights about what policies should be adopted or rejected.

Chapter 2

The 1960s: A Turning Point in How We View Race, Gender, and Sexuality

We share common views about what is appropriate, what is normal, and what is permissible. Sometimes these values change slowly over the course of many decades. Other times symbolic events, including court decisions, laws, presidential proclamations, and rioting, mark key turning points. The decade of the 1960s was one such time.

There are times when a society shifts its fundamental views about what is acceptable, shifts so dramatic that there are substantial changes from one generation to the next in how people live their lives. The events, laws, court decisions, peaceful protests, and riots of the 1960s symbolize shifts in the attitudes and values of many Americans with regard to three vital elements of our social structure. The first was with regard to African Americans. Not since the Reconstruction era, just after the Civil War, had the United States addressed the issue of whether blacks would participate fully in our society, enjoying the same liberties our Constitution granted to European-origin whites. Second, just after the civil rights movement raised questions about why we excluded blacks from opportunities because of their skin color, there were effective challenges to the assumption that the best jobs and most rewarding professional careers should go to men, while women should devote themselves to homes, families, and children. Many gradually accepted the principle of equal opportunities for women just as they had accepted it, at least in theory, for blacks. Third, the sexual revolution changed how many people viewed sexuality and led to an increase in premarital sex and cohabitation. Numerous state laws, dating from the Revolutionary era and reflecting traditional Judeo-Christian beliefs about personal morals and families, sought to restrict sexual activity to heterosexual married couples and to limit or prevent the use of birth control. These laws fell as attitudes changed.

Rights movements have a long history. Frederick Douglass and

W.E.B. DuBois eloquently demanded racial equity a century ago, and John Stuart Mill was one of many calling for rights for women. But liberalizing movements came to fruition in that brief span from the election of President Kennedy in 1960 to the *Roe* v. *Wade* Supreme Court decision in 1973. These shifts in values help account for changes in how people live, in who prospers, and in who falls behind economically. These are the changes clearly revealed by the census of 1990 and the ones that are reshaping this nation as we enter the twenty-first century.

Cohorts: A Key to Understanding Social Change

The decisions that young people make during adolescence and into their twenties influence them for their entire lives. They decide how much education to get and what type, whether to marry young or defer marriage until later; they make decisions about whether they will be parents; some decide to join the armed forces; a few decide about their sexual identity; and a very small number opt to migrate abroad. In making these decisions, they are influenced by their own values and the values of their parents. But they are also very much influenced by what their age mates are doing, by society's norms, and by what the government does about economic policy, war, education, housing, and a multitude of other matters. A young man graduating from high school in 1943 had few choices. He was in the military shortly after getting his diploma, but if he came back safely from that service, he was eligible for government-supported college tuition, he was able to buy a home for almost nothing down with a Veteran's Administration loan, and he entered a booming job market, so most of these men married and started large families. His wages kept going up and, at retirement, he and his wife got Social Security checks which increased annually to offset inflation, and their hospital bills were covered by Medicare. A high school graduate in 1983 could volunteer for the Army and be accepted if she or he had high enough test scores. But serving Uncle Sam at this time did not automatically bring college tuition or a low-cost loan for a new home in the suburbs, and when these men and women entered the job market they found lots of competitors and modest wages.

Generations differ most importantly in the social values and economic forces that shape them as they go through adolescence and become young adults. As sociologists put it, ". . . a generation is defined by the political and social experiences it has when its members are young" (Schuman and Scott 1989). The changes in social values discussed in this chapter and the economic shifts in the next chapter altered opportunities for young people, providing them with more opportunities in an important sense—that is, more choices in lifestyles, marriage, and parenting. But there were fewer opportunities in another sense since it became harder to find jobs that provide secure middle-class status.

Social change occurs largely—but not entirely—on a cohort basis. The word *cohort* refers to all persons born in a specified time span. They experience the same events at the same time and in much the same way as they march through their lives. I use decades to identify cohorts and give each of them a name. These are shown in table 2-1, along with the events or economic conditions the birth cohorts faced as they moved from adolescence to become adults. The baby boom refers to the very sharp and unexpected upturn in births and birth rates that began as soon as men were mustered out of military service from World War II. The birth rate began its fall in 1960, although so slowly that it took a few years for demographers to realize that the baby boom had finally come to its end.

A few readers are "grandparents of the baby boom," meaning that they were born around the time of the First Great War. Most of them were unfortunate enough to look for their first jobs or for spouses during the Depression of the 1930s. More readers will be from the small-sized cohorts born during the Depression or during World War II, cohorts fortunate enough to complete their schooling and search for jobs during the economic boom of the 1940s and 1950s. Younger readers—the most recent cohorts to go through adolescence and become adults—might be named the "baby bust generation," or the term I use—"Generation X." Born between 1966 and 1975, they grew up after social values had changed, but they entered a competitive job market, one in which those with specialized training would do well, but those lacking it would have a much tougher time finding a high-paying job than did their parents. Their standard of living will, quite likely, fall below that of their parents—the early baby boomers.

The Civil Rights Revolution: The Decision to Include Blacks

Writing a century ago in the first authoritative investigation of urban blacks, W.E.B. DuBois described a young man who graduated from the University of Pennsylvania with a degree in mechanical engi-

Table 2-1. Information About Birth Cohorts

Years of Birth	Name of Cohort	Became Young Adults	Key Events at That Time	Ages in Census of			
				1960	1970	1980	1990
1966–1975	Generation X	Mid-1980s through 1990s	Era of Economic Polarization			5–14	15–24
1956–1965	Late Baby Boom	Mid-1970s through 1980s	Era of Employment Restructuring		5–14	15–24	25–34
1946–1955	Early Baby Boom	Mid-1960s through 1970s	Era of Civil Rights and Sexual Revolutions	5–14	15–24	25–34	35–44
1936–1945	World War II	Mid-1950s through 1960s	Post–World War II Boom	15–24	25–34	35–44	45–54
1926–1935	Parents of the Baby Boom	Mid-1940s through 1950s	Post–World War II Boom	25–34	35–44	45–54	55–64
1916–1925	Parents of the Baby Boom	Mid-1930s through 1940s	World War II	35–44	45–54	55–64	65–74
1906–1915	Grandparents of the Baby Boom	Mid-1920s through 1930s	Depression	45–54	55–64	65–74	75–84

neering. On the basis of his excellent college record, he applied for and got a job as an engineer in Philadelphia. He lasted less than one day, fired when the employer realized he was black. When interviewed by DuBois, he was working again—employed as a waiter at the University Club, serving lunch to his former classmates.

After spending a year studying African Americans in that city's Seventh Ward, including interviews with quite a few holding advanced degrees, DuBois concluded:

> No matter how well trained a Negro may be, or how fitted for work of any kind, he cannot in the ordinary course of competition hope to be much more than a menial servant. [1899, p. 323]

After a terribly unpleasant year as a freshman at Columbia University in 1920, Langston Hughes decided to search for a job in Manhattan. He reports a similar outcome:

> In those days there was no depression—at least, not much of a one—so there were lots of ads in the morning papers. I bought the papers and began to answer ads regarding jobs I thought I could handle—office boy, clerk, waiter, bus boy and other simple occupations. Nine times out of ten—ten times out of ten, to be truthful— the employer would look at me, shake his head and say, with an air of amazement: "But I didn't advertise for a colored boy."
>
> It was the same in the employment offices. Unless a job was definitely marked COLORED on the board outside, there was no use applying, I discovered. . . . And only one job in a thousand would be marked COLORED. [1940, p. 86]

Paul Robeson, whose feats on Rutgers' football field made him the second African American to win all-American honors, obtained his law degree in 1923 and eventually got a position with a New York firm specializing in estates, Stotesbury and Miner. After a few weeks, his color made it impossible to work as even the stenographers refused to take dictation from a "nigger," albeit an all-American "nigger" with an LL.B. from Columbia University. Stotesbury, reflecting the views of this age, considered opening a Jim Crow office in Harlem so that Paul Robeson could solicit black clients, but realizing there was no future for him in law, Robeson quit and went on to earn accolades for his accomplishments as a singer and actor (Duberman 1988, p. 55).

Writing forty years later, also with a focus on New York City, Nathan Glazer and Daniel Patrick Moynihan argued that the problem for the Negro in America was the shortage of jobs for black men.

It means a particularly desperate problem for the Negro boy coming out of high school, with or without a diploma, and looking for a job in a market where there are few jobs for the unskilled, and in a neighborhood and a community in which there are few businessmen or professionals or skilled workers to give him a break or tell him about breaks (this is the way the unqualified of other groups get started). [1963, p. 38]

The Failure of Nineteenth Century Efforts

Blacks have always been included in our society in a demographic sense. At the time of the Revolution, they made up a larger share of the population—20 percent—than at present—12 percent, but during slavery and the century thereafter, blacks were generally denied most of the opportunities available to whites. Legal decisions and events of the 1960s crystallize the changes in our beliefs about the rights of both blacks and women. We began to realize that the principles of our democracy implied that blacks and women should be included in the governance and management of our society. In essence, they should have the same rights as white men.

Much that occurred in the 1960s with regard to rights for African Americans was foreshadowed by earlier laws and proposals. After the Civil War, those in Congress interested in equity for blacks knew that freedmen would be equal participants in American society only if they had the protection of the federal government. They appropriately feared that former slaveholders would impose a system of racial oppression in the South. Thus, Congress passed the Civil Rights Act of 1866 to protect the rights of blacks to buy property, make contracts, and engage in commerce on an equal basis with whites. In 1868 the Fourteenth Amendment guaranteed blacks citizenship rights and overturned the odious three-fifths compromise written into the Constitution. Two years later, the Fifteenth Amendment prohibited discrimination against blacks in voting, and the next year Congress passed the Ku Klux Klan Act, making it a federal offense to intimidate blacks. The last of these encompassing Reconstruction era laws—the Civil Rights Act of 1875—guaranteed blacks the right to use public accommodations and public conveyances (Foner 1988).

Despite three constitutional amendments and new federal laws, by the end of the nineteenth century the nation adopted a system of segregation ensuring that blacks were in a subordinate status, a unique system never imposed upon immigrants from Europe, Asia, or Latin America. The return of whites to power in southern states in the 1870s and 1880s, the withdrawal after 1877 of those federal troops who protected freedmen, and the numerous conservative rulings of the Supreme Court ratifying extreme principles of states' rights placed African Americans in the South at the mercy of whites. A system of lynching developed both to punish those blacks who violated unwritten racial codes and to intimidate those who might consider exercising their constitutional rights. In the 1890s an average of 103 blacks were lynched each year (Zangrando 1980, table 2). In their most notorious decision of that era, *Plessy v. Ferguson*, the Supreme Court upheld state laws mandating the segregation of whites from blacks by endorsing the "separate but equal" principle.

Minstrel shows in the nineteenth century made fun of blacks and immigrants. One of the popular songs insulting blacks was "Jim Crow." By the end of the century, Jim Crow came to mean black-white segregation, sometimes imposed by state laws and city ordinances, such as those calling for separate railway coaches, streetcars, cemeteries, drinking fountains, toilets; in South Carolina, separate pay windows; and in Oklahoma, segregated phone booths. In the North, customs and practices—not laws—produced the Jim Crow society that, to some degree, continues to exist in our segregated schools and neighborhoods.

When blacks began moving North in large numbers at the time of World War I, they found both similarities and differences between the two regions. Although there was no state-imposed segregation blacks could not compete equitably for jobs in New York or Philadelphia, as DuBois and Hughes remind us. Indeed, blacks were recruited for work in the northern factories and railyards only because World War I made it impossible to attract the European immigrants that employees preferred. Where the black population increased, residential segregation and the modern American ghetto developed—Chicago's South Side, Cleveland's Hough, Detroit's Black Bottom, and Manhattan's Harlem—along with its ubiquitous companion—Jim Crow schools. One important difference was that blacks could vote in the North, eventually giving blacks some clout but also creating many racially identified electoral districts.

The Civil Rights Revolution of the 1960s

The sixties—in both the nineteenth and the twentieth centuries—were civil rights decades. In both spans, Congress amended the Constitution three times to expand rights and enacted major new laws;

indeed, those of the 1960s replicated those of a century earlier. But why were the centuries-old civil rights grievances of African Americans addressed in this decade and not earlier or later?

Four reasons account for the timing of the civil rights revolution: the growth of black power, a successful civil rights movement, liberalized white attitudes, and a fundamental change in the policies of the government in Washington. First, black power—both political and economic—grew. This was largely attributable to the migration of African Americans from the South to the North. Early events directed attention to both the accomplishments and problems of blacks. On June 22, 1938, world heavyweight champ Max Schmelling fought Joe Louis in New York's Yankee Stadium. In a contest widely seen as America's patriotic challenge to the German Nazis, Louis, a Detroit Negro, won the crown handily. The next year, America's leading contralto scheduled a concert at Constitution Hall in Washington. But the owners of that building, the Daughters of the American Revolution (DAR), canceled the concert, invoking a rule that a black could never appear on their stage. Eleanor Roosevelt promptly resigned from the DAR and arranged for an even more impressive concert for Marian Anderson on the steps of the Lincoln Memorial.

A forceful demonstration of black power led to Executive Order 8802 in 1941. On the verge of America's involvement in World War II, blacks, still suffering from the record unemployment rates of the Depression, realized that they were unlikely to share in the prosperity the war effort would generate since whites would be hired first. So A. Philip Randolph, president of the Brotherhood of Sleeping Car Porters union, threatened to lead 100,000 Negroes in a march on Washington on July 4, 1941, to protest racial oppression in our democracy. Fearing that the consequences of this demonstration would damn his struggle to build support for the then-unpopular European war, President Roosevelt issued an order banning racial discrimination by defense contractors. This, plus the shortage of labor, helped blacks get some jobs and equal pay in defense industries, contributing to the growth of a black middle class.

Important symbolic changes occurred in the years after World War II, including April 15, 1947, when the Brooklyn Dodgers ran onto Ebbetts Field with Jackie Robinson at second base, the first African American to play major league baseball since the 1880s. Within a few months, Jackie Robinson became a hero to black Americans and put to rest the widely held view that sports should be organized on a Jim Crow basis (Tygiel 1983).

Black votes became significant after World War II because of inter-regional population shifts. Realizing that his chances for victory were slim in the four-candidate 1948 presidential election, President Truman, in July 1948, issued Executive Order 9981, theoretically ending Jim Crow practices in the armed forces. His victory by the narrowest of margins depended upon the votes cast by blacks in Illinois, New York, Ohio, and a few other key states.

The slow growth of a middle-class black population went hand-in-hand with the NAACP's long-term litigation strategy to make the Constitution apply to African Americans. As the middle-class black population grew, so too did their demands for better housing and schools. A series of lawsuits coordinated by the NAACP led the Supreme Court, in 1948, to declare that restrictive covenants could not be enforced. These are codicils to property deeds specifying that blacks, Asians, Jews, or other minorities could never own or live on a plot of land (Vose 1965). They had become the preferred legal and nonviolent way to maintain the American apartheid system in northern cities (Massey and Denton 1993). Equally important were the victories won by the NAACP with regard to segregation in interstate transportation and then, most significantly, in public education, leading to the May 17, 1954, *Brown* v. *Board of Education* (1954) ruling overturning school segregation. By declaring that separate could not be equal, the Supreme Court effectively overturned state-imposed racial segregation in all areas of public life. In a fundamental sense, the NAACP won the point that the Constitution was not just for white Americans. Blacks were included too.

The rapid emergence of an increasingly popular civil rights movement was the second reason. The *Brown* decision—the most important court ruling of the 1950s—set the stage for this. There are several key dates. On December 1, 1955, seamstress Rosa Parks deliberately violated Montgomery's bus segregation ordinance. On February 1, 1960, Joseph McNeil, Izell Blair, Franklin McCain, and David Richmond sat at a Woolworth's lunch counter in Greensboro, North Carolina, demanding the same food service provided to whites, a peaceful protest that was almost immediately duplicated by black college students throughout the South. It reached its high point on the afternoon of August 28, 1963, when Dr. Martin Luther King Jr., addressing a crowd of one-quarter million at the Lincoln Memorial, delivered his "I Have a Dream" speech; perhaps the most frequently cited speech given this century.

Third, white attitudes became more liberal. The civil rights movement attracted support not only from a wide array of blacks who had never previously asserted their citizenship rights but was eventually supported by many whites. It effectively turned the nation's attention upon the tremendous gap between our ideals of liberty and justice for all and the actual treatment of blacks (Branch 1988; Garrow 1986). Changes can be traced from the Second World War, but they accelerated in the 1950s and 1960s. The first civil rights bill since Reconstruction went on the books under President Eisenhower in 1957, a timid one dealing with voting rights, but one that established a federal Civil Rights Commission. After World War II, Americans became increasingly aware of the tragic outcome of the racist policies of the National Socialists in Germany, provoking reevaluation of our own policies. The effective leadership of Dr. King played a crucial role, since his appeal was to those traditional Judeo-Christian values incorporated into our national consciousness and firmly endorsed by both blacks and whites. Violence in the South also played a role in shifting whites toward support for strong federal actions in the field of civil rights. This includes the 1955 lynching of a young black Chicagoan, Emmett Till, in Money, Mississippi, who broke an unwritten rule by making comments to a white woman (Whitfield 1988); the bloody attacks upon James Farmer and the "freedom riders" in Jackson, Mississippi, who were peacefully traveling on interstate buses in the early 1960s; the extensive violence directed at Dr. King; the 1963 murder of Mississippi's NAACP leader, Medger Evers; and the deaths of James Chaney, Andrew Goodman, and Michael Schwerner in Philadelphia, Mississippi, in June of the next year. One of the fortuitous events of the civil rights movement happened on a Sunday evening in March 1965. The movie "Judgment at Nuremburg" about Nazi war crimes against the Jews was shown on national television, but it was interrupted several times for reports and clips about the day's events in Selma, Alabama—state troopers and militant whites beating blacks who were singing and praying as they attempted a voting rights march to their state capitol. At the end of World War II, many whites were reluctant to publicly support civil rights for blacks. That changed by the 1960s. (For an analysis of such changes in the South, see Edgerton 1984.)

How can we measure how much attitudes have changed? With the outbreak of World War II, the Defense Department undertook a domestic intelligence effort. They needed to monitor racial attitudes since bloody rioting between blacks and whites might vitiate the largely successful governmental attempts to portray this nation's war

efforts as the fight of our democracy against the totalitarian dictators—Hitler and Hirohito. Thus, national samples of whites have an-
swered questions about racial issues since the early 1940s.

Figure 2-1 shows the percentage of whites who gave "equal racial
opportunity" answers to questions about racially integrated schools
and buses and about equal opportunities for blacks in the labor and
housing markets.

In the early years of the war against Germany and Japan—about
two generations ago—only three whites in ten endorsed the idea of
blacks and whites going to the same schools. The majority of whites
also rejected the idea that both races should have the same opportunities to fill jobs that became available; whites even endorsed the Jim
Crow system of public transportation. In other words, U.S. citizens
generally accepted racial segregation in the 1940s. By the 1960s, attitudes had liberalized, and for the first time a majority of whites endorsed principles of equal racial opportunity. By the 1980s, more than
nine whites in ten favored equal opportunities for blacks in the job
market and in public schools. Almost all now reject the discriminatory
practices that Rosa Parks challenged by sitting in that white seat on a
Montgomery bus forty years ago.

The civil rights revolution involved a shift of white attitudes such
that racial discrimination is now seen as morally and legally wrong.
Nevertheless, improvements in the actual social and economic status
of blacks vis-à-vis whites have been much smaller than shifts in white
racial attitudes, a topic discussed in chapter 6.

Finally, there were far-reaching changes in the policies of the federal government and the attitudes of federal leaders in the early 1960s.
By 1962, officials in the Kennedy administration—especially in the
Justice Department—learned what the Radical Republicans had
known ten decades earlier: unless the federal government staunchly
defends constitutional rights, blacks in the South would have none.
With the presidency of Lyndon Johnson, the nation had a leader
knowledgeable about the tremendous costs of racial injustice and supportive of efforts to eradicate it.

In 1964 Congress passed, and President Johnson signed, one of
the most important laws of this century—an encompassing Civil
Rights Act that sought to protect the voting rights of blacks, banned
racial discrimination in employment and in public accommodations,
encouraged the integration of public schools, and put the Justice Department on the side of plaintiffs in civil rights cases. At that time
there was reluctance to accept major racial change and a belief by

Figure 2-1.   Percentage of Whites Giving the Equal Opportunity Response to Questions About Principles of Racial Equity

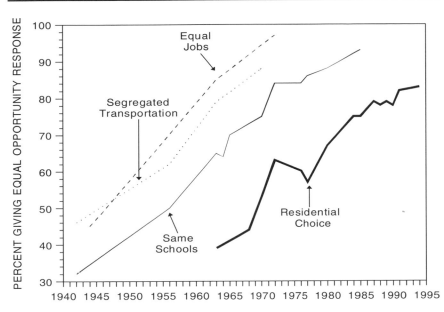

Questions:

Same Schools: Do you think that white students and (Negro/black) students should go to the same or to separate schools? (Percent saying "same schools.")

Equal Jobs: Do you think Negroes should have as good a chance as white people to get any kind of job, or do you think white people should have the first chance? (Percent saying "as good a chance as white people.")

Segregated Transportation: Generally speaking, do you think there should be separate sections for Negroes in streetcars and buses? (Percent saying "no.")

Residential Choice: Which statement on the card (showing four responses from "agree strongly" to "disagree strongly") comes closest to how you feel? White people have a right to keep blacks out of their neighborhoods if they want to, and blacks should respect that right. (Percent disagreeing.)

SOURCE: Schuman, Steeh, and Bobo 1988, table 3-1; National Opinion Research Center 1994.

many that the states—not the federal government—should protect the rights of blacks. Although now seen as a major achievement and widely accepted, there was an eighty-four-day filibuster to block passage of this civil rights law, and twenty-seven Senators, including the Republican nominee for president that year—Barry Goldwater—voted against it. One year later, after three deaths in voting rights marches in Selma, Alabama, the Fifteenth Amendment finally became effective in all states, with the Voting Rights Act symbolizing the inclusion of blacks in the system of governance. Lest one think that there was universal support for federal protection of voting rights thirty years ago, note the vote: 77 to 19 in favor in the Senate, and 328 to 74 in the House. One-fifth of Congress voted against it (Garrow 1978). Throughout the 1960s, there was debate about making it a federal crime to discriminate against blacks when they sought to purchase homes or rent apartments, a widespread practice. Many defended the idea that a man's home was his castle, so this type of discrimination was accepted. Within ten days of the assassination of Dr. Martin Luther King in April 1968, Congress passed the Open Housing Act—the final major civil rights bill of this era.

These laws reenacted legislation adopted in the Reconstruction era, but with a major difference. This time a more liberal federal court system not only upheld these laws, but extended them in important ways: by approving of busing and racial ratios as means for remedying within-district school segregation, by eradicating needless employment tests that discriminated against blacks, by approving the use of skin color as one criteria for selecting candidates for medical school, and by allowing Congress to set aside a share of federal construction spending specifically for minority contractors. In the 1960s, many Americans changed their views about racial issues and began to agree that African Americans really should enjoy the same legal, economic, and political opportunities as whites.

A Change in How We View the Adult Roles of Women: The Gender Revolution

The Civil Rights Act of 1964: New Opportunities for Women in the Labor Force

During the 1960s, views about what women might or should do with their adult lives also changed. Gradually, we adopted the belief that women should be able to compete for almost all occupations, and now a large majority agree that it is acceptable or desirable for mothers to combine their work in the labor market with their home duties. As a result, women are increasingly included in the labor force on much the same basis as men. At the outset, I emphasized the monumental differences distinguishing race and gender issues. Rooted in two hundred years of American slavery and then bolstered in this century by the seemingly scientific theory of Social Darwinism, there was widespread belief that African Americans were biologically, socially, and culturally inferior to whites. Well into the post–World War II era, state laws and customs kept blacks and whites segregated in schools, on buses, in neighborhoods, at work, and in places of public accommodations. And lest there be any miscegenation, twenty-seven states wrote laws preventing blacks from marrying whites, some staying on the books until 1967 (*Loving v. Virginia* 1967).

Women never faced circumstances exactly similar to those of blacks. No state laws kept women at the rear of the bus, nor were women lynched for transgressing unwritten rules. Although fifty years elapsed between the Fourteenth Amendment, which granted blacks the right to vote (1870) and the Nineteenth Amendment, granting women suffrage (1920), the latter amendment did not need a Voting Rights Act to make it effective. Unlike the situation for blacks, girls and boys generally went to the same schools, both benefiting from whatever investments taxpayers made in education.

In the nineteenth century, many children were cared for by both parents since most lived in rural areas where the family shared the jobs. The first childcare revolution occurred with urbanization as fathers left the home to work in factories and offices. Norms rapidly developed calling for women to devote themselves to their families while men earned money in the world of work (Hernandez 1993, chap. 11). This was uncritically accepted as a model of how society should operate, a view vested with great moral authority and strongly supported by state laws (Bianchi 1995). Women might work while they were single and spinsters might hold jobs, but once a woman married, society's norms and employer practices mandated her return to the home.

Fearing that work outside the home would adversely affect women, states passed laws limiting the hours women might work and the conditions under which they might labor. The Supreme Court, in its famous 1908 *Mueller v. Oregon* ruling, relied upon sociological evidence (in what is known as the Brandeis brief) and upheld such laws, a decision that was effective until the 1960s. In language we would now castigate as politically incorrect, the justices argued: ". . . woman's physical structure and her performance of maternal functions place her at a disadvantage in the struggle for subsistence . . . as healthy mothers are essential to vigorous offspring, the physical well-being of women becomes an object of public interest and care."

A system of now forgotten marriage bans developed in the late nineteenth century and expanded in the 1930s to ensure this sexual division of labor. Firms established regulations that either prohibited the hiring of married women or forced single women out when they married. Presumably, employers did not bear any animosity toward women nor did they believe that women were inferior in the sense blacks were presumed to be. Rather, they thought that married women would be so devoted to their spouses, children, and homes that they would be ineffective employees. Consider elementary and secondary school teaching— one of the few professions with moderately high pay and status open to women. Claudia Goldin (1990) reports that at the beginning of the Depression, 60 percent of the nation's public school systems had rules against hiring married women, while 52 percent fired single women when they married. In the 1930s, more employers adopted rules restricting the employment of women, believing that if jobs were scarce, they should go to men who really needed them to support families. In 1932, the government's Federal Order 213 said that if both members of a married couple were employed in civil service, one of them might be fired. This aimed to spread out the benefits of employment, but in almost all cases, it was the wife who got laid off. State and local governments in the Depression adopted numerous similar regulations in hopes of directing employment to men. By the time of Pearl Harbor (1941), 87 percent of local school boards refused to hire women who had husbands, and 70 percent mandated that single women quit or be fired when they married (Goldin 1990, chap. 6).

Labor market changes undermined these laws. The manpower shortage of World War II led to a temporary rise in the employment of women, including industrial jobs usually held by men, as symbolized by propaganda posters showing "Rosie the Riveter." But this was temporary; women left the labor force after 1945, with the younger ones marrying and bearing children at high rates. The census reported that the labor force participation rates of women were just about the same in the economic boom year of 1950 as they were in economically depressed 1940. Later in the 1950s, a tight labor market and the explosion of office jobs began attracting women, especially older married ones who had raised their children, so the marriage bans disappeared (Bancroft 1958, table 30).

Although some organizations and a small number of politicians championed equal opportunities for women, they were neither powerful nor prominent. No spokesperson for women's rights had the national recognition of Dr. King; no more than a few litigations concerning women's issues took place, and no one led a quarter-million people to the steps of the Lincoln Memorial to overturn the employer's right to deny employment to all women or to fire single women who married. No woman—or man—won the Nobel Peace Prize for promoting gender equity as did Dr. King in 1964 for his advocacy of racial equity.

How then did the Civil Rights Act of that year come to ban employment discrimination on the basis of both sex and race? It was a fortuitous concatenation of events—unplanned, unforeseen, unpredicted, and certainly not the outcome of protracted lobbying. Congressman Howard Smith of Virginia staunchly fought against the civil rights law. Seeing that he was about to lose, he tried a drastic move; amending the law by inserting the word "sex" into the list of characteristics that could not be used to discriminate in employment. He believed that the white males in Congress would not pass legislation overturning the regulations, state laws, and customs segregating the workplace by gender. Furthermore, it would place a great burden on employers since they might face hundreds or thousands of lawsuits from female employees if they continued their standard practices, so he expected them to denounce the amended civil rights bill and then use their power to block it. As expected, older white men in Congress condemned the attempt to make sexual discrimination in employment a federal crime, defending the laws that protected women by limiting their hours of work and conditions of employment. However, five women served in Congress. They applauded Congressman Smith's unexpected strategy and immediately convinced their peers that it would be desirable to ban sexual discrimination in employment, just as they were proscribing racial discrimination. Much to Congressman Smith's surprise, Congress voted 168 to 133 to prohibit sex discrimination, making the Civil Rights Act of 1964 among the most radical laws enacted this century (Whalen and Whalen 1985).

A more complete story would emphasize the long but thin history of attempts to legislate equity for women. Equal-pay proposals date from the last century, although many of the early ones were drawn up by men who feared that their wages would fall if women invaded their occupational specializations. And, in 1961 President Kennedy—prodded by Eleanor Roosevelt—appointed a Commission on the Status of Women. Their 1963 report documented that women were kept off the juries in some states, that other states denied women the property rights that men had, and that many women faced extensive discrimination in the labor market. Congress then passed an Equal Pay Act, although its scope was limited and its enforcement provisions weak.

Passing a law is one step; making it known, accepted, and enforced is quite different, as per our experiences with the civil rights laws of the Reconstruction era. Yet, attitudes about women's employment were changing, and litigation methods to challenge discrimination against blacks had been perfected by the NAACP, so conditions were favorable for making the new prohibition of sex discrimination effective. One suit brought the new law to the attention of employers in a manner they could not overlook: it threatened to take a large slice directly from their profits! In the late 1960s, American Telephone and Telegraph (AT&T) was the monopoly operator of long distance service, and the Federal Communications Commission (FCC) had to approve rate increases. In 1970, AT&T sought to charge more and the FCC held the mandated public hearings. By this time, there was a well-organized movement to force employers to treat blacks and women equitably and to seek remedies from those who violated the law, so the FCC hearings became a forum for presenting evidence about apparent violations of the 1964 Civil Rights Act. Shortly thereafter, the matter moved into federal court. Plaintiffs presented rigorous and extensive evidence showing that AT&T and the Baby Bells they owned steered blacks and whites and men and women to extremely different career paths with great differences in pay. After three years of litigation, AT&T settled out of court and agreed to end discrimination, to establish effective affirmative actions programs that would get women and minorities into good jobs, and, very importantly, to pay $31 million in back wages to some 500,000 employees who had been discriminated against after the new law had gone into effect. This was precedent for similar litigation involving many, perhaps most, of the nation's largest employers in the 1970s who had implicitly or explicitly used employment tracking systems that reserved the highest-paying jobs for white men. Within a decade, employers knew that there were real teeth in the sex discrimination clause cynically proposed by Congressman Howard Smith in February 1964 (Wallace 1976).

One other crucial link in this story was publication of *The Femi-*

nine Mystique by Betty Friedan, just one year before the Civil Rights Act was adopted. Among the most stimulating books appearing that decade, it proposed a new paradigm for how middle-class white women might or should spend their lives. Friedan began by cogently describing "The Problem That Has No Name." By that, she meant that many highly educated women found their suburban lives empty. They had the intellectual skills and interests to make important contributions, but they were not taken seriously in the world of work. They were told that despite their talents and their college degrees, they should stay home, take care of children, assist their husbands in their careers, defer to their husbands' judgments, and bake cookies. Friedan argued that education was the key to the problem—years in the college classroom gave women information about their own skills and abilities, showing them that they were the peers of men, thereby provoking their unhappiness when they found themselves confined to their suburban homes. But it was also, she argued, the key to the solution since opportunities would open for educated women.

New Careers and Full-Time Employment for Women

Betty Friedan did not know how prescient she was. Table 2-2 shows the number of degrees in medicine, law, engineering, and business administration earned by men and women since 1960, in which year it would have been possible to list on three sheets of paper the names of all the women who got degrees in these fields.

Without reading *The Feminine Mystique,* many young women no doubt realized that they had the intellectual skills to compete for the best jobs. At first, there was a modest rise in the number of women getting advanced degrees: just twenty-six women became dentists in 1960, and only thirty-four in 1970. But women in the early baby boom cohort benefited from the new attitudes. Between 1970 and 1980, the number of medical degrees earned by women jumped from 699 to 3,486; for law degrees, it was a phenomenal 801 to 10,754. Similarly dramatic rises occurred in MBA programs and in engineering. And women in the late baby boom cohort continued the process—record numbers earned advanced degrees. Between 1980 and 1990, diplomas in medicine, law, and dentistry going to men declined, while the number going to women rose spectacularly. As for the MBAs, degrees to men increased by only 14 percent in the 1980s, while those to women doubled. For engineering degrees, the increase was 18 percent for men, but 81 percent for women.

Table 2-2.   Degrees in Medicine, Law, Dentistry, Business Administration, and Engineering, by Gender for Recent Birth Cohorts

Birth Cohort	Parents of Baby Boom 1960	World War II 1970	Early Baby Boom 1980	Late Baby Boom 1990
Medicine				
Men	7,032	7,615	11,416	10,326
Women	387	699	3,486	5,128
Percentage women	5%	8%	23%	33%
Law				
Men	9,010	14,115	24,893	21,048
Women	230	801	10,754	14,519
Percentage women	2%	5%	30%	41%
Dentistry				
Men	3,221	3,684	4,558	3,139
Women	26	34	700	1,108
Percentage women	<1%	<1%	13%	26%
Master's of Business Administration				
Men	4,645	25,443	42,722	48,557
Women	169	1,038	12,284	24,597
Percentage women	4%	4%	22%	34%
Bachelor's Degree in Engineering				
Men	37,537	49,296	62,488	73,651
Women	142	382	6,405	11,622
Percentage women	<1%	<1%	9%	14%

SOURCE: U.S. Department of Education, 1991, *Digest of Educational Statistics*, tables 242 to 258.

To obtain the advanced degrees leading to the most lucrative and powerful careers, mothers of the baby boomers had to overcome immense social pressures. If they successfully got their credentials, they confronted even more problems finding jobs. It was not costly for an employer to discriminate against women since there were so few of them, and until 1964 there was no law to prevent the employer from summarily announcing that he did not hire women, even if they had degrees from the most distinguished institutions. There is the often-repeated story of the woman who graduated second in her class at Stanford Law School and sought a job with one of the leading firms in Los Angeles, only to be told that women were not hired as lawyers, but that she was well qualified to be a legal secretary. Fortunately for her, this discrimination did not prevent Sandra Day O'Connor from becoming the first of her gender to serve on the Supreme Court. By 2000 it's likely that the majority of new lawyers will be women and, in medicine, they may be getting more than four of ten degrees. These changes opened up fields once restricted to men and will probably lead even more women in Generation X to enter these prestigious fields.

Equally impressive are the shifts of women into full-time employment, a trend that occurred on a cohort basis. Table 2-3 reports the percentage of women who were full-time, year-round workers at the last four census dates. A person was classified full-time if he or she reported working thirty-five or more hours for at least fifty weeks in the year. The rows show changes in full-time employment as birth cohorts get older. The top panel reports that 29 percent of early baby boom women worked full-time at ages 25 to 34; when they got to ages 35 to 44, 43 percent worked full-time. Reading down a column from the top shows changes from one birth cohort to the next. Among late baby boom women, 42 percent worked full-time at ages 25 to 34. Among the preceding cohort—early baby boom women—29 percent worked full-time at these ages.

Mothers of the baby boom seldom worked full time, either when they were rearing children or later. Only 14 percent of these women held full-time jobs when they were at ages 25 to 34. You might expect that many of them would have gone to work full-time after their children grew up, but that was not the case since, for this cohort, only one-quarter worked full-time at ages 45 and over. Each succeeding cohort had higher rates of full-time employment, with the big shift experienced by the baby boom cohorts. In 1990, 42 percent of women at ages 25 to 34 worked full-time. As these recent cohorts move into midlife, they will have much higher rates of full-time employment than did their mothers or grandmothers. This is driven by new norms about women's employment, by the higher wages they earn, and by the need for their income since the wages of men—their husbands and potential husbands—have fallen since 1973.

This table also illustrates the proportion of men working full-time.

Table 2-3. Percentage of Full-Time, Year-Round Workers, by Birth Cohort, Age, and Sex

Birth Cohort		25–34	35–44	45–54	55–64
			Ages		
			Women		
1956–1965	Late Baby Boom	42%			
1946–1955	Early Baby Boom	29	43		
1936–1945	World War II	18	30	41	
1926–1935	Parents of Baby Boom	14	21	29	25
1916–1925	Parents of Baby Boom		18	25	21
1906–1915	Grandparents of Baby Boom			20	20
			Men		
1956–1965	Late Baby Boom	66%			
1946–1955	Early Baby Boom	62	72		
1936–1945	World War II	68	71	70	
1926–1935	Parents of Baby Boom	66	71	68	51
1916–1925	Parents of Baby Boom		70	68	51
1906–1915	Grandparents of Baby Boom			65	55
		Ratio of Women to Men (per 100)			
1956–1965	Late Baby Boom	63			
1946–1955	Early Baby Boom	47	60		
1936–1945	World War II	27	42	58	
1926–1935	Parents of Baby Boom	21	30	42	49
1916–1925	Parents of Baby Boom		26	37	42
1906–1915	Grandparents of Baby Boom			31	36

SOURCE: Bianchi 1995, table 3.5.

There has been little change over time in this indicator. It is commonly thought that almost all adult men work full-time, but this is not the case. For many reasons, including unemployment, a lack of skills, personal preferences, and physical disabilities, only about two-thirds of adult men hold full-time jobs.

The final panel shows the ratio of women to men with regard to full-time employment. There is a clear pattern of smaller and smaller gender differences. When the parents of baby boomers were ages 25 to 34, the proportion of women working full-time was only 21 percent that for men; for the late baby boomers, it was 63 percent. Gender parity in employment during childrearing years has not been and may never be reached, but the trend is moving in that direction.

New Attitudes About Combining of Work and Childraising

The movement of women into prestigious occupations and their full-time employment went hand-in-hand with changing attitudes about working and mothering. The National Opinion Research Center's General Social Survey has asked national samples about what sociologists call their sex-role attitudes. These questions basically tap ideas about the norm that women should stay at home with the children while men work for pay. Figure 2-2 shows trends in responses for three important questions about gender issues.

Most surveys about this topic date from the 1970s, but one investigation, conducted at the end of 1930s, found that three-quarters of a national sample disapproved of women working if they had husbands who could support them (Burstein 1985, table 3-1). These views were influenced by the job shortage of that era, but they summarize the nation's consensus about the place of women in the home. Between 1940 and the 1970s, change occurred but in 1972—almost a decade after the civil rights law—one-third of Americans still disapproved of working women whose husbands were capable of supporting them. This dropped to one in five in 1994, providing evidence of the dramatic long-run trend toward increasing approval of women pursuing their own careers while raising children. Note that there is not universal support for this since, in the early 1990s, 20 percent still feel that women should not work if they have employed husbands.

A common question asks whether women should take care of their homes while leaving the running of the country up to men, perhaps the maximum sexual division of labor we can imagine. The proportion giving the traditional response was cut in half in the score

Figure 2-2. Percentage of National Samples Giving a Traditional Response to Questions About Women's Employment

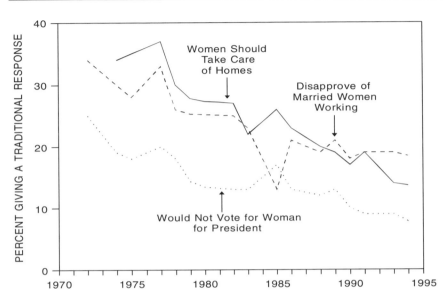

Questions:
Women Should Take Care of Homes: Do you agree or disagree with this statement? Women should take care of running their homes and leave running the country up to men. (Figure shows percent who agree.)
Disapprove of Married Women Working: Do you approve or disapprove of a married woman earning money in business or industry if she has a husband capable of supporting her? (Figure shows percent disapproving.)
Vote for Woman for President: If your political party nominated a woman for President, would you vote for her if she were qualified for the job? (Figure shows percent saying no.)

SOURCE: National Opinion Research Center 1994, items 198–200.

of years following 1972—from one-third to one-sixth. Do people support or reject the idea of a woman holding the nation's most crucial job: the presidency? Presumably, if the question had been asked in 1940, almost no one would have said they would vote for a woman for president. In the early 1970s, about one-quarter said they would not vote for a woman nominated by their party. This fell to less than 10 percent in the early 1990s. Recent shifts in attitudes about women, dating from events in the 1960s, bring us to a situation in which 90 percent say they would cast their ballot for a woman for president.

Pursuing careers generally involves full-time work, and women who have children must balance responsibilities for their home and their job. How do people feel about women who combine working with childrearing? Have attitudes shifted, or is there still a strongly held belief that children suffer when their mother works outside the home? Four frequently asked questions tap such attitudes, two focusing upon combining childrearing with work and two concerning the importance of a woman's own career. Figure 2-3 summarizes trends.

Just twenty years ago, most people did not think that it was possible for working women to get as close to their children as "full-time" mothers. Attitudes have switched and although many people continue to believe that preschool children suffer when their mother works outside the home, the majority now think that working mothers can establish as warm relationships with their children as those who stay at home with them—an idea almost everyone rejected until quite recently.

As recently as the 1970s, the majority of adults agreed that it was better for everyone if the man achieved outside the home while the woman took care of the family. While a significant minority still defends that principle, the majority feels otherwise. Among the four questions about sex roles, the greatest shift concerns gender equity in terms of careers. The idea that a wife should devote herself to her husband's career rather than her own was overwhelmingly endorsed by adult Americans in the mid-1970s; presumably an even higher proportion endorsed this traditional model of marriage a decade earlier.

Baby boom cohorts and Generation X hold more liberal views about these issues than do the parents of the baby boom. Responses to the sex role questions asked around 1990 were classified by birth cohort; the findings are shown in table 2-4. About 60 percent of the parents of the baby boom (age fifty-five and over in 1990) thought preschool children suffered when their mother worked outside the home, but among Generation X, only one-third thought so. The older cohorts were also much more likely than the newer cohorts to think that it is better if the man achieves outside the home while the wife cares for the family, leading to the intergenerational conflict about childrearing. As Katherine Newman (1993) observed, parents of the mothers who are now working full-time generally believe their grandchildren would benefit if the father worked full-time while their daughter did the traditional tasks of taking care of the house and children.

Figure 2-3. Percentage of National Samples Giving Liberal Responses to Questions About Women Combining Home and Labor Market Activities

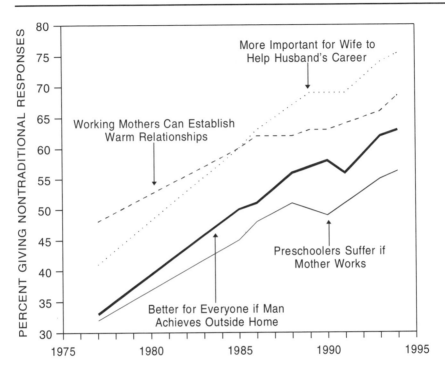

Questions:

More Important for Wife to Help Husband's Career: It is more important for a wife to help her husband's career than to have one herself. (Figure shows percent disagreeing.)

Better for Everyone If Man Achieves Outside Home: It is much better for everyone involved if the man is the achiever outside the home and the woman takes care of the home and family. (Figure shows percent disagreeing.)

Working Mothers Can Establish Warm Relationships: A working mother can establish just as warm and secure a relationship with her children as a mother who does not work. (Figure shows percent agreeing.)

Preschoolers Suffer If Mother Works: A preschool child is likely to suffer if his or her mother works. (Figure shows percent disagreeing.)

SOURCE: National Opinion Research Center 1994, item 252.

These data strongly imply a continued shift in attitudes as demographic processes replace older individuals who hold traditional ideas with younger people who hold different views of the roles of wives and husbands. Traditional views, however, have not disappeared, even among Generation X, since about one-quarter endorse the idea that it is better if the man achieves outside the home while the woman takes care of the family.

In table 2-4 there is also a clear indication of male-female differences in attitudes about these crucial issues. Men are more likely than women to hold traditional views about women's roles. For example, among the youngest cohorts, 47 percent of men but only 27 percent

Table 2-4. Attitudes About Roles of Employed Women for Birth Cohorts: Age in 1990

	Generation X <25	Late Baby Boom 25–34	Early Baby Boom 35–44	World War II 45–54	Parents of Baby Boom 55 and Over
It Is More Important for a Wife to Help Her Husband's Career than to Have One Herself (% Agree)					
Women	13%	13%	16%	24%	51%
Men	20	17	17	29	47
It Is Better for Everyone Involved if the Man Is the Achiever Outside the Home and the Woman Takes Care of the Home and Family (% Agree)					
Women	18%	24%	23%	36%	63%
Men	29	28	32	42	67
A Preschool Child is Likely to Suffer if His or Her Mother Works (% Agree)					
Women	27%	30%	34%	41%	56%
Men	47	42	46	55	69
A Working Mother Can Establish Just as Warm and Secure a Relationship with Her Children as a Mother Who Does Not Work (% Agree)					
Women	80%	77%	79%	79%	53%
Men	69	64	61	55	43

SOURCE: National Opinion Research Center 1994, item 252.

NOTE: Data are pooled by cohort from 1988 to 1992 General Social Surveys.

of women believed that preschool children suffer when mothers work. The overwhelming majority of young women reject the idea that they should forgo their careers for the sake of their husbands; they believe that their young children will not suffer if they work outside the home. But young men are less likely to endorse such untraditional ideas. These disagreements, one presumes, forestall some marriages and lead to the dissolution of others.

Changes in Values About Sexuality and Living Arrangements

I have described the changes in our views about excluding people from opportunities because of their skin color or gender. The third major shift in our views dating from the 1960s involves norms about sexuality and marriage. There are many different dimensions to this issue and little consensus about the driving forces. One popular book proclaimed that we had a divorce revolution (Weitzman 1987). Another described a contraceptive revolution (Westoff and Ryder 1977). A third view contended that society privatized sexuality by removing laws that sought to restrict what adults did behind closed bedroom doors (Garrow 1994). Some call this and the changes in living arrangements the sexual revolution (McLanahan and Sandefur 1994, p. 142). There is also the powerful argument that individuals came to place much more emphasis on their personal growth and fulfillment and less emphasis on adherence to rules or commitments. In the view of Christopher Lasch (1979), America entered an age of narcissism.

The major point is that as baby boom cohorts became young adults, they had a different array of options about how to live their lives and with whom. The years immediately following World War II were unusual because of the way sex, marriage, and childbearing were clustered together, and divorce was rare. Economic opportunities of that era allowed a young white man with a high school education to marry a classmate he loved and then establish a secure middle-class lifestyle on the basis of one good blue-collar job. The template symbolizing middle-class life of that era was the Nelson family—Ozzie and Harriet with two children and no major worries about either finances or divorce—a lifestyle also lovingly portrayed in the movies and television. Television, in particular, spread across the nation between 1947 and 1954, bringing this idealized image of the American Dream and the American Family into most homes. This image faded in subsequent decades as demographic trends affected the family: delayed marriage, more divorce, better birth control, legal changes about sexuality, and new attitudes about divorce and premarital sex.

Delayed Marriage

For thirty years, the age at marriage has been increasing. The upper panel of figure 2-4 shows annual marriage rates since the end of the Depression by reporting first marriages per 1,000 unmarried women aged 15 to 44. Economic strains of the 1930s and conscription of young men during World War II reduced marriage rates, and thus there were numerous young unmarried women when World War II ended. The result was a spike in the marriage rate in 1946 as people made up for marriages postponed during the Depression and the war. In that year, a record was set when just under 20 percent of unmarried women aged 15 to 44 became brides. The first-marriage rate stayed high in the late 1940s, the 1950s, and into the 1960s. After the 1960s, marriage rates began to fall for reasons not fully understood. The best explanations involve shifts in norms, the increasing college enrollment and earnings of women, falling wages for men, and the popularity of effective birth control. This trend toward a much lower marriage rate continues. By the 1990s, women were marrying at a rate half that of the post–World War II era.

Every year Census Bureau demographers determine the age by which 50 percent of the population had married; that is, the median age at marriage. At the end of the Depression, this median age was 21.5 for women, meaning that one-half of women married by that age, while for men it was 24.3 years. Post–World War II economic and social trends drove down the age at first marriage; by 1956, the age fell to a record low—20.1 years for women and 22.5 for men. It will be a surprise to members of Generation X to learn that in the mid-1950s, almost one-half of all women married while still in their teens; one-half of all men by age 22.5. We had a great deal of teenage childbearing in those years, but it was by married women.

New trends developed, slowly at first and then much more rapidly in the 1970s, as the baby boom cohorts entered their twenties. The median age at first marriage ascended to a record high of 24.5 years for women and 26.5 years for men in 1993. Now, the majority of people in their twenties are single, whereas the overwhelming majority were married in the 1950s and 1960s. Women in that era who were unmarried by age 24 probably heard their anxious mothers using the word *spinster.*

Figure 2-4. First Marriages Per 1,000 Unmarried Women Aged 15 to 44, and Divorces Per 1,000 Married Couples: 1940 to 1994

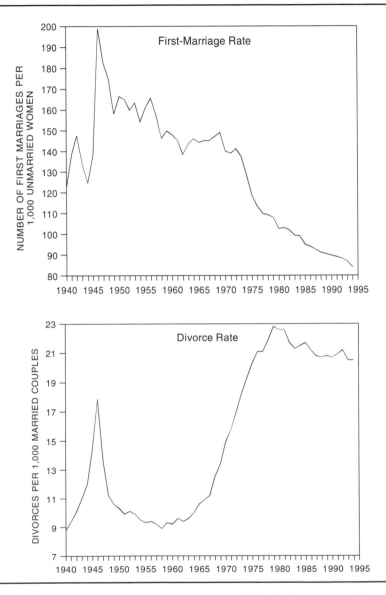

SOURCE: U.S. National Center for Health Statistics, 1991, *Vital Statistics of the United States, 1987,* Vol. III, table 2-1; 1995, *Monthly Vital Statistics Report,* Vol. 3, No. 13, pp. 3–5.

MORE DIVORCE   When the nation was new, divorces were permitted but difficult to obtain. In New York State, they required approval of the legislature. To free their agenda, Alexander Hamilton in 1787 wrote a law that gave local courts the power to dissolve marriages, but for only one reason—proven adultery. This remained the only grounds for divorce in New York until 1966. Such restrictive laws reflected widely held values emphasizing the sanctity of marriage, the immorality of divorce, and the need to protect the economic status of mothers and children in an era when women did not work (Jacob 1988).

Many forces propelled states to modernize their laws so that unhappy marriages could be more easily terminated. The greatest change was eliminating the idea that one partner was responsible for the failure of the marriage while the other spouse was the innocent victim. No longer was marriage seen as a civil contract to be dissolved only if one spouse could prove to a judge that the other had violated the contract. By the 1960s, this led to "no fault" divorce; and states gradually followed the lead of California where such a law was adopted in 1969. At that time, women entered the labor market in great numbers, so more of them could support themselves if their marriage ended in divorce. Although divorces are still complicated when children and property are involved, they are much easier to obtain now.

Marriages and divorces are recorded in several thousand county offices using a variety of forms and procedures, rather than by the federal statistical system, so it is more challenging to get precise information about marriage rates or trends in divorce than it is to learn about changes in unemployment or school enrollment. There is consensus, however, about three trends in divorce: first, the divorce rate rose rapidly, especially in the 1970s; second, divorced individuals now constitute a much larger share of the adult population than they did in the past; and, third, the majority of the marriages formed in the 1970s and 1980s will likely end in divorce.

The lower panel in figure 2-4 reports the ratio of registered divorces in a year to the number of married couples. Each year in the 1940s there were about nine divorces per 1,000 married couples. Many young couples married in haste during World War II—sometimes while a soldier was home on leave—or just after a man was mustered out of service. Quite a few of those marriages turned out to be unfortunate "starter" marriages, so they were quickly terminated. The divorce rate spiked in 1946, then settled back to the low levels typical of the Depression decade and early 1940s. In the late 1960s, after laws were changed, divorces occurred more frequently, and the divorce rate doubled in the short span between 1960 and 1975. Since the end of that decade, the rate has stabilized at twenty-two divorces per 1,000 married couples; that is, about 2 percent of the nation's marriages are ended by divorce each year, twice the rate of the 1940s or 1950s.

In 1960, a divorced person must have been rather lonely since most of his or her peers lived with a spouse. Rising divorce rates changed that. One way to appreciate this shift in the social climate is to examine the number of divorced persons per 1,000 married–spouse present individuals as shown below (U.S. Bureau of the Census 1991a, figure 2): the divorced adult population was just about 3 percent as numerous as the currently married population in 1960, but thirty years later is was about 14 percent as numerous. So in just three decades, the ratio of divorced-to-married persons quadrupled. A divorced individual in 1960 may have felt out-of-place and outnumbered, but not now. As McLanahan and Casper (1995) observed:

> The increase in the divorce ratio is likely to have a feedback effect on marriage. By increasing the chance that married and single people will interact with people who had ended their marriages through divorce, a high divorce ratio makes divorce more acceptable and marriage more uncertain.

Divorced Persons per 1,000 Married–Spouse Present Persons

Year	Number of Persons
1960	35
1970	47
1980	100
1990	142

There is no long history of survey data describing trends in attitudes toward divorce. With the sharp increase in the divorce rate, one might think that attitudes have become much more supportive of dissolving marriages that are unhappy. One careful study of a large sample of white respondents from the Detroit area suggests a great shift in attitudes (Thornton 1985). In 1962, new mothers were asked, "When there are children in the family, should parents stay together even if they don't get along?" Forty-nine percent of these mothers agreed that parents should stay together for the sake of their children.

Eighteen years later, only 19 percent of these same women—then in their forties and fifties—agreed that unhappy married couples should stay together for their children. When the daughters who were born in 1962 attained age 18 only 17 percent of them endorsed the idea that unhappy parents should not divorce for the sake of their children. So both the mothers themselves and their daughters changed their views about divorce. We cannot generalize to the nation from a Detroit sample, but this study strongly suggests a huge shift in attitudes about remaining in unhappy marriages.

A Contraceptive Revolution

Women now have many different effective strategies for preventing unwanted childbearing. Although birth rates were very low in the Depression, we do not know what couples actually did to prevent excess fertility since questions about sexuality were once deemed far too personal to ask on surveys. The original national investigation was conducted—with great trepidation—in 1955 and limited to married couples (Freedman, Whelpton, and Campbell 1959). From the perspective of the 1990s, it appears that couples then depended upon ineffective and burdensome methods. Just over one-half of the contracepting married couples used condoms and diaphragms, while the rest depended upon rhythm, douche, withdrawal, spermicides, and similar methods often thought to be unpleasant or ineffective.

A major change occurred as women born in the early years of the baby boom reached their teens and twenties. A woman could adopt oral contraceptives—a highly personal technique, so personal that her husband or lover might not know of her use. A few years later, she could choose another new effective method—the intrauterine device.

The leading investigators of family planning, Charles Westoff and Norman Ryder (1977), argue that there was a contraceptive revolution in the 1960s. In 1960, the Food and Drug Administration approved the birth control pill. Within three years, almost 2.5 million women were taking it, and by 1965 perhaps one-quarter of all married women under age 45 had used or were using oral contraceptives (Asbell 1995, p. 168). Within a decade it was, by far, the most popular birth control method.

In his history of the pill, Bernard Asbell (1995) stresses the social and psychological consequences of this development. Into the 1960s, defenders of tradition and religious leaders condemned birth control as immoral and associated it with prostitution. The appearance of the pill, widely discussed in the press and on television, made birth control an acceptable topic of conversation for both men and women. As with many other innovations, the pill was first adopted by highly educated younger people, but couples who in the past had not used contraception effectively quickly adopted the pill—couples with little education, women who had many children early in life, and Catholics. As you might expect, a debate raged briefly about the appropriateness of public clinics and student health clinics prescribing pills to unmarried women. For a while, there was an effort to restrict their use to married couples, but very quickly this shifted, and most woman who sought them could obtain them. As women in the late baby boom cohort approached age 20, getting a prescription for pills was a normal thing to do, not something condemned by society and certainly not something that indicated they were "fallen" women.

The pill was not the only major technological change of that decade. By 1970, one out of every twenty married couples of reproductive age used the highly effective intrauterine device (IUD), a method of birth control that came on the market in 1965. Again, this was a technology first adopted by educated young women, but which spread rapidly. In the 1970s, there was concern that taking oral contraceptives for long periods would lead to an increased risk of heart disease, a concern that was apparently unfounded. Women who wanted to discontinue using the pill had the IUD as an alternative (Westoff and Ryder 1977, pp. 40–43).

The third major change in birth control in the 1960s did not involve something new, nor did it involve young women. Rather, it was the increasing popularity of sterilization by couples who had all the children they wanted. Sterilization eventually became the most widely used birth control method, reflecting a change in norms. But it was used by older couples who had all the children they wished (Mosher and Pratt 1990).

Technology is part of the story of the contraceptive revolution, but more significant were the changes that made the use of birth control a socially approved activity for almost all couples, thereby giving women effective control over when they would become pregnant. With regard to sexuality, baby boomers and Generation X moved from adolescence to adulthood with more opportunities to limit their fertility than did their mothers or grandmothers.

Changes in the Law: The Privatization of Sexuality?

During the 1960s, laws changed in an important area of our personal lives—that regarding sexual behavior. It is not so much that new laws were written; rather, old ones were stricken.

Many laws in the United States try to outlaw vice; and in the Victorian age, sexual activity, except that of married couples, was defined as vice. Even the use of birth control was seen in this light, both because of religious views about its immorality and because of its close association with commercial sex. Continuing with the American tradition of fixing problems—in this case, ending vice—Congress in 1873 passed "An Act for the Suppression of Trade in and Circulation of Obscene Literature and Articles of Immoral Use." This law, named after Anthony Comstock, the New York anti-vice crusader, made it a crime to send obscene materials through the mail. When the men in Congress drew up the list of obscene materials, birth control was included. Those convicted of mailing such information faced up to ten years in a federal penitentiary. In 1897, Congress tightened the law by making it a federal crime to ship contraceptives across state lines or import them from abroad. Many states adopted Comstock laws, not only restricting contraceptives but prohibiting bestiality, homosexuality, cunnilingus, and fellatio.

Margaret Sanger, a nurse from a Catholic family in upstate New York, believing that poor married women could preserve their health and improve their lot if they had fewer children, founded the modern birth control movement. She went to prison for her beliefs: in the 1920s, she and her colleagues were prosecuted for telling immigrant women in Brooklyn about pessary caps, which was a violation of New York state law. By the 1930s, these laws were seldom enforced and federal courts removed some of them. But the laws had their defenders—especially those who forcefully argued that contraception violated God's laws and would, if used, destroy our family system—so there is a long history of litigation about state regulations limiting sexual activities. In 1943, for example, the Supreme Court let stand an Illinois anti–birth control law (*Tileston v. Ullman* 1943), but by 1958, the Postal Service announced that they would not prosecute anyone who mailed information about contraceptives. Consider that just forty years ago it was a violation of federal law for a mother to write a letter to her married daughter providing specific information about effective family limitation!

Into the early 1960s, seventeen states retained laws restricting the use of birth control. A Massachusetts statute flatly and absolutely prohibited the sale of contraceptives. Connecticut went even further, making it a misdemeanor for anyone—even married couples—to "use any drug, medical article or instrument for the purposes of preventing conception." A Connecticut married woman who took oral contraceptives in 1964 and the doctor who prescribed them, each committed a crime.

It is not surprising that restrictive laws were challenged during the decade of civil rights legislation. But it is surprising that they survived so long. On the one hand, these were unimportant laws, almost unenforceable. The governor of Connecticut did not dispatch patrolmen to bedrooms looking for diaphragms, nor did gynecologists live in fear of police raids. On the other hand, the challenges to the laws raised issues that constitutional experts debated and which the courts have yet to fully resolve. Does the Constitution contain an implicit guarantee of privacy, a guarantee that permits consenting adults to engage in whatever sexual activities they wish? Or may the state, in the interests of protecting citizens, regulate sexual activity, including proscribing sex acts some find offensive and immoral but others enjoy?

In a 1965 decision greatly complicated by the Justices' uncertainty about whether there is an implied privacy clause in the Constitution, the Supreme Court overturned the Connecticut birth control statute seven to two, thus ending state efforts to outlaw contraceptives (*Griswold* v. *Connecticut* 1965). Just three decades ago, two members of the Supreme Court upheld a state's right to prohibit birth control use by married couples.

About the same time, there was a growing recognition of the problem that motivated Margaret Sanger. Middle-class persons with access to private medical services got the contraceptives they needed, but the poor lacked such access and had unwanted children. Proposals that the federal government, in the interest of health and welfare, provide family planning services to the poor were denounced by Roman Catholic bishops. In 1959, President Eisenhower agreed with the bishops, announcing that birth control was "not a proper political or governmental activity or function or responsibility" (Garrow 1994, p. 164). Less than a decade later, President Johnson declared his War on Poverty. Advocates for the poor stressed that health services should provide birth control to those who wished to limit family size. Congress agreed. In 1970, ninety-seven years after they passed the Comstock Law, Congress passed the Family Planning Services and Population Research Act, providing about $130 million each year for birth control.

A foreseeable consequence of the Supreme Court's 1965 *Griswold* decision was the demise of many state laws that restricted sexual activity to heterosexual married couples. In doing so, plaintiffs gradually popularized the idea that the Constitution implicitly contains a privacy clause. If there is such a privacy right, shouldn't a woman be able to decide about the outcome of her own pregnancy? Most states outlawed abortion except when the mother's life was threatened, but in the 1960s, some states expanded the conditions under which abortion was permissible, allowing it when the pregnancy resulted from rape or incest. These laws required that women obtain approval of a medical board for such abortions. Plaintiffs challenged anti-abortion laws, including the exceptionally restrictive one in Texas, and so the matter of Jane Roe's right to abortion came to the Supreme Court. On Monday, January 22, 1973, after much internal controversy and disagreement, the Justices produced a complicated seven to two decision that pleased no one. They divided the period of pregnancy into thirds and ruled that during the first trimester women had unrestricted rights to abortion. During the next trimester, she had the right to terminate the pregnancy if she wished, but the state could regulate this to a limited degree. For the final trimester, the Supreme Court ruled that states—if they wished to do so—could protect the interests of future citizens and restrict abortion. The Supreme Court, however, prohibited states from adopting laws specifying when life began (*Roe v. Wade* 1973). This provoked continuing litigation about what ordinances states or municipalities could enact to limit abortions. Despite the confusion, *Roe v. Wade* is seen by its defenders and opponents as legitimating abortion, and so it symbolizes a major sexual change since it granted women the right to make their own decisions about bearing a child once they became pregnant.

A further development in the sexual revolution dates from the Stonewall Rebellion: June 28, 1969. The nation's many anti-sodomy laws never prevented homosexuality, although there is debate about how common a practice it was. By the 1960s, in New York and San Francisco, many bars, restaurants, bath houses, and stores attracted a gay clientele. Indeed, such places became meccas for homosexual men from across the nation. Although they seldom arrested men for violating sex laws, police in some cities harassed gay men, especially those who frequented the bars and sex clubs that catered to them. In New York, the police, from time to time, insulted, pummeled, or beat the habitues. On a June night in 1969, men enjoying their drinks and camaraderie at Stonewall Tavern decided they would not take such abuse any longer and fought back when the police arrived, leading to a bloody battle—great numbers of gay men versus police officers. Luckily, it was fought with fists and clubs, not guns, so there were no deaths. This gave birth to a public gay and lesbian liberation movement and the assertion that they should no longer be treated as second-class citizens. Just as other movements challenged exclusion on the basis of sex or skin color, this movement challenged discrimination on the basis of sexual orientation.

The Stonewall Rebellion raised the question of whether the state could use its police power to restrict the voluntary sexual behavior of consenting adults. This is linked to the issues of the civil rights decade, and these issues are far from settled. It is not yet clear that gays, lesbians, and bisexuals will be granted all the opportunities of heterosexuals. Can lesbian or gay couples adopt a child, or is this the prerogative of heterosexual married couples only? Should a gay partner of an employed man be granted the same insurance coverage as a wife? Under what circumstances and conditions may lesbian women or gay men serve in the Armed Forces? The most recent Supreme Court ruling (*Bowers v. Hardwick* 1986) rejected the principle that there was a constitutional right to privacy protecting homosexuality. If states wish, they may prohibit such behavior, but these laws will likely be as ineffectual and unenforced as Connecticut's birth control statute was three decades ago.

Changes in Attitudes About Sexuality

If a sexual revolution occurred, it involved much more than changes in laws and birth control technology. We would expect new views to become popular about what sexual activities are permissible or should be forbidden. Furthermore, we would expect substantial changes in actual sexual behavior.

Although questions about racial attitudes date from the 1940s, until recently few surveys were bold enough to ask people how they felt about sexual practices, especially those that violated state laws. The most informative time series dates from 1972. Figure 2-5 shows trends in how national samples judged sexual relations between adults of the same sex, extramarital sex, and premarital sex. They evaluated each of these on a five-point scale ranging from "always wrong" to "never wrong at all." Figure 2-5 reports the proportion saying "always wrong."

There are fascinating trends and differences here since homosexuality and unfaithfulness to one's marital partner are viewed extremely differently from premarital sex. Consistently, three-quarters have said that extramarital sex is "always wrong," so changes in sexual mores, if they have occurred, certainly do not approve of adultery. Most think it is wrong. An almost equal proportion think that homosexual sex is

Figure 2-5. Percent Giving the "Always Wrong" Responses to Questions About Three Kinds of Sexual Activity: 1972 to 1994

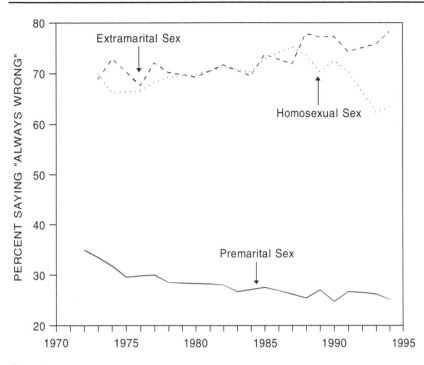

Questions:

Premarital Sex: There's been a lot of discussion about the way morals and attitudes about sex are changing in this country. If a man and a woman have sex relations before marriage, do you think it is always wrong, almost always wrong, wrong only sometimes, or not wrong at all?

Extramarital Sex: What is your opinion about a married person having sexual relations with someone other than the marriage partner? Is it always wrong, almost always wrong, wrong only sometimes, or not wrong at all?

Homosexual Sex: What about sexual relations between two adults of the same sex—do you think it is always wrong, almost always wrong, wrong only sometimes, or not wrong at all?

SOURCE: National Opinion Research Center 1994.

"always wrong," although the percentage giving that answer declined from 74 percent in 1988 to 62 percent in 1994. Future surveys will reveal whether the 1990s are the years in which the traditional condemnation of homosexual activity weakens. Generation X and their successors may adopt the view that sexuality is a private matter, and they may become more approving of homosexuality and bisexuality.

There is much more approval of premarital sex. Perhaps this is where the great change has occurred, and it may be the key to the sexual revolution. The proportion saying that premarital sex is always wrong dropped from 35 percent in the early 1970s to 26 percent twenty years later. For two decades, the typical answer to this question has been "not wrong at all." If there once was a strong view that sexual enjoyment should be delayed until after the wedding, it waned—but did not completely disappear. By the 1990s, most accepted or approved premarital sexuality.

What about approval of abortion? Did attitudes change dramatically after *Roe v. Wade?* The findings will surprise many. Despite the strenuous efforts of both the pro-choice and pro-life advocates, attitudes about abortion have hardly changed since the Supreme Court ruled. We became neither more liberal nor more conservative with regard to abortion. A clear and consistent pattern is shown in figure 2-6. Most Americans believe that abortion should be available if the mother's life is endangered (90 percent approve); if the pregnancy resulted from rape (about 80 percent approve); or if the child will be defective (about 80 percent also). But there is much less approval of the abortion option when it is used as a form of birth control. Only four adults in ten think that abortion should be an option when a woman cannot afford any more children, or because a married woman wants no more children. Approximately the same percentage approve abortion when a pregnant unmarried woman does not want to marry the father (data not shown in figure 2-6). And the question asking about abortion for any reason at all—the complete pro-choice option—is endorsed by less than 40 percent. *And these attitudes have hardly changed in the last twenty years.* Only a minority endorse abortion for any reason at all, but the overwhelming majority endorse it when the mother's life is threatened, when conception resulted from sexual crime, or when the child will be defective.

Stability over time in abortion attitudes is matched by a fairly stable abortion rate. A common index is the ratio of registered abortions to live births in a year. Just after *Roe* this ratio was about 330 abortions for every 1,000 live births. This gradually increased to a peak of 440 abortions per 1,000 live births in 1983, and then fell back to about 380 in 1992, suggesting a fall of 14 percent in the last decade (Henshaw and Van Vort 1994, table 1). It is not clear whether this

Figure 2-6. Percentage of National Samples Thinking It Should Be Possible for a Woman to Obtain an Abortion for Specific Reasons

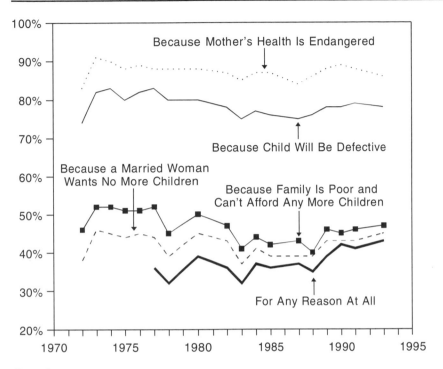

Questions:
Please tell me whether or not you think it should be possible for a pregnant woman to obtain a legal abortion (**reasons read from card**):

- If the woman's own health is seriously endangered by the pregnancy?
- If there is a strong chance of serious defects in the baby?
- If the family has a very low income and cannot afford any more children?
- If she is married and does not want any more children?
- The woman wants it for any reason?

SOURCE: National Opinion Research Center 1994, item 206.

results from better use of birth control or the increasing difficulty that some women face in finding abortionists.

Have actual sexual practices changed? Is there much more pre-marital, extramarital, and homosexual activity than before? Although there is a history of attempting to measure sexual activities, including the Kinsey studies of the late 1940s and the more recent Janus Report on sexual behavior (Janus and Janus 1993), most of these efforts have been severely criticized for their methodological errors, especially the lack of representative samples (Greeley 1994). With changing social values and concerns about the spread of AIDS, there has been a recent development of rigorous studies providing information about the current proportions of people engaging in specific activities, but these cannot provide much information about changes over time (Michael et al. 1995). One important exception is the National Study of Family Growth. Representative samples of adult women have been asked questions about the date of first intercourse, their age at marriage, and many questions about their current sexual activities. Findings from this survey are consistent with the idea that premarital sexual activity increased very much in recent decades. There are convincing reasons to believe that this would happen since the average age at first marriage for women moved up five years since the 1950s and since better contraceptives became popular. Premarital sex among teenagers became more common as the baby boom cohorts entered their teens. Shown below are the percentage of women who said they had sex for the first time, while unmarried, before their fifteenth, their seventeenth, and their nineteenth birthdays:

Sexual Activity of Young Women in Three Birth Cohorts

	World War II	Early Baby Boom	Late Baby Boom
Before Age 15	3%	5%	9%
Before Age 17	14	20	33
Before Age 19	32	48	64

SOURCE: Hofferth, Kahn, and Baldwin 1987.

Among the World War II birth cohorts, just 3 percent engaged in sex before their fifteenth birthday while unmarried and 32 percent before age 19. Thus, two-thirds of the unmarried women went through high school without a sexual partner. It was greatly different for the late baby boom women. Nine percent were sexually active before age 15 and 64 percent before age 19, so only one-third got to age 19 without a sexual partner. The majority of women in the late baby boom cohort and in Generation X engaged in sex before high school graduation, a sharp change from the practices of earlier cohorts. (For corroborating information from the survey of American sexual practices, see Michael et al. 1995, pp. 88–94; Laumann et al. 1994, pp. 322–333.)

Conclusion

We share common views about what is appropriate, what is normal, and what is permissible. Sometimes these values change slowly over the course of many decades. Other times symbolic events, including court decisions, laws, presidential proclamations, and rioting, mark key turning points. The decade of the 1960s was one such time. Our views about including African Americans and women in our society on the same basis as white men changed, albeit gradually with the shift culminating in the events of the 1960s. In that decade, our elected representative sought to fix the denial of equal opportunities with new laws. Simultaneously, the 1960s apparently mark a turning point in our views about marriage, divorce, and what sexual behavior is appropriate and legal. As the consequence of these changes, baby boom cohorts and Generation X had more options about how they lived their lives. Women and blacks could, more realistically, aspire to climb the occupational ladder and they, as well as white men, had more choices about their living arrangements. But these aspirations and choices are also strongly influenced by economic opportunities. The next chapter explains how ground rules concerning economic success and failure were rewritten after the energy crisis of 1973.

Chapter 3

The 1970s: A Turning Point in the Nation's Economy and Whom It Rewards

From the viewpoint of the 1990s, the long interval stretching from 1945, when Germany and Japan surrendered, to 1973, when the OPEC finance ministers met, seems characterized by highly favorable economic trends, trends that permitted most young white men with high school educations to marry, raise children, and buy starter homes in the suburbs before they reached their early thirties. Extensive changes in the subsequent two decades have made it more challenging for similar men—and the women they marry—to be included in the middle class.

In 1972, Americans could buy a gallon of gasoline for about thirty-five cents, but in 1973 the finance ministers of the major oil-producing countries restricted the flow of petroleum to the United States. And for a few years OPEC (Organization of Petroleum Exporting Countries) maintained a highly effective cartel (Thurow 1980, p. 21). The price of gasoline jumped, eventually going above a dollar and a quarter a gallon in the United States. Worse yet, the shortfall in imported oil led to a brief period when gasoline was hard to find, and long queues formed around filling stations. For many, the cost of daily commuting doubled, and the government even printed ration stamps for gasoline just as they had in World War II, but they were never used. The cheap transportation that Americans had taken for granted suddenly became much more expensive. All manufactured products increased in price since firms had to pay more to ship their goods from factories to stores. In less than two years, we switched from a nation of plentiful, cheap energy to one in which energy supplies were costly and uncertain.

The oil price shock separates two economic eras. Between 1940, when manufacturing output boomed because of warfare in Europe, and the early 1970s, the modern American middle-class was created. Millions of men—many of them from rural backgrounds with just a

few years of secondary school education—found steady jobs in the
thousands of factories that produced steel, autos, and appliances, or
they got good-paying work on the trucks and trains that shipped these
products to the corners of the nation. Many other men worked jobs
in construction, a booming sector since federal fiscal policies encouraged the building of the new suburban rings after World War II, an
interstate highway system in the 1950s, and then, later, the modern
office buildings found in many downtowns and the new "edge" cities
that sprung up on what used to be farmland.

Figure 3-1 portrays this growth of the middle class. Using data
from the Census Bureau pertaining to pre-tax cash income, I classify
households into one of five categories of poverty or prosperity:

> *Very poor.* Pre-tax cash incomes are below one-half the poverty line
> for households of their size.
> *Poor.* Cash incomes are between one-half the poverty line and the
> poverty line itself. For a household of four in 1995, the poverty line
> was $15,700.
> *Near Poor.* Cash incomes are between the poverty line and twice the
> poverty line.
> *Middle Class.* Cash incomes are between twice the poverty line and
> five times the poverty line.
> *Comfortable.* Cash incomes are five times or more the poverty line;
> that is, with incomes exceeding $63,400 for a family of four.

Figure 3-1 reports the findings. Coming out of the Depression
decade, almost two-thirds of the population lived in households with
incomes below the current poverty standard. Only one person in eight
lived in a household with a middle-class income; that is, an income
two to five times the poverty line. But World War II and the many
prosperous years that followed changed this, so the middle class included a much larger share of the population, and the census of 1960
reported that, for the first time, a majority were in the middle economic class and that about 5 percent were comfortable: their household incomes were more than five times the poverty line. One of the
most important symbols of middle-class status—homeownership—became common. In 1940, only 37 percent of urban households lived in
homes they owned or were buying. By 1970, this was up to 58 percent
(U.S. Bureau of the Census, 1943a, table 9; 1971, table 10). Every
census from 1940 through 1970 recorded declines in the impoverished population and rises in the middle class, but this beneficial trend
came to an end in the early 1970s.

Figure 3-1.   Economic Status of the Total Population: 1940 to 1994

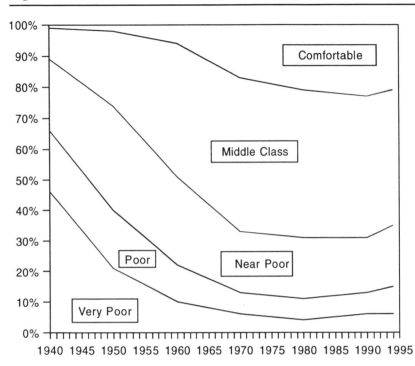

Very Poor. The percentage of population in households with pre-tax cash incomes less than 50 percent of the poverty line for households of their size.
Poor. The percentage of population in households with pre-tax cash incomes between 50 percent and 99 percent of the poverty line for households of their size.
Near Poor. The percentage of population in households with pre-tax cash income between 100 percent and 199 percent of the poverty line for households of their size.
Middle Class. The percentage of population in households with pre-tax cash incomes between 100 percent and 499 percent of the poverty line for households of their size.
Comfortable. The percentage of population in households with pre-tax cash incomes 500 percent or more of the poverty line for households of their size. In 1995, a household of four fell below their poverty line if their pre-tax cash income was less than $15,719 (1995 dollars).

SOURCE: U.S. Bureau of the Census, Public Use Microdata Samples from the censuses of 1940 to 1990; and the 1994 Current Population Survey.

The Post–World War II Era of Growth and Prosperity

From the viewpoint of the 1990s, the long interval stretching from 1945, when Germany and Japan surrendered, to 1973, when the OPEC finance ministers met, seems characterized by highly favorable economic trends, trends that permitted most young white men with high school educations to marry, raise children, and buy starter homes in the suburbs before they reached their early thirties. Extensive changes in the subsequent two decades have made it more challenging for similar men—and the women they marry—to be included in the middle class.

Continued Economic Growth and Expansion

Employment boomed during World War II, but consumers could buy little since the nation's factories mostly turned out guns, ships, warplanes, and jeeps. No new automobiles rolled off Detroit's assembly lines and almost no new single-family homes were constructed. Like it or not, people saved money, often by buying war bonds. As a result, they had money to spend on cars, new homes, and furnishings in the years just after VJ day. Indeed, the need for consumer durables was great since, during the Depression decade, families had spent only for necessities.

The gross domestic product (GDP) measures the size of the economy. This is the total market value, expressed in dollars, of goods and services produced by workers in factories, shops, and offices in the United States. In 1995, for instance, the GDP was $5.5 trillion, or about $21,000 per capita. The nation's GDP increased at the healthy rate of about 4.0 percent annually during the 1950s and 4.1 percent annually in the 1960s (Council of Economic Advisors 1996, table B-6). At these rates, the nation's output would double in seventeen years.

Many factors encouraged this rapid economic growth. Throughout the 1950s we had a marriage and baby boom, creating a high rate of household formation. These new households first rented apartments and then bought homes, appliances, and television sets, thereby stimulating further economic expansion. The government had developed programs in the 1930s to encourage homeownership, and these aims were realized after World War II. The Federal Home Administration (FHA) and the Veteran's Administration (VA) allowed blue-collar families to purchase new homes with minimum down payments, and the

Federal National Mortgage Association (FNMA) lured capital to the housing market with attractive packaging of home loans for large investors. The nation invaded and conquered the "crabgrass frontier" by constructing millions of suburban homes for the new middle class (Jackson 1985), and then local governments built roads, sewer systems, parks, and schools for the baby boom cohorts. The school age population more than doubled in the twenty years following 1950 (U.S. Bureau of the Census 1975, p. 15), so demographic processes fueled economic expansion. Just as the post–World War II spending boom was approaching its end, the United States fought a land war in Korea. And then, in the late 1950s, the government built the extensive new system of interstate highways, an economic development project similar to the support provided railroads seventy-five years earlier. In the mid-1960s, the United States began its long participation in the Vietnam War. Unlike the situation in World War II when domestic production was curtailed, the Korean and Vietnam wars were "guns and butter" conflicts. The government spent generously on military appropriations without forcing consumers to cut back on purchases, so the domestic economy continued its booming growth.

Full Employment

On the first Friday of every month the Bureau of Labor Statistics reports the unemployment rate. This is the proportion of the labor force, that is, the sum of those working and those looking for work, who did not find jobs in the last month. Rapid economic growth in the post–World War II years led to consistently short unemployment lines—a high proportion of those who looked for jobs found them. The national unemployment rate averaged only 4.4 percent during the 1950s and fell under 3 percent during 1952 and 1953 when U.S. servicemen battled Korean and Chinese troops. In the 1960s, the average unemployment rate was 4.7 percent, but it sunk below 4 percent during the prosperous Vietnam War years.

The definition of a high, a moderate, or a low unemployment rate depends upon the expectations of the time. Unemployment was a central issue when John Kennedy campaigned against Richard Nixon in 1960. Many observers felt that Kennedy squeezed out his narrow victory because he effectively blamed the Eisenhower-Nixon administration for high unemployment. But in October of that election year, the unemployment rate was 5.0 percent, a rate that presidential candidates now would boast about (Killingsworth 1968, chap. 1; U.S. Bureau of Labor Statistics 1988, table A-31).

Demographic trends help explain the low unemployment rates of the 1950s and 1960s. The labor force participation of women remained minimal since they married young and then raised their children while staying at home. And foreign immigration was low, so few workers came from Latin America or Asia to compete with the native-born.

Rising Productivity: The Key to Higher Wages

Labor productivity is defined as the value of goods and services produced per hour of labor input. For example, a factory employing 150 men builds 10,000 refrigerators in one year worth $3.5 million wholesale. The next year 150 men employed in that same factory produce 12,000 refrigerators worth $4.2 million. Since the labor input is the same but the value of the output, in constant dollar amounts, increased by 14 percent, the productivity of these workers went up by 14 percent. Productivity in this plant might increase for several reasons. Management may have installed new machinery to let the same workers produce more ice boxes, management may have provided more training to the same workers, or management might have fired the sluggards and slackers and replaced them with the same number of diligent workers.

Increasing productivity is crucial to employment and prosperity because it stimulates higher wages. If the manufacturer has greater sales with the same number of workers, she can pay higher wages and still see her profits increase. And if she does not pay them more, these increasingly productive men will look for different employers who will reward them more appropriately. But if the productivity of her workers declines, she will have to freeze wages and then reduce them since her sales revenue falls but her work force remains the same. In the long run, our ability to increase our consumption and spend more, be it for new clothes or for research to cure cancer, depends upon increasing productivity. With constant or declining productivity, our standards of living will stagnate or fall (Levy 1995, pp. 6–10).

Labor productivity rose steadily and at a sustained high rate following World War II. Considering all workers in the private economy, productivity increased by about one-third during the 1950s and then by an additional 30 percent in the 1960s. Each year, output per hour of work went up about 3 percent, allowing employers to consistently raise wages. This trend ended with the oil price shock of 1973.

U.S. Domination of World Markets

By 1945, bombing by the Allies had destroyed the industrial capacity of our present economic rivals: Germany and Japan. Many nations who now sell us their manufactured products, such as Korea, Brazil, and China, had almost no ability to make and export desirable goods for the U.S. market. Consequently, U.S. manufacturers dominated world markets for many goods even though there were many imports since Americans have always bought French wines, English woolens, and, starting in the mid-1950s, Volkswagon Beetles. But, in the 1950s and 1960s, for every $1,000 of imports, there were about $1,150 of exports. This consistently favorable balance of trade boosted the domestic economy, helping to create the good jobs that enlarged the middle class.

Low Rates of Inflation

Families and businesses look forward to steady prices—that is, to low rates of inflation. We ordinarily make projections about our future living expenses, so if the price of meat, milk, or gasoline jumps 10 percent in one month, we become cautious with our spending, fearing that more price shocks are coming. Lenders are troubled by the prospect of inflation since if they loan money to a family for a new house or to a business for a new factory at a fixed rate of interest and there is great inflation, they will be paid back with dollars worth much less than they expected. To protect themselves, lenders will raise interest rates when they expect inflation, which, in turn, will discourage investments by consumers and firms because of the high cost of interest.

Measuring inflation—or the changing value of a dollar—is a complicated and often controversial endeavor. The most common indicator is the consumer price index. The cost of a standard basket of goods and services representing the purchases of a typical household is regularly priced in sample surveys conducted by government interviewers. If the identical basket of goods and services costs $100 one year and $106 the next, the cost of living has gone up by 6 percent. Or, stated differently, the value of the dollar falls by 6 percent since it costs $106 to purchase exactly what $100 purchased in the previous year. This doesn't necessarily mean that everyone's expenditures went up 6 percent. If the price of meat skyrockets while that of fowl stays low, people will adjust and eat more chicken legs and less filet mignon.

For several decades after World War II, prices rose modestly from one year to the next. In the 1950s, the consumer price index went up an average of about 2 percent annually; in the next decade, by about 2.7 percent every year. Consumers and lenders felt that they were in an era of predictably stable prices, making them confident about continued economic growth.

Generally Increasing Earnings

There are many appropriate indicators of trends in earnings. One is the hourly wage rate of production line and nonsupervisory workers in the nonagricultural sector. In 1947, such workers earned an average of $7.28 per hour (in constant 1993 dollars). By 1960, this had risen to $10.15, and then it peaked at $12.76 per hour in 1973. Or consider the weekly wages for production line workers in manufacturing industries. In 1947, this was $295 (in constant 1993 dollars), going up to $393 in 1960, and then to the high-water mark of $472 in 1973 (Council of Economic Advisors 1996, table 43). Remember that if a worker earns about $500 every week, the annual earnings are about $25,000. The real purchasing power of earnings went up an average of more than 2 percent per year between the end of World War II and the oil price shock. This may not sound like much, but it is a major economic accomplishment since it means that, at the end of the decade, the typical worker spending the same amount of time on the job was able to purchase about 25 percent more than he or she could at the start of the decade. It is particularly impressive in light of what came after 1973—generally falling wages.

Were all groups included in these trends? If not, then who became economically prosperous and who did not fare so well? Prior to the 1970s, little information was gathered about Hispanics or Asians since their numbers were sparse. While the earnings of blacks rose rapidly, the racial gap remained large. Black men earned an average of only 55 percent as much as white men in 1950, 58 percent as much in 1960, and then—with a major boost from the booming economy and, perhaps, from innovative civil rights legislation—to 64 percent as much as white men in 1970 (Smith and Welch 1986, table 1). So wages for blacks went up faster than those for whites, but black men continued to take home much thinner pay envelopes than white men.

The gender gap in earnings did not close in this era. The story here is complex. Few women worked in 1950. Younger women were staying home to take care of their children and older married women rarely entered the labor force. A relatively high proportion of the few women who worked in 1950 had been on their jobs for a long time, so they had rather high earnings (Goldin 1990, chap. 2) In the early 1950s women earned about 64 percent as much as men. But later in that decade older married women who had raised their children started working, often at part-time jobs in retail shops and offices. Few of these women had extensive job histories or much in the line of specialized training, so their earnings were meagre. Thus, by 1960 the ratio of women's to men's earnings fell to .59 and it remained there until the 1980s (Bianchi and Spain 1986, table 6.2). The gender gap in earnings did not start to close until the Reagan years.

The Switch from Agriculture to Manufacturing

A uniquely favorable opportunity developed in the 1940s and 1950s for millions of men in rural areas who had limited educations. There has always been a trend toward mechanization in farming, but in the twenty-five years after World War II, farm employment dropped sharply, causing agricultural productivity to rise spectacularly. The proportion of cotton picked by hand dropped from 92 percent in 1950 to 30 percent twelve years later (Smith and Welch 1986, table 34). Larger tractors, better seeds, more effective ways to control pests, and improved fertilizers meant that fewer and fewer farmers grew the crops sold in supermarkets. This also created a large surplus of corn, wheat, and oats to be sold abroad or used to feed the burgeoning populations of developing countries in this era before the Green Revolution turned quite a few Third World countries into food exporters.

At the end of World War II, more than eight million persons labored on farms, accounting for one in eight workers. Among men, one in six worked in agriculture (U.S. Bureau of the Census 1975, series D-16). Within fifteen years, that number was cut in half. Fortunately, many of the men displaced by mechanization on farms found city jobs since the skills needed for working on farms—a dedication to hard work in difficult circumstances, an ability to do what the boss wants, and physical strength—were ideally suited for many industrial jobs. If urban employers had demanded a highly literate, computer-ready work force, the basic economic trends would have been very different.

From 1973 to the Present: An Era of Rapid Economic Shifts

The two decades following 1973 differ from the early period in important ways. The skills and abilities that guaranteed white men middle-class status in the early era were less rewarded, so for many it became extremely difficult to enter or remain in the middle class because of new occupational demands. But these have not been bleak economic years. To the contrary, they have been years of growth and higher living standards. Employment, that is, the number of workers holding jobs, went up an average of 1.6 percent each year between 1973 and 1995—just about the same as the growth rate of employment in the previous twenty years (Council of Economic Advisors 1996, table B-32). The rate of job creation hardly slowed down. Per capita income—$15,600 in 1993—went up and was 23 percent greater than in 1973 in constant dollar amounts, so the typical person is now much better off than before we entered this era of economic change and uncertainty (U.S. Bureau of the Census 1991; 1995a, Appendix D). This increase in per capita income is due, not to rising wages but rather to the increase in labor force participation by women and to the demographic shift toward more workers and fewer dependents. *Per capita income has gone up steadily, not because wages are rising but because a higher percentage of people are working.*

Fundamental differences distinguish the two eras. The post–World War II boom was a rising economic tide that lifted all boats, albeit one that left female and black workers far behind white men (Danziger and Gottschalk 1993, introduction). In this recent period, many have found expanded opportunities and much higher wages, but some who prospered in the past found themselves just holding on in the restructured economy. Let's begin by looking at the major trends influencing employment in this period.

A Shift Away from Manufacturing

Employment opportunities are strongly influenced by how consumers spend their money. In the United States there has been a fundamental shift toward more consumer spending for services. One clear way to describe what happened is to allocate all spending by consumers into one of two categories: manufactured products, including housing, and services, including healthcare from nurses and doctors, personal care

Figure 3-2a. Share of Personal Consumer Expenditures Spent for Manufactured Goods or Services: 1960 to 1994

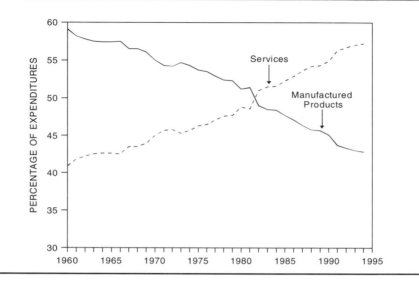

SOURCE: Council of Economic Advisors 1995, table B-1.

Figure 3-2b. Value of Manufactured Goods Exported Minus Value of Manufactured Goods Imported: 1960 to 1994 (amounts in constant 1989 dollars)

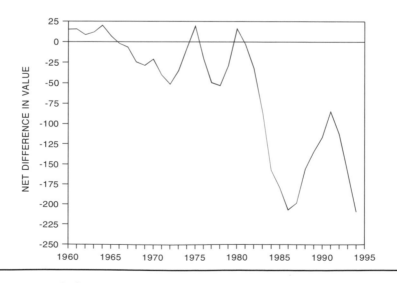

SOURCE: Council of Economic Advisors 1995, table B-22.

from barbers and beauticians, and repair work from shops (see figure 3-2a). In 1960, we devoted about 60 percent of our income to manufactured goods and about 40 percent to services. Service spending grew consistently, both before and after the 1973 turning point. By the early 1990s, services and manufactured goods had reversed their standings, and consumers now devote almost 60 percent of their spending to services.

The increasing share of moneys spent on health and medical care is of concern to all of us. When John Kennedy was elected president, Americans typically spent $695 per year for this purpose. In 1990, this had more than tripled to $2,135 per capita (in constant 1993 dollars). This money has been well spent: the life span went from 69.7 years in 1960 to 75.4 years in 1990—an addition of almost six years (U.S. National Center for Health Statistics 1993, table 4). In 1960, 5.3 percent of the national product went to healthcare; in 1995, 14.9 percent (Council of Economic Advisors 1996, table B-13). At the earlier date, total purchases of manufactured goods were about 20 percent greater than purchases of medical care, but by the early 1990s spending for health and medical care exceeded the purchases of durable goods. We decided either deliberately or unconsciously to devote much more of our income to medical care, thereby creating many very good jobs in that field, but it has not been such a good time for factory workers.

The internationalization of markets and production also influences employment trends, especially in manufacturing. In the 1960s, foreign producers started selling their goods here in great amounts. Sometimes they had a price advantage since they paid their workers much less than did employers in this country. Increasingly, clothes and textile products came from Southeast Asia, and the toys we buy now come from China. A strategy used by some domestic firms was to shift their production offshore so that they could benefit from low wages of foreign workers. Many manufacturing plants were built just south of the Rio Grande. This boosts imports and makes it more difficult for some U.S. workers to find good manufacturing jobs. For other products, it was the quality of foreign-made goods that explained their success in this country. From the late 1970s into the 1980s, Japanese cars were often more stylish and of higher quality than those made in American plants, so imports eventually captured one-third of the automobile market, greatly troubling many workers in the Rustbelt states (U.S. Bureau of the Census 1995b, table 1024).

Manufactured goods account for the lion's share of imports and exports, about three-quarters of our merchandise exports and more than four-fifths of imports. Figure 3-2b shows the balance of trade in manufactured goods from 1960 to the present and illustrates a change that strongly influenced employment and earnings of those men and women who produced manufactured goods. In the 1960s, the United States had a favorable balance of trade, but in the 1980s we imported $1,349 of manufactured goods for every $1,000 sold abroad.

Gender Changes in Labor Force Participation

A continuing trend of crucial importance to our story about economic change is the increasing labor force participation of women. During the post–World War II baby boom era, few women worked, but by the 1960s women began to enter the labor force in large numbers. This is shown in figure 3-3, which reports the percentage of men and women aged 16 and over who were employed or who were looking for jobs each year. Women began entering the labor market in large numbers after 1970, and by the late 1980s a majority of women worked. Among men there were declines in labor force participation, largely attributable to earlier retirement. Thus, the gender gap in labor force participation narrowed but it did not close since, in 1995, 59 percent of women and 75 percent of men (aged 16 and over) were participating (Council of Economic Advisors 1996, table B-35).

A similar trend is evident when we exclude the younger population—many of them still in school—and older persons approaching retirement age. The figures below show the modest decline in percentage of men aged 25 to 54 in the labor force and the sharp rise among women (U.S. Bureau of the Census 1964, table 194; 1973b, table 218; 1983, table 272; 1993a, table 44).

While there has been an increase in the labor force participation of women in all marital statuses, a dominating change of the last three decades is much more work by married women and those with young

Labor Force Participation Rates for Persons Aged 25 to 54

Year	Men	Women
1960	95%	41%
1970	94	49
1980	92	64
1990	91	74

Figure 3-3. Labor Force Participation Rates for Civilians Aged 16 and Over, by Sex: 1960 to 1994

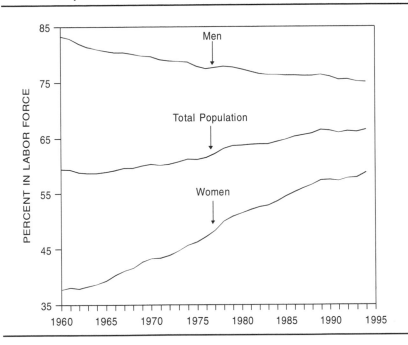

SOURCE: Council of Economic Advisors 1995, tables B-33 and B-37.

children. In 1960, only 31 percent of married women living with their husbands were at work or looking for jobs; by 1994, this rose to 61 percent. And the presence of young children no longer deters women. In the 1960s, fewer than one mother in five with a child under age 6 was in the labor force, but by 1994 this increased to 62 percent; that is, an even higher rate of labor force participation than for all married women (U.S. Bureau of the Census 1995b, table 638). Being married and having preschool children does not limit women's labor force activity the way it did just a generation ago.

Three forces account for this massive change. First, American values about the social and economic roles of women switched. Increasingly, women found it fulfilling to utilize their talents and skills, first in getting an education and later in working. No longer do our norms and values condemn married women with children who work. Second, wages of women generally rose. As their earnings went up, women found it more financially rewarding to be at work and, simultaneously, more costly to remain at home. Third, falling wages of men undoubtedly led many wives and mothers to take jobs to supplement family incomes.

Stagnating or Declining Wages

After three decades of generally increasing wages, recent changes led to a new pattern of stagnating wages, especially for men. Figure 3-4 illustrates this trend and shows clearly why 1973 marks the end of the post–World War II era of economic growth and prosperity: earnings have not gone up since the oil price shock. Since most workers are nonsupervisory personnel employed in the private sector, this figure lays out trends affecting the majority of American workers. After reaching a peak in 1973, the long climb of earnings came to its end, and wages stagnated during periods of both economic growth and contraction. Periods of economic recession are indicated by a shaded vertical bar. Bennett Harrison and Barry Bluestone aptly use the title, *The Great U-Turn,* to describe this shift from rising earnings to stagnation and then decline.

Lest someone think this trend is dominated by those part-time employees who serve us food in restaurants and check out our groceries, consider the earnings of those persons who worked full-time throughout the year. The earnings of full-time men peaked in 1973, fluctuated a bit in the years thereafter, and then slowly declined. By the early 1990s, men who worked full-time every week had paychecks with 10 percent less purchasing power than did men who worked full-time twenty years earlier. For women, the news was slightly more optimistic: the trend of the 1960s toward higher earnings slowed down after 1973. But the 1980s were moderately good years for women and, by 1993, full-time women workers were earning about 15 percent more than similar women had two decades earlier. *On average, employed men in the 1990s earned less than men did in the early 1970s, but employed women earned more.*

An Economic Roller Coaster

Long-run trends in consumer spending, such as the purchase of Japanese-made Toyotas rather than Chevrolets, help account for employment opportunities. But short-run fluctuations in the business cycle, such as sharp increases in inflation, dramatic changes in interest rates, or sudden falls in the value of the dollar, motivate employers to

Figure 3-4. Average Hourly and Weekly Earnings for Private Sector Workers: 1960 to 1993 (amounts in 1993 dollars)

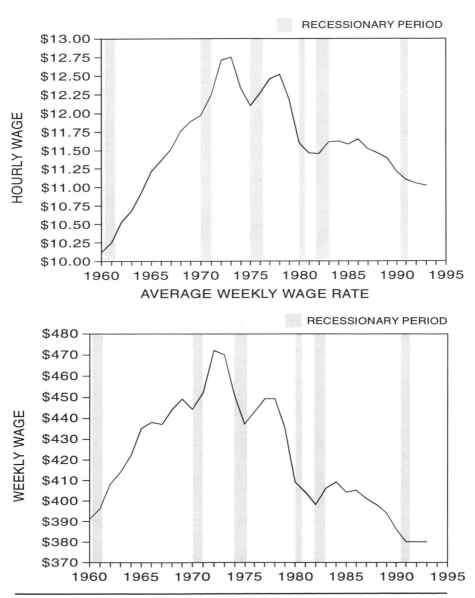

SOURCE: Council of Economic Advisors 1995, table B-45.

change the way they do business. Radical changes may be forced upon employers because new economic conditions make old practices obsolete. Indeed, some of the largest and best-known firms of the early 1970s are out of business, including Pan American Airlines, Penn Central Railroad, and Eastern Airlines. The country would have been reduced to two major domestic auto firms had not the federal government bailed out Chrysler.

More so than in the post–World War II era when economic trends operated steadily, abrupt changes occurred in the last two decades, sending the message that it was no longer business as usual. Employers reacted to these changes; the consequences, as revealed by the census of 1990, were more opportunities for women and for workers with advanced training. But job prospects and earnings became worse for people with little education, especially for men.

Figure 3-5 summarizes basic economic trends since 1960 by showing the year-to-year change in the gross domestic product (controlling for inflation). It also reports the overall unemployment rate. In prosperous periods, the GDP grew at 4 to 6 percent from one year to the next, and the unemployment rate was low—5 percent or less. When the nation entered a recession, the GDP declined and unemployment shot up. The six recessions since 1960 are marked by shaded vertical bars. The 1960s were an exceptionally prosperous decade with only a brief recession at the start; and the GDP grew at an annual rate of about 6 percent in the late 1960s while the unemployment rate sank under 4 percent.

The economy entered a brief recession in 1970 characterized by higher interest rates, inflation, and a temporary rise in joblessness. The conditions at that time were considered serious and unusual, so much so that there was consensus about taking drastic actions. In 1971, President Nixon abolished the gold standard for our currency in hopes that this would stimulate growth. Perhaps it did, since this recession was a short one. In retrospect, the oil crisis was much more of a turning point than was the jettisoning of the gold standard.

1973 to 1979: Years of Economic Change and Uncertainty

Immediately after the oil price shock, the rate of inflation jumped and then interest rates soared, causing consumers to cut back on their spending and employers to reduce their investments because of the high costs of borrowing (Thurow 1984, p. 57). The result was a serious recession: the growth rate of the GDP went from a healthy

Figure 3-5. Annual Change in Real Gross Domestic Product and Annual Unemployment Rate for Total Labor Force: 1960 to 1994

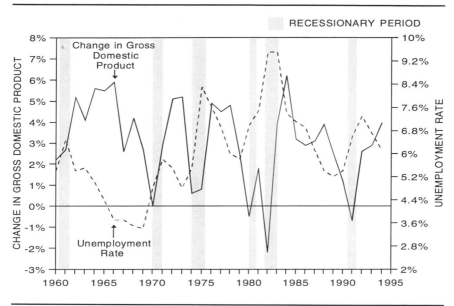

SOURCE: Council of Economic Advisors 1995, tables B-2 and B-33.

+5 percent in both 1972 and 1973 to a −1 percent in each of the next two years. Troubling for many workers and families was the inevitable rise in unemployment. In a typical month of 1975, about 8 million people were out of work, compared to about 4.3 million each month two years earlier.

But the economy resumed growth in 1975. Several forces account for this. One was the government's decision to let the dollar decline, especially against the yen and the mark. As a result, manufactured products from the United States fared well on world markets since it took fewer yen or marks to buy our products. Conversely, imported products became more expensive since foreign producers wanted more of the devalued dollars, and thus fewer German or Japanese cars were sold here. The weakened dollar was a boon to manufacturers in this country and allowed firms to put off increasing productivity.

Interest rates stayed rather high during the 1970s, making it costly for firms to introduce the labor-saving equipment that might have increased labor productivity. Another force in the same direction was the high rate of inflation, which made for uncertainty about the future. Indeed, employers could hold costs in check during this era by keeping wage increases below inflation.

These economic trends of the later half of the 1970s had three specific consequences (Levy 1995). First, these years are marked by a slowdown in the long-term trend toward greater labor productivity. Figure 3-6 shows trends in productivity: output per hour for private-sector employees. Additionally, it presents an index of productivity for manufacturing industries. After consistently rising by 3 percent per year in the post–World War II years, productivity increased little between 1973 and 1983—the average change being a humble increase of 0.7 percent annually. This decade-long stagnation in productivity exerted strong downward pressure on wages.

Figure 3-6.   Index of Output per Hour for Private Sector Employees: 1960 to 1994

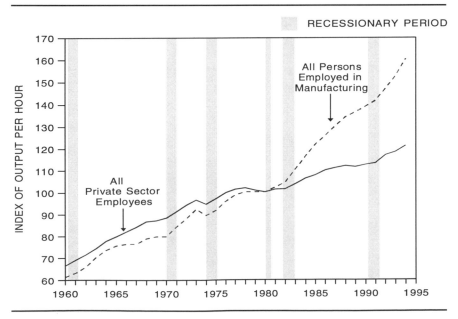

SOURCE: U.S. Bureau of Labor Statistics, 1989, *Handbook of Labor Statistics*, Bulletin 2340, table 98; 1994, *Monthly Labor Review*, Vol. 117, No. 12, table 44.

NOTE: 1980 = 100

Second, there was a rural renaissance in these years (Fuguitt, Brown, and Beale 1989, pp. 27–31). Reversing a trend of more than a century, small towns, a few rural areas, and many smaller metropolises in the hinterlands began to grow more rapidly in population than the nation's largest urban centers. This resulted from higher prices for energy, which led to greater employment and prosperity in the oil patch, in coalfields, and in locations where crews of geologists explored for petroleum. In addition, the boost given by the weakened dollar sustained employment in the smaller manufacturing centers such as the farm equipment centers in Iowa. Finally, U.S. agricultural products did well on world markets in this span since the Green Revolution was just beginning to make developing lands competitive. This helped to stabilize population trends in rural areas. Farm employment dropped by two million in the 1960s, but by only 100,000 in the 1970s (Fuguitt, Brown, and Beale 1989, p. 29).

Third, as a result of the economic trends of 1975–79, the demand for unskilled labor rose more rapidly than that for college-trained workers. There was, in fact, something of a surplus of college-educated men. One of the unintended consequences of the Vietnam War was a sharp increase in college completion among men in the early baby boom cohorts, since one way to avoid the life-threatening risks of that unpopular Asian war was to stay enrolled in college. The rate of college completion was higher for men entering the labor market in the 1970s than for those born a decade earlier or a decade later. But the job market did not expand so rapidly, so the financial benefit of having a college education declined in the 1970s. In 1969, college-educated men (aged 25 to 54) earned 46 percent more than men who just completed secondary school. In 1979, their advantage declined to 36 percent.

July 25, 1979: The Adoption of High Interest Rates

The restructuring of manufacturing that eventually produced declining opportunities and smaller paychecks for low-skilled workers but better wages for highly trained persons was greatly hastened by a decision announced on July 25, 1979. President Carter realized that although the economy was growing, trends were not at all favorable for a sitting president. The unemployment rate exceeded 6 percent, almost double what it had been a decade earlier, and both interest and inflation rates were so high that they discouraged new investments, thereby depressing employment. Even more troubling for a presidential candidate were the annual rises in consumer prices. They had gone up less than 3 percent each year in the 1960s but about 8 percent in the late 1970s. Whenever a voter bought groceries or gasoline, she or he was reminded of the sharply rising cost of living—a problem that voters were likely to blame on the administration's economic policies.

On July 25, President Carter removed William Miller from his position as head of the Federal Reserve Board (the Fed) and appointed him Secretary of the Treasury. Paul Volcker was selected to chair the Fed and given marching orders to bring down skyrocketing consumer prices. Chairman Volcker and the Fed promptly set out to accomplish this by drastically increasing interest rates. Just before the oil price shock in 1973, a couple looking for a new home could have locked in an interest rate of 8 percent, which was pretty high by the standards of the post–World War II era, but much, much lower than the 13 percent interest rate they would have had to pay in 1980. During this fight against inflation, the Fed's tight money policies led banks to triple the interest rate charged their most reliable commercial customers to an eventual high of 19 percent (Council of Economic Advisors 1996, table B-69).

These policies reduced the rate of inflation, but not rapidly enough to save the Carter presidency. The economic troubles of the late 1970s help explain one of the most lopsided elections of this century: the incumbents won only five states, two of them being the home states of the candidates themselves.

Economic Policies of the Reagan Years

Upon taking office, the Reagan administration faced crucial economic decisions. An early decision to continue the fight against inflation caused interest rates to rise during the first eighteen months of the new president's term. In 1982, for example, a mortgage for a new home carried a record high of 15 percent as an annual rate. Families could not afford such high interest rates, so they stopped buying new cars or homes, and employers could not afford to borrow what they needed for new plants or equipment. Sales of domestic automobiles plunged from 9.3 million in 1978 to 5.8 million four years later. In the same period, the sale of homes was cut in half (U.S. Bureau of the Census 1985, table 1036). The outcome was the most severe recession since the Great Depression, with more than 10 percent of the labor force out of work from September 1982 through the summer of the next year—double or triple the rates of most of the post–World War II years. By this time, economists devised a new index—the misery index—the sum of the consumer price index and the unemployment rate (Bluestone and Harrison 1982, p. 5). That misery index rose mightily in the early 1980s, reflecting the economic pain and troubles experienced by millions of Americans.

But there was another component to the economic policies of the new administration. By the early 1980s, workers and politicians became aware of stagnant wages. Consumers wanted an increase in what they could spend so that they could stay solvent in an era of rapid inflation. One strategy to accomplish this and to simultaneously stimulate the economy was to cut federal income taxes. So, in the summer of 1981, federal income taxes were cut by almost one-third, as Congress and the administration enacted the Economic Recovery Act, an economic policy popular with almost everyone. Rather than reducing governmental spending to compensate for the loss of revenue, planners assumed that the tax cut would so stimulate the economy that tax revenues would soon grow back to where they had been before the cut. Thus the decision was made to continue generous governmental spending, including a major boost in defense, using borrowed dollars when necessary.

These policies began to have favorable effects. Consumer spending increased, lower interest rates let businesses expand their plants, households once again thought about buying or building new homes, and the unemployment rate began to fall, ushering in a seven-year period of economic expansion. The popularity and success of the policy of combining federal tax cuts with continued federal spending led to an even more lopsided election in 1984, as President Reagan carried every state but that of his challenger.

This period of sustained growth—1982 to 1989—differed from earlier ones. There were, of course, the continuing shifts toward the service industries and the growing numbers of women in the work force. But, in an important sense, the economic crises of the late 1970s and early 1980s were a wakeup call to entrepreneurs. Increasing productivity and maximizing profits depended upon doing business very differently. In particular, they required introducing new labor-saving equipment and wringing more productivity out of the existing labor force. Typically, this meant laying off those workers who did repetitious work on assembly lines and moving from old inner-city plants (where goods had to be shifted up and down floors) to new, efficient plants (where modern machines did much of the work). As figure 3-6

shows, labor productivity stagnated from 1973 to the early 1980s, but
it began to rise after that. It has increased about 1.2 percent annually
since 1982: about double that of the troubled 1970s. Productivity in
the manufacturing sector rose spectacularly after 1982 as firms used
effective new equipment, shifted production to modern plants, and
laid off thousands of redundant workers.

We are familiar with many successful efforts to increase productivity. Fifteen years ago, gasoline stations were staffed with young men,
who often had little formal training, who pleasantly filled the tanks
and made change. Now, we pump our own gasoline in most places.
And when we cashed a check for the weekend, we dealt with a teller
who made certain that our account had sufficient funds. Now we in-
sert a plastic card into a machine, a computer checks our balance
more accurately and rapidly than a teller could, and the machine dis-
penses currency. Banks, therefore, employ fewer tellers but more technicians, to make sure the machines work. In the early 1980s, when
we came to a railroad crossing, we knew that a red caboose with two
or three trainmen followed a long line of boxcars. Now, a technical
device on the last car of the freight train provides the engineer with
the information. Other dramatic increases in productivity are evident
only to those who monitor changes reported in ponderous tomes of
federal statistics. For example, in 1980, 400,000 men and women in
the steel industry produced eighty-four million tons of metal; thirteen
years later, 127,000 workers produced eighty-nine million tons (U.S.
Bureau of the Census 1995b, table 1265).

Increasing productivity is easier to plan and describe than it is
to accomplish since it requires fundamental social and economic
changes. Often, there are good reasons to continue with the status
quo rather than to make radical changes. For manufacturing firms,
increasing productivity involved laying off thousands of blue-collar
workers, closing old plants, and building new, more efficient ones. But
this is complicated, messy, and expensive since it involves lawsuits,
environmental impact statements, and the raising of much capital.
There is also an important human dimension to raising productivity.
Unions, as well as white-collar workers, fight hard to retain their jobs,
using political pressures and litigation to keep workers on the payrolls. White-collar managers fight hard to keep their own staffs, be
they assembly-line employees or university professors. Over the years
most firms built large office complexes and filled them with white-
collar employees processing information about payroll, accounting,
purchases, taxes, and output. In the past, all of this information was

put on paper and stored for years. Large staffs made sure that this was done correctly. But in the 1980s, computers began to make that type of recordkeeping obsolete. It was not easy for bureaucracies to rapidly get rid of the hundreds of managers and the thousands of employees who kept records. Defenders of the old system, in protecting their jobs, would point out the uncertainty involved in the new computerized environment. But productivity increased, and in the future there will be more changes as bureaucracies shift from the pencil/paper/typewriter system dating from the nineteenth century to modern systems involving terminals, hard disks, and file servers.

The recession of the early 1980s was the crucial trigger that forced firms to make the difficult decisions that increased productivity—decisions that they had put off in the 1970s. Manufacturing firms were challenged by foreign producers who were beating them in both quality and price. After making the hard decisions, productivity rose in the 1980s, but this involved great shifts in employment. Both manufacturing firms and most service industries needed a more technically trained labor force, often people who were ready to use computers in their jobs. But men who worked blue-collar factory jobs in the 1970s could not easily take jobs as computer technicians or programmers a decade later.

Cutting labor costs and eliminating redundant workers in the 1980s may have been easier than in the 1960s because of the increased labor pool of women and immigrants. Unions lost their strength as the educational attainment of workers went up and manufacturing employment declined.

One important event symbolizes a major change in the historic struggle of labor unions to influence the government's policies. The Professional Air Traffic Controllers Organization was an exceptional union since its members were highly paid, most of them with college training, and—not surprisingly—it was a union whose members gave unusual support to President Reagan in his 1980 election. However, when they attempted to strike in 1981 for better working conditions and more benefits, the new administration not only rejected their demands but ordered that those air traffic controllers who struck be fired and never rehired. This sent a message to employers to proceed rapidly with employment restructuring.

From 1982, when the recovery began, until 1989 the nation's GDP grew at the healthy rate of 3.8 percent per year. This was the largest and longest peacetime economic expansion in the nation's history. In many ways, this recovery was similar to other prosperous spans in the post–World War II era. Employment rose rapidly and income went up. Average household income in 1989 was 16 percent greater than in 1982, and per capita income was up 21 percent in constant dollars (U.S. Bureau of the Census 1991b, tables B-5 and B-16). Writing in the early 1980s, Bluestone and Harrison (1982, p. 5) argued there had been no income gain for a decade. Such a statement could not be written in the 1990s because of the sustained economic growth of the 1982–89 interval.

Why is this prosperous decade often seen as an era in which America was in economic decline or an era in which the middle class was threatened? Why are books, including *The Age of Diminished Expectations* (Krugman 1994), *Declining Fortunes* (Newman 1993), and *The End of Affluence* (Madrick 1995), so popular? The answer is that this recovery differed in four fundamental ways from earlier periods of prosperity.

1. Unemployment persisted at a relatively high rate throughout this period. It never fell as low as 5 percent; indeed, for most of the prosperous years of the 1980s, 6 to 7 percent of the labor force sought jobs but could not find them. At its lowest point in the decade, the unemployment rate fell to 5.1 percent in February 1989. This is higher than the average unemployment rate for the entire 1950s or 1960s.

2. Although overall labor productivity began to rise in 1983 and then grew steadily, wages did not go up. The average earnings of men stagnated, while those of women increased moderately. After seven years of economic growth (1982 to 1989), the median earnings of full-time men were up less than 1 percent; those of full-time women up 11 percent (U.S. Bureau of the Census 1993b, table B-16). This expansion was characterized by rising labor productivity but rather stagnant wages.

3. There was no growth in the proportion of people in the middle class in this recovery and little change in the proportion impoverished. During the recession of the early 1980s, the poverty rate ascended to a peak 15.2 percent in 1982. It fell back to 12.8 percent in 1989, but this was a still a poverty rate two points higher than that of 1973. In 1980, 49 percent of whites were middle class—that is, in households with incomes two to five times the poverty line; in 1990, 48 percent were middle class (see figure 3-1). For blacks, the percentage in the middle economic class went from 37 to 36 percent in this decade. In earlier economic booms, the middle class grew and poverty declined.

4. During this recovery, there was an increase in income but also an increase in income inequality. We expect incomes to grow in the economic expansion but not income inequality. What do we mean by inequality? This refers to the distribution of earnings or income. Using data from the Census Bureau's surveys, we can array all households by income. In 1980, the poorest 20 percent of households received only 4.2 percent of the total cash income received by all households. Households in this bottom rank of the income distribution had average incomes of $7,540—just about the poverty line for a single-person household (in 1993 dollars). In 1980, the wealthiest 20 percent of households received 44.1 percent of all household income. They had average incomes of $80,000, or more than five times the poverty line for a family of four (in constant dollars).

When we look at income distribution after the nation went through its sharpest recession since the Depression and then the prolonged recovery, we find that in 1989 the poorest 20 percent of households received only 3.8 percent of all income—down from 4.2 percent at the start of the decade—and they had average incomes of $8,120. Those households in the top 20 percent of the income distribution in 1989 got 46.6 percent of all income in 1989—up from 44.1 percent in 1980—and had average incomes of $98,600.

Those in the bottom quintile of the income distribution might rejoice in the fact that their average purchasing power went up 9 percent during the prosperous 1980s. However, the purchasing power of those in the top quintile went up much faster—24 percent—so the poor might feel they fell deeper into the well since they dropped quite a bit further behind those at the top. (For other analyses of trends in income and earnings, see Danziger and Gottschalk 1995, chap. 3; Karoly 1993; Levy and Murnane 1992.)

Who Gained and Who Lost in the New Economic Era

The large-scale economic changes now reshaping this nation benefit some people greatly, but for others, their impact is highly unfavorable. This section describes what is happening and why, beginning with employment itself.

There are several different ways to count jobs, including surveys of employers and the analysis of tax records. The approach used here is clear and unambiguous: it is based upon what people actually report about their own work. The census first determines whether a person holds a job and, if so, additional questions are asked about its characteristics. As a result, we have excellent information about who works, what they do, and how much they earn, but there is some undercount of jobs. Moonlighters generally report only their chief jobs, and we also miss the jobs of those who are not included in the census, about 1.8 percent of the population in 1990 (Hogan and Robinson 1993, table 1). There are several numbers to keep in mind. In 1990, the labor force included 125,000,000 persons out of an adult (age 16 and over) population of 192,000,000. One hundred and sixteen million held jobs in 1990 compared to 99,000,000 a decade earlier, or a net addition of 1,700,000 jobs each year.

Industrial Changes

When we wish to study the decline in manufacturing and the rise of services, we are interested in changes in the industries of employed workers. Employed persons are asked three questions to determine what product their employer makes or what services he or she provides. Jobholders are then classified into one of 235 detailed industrial categories ranging, alphabetically, from agricultural production to yarn, thread, and fabric mills.

Table 3-1 provides information about fifteen major industrial categories ranked by their growth rates in the 1980s. Industries classified as services are in bold type.

Legal/engineering and other professional services; social/welfare/religious services; and entertainment and recreational services grew most rapidly, by two-thirds in one decade. Looking at specific kinds of employment within these broad categories, we find some remarkable increases. Your impression about the explosion of litigation is correct since the total number of jobs in legal services rose by 71 percent, while the number of persons working in accounting and auditing services went up by 63 percent. Jobs in securities, brokerage, and investment firms just about doubled from 351,000 to 692,000. There were many more jobs in 1990 than in 1980 for highly trained, white-collar workers.

Given our shift in spending, it is no surprise that employment in healthcare/hospitals rose by two million. But there was also a net addition of more than two million jobs in the FIRE industries (finance/insurance/real estate). This is not just more Wall Street brokers doing arbitrage or raising funds for leveraged buyouts. Our tax laws

Table 3-1. Employment by Industry in 1990 and Changes in the 1980s

	Employment in 1990 (000)	Percent Change in 1980s	Percentage of Workers Female in 1980	Net Change in 1980s (000)	
				Men	Women
Rapidly Growing Industries					
Legal, engineering, and other professional services	**4,156**	**+101%**	**41%**	**+968**	**+1,119**
Social, welfare, and religious services	**3,526**	**+67**	**62**	**+518**	**+1,506**
Entertainment and recreational services	**1,636**	**+63**	**40**	**+345**	**+284**
Business and repair services	**5,577**	**+37**	**34**	**+828**	**+667**
Finance, insurance, and real estate	7,985	+35	58	+749	+1,337
Hospitals and health services	**9,683**	**+34**	**76**	**+496**	**+1,936**
Personal services	**3,040**	**+28**	**75**	**+248**	**+346**
Construction	7,214	+26	8	+1,229	+245
Retail trade	19,486	+24	51	+1,805	+1,965
Wholesale trade	5,071	+20	27	+444	+410
Slow Growing or Declining Industries					
Transportation, communication, utilities	8,205	+16	24	+471	+647
Educational services	**9,633**	**+15**	**65**	**+242**	**+1,014**
Public administration	5,538	+8	41	+117	+274
Agriculture, forestry, fisheries	3,115	+7	18	−60	+90
Nondurable manufacturing	8,053	−5	41	−273	−109
Durable goods manufacturing	12,409	−8	26	−969	−103
Total Employment	115,681	+19%	43%	+6,700	+11,342

SOURCES: U.S. Bureau of the Census, *Census of Population: 1980*, PC80-1-C1, table 105; *Census of Population: 1990*, CP-2-1, table 35.

NOTES: Service industries are in boldface. Mining employment is not shown.

changed, creating diverse new approaches to savings with IRAs, Keogh plans, 401Ks, and ESOPS; and banks that once handled just checking and savings accounts now sell numerous financial instruments, requiring more financial sales personnel. Importantly, almost three-quarters of the net jobs added in the health and FIRE industries in the 1980s were filled by women.

Industries growing at less than the national rate of 19 percent are shown in the bottom panel. Because there was a taxpayer's revolt in California and Massachusetts, and because other states enacted legislation to limit spending, public administration jobs grew slowly. The Reagan administration did not succeed in actually cutting the federal payroll, but it succeeded in drastically slowing its growth, so the number of civilians working for Uncle Sam increased by less than 5 percent during the decade. Demographics also limited educational employment since the population at ages 5 to 17 fell from forty-seven to forty-five million in the 1980s, resulting in a need for fewer teachers. Manufacturing industries are at the tail end of the list and were the only ones to experience a net loss of jobs: nondurable goods manufacturing went down 5 percent, and durable goods manufacturing fell by 8 percent. Employment in the nation's textile mills fell by 19 percent, by 44 percent in steel mills, and by 49 percent in those factories making tractors, farm equipment, and earth movers. If you consider total employment in manufacturing, it was still the largest industry in 1990, but its lead over the next largest—retail trade—was much smaller than at the start of the decade.

Trends were more favorable to the employment of women than to men. While the nation gained eighteen million new workers, eleven million of them were women, fewer than seven million were men. Women made up 43 percent of employment in 1980, but they were highly represented in the most rapidly growing industrial sectors. The number of women working in legal/engineering/professional services increased by more than one million, and more than 1.5 million new jobs in social/welfare/religious services were filled by women. Decisions to spend much more on healthcare were not made with the intention of creating good new employment opportunities for women, but they had that consequence. The number of women added to the payrolls of hospitals and health services in the 1980s was more than double the number of jobs lost by men in durable goods manufacturing. Job prospects improved for nurses and X-ray technicians, but not for production line workers and their foremen.

Occupations

Occupation refers to what you actually do on your job, while industry refers to the products or services made by your employer. A person in the occupational category of secretary might work for a lawyer, a railroad, or a hospital. And a carpenter (occupation) might work for a school system or a construction company (industry).

It is ordinarily difficult for an individual to shift far across the occupational spectrum because occupations place very different demands upon their incumbents and offer different rewards. While they are young, people make decisions about their occupations, some remaining in school for many years to obtain the specialized technical training needed for specific occupations, while others may drop out early, thus restricting the range of jobs they might fill when they are middle-aged. Although individuals have some ability to choose their occupation by gaining the skills and training they need for particular jobs, they typically have no control over those large-scale economic processes that determine which industries or occupations thrive and which decline.

Table 3-2 provides information about sixteen broad occupational classes; all five hundred detailed occupations are included here. Once again, services are in boldface, emphasizing the need to be specific when we describe service employment. Many industries are categorized as services by the federal statistical system, including hospitals, schools, law offices, and medical laboratories. But there are also occupations that are labeled services: specifically, protective service occupations (police and fire) and private household occupations (domestic service provided by maids and butlers). The most numerous service occupations are "other service": food service workers, health service workers, such as nurses' aides and practical nurses, and workers who provide personal services, including barbers, hairdressers, and childcare workers.

Table 3-2 ranks occupational categories by their growth during the 1980s. The small category of technologists increased most rapidly, followed by sales jobs, then by executive/administrative/managerial and professional speciality occupations. It will not be a surprise to learn that the number of doctors (+34 percent), lawyers (+47 percent), and stocks and bonds sales people (+114 percent) went up rapidly during this decade.

Blue-collar occupations stagnated or declined. The number of precision production and crafts workers—boilermakers, heavy equipment machinists, and the like—rose by only 4 percent, far below the na-

Table 3-2. Employment by Occupation in 1990 and Changes in the 1980s

	Employment in 1990 (000)	Percent Change in 1980s	Percentage of Female Workers in 1980	Net Change in 1980s (000)	
				Men	Women
Rapidly Growing Occupations					
Health technologists	1,397	+45%	84%	+106	+324
Technologists except health	2,860	+42	25	+508	+337
Sales occupations	13,635	+40	48	+1,961	+1,913
Executive, administrative, and managerial	14,228	+40	30	+1,172	+2,923
Professional specialty occupations	16,306	+36	49	+1,414	+2,874
Protective services	**1,992**	**+35**	**11**	**+375**	**+142**
Other service occupations	**12,782**	**+21**	**64**	**+813**	**+1,404**
Transportation occupations	3,761	+20	9	+332	+140
Slow Growing or Declining Occupations					
Administrative support occupations	18,826	+12	77	+399	+1,573
Precision production and crafts	13,098	+4	8	+246	+258
Helpers, handlers, and laborers	4,563	+4	20	+144	+35
Farming, forestry, and fishing occupations	2,839	+1	14	−18	+46
Fabricators and assemblers	2,922	−6	40	−46	−156
Material moving occupations	968	−12	6	−117	−15
Private household service occupations	**521**	**−12**	**95**	**−1**	**−67**
Machine operators	4,982	−16	40	−590	−389
Total Employment	115,681	+19%	43%	+6,700	+11,342

SOURCES: U.S. Bureau of the Census, *Census of Population: 1980*, PC80-1-C1, table 104; *Census of Population: 1990*, CP-2-1, table 34.

NOTE: Service occupations are in boldface.

tional growth rate of 19 percent. The transportation occupations, now known as material moving jobs, were down by 12 percent. The number of people working on trains and in railyards, for example, fell by 40 percent. As the emphasis upon greater labor productivity and cost-cutting spread throughout manufacturing, the number of machine operators dropped by one-sixth.

Educational Attainment and Employment

The economic trends that led to rapid growth in some industries and occupations but to declines in others operated selectively with regard to education and gender. They provided many opportunities for highly educated persons, leaving behind those who dropped out of school early.

Figure 3-3 summarized the long-run trend toward more women, but proportionally fewer men, working. Table 3-3 elaborates by showing how this played out according to the investments that individuals made in their own educations. This information, and that in several subsequent tables, pertains to people of prime working age—25 to 54—thereby eliminating younger persons who may mix school with work and older ones who may be phasing into their retirement. Five educational attainment categories are used.[1]

Economic trends led to substantial declines in employment for men at the lower end of the educational distribution. The percentage of adult men with less than high school educations holding jobs when the 1990 census was taken was 74 percent, down sharply from the 89 percent at work in 1970. For men who earned college degrees, there was almost no fall off in employment. Among women there was increasing employment at every educational level, but the biggest increase were among the most highly educated.

Per capita hours of employment worked in the year before the census are also reported. Recall that those who work forty hours for fifty weeks accumulate two thousand hours on the job in a year. Changes in employment opportunities—fewer good jobs and lower pay rates—reduced per capita hours for men with less than high school diplomas by 250, but added more than 200 hours of work for

1. The educational question on the census of 1990 differs from that used in 1980. From 1940 through 1980 the inquiry sought to determine how many years of formal schooling a person had completed. In 1990, the question focused upon years of attainment for those low on the educational continuum and on degrees for those at the high school level or above (see Mare 1995).

Table 3-3. Labor Force Information for Men and Women Aged 25 to 54, by Educational Attainment: 1970 to 1990[a]

Educational Attainment	Percent Employed				Per Capita Hours Worked			
	1970	1980	1990		1969	1979	1989	
Men								
Postgraduate training	96%	95%	95%		1,993	2,096	2,213	
College, 4 years	96	95	94		2,030	2,115	2,150	
College, 1 to 3 years	94	91	91		2,007	2,034	2,056	
High school, 4 years	95	90	88		2,027	2,016	1,956	
High school, less than 4 years	89	80	74		1,796	1,719	1,550	
Total	92	89	88		1,935	1,976	1,984	
Women								
Postgraduate training	72%	80%	87%		1,026	1,366	1,647	
College, 4 years	53	70	80		715	1,169	1,488	
College, 1 to 3 years	49	66	76		726	1,149	1,426	
High school, 4 years	48	60	68		726	1,053	1,251	
High school, less than 4 years	43	46	47		620	800	851	
Total	47	60	71		699	1,046	1,314	

SOURCES: U.S. Bureau of the Census, Public Use Microdata Samples from censuses of 1970, 1980, and 1990.

[a]Figures indicate the percentage of men and women employed at census date and per capita hours of employment for the noninstitutionalized population in the year prior to the census.

men who spent five or more years in college. The differential in amount of work by educational attainment increased sharply since, in 1970, men with postgraduate training typically worked two hundred more hours per year (four more hours each week) than high school dropouts; in 1990, about seven hundred hours more (fourteen more hours each week).

The increased employment of women, their growing representation in many occupations, and their rising earnings are among the most important changes of this era. Adult women are spending time very differently than women did just a quarter-century ago. At every educational level, changes in labor supply by women differ from those of men. Even at the lowest levels, employment and hours of work went up for women. The sharpest gains were among those women who had the skills to excel in the new labor market: those who obtained the specialized training that college provides. Women with five or more years of college now work an average of more than 1,600 hours per year, or just about double the work effort of women who dropped out of high school.

Despite these remarkable increases, women continue to work less than do comparably educated men. The gender gap in 1990 was small among men and women who had five or more years of college, but even here employed women spent about twelve fewer hours each week in the office or shop than did men.

Educational Attainment and Earnings

Changes in earnings track changes in employment: the paychecks of those who invested extensively in education went up the most. Table 3-4 reports average earnings for persons aged 25 to 54 who worked at all during the year before the census-taking. The amounts include wages and salaries as well as net self-employment earnings for those who owned their own farms or businesses. Overall, men reported an average of $39,300 in earnings in 1970, but ten years later this fell to $35,700 and then to $34,200 in 1990 (amounts shown in constant 1993 dollars). By 1993, average earnings for men fell to $31,600. However, this trend toward smaller earnings conceals dramatic differences by educational attainment. In the 1970s, earnings fell for men in all attainment categories, but declines were sharpest among the extensively educated. Thus, the premium associated with college degrees declined, as shown in table 3-4. In the 1980s, earnings continued to go down for high school men but increased for those with college educations. In ten years, men with college educations went

Table 3-4. Average Earnings for Men and Women Aged 25 to 54 Who Worked at All in Year Prior to Census or Survey (amounts in 1993 dollars)

	Census of			Current Population Survey 1994	Change in Earnings 1970 to 1994
	1970	1980	1990		
Men					
Average Earnings	$39,528	$35,870	$34,321	$31,747	−20%
Postgraduate training	60,930	51,353	65,380	53,715	−12
College, 4 years	55,105	45,901	47,357	41,927	−24
College, 1 to 3 years	43,420	36,336	34,752	30,570	−30
High school, 4 years	37,828	34,415	29,440	25,427	−33
Less than 4 years of high school	30,767	27,121	21,797	16,389	−47
Ratio of College Grad to High School Grad	1.46	1.36	1.60	1.65	
Women					
Average Earnings	$18,291	$16,613	$20,283	$20,086	+10
Postgraduate training	33,028	26,143	30,210	36,236	+10
College, 4 years	25,304	20,434	22,740	26,448	+5
College, 1 to 3 years	20,422	17,592	17,310	19,467	−5
High school, 4 years	17,825	15,564	13,830	15,644	−12
Less than 4 years of high school	14,563	12,640	10,000	10,012	−31
Ratio of College Grad to High School Grad	1.42	1.31	1.64	1.69	

SOURCE: U.S. Bureau of the Census, Public Use Microdata Samples from the censuses of 1970, 1980, and 1990.

NOTE: Data refer to the average earnings of all persons who reported they worked in the year before the census.

from earning 36 percent more than men with high school diplomas to earning 60 percent more—a trend that continues into the 1990s. This is accounted for by downsizing in the industries and occupations that employed blue-collar men and the run-up of employment in health and financial services.

The earnings of employed adult women also rose in the 1980s. Women with college training fared best, but the earnings of women with just high school educations stayed constant, while those of their brothers with similar educations declined, on average, by 13 percent. So women with less than a college education held their own in terms of earnings, but men did not.

The Important Young Adult Years

Social changes occur to specific age groups, and the decisions that individuals make in the years between adolescence and young adulthood influence their economic status for the rest of their lives. For many, the most salient decisions about careers, marriage, and starting families are made as they age from 25 to 34.

Information about the labor force status and earnings of successive cohorts of persons aged 25 to 34 is presented in table 3-5. Turning to trends among young men (upper panel), we see the fall-off in employment among those with high school educations or less. To be sure, most of these men worked in 1990 and many of them spent numerous hours on the job, but economic opportunities for recent high school graduates were much more constrained than just a quarter-century ago. Men from the World War II cohorts who obtained high school diplomas could expect to earn about $33,900 by the time they attained age 30, or considerably more than double the poverty line for a family of four. This was the last birth cohort of men who could expect to enter the middle class by age 30 on the basis of just a high school education. Men from the late baby boom cohorts with such educations might expect to earn only $24,800 by age 30, or just about one-and-one-half times the poverty line for a family of four. It is no surprise that many put off marriage while those who married had working wives. To get a family of four safely into the middle economic class by 1990 on the husband's earnings alone, men from the late baby boom cohorts (born 1956 to 1965) needed college degrees. Even though the trend is toward much greater educational attainment, only one-fourth of the late baby boom men stayed enrolled long enough to obtain that credential, so this trend toward lower earnings limits opportunities for the three-quarters of young men who did not graduate from college.

Table 3-5. Percent Employed, Per Capita Hours Worked, and Average Earnings for Employed Persons at Ages 25 to 34: 1970 to 1990 (amounts in 1993 dollars)

	Percent Employed			Per Capita Hours Worked			Average Earnings for Employed Persons		
	World War II 1970	Early Baby Boom 1980	Late Baby Boom 1990	World War II 1969	Early Baby Boom 1979	Late Baby Boom 1989	World War II 1970	Early Baby Boom 1980	Late Baby Boom 1990
Men									
Postgraduate Training	93%	92%	92%	1,803	1,962	2,098	$44,532	35,380	45,228
College, 4 years	95	94	94	1,902	2,067	2,103	43,164	33,733	36,818
College, 1 to 3 years	93	90	91	1,925	1,976	2,030	36,621	29,197	28,095
High school, 4 years	95	88	88	2,002	1,959	1,947	33,872	27,898	24,743
High school, less than 4 years	88	78	74	1,752	1,631	1,516	27,863	21,414	17,760
Total	93	88	88	1,892	1,930	1,947	34,684	29,116	28,269
Women									
Postgraduate training	67%	80	86	913	1,393	1,668	$28,687	22,632	30,960
College, 4 years	52	73	82	682	1,298	1,588	24,105	19,732	25,416
College, 1 to 3 years	46	67	75	649	1,179	1,408	19,488	16,437	18,189
High school, 4 years	42	58	65	608	1,039	1,205	16,785	14,268	14,338
High school, less than 4 years	37	42	42	484	725	753	13,305	10,695	9,814
Total	43	61	70	595	1,082	1,308	17,446	15,996	18,432

SOURCES: U.S. Bureau of the Census, Public Use Microdata Samples from the censuses of 1970, 1980, and 1990.

NOTE: This table refers to the noninstitutionalized population and shows the percent employed at the time of the census, per capita hours worked in the year before the census, and average earnings for all workers who reported any earnings in the year before the census.

Young women adapted to the changing economic conditions by working more. Around age 30, 43 percent of the World War II cohorts held jobs, but this increased to 70 percent for women in the late baby boom. Employment and hours spent on the job increased most rapidly for young women who invested in college educations, but there were substantial increases even among women with limited educations. Economic trends have not been kind to young women with high school educations or less, so their earnings have fallen, but to a much lesser extent than those of their brothers. And women who made the decision to obtain college degrees saw their earnings go up quite a bit in the 1980s. Despite these favorable trends, women continue to earn much less than ostensibly similar men. For example, women with postgraduate training from the late baby boom cohorts at age 30 in 1990 reported average earnings of about $31,000. This is only two-thirds as much as similar men in these birth cohorts. Even highly educated young women who depend upon their own earnings to support themselves and several children may find themselves closer to the poverty line than they would like.

Good Jobs and Bad Jobs: Job Creation in the 1980s

I described several seemingly contradictory economic trends. Employment—the total number of jobs—was up substantially in the 1980s as economic changes simultaneously provided work for our growing male population and jobs for the sharply increasing proportion of women in the labor force. In April 1990, there were also 4.5 million immigrants at work who entered during the 1980s; that is, 25 percent of the seventeen million net new workers added to payrolls were people who lived in a foreign land at the beginning of the decade.

Jobs were created at a high rate in the 1980s. But are we in a situation in which the many new jobs are ones that pay little and offer few benefits? Bluestone and Harrison (1982) powerfully argued that America's deindustrialization meant that high-paying, desirable jobs in manufacturing industries were replaced by low-skill, low-paying jobs, that "good" jobs disappeared while "bad" jobs proliferated. A glance at table 3-1 seems to bear this out. Employment in manufacturing in the 1980s fell by 1.5 million jobs, while 3.8 million new jobs appeared in retail trade.

There is no consensus about what constitutes a good job or a bad job. (For a discussion of this issue, see Wetzel 1995.) One direct way to get at this important issue is to look at the jobs people actually have, classify these jobs by their wage rates, and look at changes in the 1980s. Of course, not every job paying $25 per hour is better than every job with a $5 rate, but most of us strongly prefer the higher-paying one. And since fringe benefits and perquisites are directly related to earnings, high-paying jobs, relative to low-paying ones, are even better than the hourly rate suggests.

Persons who worked in the year before the 1980 or 1990 censuses are classified in figure 3-7 by how much they earned, ranging from less than $5 per hour to $30 or more (amounts shown in constant dollars). To eliminate the confounding effects of people who mix education with employment or who are approaching retirement, this analysis is limited to persons aged 25 to 54.

Overall, the number of jobs rose by 30 percent for these adults. There is evidence that "bad" jobs, such as low-wage jobs, were created in great numbers since the fastest growth was in jobs paying under $5 per hour—a growth rate of 51 percent. The impression that many more people are working in fast-food restaurants and at checkout counters is correct, but this is only half the story. There was also rapid growth of new jobs paying more than $25 per hour. Job growth was substantial across the economic spectrum but greatest at the extremes.

The picture gets more complex when we consider full-time jobs and gender. Turning to information about men who worked fifty or more weeks and usually spent thirty-five or more hours on the job, there is strong support for the Bluestone-Harrison hypothesis about deindustrialization. The number of men working all year for less than $10 an hour went up at a high rate. And the number of men working full-time for $15 to $25—the very good unionized blue-collar jobs in heavy industries—hardly increased at all between the censuses. But at the top end, there was also substantial growth since the number of men earning more than $30 went up as rapidly as the number earning less than $10. Rather than just creating low-paying jobs, both "good" and "bad" jobs grew most rapidly for men. Jobs with earnings in the middle range became scarcer compared to jobs that either paid a little or a lot (Gittleman and Howell 1982), contributing to the image that the middle class is now greatly challenged.

Trends among women who worked full-time are summarized more easily: modest growth of jobs in the low-wage range, and rapid increases for jobs in the middle and upper ranges. The number of jobs paying $20 or more per hour—$40,000 if she works all year—more than doubled. Among men, it increased by about 20 percent.

Discussions of the restructuring of employment and deindustrial-

Figure 3-7. Job Growth Among Persons Aged 25 to 54, by Hourly Wage Rates: 1979 to 1989 (wage rates in 1989 dollars)

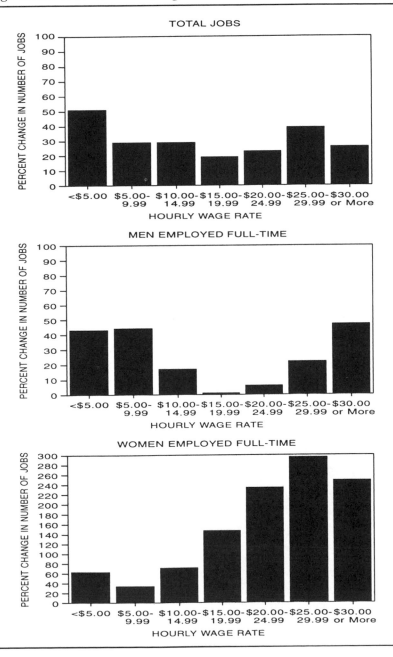

SOURCE: U.S. Bureau of the Census, *Census of Population and Housing: 1980 and 1990*, Public Use Microdata Samples.

ization focus upon the disappearance of good jobs in the nation's basic
manufacturing industries, jobs primarily held by white men. Perhaps
the minimum pay for a full-time job you could label "good" would be
$29,500 (in 1993 dollars). This would allow a person to support a
family of four at twice the poverty line. The number of such good
jobs held by men in manufacturing declined by 600,000 in the 1980s.
Many of these men must have been devastated by the loss of their
jobs when they found themselves unable to support their families as
they had in the past. If unions had been stronger or if federal policies
had encouraged a different type of economic development, the number of jobs lost might have been fewer. But a more complete picture
of industrial restructuring and its gender components would show a
net increase of 1.5 million such "good" jobs held by women in
healthcare and in finance/insurance/real estate. More than 700,000
similarly rewarding full-time jobs held by men were added in those
two industrial sectors, more than offsetting the loss of "good" jobs in
manufacturing.

James Wetzel summarized this debate about the creation of "good"
or "bad" jobs:

> Professional services and finance, insurance, and real estate ac-
> counted for half of all net new jobs created during the 1980s, and
> an even larger portion of the "good" jobs. Which group was waiting
> in the wings to fill such jobs? The baby boom generation, of course,
> and particularly the women, who had acquired much more college
> training and were much more career-oriented than earlier genera-
> tions of women. New entrants found their training for the tradition-
> ally female-dominated health care and education occupations sup-
> ported by strongly rising demand. Also, more women advanced into
> executive and senior managerial positions as their sustained work
> experience, educational preparation, and career orientation readied
> them for leadership roles. [1995, chap. 2]

What Does It All Mean?

Individuals participated in and adapted to changes dating from the
1960s concerning how women and minorities should be included in
our society and to another set of macroeconomic changes dating from
the 1970s. These trends may be summarized in several points:

1. Employers consistently emphasize productivity, but how and when
   they do so change over time. Economic shocks occurring around

1980 were an important turning point for increasing productivity. Some describe these shifts as the fundamental deindustrializing of America, stressing that policies adopted by a conservative administration in the Reagan years encouraged firms to lay off thousands of workers, close plants in the United States, and move jobs offshore (Harrison and Bluestone 1988; Bartlett and Steele 1992). They argue that this allowed those individuals who controlled capital and wealth to prosper, while the working class suffered (Dudley 1994). Others view the emphasis on greater productivity as the continuation of a long trend in which the economic fits and starts of the early 1980s forced employers, including the government, to make those tough and unpopular decisions required to increase productivity, decisions that were avoided in earlier decades. Whatever the reason, although good blue-collar jobs continue to exist in great numbers, they are much harder to find. Thus, the late baby boom cohorts entered a job market extremely different from the one the World War II birth cohorts entered.

2. Long-run trends in employment, driven by shifting patterns of consumer expenditures, now strongly favor those with high skills and advanced training. Because blue-collar jobs are diminishing relative to white-collar jobs, the employment rate and hours of employment have stagnated or declined for men with high school educations or less. The drop in employment in manufacturing is one of the lead stories of the 1980s. The rise in employment in healthcare, FIRE, and retail trade merits equal attention.

3. Secular trends in employment favored women more than men since the occupations and industries growing rapidly were those where women were well represented. The emphasis on technology also means that a strong mind will be more highly rewarded than a strong back. To put it differently, men did not switch rapidly enough into the expanding occupations and industries. The net number of persons working as unskilled machine operators, for example, dropped by one million in the decade, with the majority of these lost jobs held by men. But the number employed as registered nurses went up by 600,000, and women accounted for 90 percent of the net increase in nursing.

4. The economic recovery of the 1980s led to moderately rising incomes for families, to somewhat larger paychecks for women, and to much higher salaries for persons with postcollege training, but it was, apparently, an economic expansion unlike those before 1973. Its benefits were not distributed across the entire income

distribution: the top 40 percent of the income distribution did well; for the next 40 percent, the recovery was something of a wash; while those at the bottom found their economic status in 1990 not improved at all over 1980.

There was a brief recession in 1990 and 1991, followed by another economic expansion that started out slowly but gained momentum by 1994. It is too early to determine whether this expansion will be similar to the 1980s. On the favorable side, it is marked by a rapid and sustained increase in employment and by a growth of the GDP in the 4 percent range. But this economic growth will not mean the return of many good blue-collar jobs. Manufacturing employment fell by 7 percent in the first three years of the 1990s—a faster rate of decline than in the 1980s. Firms will probably try to squeeze greater productivity from their current work forces and will continue to introduce labor saving equipment. And there are no signals that voters want to pay higher taxes to increase employment in that one-sixth of our economy devoted to the government. Frank Levy (1995) contends that the continued emphasis upon greater productivity interacted with the 1990 recession to bring about new shifts in employment, shifts that continue to favor those with specialized skills and training. Employers seeking greater labor productivity now look to thin out and eliminate middle management, threatening the jobs of many early baby boom men. The idea of creating lean, flat organizations—organizations with few managers—is not new, but the most recent recession (1990–91) may have been the catalyst prodding executives to make those difficult decisions involved with firing white-collar employees who had been with their firms for years. Adopting the principle of equal employment opportunity may also account for this trend since it may be possible to hire recent college graduates—female as well as male—who are better able to do the jobs now held by older men. The effective use of computers in this decade and the next will quite likely permit management to cast off those thousands of workers who processed paper and their hundreds of supervisors. If this is occurring— and it is if sales of *Reengineering the Corporation* (Hammer and Champy 1994) are an indicator—then the effects will be felt most by older, well-educated white men in middle-management positions. During this most recent recession and the period that followed, the unemployment rates of blue- and white-collar workers were more similar than before (Levy 1995). Furthermore, in 1989 men aged 45 to 54 with exactly four years of college earned $49,400. Three years later, the average earnings of this same group were down 10 percent to $44,500 so the new move toward greater labor productivity has not spared the older college-educated work force (see also table 3-4).

When economic opportunities change, so too do living arrangements, although these are also influenced by changes in social norms. Next we turn to what the census reveals about how children and their parents live.

Chapter 4

Changes in American Families

The largest numerical shift for children in recent years has been into mother-only families, and here the poverty rates are high—47 percent in 1990. Almost one-half of all children in mother-only families are impoverished.

I t has long been assumed that married men would spend their adult lives working to support themselves, their wives, and their children. In the post–World War II years, beneficial economic conditions enabled men to marry young and support their families, marking this era by exceptionally early marriage, high fertility, and, from the present perspective, little divorce. Chapter 2 described the far-reaching changes in society's views about women and work and about working women and childrearing. Chapter 3 described changes in the economy, the important ones being declining employment opportunities and wages for men lacking college degrees and better job opportunities and higher wages for women.

As a consequence, the living arrangements of children and their parents in the 1990s are quite different from those of children and parents three decades ago. Then, the image of the typical American family included an employed father, a homemaker wife, and two children. There is no such popular image of the typical family today. Many families continue to resemble that 1950s icon, but they are in the minority, and their number is decreasing steadily. Much more common is the family in which both parents work or, increasingly, the family headed by a single parent. Most children born in the 1980s and 1990s will live in a single-parent family for some time before they graduate from high school.

A family as defined by the statistical system includes two or more individuals related by blood, marriage, or adoption who share a home. Unrelated individuals living together constitute a household but not a family. At the end of President Eisenhower's term, about two-thirds of American families consisted of a married couple with the wife staying at home. But family structure changed rapidly in a short span, as illustrated in figure 4-1.

Figure 4-1.   Number of Families, by Type: 1960 to 1994

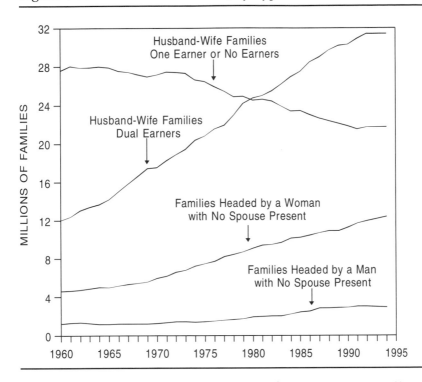

SOURCE: U.S. Bureau of the Census, *Current Population Reports*, series P-60, no. 184, table B11.

As women entered the labor force in great numbers—the mothers of the baby boomers doing so at older ages and the baby boom women doing it just after school—married-couple families with a working wife became much more common. By 1980, there were equal numbers of married-couple families with and without wives in the labor force, but since then the trend has been toward much more employment of wives and dual-earner families. The most common American family is now one in which both spouses work.

Divorce and, more recently, rising rates of childbearing by never-married women produced sharp increases in the numbers of families headed by women without husbands. By the early 1990s, about one family in five was of this type. The rise in divorce also led to a steady increase in the number and proportion of families headed by men without wives living with them. If a man retains custody of his children he becomes a single parent, and increases in cohabitation may make it more feasible for men to retain custody of their children. This is a producing a new type of family: a heterosexual but unmarried couple with children. In 1990, 1.5 million families consisted of a father and his children, but no wife. In more than one-third of these, there was an adult woman identified as a partner.

New Patterns of Marriage and Cohabitation

The timing of marriage changed in a short span. Parents of the baby boom married early, with the typical woman getting married for the first time at age 20 and the typical man at age 23, but their children, holding different views about premarital sex, facing a much less certain economic future, and able to use more effective contraceptives, followed a different script. They delayed their marriages and devoted much less of their twenties to being husbands or wives. Table 4-1 shows the percentage who had married at different ages for each birth cohort. Reading down the columns of this table reports changes from one cohort to the next in the percentage married, thereby describing the advancing age at which women marry. For women in Generation X, 37 percent had married by ages 20 to 24, a low proportion compared to the 69 percent married at these ages for parents of the baby boom. The shift away from such early weddings began with women in the early baby boom cohorts and continues to the present, each cohort putting off marriage longer than the previous one.

Among parents of the baby boom cohorts almost all women married before their fortieth birthdays. There has been controversy about whether the pervasive trend toward delayed marriage means that a high proportion of men and women will never marry (Faludi 1991, pp. 9–19). It is impossible to know the outcome. Among those women who got to age 40 in the early 1990s, 91 percent had married, only a modest decline from the proportions married in earlier birth cohorts. Members of Generation X are delaying marriage to record late ages, but many still marry. Current Census Bureau projections imply that about 90 percent of white women and just under 75 percent of black women will eventually marry (Norton and Miller 1992, p. 4). There is no current evidence suggesting that high proportions of men and women will forgo marriage entirely.

An important outcome of recent changes in social values has been

Table 4-1. Information About Women's Marital Status, by Birth Cohort and Age

	Ages				
Generation	15–19	20–24	25–29	30–34	35–39
Percent Ever Married[a]					
Generation X	6%	37%			
Late baby boomers	10	46	71	84	
Early baby boomers	12	62	83	89	91
World War II	15	69	90	93	95
Parents of baby boomers	16	69	89	94	95
Percent Married and Living with Husband					
Generation X	5%	31%			
Late baby boomers	9	38	58	67	
Early baby boomers	10	54	69	70	71
World War II	15	62	81	81	78
Parents of baby boomers	15	62	80	84	82
Divorced or Separated Women per 1,000 Married–Spouse Present Women[a]					
Generation X	...	161			
Late baby boomers	...	158	207	224	
Early baby boomers	...	111	174	229	254
World War II	...	65	86	123	179
Parents of baby boomers	...	81	75	83	98

SOURCE: U.S. Bureau of the Census, *Current Population Reports*, series P-20, nos. 62, 105, 144, 212, 287, 365, 410, and 450.

[a]These percentages exclude women who were separated because their husbands were in military service.

the development of cohabitation as a substitute for marriage. There are four points to stress about cohabitation. First, it apparently is a recent development. The text table below shows Census Bureau estimates of the number of heterosexual cohabiting couples since 1960. Their number reached one-half million in 1970 but then grew very

Date	Number of Cohabiting Couples	Cohabiting Couples as a Percentage of Total Married and Cohabiting Couples
1960	439,000	1.1%
1970	523,000	1.2
1980	1,589,000	3.1
1990	2,856,000	5.2
1993	3,510,000	6.2

rapidly. During the 1980s and 1990s, the number of cohabiting couples increased by 6 percent annually while the number of married couples went up 1 percent each year.

Second, cohabitation has now become the typical way to begin a live-in sexual relationship. The Sex in America survey conducted by the University of Chicago's National Opinion Research Center gathered information from a large national sample about when a couple first lived together and when they married. Among the Depression birth cohorts, about 94 percent of the women and 85 percent of the men were married when they began to live with someone of the opposite sex. But that pattern changed, and among those in Generation X only one-third of women and men were married when they started to live together, implying that two-thirds began their live-in sexual relationships as cohabitors. It is the late baby boom cohorts that differ from earlier cohorts in their choice of cohabitation rather than marriage (Michael et al. 1994, pp. 97–99).

Third, even if you assume that all young cohabiting couples should be considered as if they were married, there is a clear trend toward much delayed entry into marriage. Men and women from the late baby boom cohorts and Generation X put off getting into live-in sexual relationships, be they marriages or cohabitations (Laumann et al. 1994, pp. 476–480).

Finally, cohabiting couples are still relatively rare compared to married couples. The text table above shows such couples as a percentage of total married and cohabiting couples. Despite the increasing popularity of cohabitation and its replacement of marriage as the way men and women begin living together, there were, in the 1990s, about eighteen married couples for every one cohabiting heterosexual couple.

The Increasing Likelihood of Divorce

In 1964, and again in 1968, many Republican leaders thought they had the ideal candidate for the White House—Nelson Rockefeller. He demonstrated his popularity and campaign stamina by getting elected governor of the nation's largest state and had served his party and his nation faithfully. He had the resources to sponsor a masterful campaign. But Republicans outside New York State emphasized that he was a flawed and possibly unelectable candidate because of the stigma of his divorce, so he never got his party's nomination. Three elections later, the Republicans nominated and the voters overwhelmingly cast their ballots for Ronald Reagan, a candidate not hampered by an early divorce. Changing views about whether divorce disqualifies a candidate for the nation's highest office reflect changes in behavior by people many decades younger than those who seek the presidency.

Not only did baby boomers delay their marriages, once they got married they were more likely to divorce than were their parents or grandparents. Figure 4-2 is one of the most informative and frequently repeated graphs describing social change. Using historical data, Preston and McDonald (1979) determined what percentage of marriages taking place in specific decades were terminated by divorce. Our image of once-stable and lifelong marriages is not wrong if we go back far enough, since no more than 5 percent of the marriages taking place in the years right after the Civil War ended in divorce. Most people who married took their spouses "for better or for worse" and lived together until one spouse died. The divorce rate rose to about one marriage in four for those who married shortly before World War II. Although we do not know exactly what percentage of the marriages of the 1970s will end in divorce, it is probable that more than one-half will.

As a society, we adopted new views about personal fulfillment and about whether unhappily married couples should stay together. As values changed, so too did the laws making it easier to divorce. Will the curve showing the percentage of marriages terminated by divorce keep rising? Martin and Bumpass (1989) updated the trends by considering dissolution rates in the 1980s. They argued that a conservative estimate for recent marriages was that 56 percent will be terminated by divorce, while their most realistic estimate was that *two-thirds* will end in divorce. But there is no agreement about so high a probability. Generally, the older people are when they marry, the less likely they are to divorce, and thus the sharp advance in the age at first

Figure 4-2.   Proportion of Marriages Begun in Each Year Ending in Divorce: 1867 to 1973

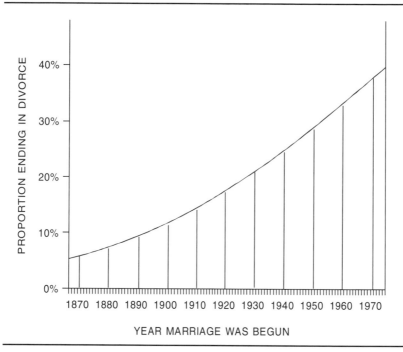

YEAR MARRIAGE WAS BEGUN

SOURCE: Preston and McDonald 1979.

marriage among Generation X may dampen the divorce rate. Norton and Miller (1992, p. 5), using information from the late 1980s and early 1990s, suggest that the percentage of marriages ending in divorce has reached a peak and may fall to around 40 percent for Generation X. Compared to the recent past in this country and compared to other nations, this is still a remarkably high proportion of marriages ending in divorce. The rising divorce rate itself may lead to a deferral or avoidance of marriage. If young people think that 40 to 60 percent of current marriages will end in divorce, they may be reluctant to wed, especially when cohabitation is socially acceptable.

    One outcome of these changes is a decline in the percentage of women living with a husband. Table 4-1 lays this out: the middle panel showing the proportion of women by birth cohort and age living with a husband and the bottom panel showing the ratio of divorced to currently married women. Women in the World War II birth cohorts married early, and few of them divorced, so by the time they got to their late twenties, there were only 86 divorced women for every one thousand married women, meaning that young divorced men and women in those cohorts had relatively few peers. Women in the late baby boom cohorts deferred marriage, but many of them divorced: when they reached their late twenties, there were 207 divorcées for every one thousand married women. The increasingly large proportion who are divorced undoubtedly plays a role in weakening marriage (McLanahan and Casper 1995). An individual considering divorce several decades ago may have observed that most of his or her age mates were married and probably feared that divorce would make him or her a social outcast. Now a higher proportion are single or divorced, so there are fewer social pressures to stay married and more social opportunities for the divorced.

This ratio of divorced to married persons will remain high since the remarriage rate has fallen quite rapidly in the recent past. Divorce in the 1960s was often a pause between one marriage and the next! In that decade, about one in six divorced women aged 15 to 54 got remarried each year. Just as the first marriage rate fell in the 1970s, so too did the remarriage rate, and by the late 1980s the remarriage rate was just about cut in half. As commitment to marriage wanes, it is likely that divorced people will increasingly find cohabitation an attractive alternative to a second or third marriage.

The Baby Boom, the Birth Dearth, and New Fertility Patterns

The baby boom after World War II surprised no one. Young couples put off marriage during the war, while older couples found that post-war prosperity allowed them to have the children they had deferred during the Depression. Given the long-run trend toward lower fertility and smaller families in the United States, it was surprising that birth rates remained very high in this country for a full decade-and-a-half after World War II. Larger families came back into style as women born in the Depression, mothers of the early baby boomers, averaged 3.2 children. The last native-born women to have that many children were those born during the 1880s (Cherlin 1981, p. 21).

The post–World War II baby boom came to its end late in the 1950s. The annual number of births peaked at a record high of 4.3 million in 1957, and after 1960 the rate at which women had children steadily declined for fifteen years. At first glance, you might think that this was the direct result of the contraceptive revolution (Westoff and Ryder 1977). Certainly the availability of birth control pills and IUDs gave women much more effective control over their childbearing; but other changes were occurring as young women increasingly put off their marriages, enrolled in school longer, and then began careers. It is important to emphasize that birth rates completed their drop from high to moderate levels before the wages of men started their fall.

The dramatic shift toward lower fertility is shown in figure 4-3. It reports births per one thousand women in the four prime age groups for childbearing. At the high point of the baby boom, one women in four at ages 20 to 24 had a child each year. And while going through her twenties, the typical woman in the baby boom era bore more than two children. When social values changed, birth rates were just about cut in half in the brief span of fifteen years. Women at older ages reduced their childbearing just as teenage women did, so the shift toward much lower fertility involved all age groups.

Figure 4-3 hints at two other more modest fertility trends. First, since 1985 birth rates have gone up for women of all ages. The rise in fertility among teenagers gets the most attention since, unlike the situation in the 1950s and 1960s, teenagers who become mothers now seldom have husbands. In 1993, 72 percent of all teenage mothers were unmarried, whereas in 1960 only 15 percent were single. Second, perhaps as a result of women's increased dedication to educational attainment and their need for earnings, childbearing is gradually being shifted to older ages. In the 1980s, the birth rate rose most rapidly among women in their thirties: women in the late baby boom cohorts are making up at these older ages for the childbearing they did not do while younger. Despite their recent rise, birth rates for women over age 30 are still much lower than they were for women at these ages during the baby boom, and childbearing at ages over 40 remains rare (O'Connell 1991).

National statistics about the marital status of mothers have been kept since the 1930s. For several decades after 1940, about 2 percent of births were delivered to mothers who were not married. A grave negative stigma was attached to an unmarried mother and her child, who was then designated as illegitimate. Middle- and upper-class parents did whatever they could to hide the pregnancies and childbearing of their unmarried daughters. Marital childbearing was the norm, even if many weddings were hastened by a pregnancy. But then the proportion of out-of-wedlock births rose gradually, reaching about 4 percent in 1960. Since then this proportion has escalated, and by 1993 unmar-

Figure 4-3. Birth Rates for Women by Age: 1960 to 1993 (births per 1,000 women)

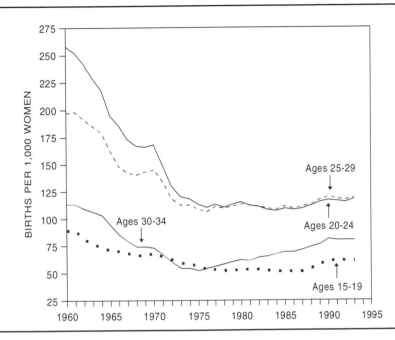

SOURCES: U.S. National Center for Health Statistics, 1995, *Vital Statistics of the United States, Vol. I Natality,* table 1-14; 1995, *Monthly Vital Statistics Report,* Vol. 44, No. 3 (supplement), table 4.

ried women accounted for 31 percent of births. This trend is shown with the ascending line in figure 4-4.

The proportion of births occurring to unmarried women may increase for several reasons, and it is important to identify them since they are the outcome of different social trends. This proportion may go up because:

1. The rate at which married women have children goes down.
2. The rate at which unmarried women have children goes up, a change that occurs when "shotgun" marriages go out of style.
3. The proportion of women who are married decreases, meaning that more women are at risk of unmarried childbearing and fewer are at risk of marital fertility.

Between the 1950s and the 1980s, the delay of marriage and the sharp decline in birth rates of married women accounted for the in-

Figure 4-4.   Birth Rates for Married and Unmarried Women Aged 15 to 44, and Percentage of Total Births to Unmarried Women: 1960 to 1993

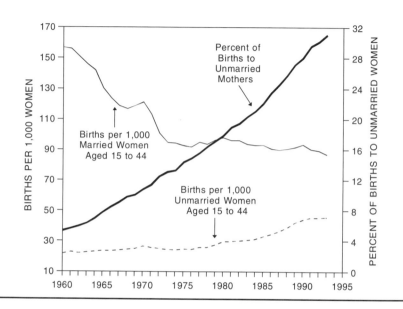

SOURCES: U.S. National Center for Health Statistics, 1995, *Vital Statistics of the United States, Vol. I Natality,* table 1-76, 1-77, and 1-78; 1995, *Monthly Vital Statistics Report,* Vol. 44, No. 3 (supplement), table 14.

creasing proportion of births to unmarried women. This was not an era in which single women increased their rate of childbearing.

A much different social trend characterized the 1980s—rising birth rates for unmarried women. The increase from 16 percent of births occurring to unmarried mothers in 1980 to 31 percent in the early 1990s resulted from higher birth rates by unmarried women as well as the continued advance in the age at marriage. At all ages, marital birth rates were very much lower in 1990 than in 1960: married women in the 1990s are having children much less frequently than their mothers did three decades ago. The opposite trend characterizes women who do not have husbands. The birth rate for unmarried women aged 15 to 44 doubled in the last thirty years, with most of the increase occurring in the 1980s. Childbearing and marriage are less bundled together now, and as the sanctions against single parents wane, a new and different pattern of fertility develops. Upward of one-third of the children born in the 1990s will be delivered to unmarried women (Moore 1995).

Implications of the Changing Living Arrangements of Children

In an era of economic growth and prosperity, jobs should be readily available and wages should be rising. If this happens and if the social norms call for men to support their families, the economic condition of children should improve. But when wages stagnate, when the social mores upholding marriage weaken, and when sanctions against women bearing and raising children on their own fall, many children may be at risk of spending their youth in low-income families. Rising earnings for women may help, but women who work still earn considerably less than men do, and the woman who has a full-time job and childrearing responsibilities will face serious time constraints.

Problems of poverty in single-parent families are not new. With industrialization came moderately high levels of on-the-job mortality; hence, long before the Depression, some states enacted mother's pensions to support widowed women and their children. Later, President Roosevelt and Congress created the federal program that subsequently became Aid to Families with Dependent Children, whose beneficiaries were presumed to be widowed mothers. When it was enacted, divorce was rare, out-of-wedlock childbearing uncommon, and few mothers were employed. Programs of this type were modestly expanded during the War on Poverty in the 1960s, and then an unexpected change occurred. The children who needed financial support were not the sons and daughters of impoverished widows, but the children of women who never married or who had terminated their marriages.

These demographic changes led some observers to believe that welfare programs are a large part of the problem of childhood poverty rather than the solution. Charles Murray (1984) argues that unmarried women became mothers knowing that the state would supply financial aid even if they did not marry the fathers of their children. And welfare encouraged irresponsibility in men, he believed, since they knew that money from the government would be available if they left their wives and children, undercutting the commitment to traditional responsibilities.

One of the major stories of this era is persistent childhood poverty, despite rising incomes and relatively low unemployment. Figure 4-5 shows trends in the poverty rate for both the total population and for children under age 18. Because trends for the older population differ so greatly, the poverty rate for people age 65 and over is also shown.

In 1960, 27 percent of children were poor, but this sunk to a low of 14 percent in 1969, illustrating the beneficial effects of an economic boom in an era when most children lived with two parents. Since then, childhood poverty has increased, especially in years of recession. Even in the prosperous 1980s, childhood poverty was at a higher rate than in the late 1960s or 1970s, with more than one-fifth of the nation's children living in households with cash incomes below the poverty line. The number of poor children sank to a low of ten million in 1969 but then climbed to 15.7 million in 1993.

High poverty rates can be reduced, as shown by what happened to the older population. In 1960, the poverty rate for the elderly was

Figure 4-5. Percent Below the Poverty Line: Total Population, Persons Aged 65 and Over, and Children Under Age 18: 1960 to 1994

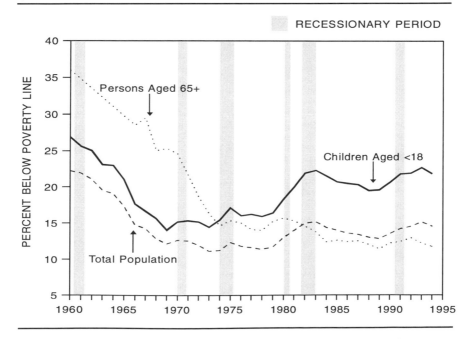

SOURCE: U.S. Bureau of the Census, 1995, *Current Population Reports,* series P60, no. 188, tables D-4 and D-5.

much above that of children, but by 1974 children and older people were equally likely to be poor. Since that time, the elderly, but not children, have benefited from Social Security payments indexed for inflation, from better pensions, and from the sale of homes in a booming real estate market. The economic gap separating the ends of the age distribution has widened markedly: higher poverty rates for children, moderately lower ones for persons aged 65 and over (Preston 1984).

Three trends now influence the economic status of children. Two of them increase poverty, the other reduces it. First, there is the shift of children away from relatively prosperous two-parent families and into lower-income, single-parent families, usually headed by the mother. Second, younger fathers, unless they have college degrees, have lower earnings than young fathers did in the past, so the declining wages of men plays a role. But there is an important trend working in the opposite direction: the increasing employment of mothers and their greater educational attainments.

Let's first take a look at the most important of these trends—the shift of children away from two-parent families. Although few marriages were terminated by divorce early in the century, adult death rates were high by current standards, causing many children to live in one-parent families, most often with a widowed mother. Hernandez (1993, p. 85) estimated that about one-third of children born at the turn of this century experienced marital disruption before attaining age 18. Declining mortality rates for adult men had a beneficial effect, which was offset by the long-term trend toward more divorce. The children least likely to live with one parent as they grew up were the early baby boomers. Just under 30 percent of them lived in a one-parent family sometime before age 18.

Social changes dating from the 1960s drastically altered this. In 1960, 90 percent of children under age 18 lived with a father and a mother. The sharp increase in divorce in the 1970s and the shift toward more childbearing by single women reduced this percentage. By 1980, 80 percent lived with two parents, declining further to 70 percent in 1993. The majority of children still live in two-parent families, but the proportion is steadily declining.

In the future, only a minority of children are likely to reach age 18 while living consistently with their two parents. Using information from the rates of the 1970s, Hernandez (1993, p. 87) projected that 53 percent of children born in that decade will live in a one-parent family at some point before their eighteenth birthday. Because of the rise in the birth rates of single women in the 1980s, it is inevitable that an even higher proportion of children born in that decade and in the 1990s will spend time in one-parent families (Bumpass 1984).

Common stereotypes about welfare and AFDC cause us to assume that all children in single-parent families live with their mothers. This is not accurate. The number of children in father-only families has risen at about the same rate as the number in mother-only families, and now about one-seventh of youngsters in single-parent families live with their father not their mother. Recall that these families include one parent and his or her own children, but not his or her spouse.

The Economic Status of Children: Family Type Makes a Difference

Changes in family living arrangements and the rising birth rates of unmarried women put an increasing fraction of children below the poverty line and into family constellations associated with serious adolescent problems.

In the last 125 years we have had two childcare revolutions. In the first, fathers went from working on family farms to jobs in factories and offices. Rather than being cared for by both parents in or near their homes, America's children were cared for by their mothers and by the schools. The second childcare revolution happened after 1965, as married women with children left their homes to take jobs in shops, factories, and offices (Hernandez 1993, chap. 5). Increasingly, parents pay someone else or use a barter system to care for their children while they work. This second childcare revolution should have beneficial financial consequences since the mother's work for pay adds to the family's income, providing the child with more insurance against poverty. However, the shift of children away from living with both parents and into families headed by women had the opposite effect since single-parent families have modest incomes, and many of the children in them are at risk of poverty.

An ideal way to summarize the outcome of these trends is to examine the status of children in 1990. Table 4-2 classifies children by their family living arrangements and reports their economic status. It shows the average income of families and the percentage of children who were either poor or economically comfortable. The poor are those living in families with cash incomes below the poverty line. To be comfortable, a family had to have a pre-tax cash income five times or more the poverty line.

Children living with both their parents in 1990 were quite well

Table 4-2. Economic Status of Children, by Living Arrangements: 1990

Living Arrangements	Distribution of Children by Family Type	Average Family Income in 1989 (000)	Percentage of Children	
			Below Poverty Line	Comfortable
In Two-Parent Families	72%	$53.6	9%	18%
Both parents work full-time[a]	24	60.9	3	24
Father full-time, mother part-time	16	56.3	5	18
Father full-time, mother doesn't work	22	52.7	10	15
Mother full-time, father part-time	2	43.8	17	7
In Mother-Only Families	21	21.6	47	3
Mother works full-time	9	28.9	21	4
Mother works part-time	5	18.8	57	2
Mother doesn't work	7	14.4	75	1
In Father-Only Families	4	32.8	25	8
Father works full-time	3	37.5	14	11
Father works part-time	1	25.6	41	5
With Neither Parent	3	30.6	41	6
Total Children Under 18	100%	$45.4	19%	14%

SOURCE: U.S. Bureau of the Census, *Census of Population and Housing: 1990*, Public Use Microdata Sample.
[a] Data not shown for all combinations of parental employment. Amounts shown in 1993 dollars.

off since they had a poverty rate of 9 percent, less than half the national poverty rate for children, and shared average family incomes of $46,000. They were even more prosperous if their mothers worked. For families in which both parents usually worked thirty-five or more hours per week, the poverty rate was just 3 percent, and one-quarter of those children could be termed economically comfortable. The inclusion of mothers in the labor force had economic benefits for children living with two fully employed parents. But employment of parents implied less time spent with children. Juliet Schor (1991, pp. 20–21) emphasizes the tremendous time pressures on mothers who work full-time, describing them as mothers in perpetual motion who in reality have two jobs—one in the workplace and one at home. Harriet Presser (1989, p. 523) summarized her investigation of this as follows:

> Not only are Americans having fewer children than ever before, they are spending less time with the children they have. This is due in large part to the growth in the labor force participation of women, which is most evident among mothers of young children, and to the decline in the proportion of families with fathers present.

The largest numerical shift for children in recent years has been into mother-only families, and here the poverty rates are high—47 percent in 1990. Almost one-half of all children in mother-only families are impoverished.

There is a measurement issue to keep in mind. When estimating poverty and prosperity, the Census Bureau counts cash income, including welfare payments, Supplemental Security Income, Social Security payments, and alimony, but not noncash benefits, such as food stamps or school lunches. A poverty rate of 47 percent for those sixteen million children in families headed by their mothers may be hard to reconcile with our image of a prosperous nation dedicated to providing opportunities to the next generation. Some might think that if we took into account noncash benefits—benefits that increased with the War on Poverty—the poverty rate for children in mother-only families would be much lower. This is erroneous. Imputing a value to those noncash transfers reduces the poverty rate, but a simultaneous adjustment should be made for the taxes they pay—sales tax, Social Security, and the like. The overall poverty rate for children changes little when both adjustments are made. It decreases by about three points, so the corrected poverty rate for children in mother-only families is 44 percent (U.S. Bureau of the Census 1991c, table 10). Even with noncash benefits, the majority of the increasingly large share of children living in these families are near poor or poor.

If a woman has the responsibility for raising her children, working full-time is a good way to avoid poverty. But the earnings of women, except those with college degrees, remain moderate or low, so many working mothers still fall into poverty. The census counted 5.9 million families headed by women who had children under age 18. In 40 percent of these, the woman worked full-time. Among these families, the poverty rate was still a high 21 percent (see table 4.2). Consider the typical jobs that women hold. Women who worked full-time in 1989 as cashiers earned $13,000; waitresses, $12,500; childcare workers, $11,700; and cosmetologists, $10,237. If a mother had two children, these amounts would have left her and her children near or below the poverty line. If a woman raises children without a husband, she will avoid poverty only if she works full-time and has the training and skills to get a high-paying job.

Children living with their fathers only are much better off economically than children living with their mothers only for several reasons. The father is more likely to work full-time, the wages of men continue to be 20 to 30 percent higher than those of similarly educated women, and the typical father-only family has fewer children than the typical mother-only family, so income is divided among fewer persons. Additionally, father-only families are more likely than mother-only families to include a cohabitant, presumably a woman who contributes some earnings. But children living with their fathers only are much less prosperous than those living with both parents.

Not only are there more children in one-parent families but there has been a shift into the types of single-parent families with the lowest incomes. Figure 4-6 shows the distribution of children in one-parent families by the marital status of the head of their family. In 1960, about one-half of these children lived with a divorced or widowed parent, many of them benefiting from annuities or alimony linked to the absent parent. The birth rate of unmarried women went up in the 1980s, so children are increasingly living with never-married mothers. They, and their mothers, typically have weaker claims on the father's economic assets. At present, paternity is established for fewer than 40 percent of the births to unmarried women, so these children are at great risk of poverty (Blankenhorn 1995, p. 236). In 1989, 59 percent of divorced women with children got financial support from the absent fathers, but only 18 percent of never-married women received

Figure 4-6. Children Under Age 18 Living with One Parent, by Marital Status of Parent: 1960 to 1993

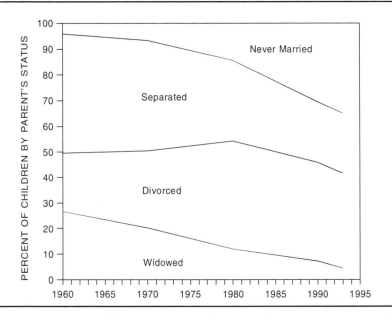

SOURCE: U.S. Bureau of the Census, 1996, *Current Population Reports,* series P-20, no. 484, table E.

such support (Bianchi 1995). The poverty rate for children living in families headed by their never-married mothers in 1990 was 53 percent, much higher than the poverty rate for children living in families headed by their divorced or widowed mothers—31 percent.

Recent changes in the living arrangements of children pose many challenges. Longitudinal investigations report the numerous advantages of growing up in a stable family and corresponding disadvantages for children experiencing their parents' marital disruption or never living with their fathers. Some children, of course, are much better off with a single parent, and most children from such families will become successful adults, but, in the aggregate, family breakups are costly to children. After taking into account those differences in parents' educations, number of siblings, and other socioeconomic factors that distinguish children from stable two-parent families from those that experienced family disruption, Sara McLanahan and Gary Sandefur (1994, chap. 3) found that children who spent time in one-parent families had lower grade point averages and were about twice as likely to drop out of high school before getting diplomas than those who grew up in two-parent families. Daughters from single-parent families were 2.5 times as likely as daughters from two-parent families to become teen mothers themselves; that is, among teenage white girls in the 1980s, 22 percent of those from single-parent families became teenage mothers compared to 8 percent for daughters from two-parent families. Teenage boys from single-parent families were 1.4 times as likely to be idle—neither enrolled in school nor employed—than children from two-parent families. Children whose family of origin was disrupted by the death of a parent were least disadvantaged by their father's absence; those born to unmarried women, the most disadvantaged. The presence of a stepparent or a grandparent did not make up for the loss of their own father (McLanahan and Sandefur 1994).

Although these studies cannot take into account all differences that might distinguish one-parent and two-parent families, such as psychological problems or alcoholism, they strongly imply that the breakup of families or the total absence of a father has adverse consequences for children. Family disruption usually means that parents spend less time with their children, presumably providing less supervision, discipline, and social support. Family disruption is also associated with frequent geographic mobility, and this too has an adverse effect upon children as they frequently switch from school to school. These new findings are consistent with studies of a generation ago in reporting that family dissolution disadvantages children, especially by truncating their educational attainment (Blau and Duncan 1967, pp. 331–337; Duncan, Featherman, and Duncan 1972; Featherman and Hauser 1978, pp. 303–306).

We should be concerned about the rise in the poverty rate of children since 1980 since they were years of economic growth and expansion. A demographic trend—the shift of children away from two-parent families and into mother-only families—accounts for this recent rise in childhood poverty. Yet it is rash to conclude that the 1980s were bad economic years for children. Some children benefited from sharply rising incomes while others did not, so there are now proportionally fewer children living in families in the middle of the income distribution. The optimistic and encouraging news is that the percentage of children living in households with incomes five or more times the poverty line went up from 12 to 14 percent in the 1980s. This is entirely due to the higher incomes of husband-wife families, reflecting the much greater employment of mothers and their slightly rising earnings. This also means that economic polarization is occurring since, on average, children in two-parent families are increasingly better off than those living with their mothers only. The discouraging news is that the percentage of children in poverty-level families also rose—from 16 to 18 percent according to the censuses. Fewer children are now in middle-income families. Thus, the clearest evidence of a decline in the size of the middle class in the 1980s involves children.

Living Arrangements of Adults

In the 1950s and 1960s, most children moved away from home shortly after high school to get married, go off to college, fulfill military obligations, or live with their pals as they started their jobs. But now children commonly live with their parents for quite a few years after high school or return home after college or following divorce. By 1993, 53 percent of young adults aged 18 to 24 were living in their parents' homes, an increase from 42 percent in 1960. On most indicators, there is more family disruption in the 1990s than in the 1950s, but on this one—adult children living with their parents—the change is toward much more family stability. In the past, many parents finished their financial obligations to their children when the children graduated from high school or college. Now it is common for parents to continue providing shelter and some financial support when their children get into their mid-twenties or even thirties.

Three social and economic shifts account for this. First, there was the delay of marriage. Second, the rising cost of housing in the 1980s made many young people reconsider moving away from home. In many large metropolises, the cost of an attractive apartment or starter home went up rapidly, while the salaries of young workers declined. Finally, college enrollments went up in the 1980s, but tuitions increased much faster than inflation, so to keep college costs in line, more students lived at home rather than in dormitories or their own apartments. The percentage of 18- to 24-year-old college students living in dorms fell from 26 to 22 between 1980 and 1990.

Next, we turn to adults aged 25 to 64. It is easy to capsulize their changing living arrangements: an increasing diversity with fewer husband-wife families and many more people living by themselves. Shifts in values about marriage and divorce, combined with changes in job opportunities and housing costs, produced a much more differentiated array of living arrangements.

To describe such changes and explain trends in prosperity and poverty, we need a good classification system. Current procedures start with the household. A household includes all the people who live together in a dwelling unit—a home, apartment, or condominium. The people are often related to each other, but in some circumstances they are not. Almost all people—97.3 percent in 1990—lived in households. Presumably, they shared meals, used the same living space, and, to a greater or lesser degree, shared the household's income and its obligations. Those not in households lived in group quarters or institutions, such as dormitories, barracks, and prisons. In 1990, this included 3.3 million persons counted in correctional institutions, two million in college dormitories, and approximately one-quarter million homeless as enumerated by the Census Bureau's special procedures in March of that year.

Most households include a family: two or more persons related by blood, marriage, or adoption. Seventy-one percent of households did so in 1990. A husband and wife who live in their own house are classified as both a married-couple family and a married-couple household. A divorced or never-married woman living in her own apartment with two children would be a female-headed household and a female-headed family. Some households do not contain a family. A person living alone or three unrelated young people sharing an apartment while they attend college would be households that do not include families. A cohabiting couple with no children gets counted as a household but not as a family since they are not related to each other.

The living arrangements of adults differ from those of the past, as shown in figure 4-7, which provides information about trends in types of households. When John Kennedy was president, two kinds of households were dominant—married couples and women living by themselves, typically older women who had outlived their husbands—but this no longer holds. Husband-wife households as a share of total households have declined steadily, and by the late-1990s may make up only one-half of all households. The drop has been greater for married couples with children than for those without children, because of postponed childbearing by young couples as well as falling death rates, which produce more older married couples. In 1960, about three-quarters of all households were husband-wife families. By the early 1990s, just over one-half were.

Other household types have increased, with a particularly large rise in persons living alone, reflecting, at one end of the age spectrum,

Figure 4-7. Distribution of Households, by Type: 1960 to 1994

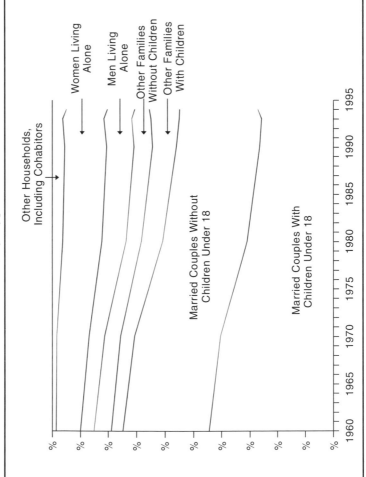

SOURCE: U.S. Bureau of the Census, 1990, *Current Population Reports*, series P-20, nos. 447 and 477.

the delay of marriage and, at the other, the greater life expectancy of men and women, resulting in more widows and widowers living by themselves. Mothers of the baby boomers typically lived with their own parents until they married and then lived with their husbands, and many will continue to do so until they are widowed. But among the late baby boomers, it was common to move away from the parental home, live alone or with nonrelatives, marry, divorce, move back home, and then into some other type of household, perhaps with a second spouse or with an unmarried partner. This explains the much greater diversity of living arrangements for adults.

These trends have great implications for the welfare of adults and children since the family is this society's major means for redistributing income from earners to dependents, be they children, spouses, or adults who cannot or do not work. Recent changes in living arrangements led to the growth of both prosperous and low-income households.

Table 4-3 shows what happened in the 1980s. Because the focus here is on adults, this table is restricted to households headed by people aged 25 to 64. Overall, the number of households increased by 15 percent in the decade, but married couples with children dropped by 2 percent. Nonfamily households—men and women living either by themselves or with nonrelatives—increased rapidly. Family households involving children but no spouse—mother-only or father-only families—also became more numerous. Married couples are still the most common household type, but adults are increasingly spending more years living by themselves or with nonrelatives.

Married-couple households did quite well economically in this decade: the average purchasing power rose 18 percent for those without children and 12 percent for those with children. Income also went up sharply for women who lived by themselves. With higher earnings, women may be deferring marriage, and those who are quite prosperous can readily afford to live alone. Women who headed their own families with children did not fare as well since their average incomes declined. The average income of men who headed families with children alone also decreased. *During the 1980s the only types of households whose average incomes fell were single-parent families.*

Poverty rates are shown to the far right in table 4-3. Husband-wife families and those rare families headed by a man who has neither a spouse nor children—perhaps two brothers—had the lowest poverty rates, while single mothers who headed their own families were most likely to be poor. The largest increases in poverty rates in the 1980s were in the single-parent families.

Table 4-3. Households Headed by Persons Aged 25 to 64: Income and Poverty: 1980 and 1990 (amounts shown in 1993 dollars)

	Households		Household Income			Percent Poor	
	Number in 1990 (000)	Percent Change Since 1980	Average Income in 1989 (000)	Percent Change Since 1980		1990	Percentage Point Change Since 1980
Married-Couple Family Households							
With children	22,840	−2%	$56.0	+12%		7%	0%
No children	17,719	+13	62.1	+18		3	−1 Point
Family Households Headed by Women							
With children	5,271	+22	20.1	−9		41	+4
No children	2,937	+51	35.6	+6		14	0

Family Households Headed by Men						
With children	1,167	+74	32.0	−18	20	+6
No children	1,121	+43	45.4	0	8	+1
Nonfamily Households Headed by Men						
Living alone	6,270	+33	33.1	+10	12	0
Living with others	1,930	+70	53.5	+12	11	0
Nonfamily Households Headed by Women						
Living alone	6,035	+27	25.4	+22	17	−3
Living with others	1,157	+99	50.9	+19	14	−2
Total Households	66,447	+15%	$48.7	+12%	11%	0%

SOURCE: U.S. Bureau of the Census, *Census of Population and Housing: 1980 and 1990*, Public Use Microdata Samples.

The New Requirement for Middle-Class Status: Working Wives

From the end of World War II through the early 1970s, the incomes of married-couple families with a wife in the labor force marched up at the same rate as the incomes of those families depending on the husband's earnings alone because working wives contributed so little. But this changed. The income of married couples where the wife stayed at home peaked in the early 1970s, stagnated for a while, and then declined. So these husband-wife families did not benefit from the record peacetime economic expansion of the 1980s. But married couples with employed wives who saw their earnings go up just a little in the 1970s, experienced much more rapid earnings growth after economic growth resumed in the 1980s.

According to the old rules, a man who got a job and worked diligently could expect to support his family while his wife raised the children, but this is no longer the case. For married couples to get into the higher income brackets or to keep their secure hold on middle-class status, two earners, preferably full-time earners, are needed. In 1960, only 30 percent of married couples had wives in the paid labor force, but by 1994 it was 61 percent. Given the downward trajectory of men's earnings, married couples will likely see their incomes rise in the future only if wives work longer and earn more.

Many social and economic pressures encourage wives to work. But work competes with childcare responsibilities and with the time-consuming tasks of maintaining a home, tasks that are still done primarily by wives, not by husbands. As Arlie Hochschild puts it, the married woman who works a full-time job is working a second shift (Hochschild and Machung 1989; Presser 1989). What are the factors that determine whether a wife is employed or not? Findings from the census show an unambiguous cohort trend, with younger wives and those with extensive educations most likely to be earning money.

Table 4-4 summarizes results for married couples in 1990 with wives aged 25 to 64. Wives were classified by their ages, their educations, the presence of children, and by their family's incomes from sources other than their earnings, primarily from the husband's earnings. I show the net impact of having a specific characteristic by reporting the odds that the wife had earnings in 1989 in comparison to the odds for a baseline category of the variable. An example makes this procedure clear. Having either no children in the family or having children over age 6 greatly increased the likelihood that the wife worked for pay in 1989. This conclusion comes from observing that

Table 4-4.   Likelihood (Odds) of a Married Women Having
Earnings in Married-Couple Families: 1990

	Odds of Having Earnings
Presence of Children (odds relative to having children under age 6)	
Children under age 6	1.0
Children ages 6 to 17, but none under age 6	2.4
No children under age 18	3.0
Birth Cohorts (odds relative to wives aged 55–64)	
Age 25–34: late baby boom	5.8
Age 35–44: early baby boom	4.5
Age 45–54: World War II	2.9
Age 55–64: mothers of baby boom	1.0
Education (odds relative to not high school graduates)	
Not high school graduate	1.0
High school graduate	2.0
Some college	2.9
College graduate	3.5
Postgraduate education	5.7
Other Family Income, Primarily Husband's Earnings (odds relative to $40,000 or more)	
Less than $15,000	1.8
$15,000 to 24,999	2.1
$25,000 to 39,999	1.8
$40,000 or more	1.0

SOURCE: Bianchi 1995, table 3.15.

the odds of having earnings were much greater for wives with no
children or for those with older children than they were for wives
who had children under age 6. Wives with no children were three
times as likely to have earnings as wives with children under age 6.
Having young children is costly for married couples, not just because
it is expensive to pay the expenses of the child, but also because it
reduces the likelihood that the wife works.

Cohort trends described in previous chapters strongly affect wives' employment since those in the late baby boom cohorts were, net of other factors, about 5.8 times as likely to have earnings as were the mothers of the baby boomers. With the changes in social values, many younger women expect that they will be working wives most of their lives, an idea firmly rejected by women born during the Depression decade. Wages go up with increases in education, so it is not surprising to find that wives with postgraduate educations were 5.7 times as likely to be earning money as wives with less than high school diplomas. Women who receive specialized training or advanced degrees generally work to improve their family's economic welfare. Given their high potential earnings, it is costly for them to stay at home.

Economic necessity is also a motivating factor, so the success of a husband in the labor market influences whether a wife works, regardless of her own education. Women whose husbands earned less than $25,000 were about twice as likely to be working as women whose husbands earned more than $40,000. Net of other characteristics, women who marry men with great earnings are more likely to remain at home.

Increases in the educational attainment of women, higher wages for women, and the stagnation of men's earnings generally have resulted in a long-run shift toward more married couples with working wives. This should have beneficial economic effects for children living in such families. But a complete appraisal of the trends would also emphasize that married-couple families are a decreasing share of all households and that children increasingly live in single-parent families. If the wages of women were to go up rapidly, presumably more mother-only families would be lifted above the poverty line, but wage gains for women were modest in the 1980s, and the poverty rate of mother-only families actually increased.

What Causes Changes in Marital Status, Families, and Living Arrangements?

The traditional American family depended upon certain social values and economic opportunities. There had to be consensus that this system of traditional gender roles was ideal, with norms supporting it and censuring those who opted for a different lifestyle, be it having children out-of-wedlock or living with an unmarried partner. It also depended upon there being high-wage jobs for men. It was aided—

and this may be the key factor—by social values specifying that if a woman desired a stable, secure, middle-class lifestyle, she had to marry and depend on her husband's earnings. So employment policies kept the best jobs for men and laid off women when they married or had a baby. Simultaneously, mores and social pressure restricted sexual activity to the married population but were applied more stringently to women than to men.

These private values and governmental economic policies of the 1940s, 1950s, and 1960s reduced poverty and created the modern American middle class in large part because of the two-parent family system. And because the strategy involved keeping a high proportion of men working, we have had policies seeking full employment for men since the 1930s. Public and private investments were made in education so that once men entered the labor force their productivity would rise, giving them higher wages. Then there were the favorable policies, abetted by thousands of local communities, that encouraged homeownership.

I believe that the changing living arrangements of parents and their children help to explain the unusual economic trends of the 1980s and the pervasive sense among the middle class that is not doing well. There is consensus that these problems need to be fixed, but there is no agreement about what should be done. The policies that worked so well in the past seem to have lost their potency. Any program to specifically raise the earnings of men would be labeled gender discrimination and, even if it were successful, its impact would be limited in this new era since almost one-third of births occur to single women, and husband-wife families make up just over one-half of all households.

It is important to understand what is happening to families and households since they are still society's major program for transferring income from earners to dependents. If we wish to assess what might happen were current policies terminated and new ones adopted, we need to know why the living arrangements changed so rapidly in the three decades following 1965—changes that, as all the most recent indicators show, continue apace.

Many social scientists would like to explain these shifts by pointing to a single factor—a decline in morals, a decline in commitment to responsibilities, or easy access to welfare. But there is no single factor accounting for the substantial changes in marital status and childbearing that are now occurring. Despite the richness of census data, no one can specifically determine how much of the change was due to changing moral values; to the greater acceptance of premarital sexuality, divorce, and single parenting; to the liberation of women from those traditional constraints that kept them home and at the edges of the labor market; or to the steadily falling wages of most young men. All contributed.

The most popular single-factor explanation directs attention to the availability of welfare payments and other governmental moneys sent to the poor, especially to single-parent families. It is among the weaker explanations. Women whose own prospects for high earnings are limited generally recognize that their prospective mates will also earn little. If these women wish to have children, they realize that welfare benefits may support them in a manner similar to that of a low-earning husband. For some women this may be enough motivation to put off marriage, but not childbearing. While this explanation might account for changes among those with little education or few job opportunities, it would not apply to highly educated men and women. They, too, delayed their marriages and shifted into new family arrangements similar to those of people who dropped out of high school.

The national mood has frowned upon welfare—a crucial issue in national and state elections for several decades (Quadagno 1994, chap. 8). Opponents of AFDC have not eliminated it, but they have successfully achieved their next best goal—drastically cutting benefits. Figure 4-8 shows the poverty line for a family of four, such as a divorced or separated woman with three young children. It also reports the benefits she typically would have received from AFDC. If she had been cashing welfare checks since 1970, she would have seen their purchasing power decline by more than 40 percent: women on welfare today get much less than their mothers or older sisters did a quarter century ago. If welfare were the primary cause of changes in family living arrangements, we would have expected a return to traditional families as welfare checks lost their value, but quite the opposite occurred.

Sara McLanahan and Lynne Casper (1995) carried out the most thorough recent investigation of the changes in marital status and families, using information from the 1970 to 1990 censuses, focusing upon the delays in marriage. They assumed that several factors account for what occurred. First, if the employment situation for women were favorable and if employed women had good jobs and high earnings, they assume that women would put off marriage. Presumably, many women would find their careers highly rewarding and postpone marriage, while other women would become more selective in choos-

Figure 4-8. Median Monthly AFDC Benefits for a Family of Four and Poverty Line: 1970 to 1993 (amounts in 1993 dollars)

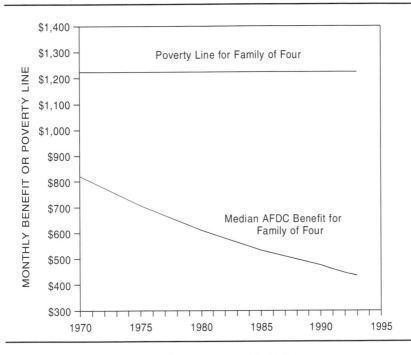

SOURCE: Committee on Ways and Means 1994, table 10-15.

ing their husbands. Second, McLanahan and Casper argue that if the employment situation were bad for men and if men of marriageable age had low earnings, marriage would be deferred, since women would shy away from marrying men with limited earnings, especially when their own economic outlooks were improving. Similarly, men in a tight job market with poor earnings prospects would be reluctant to take on the responsibilities of marriage. Finally, they took the level of AFDC payments into account, since these vary from state to state and have changed over time. Some women live in states with rather generous benefits, others in states with meager benefits. In 1993, for example, the maximum monthly cash benefit for a mother and her two children was $517 in Wisconsin and $120 in Mississippi (U.S. House of Representatives Ways and Means Committee 1993, p. 677).

The results suggest that welfare payments have a net effect in the expected direction, but a modest one. Where benefits were relatively generous, women deferred marriage more than where benefits were modest. So the effects of welfare were significant but small. More important were the employment and earnings of men. Declining earnings of men apparently accounted for much of the change in family living arrangements described in this chapter. Where many men were unemployed or where they earned little, marriage was put off. If a policy drastically raised the wages of men, especially those with less than college educations, the trend away from traditional marriage might be slowed. Women would, presumably, marry earlier and would have fewer children on their own. Even more important were the economic opportunities of women. Where many women were employed and where the earnings of women were high, women delayed marriage the most. Net of other factors, places in which the earnings of women went up most rapidly were those with the biggest declines in early marriage. This is strong evidence that women put off their marriages because of their own employment opportunities.

Three basic changes, I believe, explain new developments in the American family system. First, social values switched rapidly in just a few decades. In the 1950s, there was one acceptable way for adults to live and those who deviated from it were, to some degree, stigmatized and censured. New social values accept a wider variety of living arrangements—both heterosexual and homosexual—and with or without a formal marriage contract. Second, a liberation of women occurred as young cohorts increasingly invested in their educations and then moved into better jobs with higher wages. As Generation X women, born 1965 to 1974, become young adults, they will be more independent economically and psychologically than were the mothers of the baby boomers. They also have access to more effective contraceptives. The economic success and independence of young women today makes them reluctant to marry the kinds of men their mothers or grandmothers may have considered. Perhaps it is not surprising that two-thirds of the Generation X women are selecting cohabitation as their first live-in sexual relationship. Third—and totally unexpected—is the small but steady annual decline in the wages of men. Proportionately fewer men in Generation X will be able to take on the financial responsibilities of traditional families while they are young, so they are reluctant to marry, especially since new values make alternative lifestyles socially acceptable and economically feasible.

Table 4-5. International Comparisons of Family Status: 1990

| | Divorce Rate | Percentage of Births to Single Women | Single-Parent Families | Percentage of Young Women Employed | Poverty Rates Controlling for Age and Education | | | |
| | | | | | Married-Couple Families | | Single-Mother Families | |
					Employed Mothers	Non-employed Mothers	Employed Mothers	Non-employed Mothers
United States	21%	28%	23%	73%	10%	19%	30%	69%
Canada	12	24	15	75	6	19	21	63
Germany	8	11	14	62	2	6	13	44
Italy	2	6	n.a.	61	4	17	9	41
Netherlands	8	8	15	55	6	4	7	10
Sweden	12	47	13	89	2	8	3	20
United Kingdom	12	28	13	66	8	17	15	21

SOURCE: McLanahan and Casper 1995, tables 1.3 and 1.10.

Divorce Rate: Divorces per 1,000 married women.

Percentage of Births to Single Women: Percentage of births born to unmarried women.

Single-Parent Families: Percentage of all family households that are single-parent families. Data for Canada are for 1986; for Germany, 1988; for the Netherlands and Sweden, 1985; and for the United Kingdom, 1987.

Percentage of Young Women Employed: Data refer to women aged 25 to 34, except in Italy where the age range is 25 to 39.

Poverty Rates: These are poverty rates controlling for age and education, taking into account family size. Poverty is defined as having a total family income less than one-half the median income for families of that size in that country.

An International Comparison

The United States differs from prosperous Western European countries on the indicators discussed in this chapter, particularly in its high rates of childhood poverty. Table 4-5 provides information comparing countries on several measures of marital and family status. The United States stands out for its elevated divorce rate, but the proportion of births to unmarried women is even higher in France and Sweden than in the United States (McLanahan and Casper 1995). When it comes to poverty levels, especially in single-parent families, the United States is much dif-

Figure 4-9. Percentage of All Poor Families with Children Lifted Out of Poverty by Government Interventions

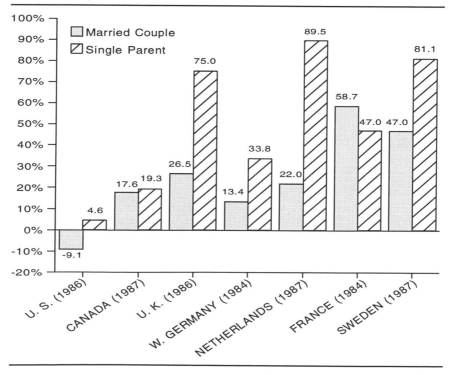

SOURCE: McFate 1995.

NOTE: Poverty is defined as 50 percent of the median income for households with heads aged 20 to 55 in each country.

ferent. It is not so much that we have a higher divorce rate, more out-of-wedlock births, or less cohabitation than the prosperous Western European countries, although these factors account for some of the difference. Basically, poverty rates are lower in other countries because governmental programs provide moneys to poor families with children.

Let's be more explicit. Figure 4-9 considers families whose cash income fell below an internationally comparable poverty line. It reports the percentage of these families lifted above that poverty line by governmental financial interventions, such as welfare benefits provided to poor families. In the Netherlands, 90 percent of the single-parent poor families had their poverty eradicated by governmental transfers, 81 percent in Sweden, and 47 percent in France. In contrast, only 5 percent of U.S. single-parent poor families rose above the poverty line because of governmental transfers. Married-couple poor families benefited much less in all countries than single-parent poor families, primarily because they are eligible for fewer benefits, but they fare worse in the United States than elsewhere. Governmental financial interventions actually do more harm than good to married-couple poor families in the United States since they pay taxes but seldom benefit from AFDC or other cash relief programs.

Living Arrangements and Economic Status of the Older Population

There is one group whose economic status clearly improved in the 1970s and 1980s, a group largely unaffected by industrial restructuring, declining wages, or changing social values. Persons aged 65 and over were much better off financially in 1990 than ever before. (For a detailed discussion of these changes, see Treas and Torrecilha 1995).

The living arrangements of this group are strongly influenced by mortality rates, health status, and their own financial resources. In the past, a sizable fraction of older persons lived with their relatives, typically their children, because they could not afford to maintain their own homes, but this is no longer the case. Table 4-6 reports the number of older persons in each type of household and provides indicators of their economic status. Because older men and women differ so greatly in their living conditions, data are shown separately for the two sexes.

By 1990, more than three-quarters of older men lived with their wives in their own homes or apartments; only 15 percent lived by them-

Table 4-6. Household Living Arrangements and Economic Status of Men and Women Aged 65 and Older

	Persons		Household Income		Percent Poor	
	Number in 1990 (000)	Percent Change Since 1980	Average Income in 1989 (000)	Percent Change Since 1979	1990	Percentage Point Change Since 1980
Men						
Married-couple household	9,480	+22%	$39.3	+22%	6%	−2%
Living alone	1,887	+31	20.5	+24	17	−7
Living with relatives	480	−8	56.3	+14	7	+1
Living with nonrelatives	173	+36	43.3	+15	30	−6
In group quarters or institutionalized	478	+17	n.a.	n.a.	n.a.	n.a.
Total	12,497	+22%	$37.1	+26%	8%	−3%
Women						
Married-couple household	7,617	+29%	$37.6	+23%	6%	−3%
Living alone	7,082	+26	15.0	+15	26	−4
Living with relatives	2,374	−8	53.6	+12	6	0
Living with nonrelatives	299	+27	49.4	+23	45	−2
In group quarters or institutionalized	1,267	+17	n.a.	n.a.	n.a.	n.a.
Total	18,639	+23%	$29.6	+23%	13%	−5%

SOURCE: U.S. Bureau of the Census, *Census of Population and Housing: 1980 and 1990*, Public Use Microdata Samples.

NOTES: Poverty status and household income were not ascertained for people living in group quarters or institutions hence the n.a.'s in the table. Poverty and household income information for the total refer to all persons in households. Amounts shown in 1993 dollars.

selves. Because women at age 65 can expect to live five years longer than men—that is, nineteen years for women, fourteen for men—their household living arrangements are very different. About 45 percent of older women lived with husbands, while another 40 percent lived on their own. Older people who live alone are overwhelmingly those who have outlived their spouses: about 60 percent of men and 80 percent of women reported "widowed" as their marital status.

For both sexes, the most important long-run trend is the continuing disinclination to the once-common living with children. In 1990, just 4 percent of people age 65 and over lived in households headed by their own children or by their sons or daughters-in-law, a drop from 6 percent a decade earlier.

Many persons aged 65 and over in 1990 did very well in the housing market since they had purchased first homes soon after World War II, often with the help of government financing, and then benefited as housing prices rose faster than inflation. The fortunate among them had the option of selling their homes and using their capital gains to purchase retirement condominiums in the Sunbelt or to stay where they always lived, often in a very spacious home. It is improbable that the late baby boom and Generation X cohorts will do as well in the housing market, since they are getting off to a much slower start in buying their first homes (Myers and Wolch 1995, pp. 292–296).

There is a popular perception that a sizable fraction of the elderly live in nursing homes, homes for the aged, and similar institutions, but that is not the case. In 1990, just 4 percent of men and 7 percent of women aged 65 and over resided in such places. Even among those aged 85 and over, the majority lived in their own households rather than in institutions, but at these very oldest ages, living in institutions was more common—17 percent for men and 27 percent for women.

Comparing tables 4-4 and 4-6 reveals how remarkably favorable the economic trends were for the older population in the 1980s. Among households headed by persons aged 25 to 64, average purchasing power went up 12 percent, so their economic conditions got better. But for households headed by people aged 65 and over, the economic gain was twice as great (see table 4-6). This rapid rise in income helps to explain the burgeoning growth and prosperity of the nation's retirement communities and recreational centers. As figure 4-5 shows, poverty rates fell among the older population while rising among youth.

Very favorable cohort trends and beneficial governmental policies explain the economic and health improvements among those aged 65

Figure 4-10. Average Monthly Social Security Payments and Poverty Lines for Single Individuals and Married Couples: 1960 to 1993 (amounts in 1993 dollars)

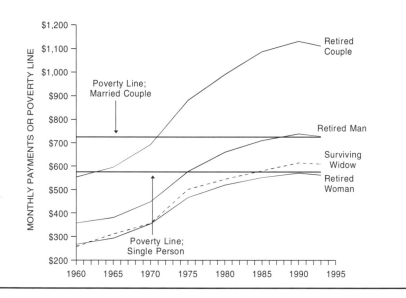

SOURCE: U.S. Social Security Administration, 1994, *Social Security Bulletin, Annual Statistical Supplement: 1993*, table 5.41.

and over. The population now coming to retirement is increasingly well educated, and more of them worked at white-collar jobs rather than on farms or in factories. Presumably, they will collect better pensions than those who retired in the 1960s and 1970s or, as an economist would put it, in their retirements they will benefit from the increased productivity of their midlife labor.

When Social Security was enacted, it was assumed that older persons would support themselves from three sources: their savings, their pensions, and Social Security. Thus, payments from the federal program were originally modest, but presidential politics eventually changed that. Figure 4-10 shows the poverty line for older single persons living on their own and for older married-couple households. It also reports the average payment made by Social Security. Since the size of the benefit depends upon the pay level of a person's employment and their years of contribution, some beneficiaries received more and some less than the amount shown in figure 4-10.

Before the 1970s, Congress increased Social Security payments from time to time, often shortly before elections. But payments were still small so an unfortunate retiree or widow who depended on Social Security alone found herself or himself far below the poverty line. When Congressman Wilbur Mills planned his campaign for president in 1972, he sought the support of the elderly, and his efforts led to a major change that continues to greatly aid the older population. Since 1973, Social Security payments have been indexed to annual changes in the consumer price index, and so they have risen steadily. They rose particularly rapidly around 1980 when the cost of living shot up. For the first time, older persons found that their Social Security checks alone were putting them near or above the poverty line. Interestingly, Social Security payments have steadily risen while the wages of adult men have fallen, leading to a decreasing gap between the income of the older population and that of the working age (Treas and Torrecilha 1995, figure 2-12).

Poverty rates for older persons are not exceptionally low, 8 percent for men in 1990 and 13 percent for women. And a widow previously married to a man with low earnings will still find herself impoverished if she depends upon just Social Security. Her condition will be much worse if she was divorced and her former husband's check is split with one or two other surviving wives. Nevertheless, the recent trend is toward a decline in poverty among the older population, a trend that may accelerate given the more favorable occupations of those who will retire in the future and the generous indexing of Social Security payments.

Will the income of the older population continue to rise more rapidly than that of the working age population? Will the poverty rate of those aged 65 and over decline to still lower levels? Current demographic, economic, and political trends present many challenges if these trends are to persist into the next century.

Two major programs of the federal government—Social Security, especially after it was indexed for inflation, and Medicare—help explain the health and prosperity of those who recently attained retirement age. Since 1965, the government has assumed chief financial responsibility for the health care costs of seniors. Part A of that program pays hospitalization bills, thereby protecting against expenses which, in the past, might have forced older persons to sell their homes, deplete their savings, or borrow from their children. Most persons over age 64 also enroll in the voluntary Part B of Medicare. In 1995, the monthly premium was $46, but it paid for 80 percent of the cost of outpatient services. These are entitlement programs; anyone in the United States who works a sufficient number of quarters pays

Social Security and Medicare taxes and thereby becomes eligible for these benefits. There is also no limit to the payments. As the life span lengthens and as costly medical procedures improve the health of the older population, government payments increase—by as much as 14 percent from one year to the next in the late 1980s and early 1990s. If hospitalization or visits to the doctor are needed, Medicare pays the costs. Neither Social Security nor Medicare is an actuarially sound insurance system. All workers and their employers presently pay 8.75 percent of their earnings for these benefits, but rather than maintaining individual accounts, the federal government each year writes Social Security and Medicare checks from that year's tax revenues. The modest trust funds earmarked for these programs are invested in federal government bonds: when they are cashed in, taxpayers will pay higher rates or the Department of the Treasury will borrow money with taxpayers paying the interest.

When Medicare went into effect in the 1960s and when Social Security was indexed for inflation, there was a long history of steadily rising wages and, most importantly, the working age population was very large compared to those of retirement age. The figures below show the number of working age persons relative to retirement age persons (U.S. Bureau of the Census 1984, table 3; 1996, table G).

When there were five working-age persons per retiree and when medical costs were much lower, tax rates could be kept modest. But the sharp decline in fertility—the shift from the three- to the two-

Year	Ratio of Working Age (25–64) Persons to Retirement Age (65 +) Persons
1950	5.0
1960	5.0
1970	4.5
1980	4.2
1990	4.1
Projected	
2000	4.1
2010	4.0
2020	3.0
2030	2.3

child family—and the extension of the life span at the older ages—
the addition of three years to the life span at age 60 since 1960—
altered the demographic balance and now jeopardizes the current system. Unless fertility and mortality rates take a sudden and unexpected
upturn by early in the next century, there will be fewer than three
working age individuals for each Social Security and Medicare benefi-
ciary. Trust funds will likely be spent since annual outlays will far
exceed annual tax revenues.

Federal expenditures have been fundamentally shifted in the last
three decades by the growth of the older population and the sharply
rising per capita cost of Medicare. The share of spending devoted to
defense declined while Social Security and Medicare increased. The
fraction spent on interest also moved up because deficit spending ne-
cessitated borrowing to enable the government to pay its bills. These
trends are clearly illustrated with the following information about federal expenditures (Council of Economic Advisors 1996, table B-79).

Percentage of Federal Government Spending Devoted to
Specific Purposes

	1960	1970	1980	1995
Total	100%	100%	100%	100%
National Defense	52	42	23	18
Social Security	13	16	20	22
Medicare	0	3	5	11
Interest Payments	7	8	9	15
All Other Items	28	31	43	34

The improved health and economic prosperity of the older population is a tribute to innovative and now very popular federal programs. This is an example of how congressional actions fixed the
healthcare and income security problems of people at great risk of
falling below the poverty line. But when the government begins to
devote one-half or more of its expenditures to the support of the older
population, there will, quite likely, be lively debate about the wisdom
of continuing such a policy. Perhaps three options will be discussed.
First, benefits for these entitlement programs might be reduced. While
some cutbacks seem inevitable (a modest advance in qualifying ages

for Social Security is already on the books), the voting strength of the retired population and those approaching retirement will temper such reductions, especially with regard to healthcare. Second, taxes might be raised to specifically fund Social Security and Medicare, but this will also be politically unpopular because the wages of those who would pay more have been stagnant or declining for two decades. Third, federal governmental support for all other programs—Medicaid, education, national parks, environmental clean-up, health research, housing programs, welfare, Amtrak, and thousands of others—might be scaled back just as defense spending was in recent years. In upcoming decades, voters will make their choices about these important matters.

Chapter 5

New Americans

The symbolism of Miss Liberty's torch for our schoolchildren is that we are a nation of immigrants and that our forebears came here searching for freedom and economic opportunities. With diligent effort, all of us could trace our roots back toward Africa, Europe, or even to Asia in the case of the first immigrants to arrive—American Indians.

Throughout American history, contentious arguments have raged whenever immigration has surged. Will immigrants reject American values and thereby destroy our country? Will they vote as a block undermining democracy? Will they work for such low wages that native Americans will be impoverished? Will they impose their religious systems on us? Will they retain their own languages, eventually making English a minority tongue?

In every era, many observers and commentators thought that the answers were yes, instigating strong efforts to close the gates and to limit the rights of the foreign-born. (For a recent statement of this view, see Brimelow 1995.) Many states enacted literacy tests for voting lest newcomers be cajoled or bribed into massive voting blocs. The Dillingham Commission early this century stressed that immigrants from Northern and Western Europe might eventually fit in, but that those from Eastern and Southern Europe certainly would not, leading to the most restrictive immigration laws that Congress ever passed.

From the perspective of the 1990s, it is obvious that these apprehensions were unfounded: findings from recent censuses document assimilation of immigrants from all parts of Europe on all social and economic indicators (Lieberson and Waters 1988; Alba 1990; Waters 1990). Ethnic neighborhoods once populated by Eastern and Southern Europeans disappeared in the post–World War II suburban boom, there are no longer distinctive ethnic voting patterns, and ethnic intermarriage is now common, so common that many whites do not give consistent or specific answers when asked about their ethnicity. To a large degree, the Catholic and Jewish religions brought by immigrants in the second great wave—1880 to 1924—have been "Americanized." Rather than being distinctively "foreign" or "immigrant," members of these religious groups and their leaders are firmly in the American mainstream. The most distinctive religious movements in recent years—the evangelical movements and the fundamentalism of born-again Christians—are not associated with immigrants.

On the basis of what happened throughout this century, we can confidently predict that a similar process will eventually incorporate the new streams now arriving. When Italians, Slavs, and Jews were the steerage passengers arriving in New York, Israel Zangwill described an American melting pot—a blending of cultures that enriched the nation while allowing immigrants to retain some of their distinctive ethnicity. The United States is still a melting pot, but now it is heavily flavored by contributions from Asia and Latin America.

The symbolism of Miss Liberty's torch for our schoolchildren is that we are a nation of immigrants and that our forebears came here searching for freedom and economic opportunities. With diligent effort, all of us could trace our roots back toward Africa, Europe, or even to Asia in the case of the first immigrants to arrive—the American Indians (Jaffe 1992). But interest in this topic waxed and waned. Descriptions of our nation written in the 1960s paid little attention to immigration (Taeuber and Taeuber 1971). During that decade, the era of immigration seemed to be over, and the United States would grow or decline on the basis of its birth and death rates. No one foresaw the arrival of millions of immigrants from Asia and Latin American or the subsequent demands for restrictive legislation.

Four developments make the United States, once again, a country with substantial immigration. First, in 1965 Congress applied the principles of the civil rights revolution to immigration laws. Throughout the nineteenth century, forces favoring immigration battled those who wished to close the ports. Laborers from South China arrived in large numbers along the West Coast to build the railroads, but natives feared that they not only brought a strange culture but that their willingness to work for low wages would impoverish American workers. So Asians became the first group targeted for exclusion, a process that Congress began in 1870 and completed with a 1917 law that banned migrants from the Asiatic Triangle—a region extending from the straits of the Bosphorus to the Hawaiian Islands. Closing our borders to Asians was the first step. The arrival of millions of immigrants after 1880 from Southern Italy and from Eastern Europe coincided with the emergence of Social Darwinism, prompting many seemingly scientific studies reporting that new Slavic, Italian, and Jewish immigrants could not be assimilated and were so biologically inferior that they would eventually undermine our democratic system. Congress, in an effort to fix the problem of too many inappropriate immigrants, appointed Vermont Senator Dillingham to chair a committee that produced forty-two volumes. They stressed the harm that immigration was doing to the country and called for restricting entry.

Emma Lazarus' poem on the Statue of Liberty describes the tired, the poor, the huddled masses, and the homeless yearning to be free who came to America's golden door. But by the 1920s, popular sentiments emphasized another line from that stanza—the wretched refuse of teeming European shores.

Laws were written and amended a dozen or more times to keep out presumed undesirable immigrants. But a new system developed after World War I: the number entering from any country was linked to the number born in that country and counted in the U.S. census of 1890 and then later linked to the number from that country counted in 1790, the first census. This, the National Origins Quota Act of 1924, severely restricted immigration from Eastern and Southern Europe while assigning a large quota to the British Isles. But immigration rapidly became a moot issue. The Depression of the 1930s and World War II in the 1940s cut off immigration from Europe. Indeed, during the 1930s more foreign-born persons left the United States than entered (Taeuber and Taeuber 1971, p. 968).

In 1952, Congress debated the immigration laws once again and, over the veto of President Truman, retained the National Origins system. Social Darwinists won that round since the law called for 270,000 immigrants annually, with Northern and Western European countries given the lion's share. The long-standing prohibition of immigration from Asia ended with token quotas of one hundred per year from China and Japan (Archdeacon 1983, p. 181; for a brief history of immigration, see Borjas 1994).

The effective civil rights movement of the 1960s challenged the practices that discriminated on the basis of race or ethnicity. Once that issue was raised, Congress not only passed laws to provide equal opportunities to native-born blacks but scrapped the favoritism shown to Western Europeans. The Reform Immigration Act of 1965 established a low limit of 290,000 annual migrants, with no more than 20,000 coming from any one country. A different preference system was also elaborated, with the highest priority given to foreign-born relatives of U.S. citizens and the second preference to individuals who had skills in short supply in this country. For the first time, a limit was established for the Western Hemisphere: 120,000 per year from the Americas. This law reflected a fundamental change in thinking about immigration. No longer were the residents of one country or area favored or damned and, for the first time, numerical limits were applied to Canada, Mexico, and other American lands.

Changes in the law are important, but they are only part of the story about how the number of legal immigrants escalated from 170,000 in 1953 to a peak of 1.8 million in 1991. A second development in the 1970s and 1980s was identical to the one that led to great immigration from Italy and the Slavic lands a century ago—demographic pressures abroad resulting from high fertility. Mortality rates fell in Mexico, Central America, and the Caribbean in the 1950s and 1960s, a decade or more before birth rates in these lands started to plummet. Large birth cohorts came of age but found few employment opportunities.

Although manual labor at minimum-wage jobs with no fringe benefits in the United States do not appeal to native-born citizens, they are more attractive than no job at all to people living in Port Au Prince, Santo Domingo, Managua, or San Salvador. Much of this international migration involves modest transportation costs—it is less expensive for most Latin Americans to come to the United States now than it was for Europeans to sail the Atlantic—but the driving forces for these migrants are identical to those in the previous great wave of immigration.

Chapter 3 stressed the growth of employment in the United States in the 1980s, with the highest rates of increase for either quite low-paying jobs or very high-paying jobs. The structural change in the economy is the third development accounting for the increasing volume and diversity of immigration. The expanding job market in the United States has many niches to be filled by immigrants with little formal training, and their presence here helps create job opportunities for others. Employment restructuring means that large firms subcontract much work and seek the lowest-cost suppliers. Population growth is concentrated in the South and Southwest, creating millions of jobs for construction laborers, for cooks in fast-food restaurants, and for low-level workers in healthcare. No strong union movement now demands restrictions on immigration or insists that newcomers go through a time-consuming and costly process to get work permits—a procedure adopted in some countries.

At the same time, many highly skilled technological jobs are now filled by immigrants, since jobs at the top end of the occupational spectrum increased. Derek Bok (1993) emphasizes that English became the language of science, medicine, and finance throughout the world after World War II. Engineers and technical specialists trained in Asia can fill good jobs in Silicon Valley, and physicians from India can readily staff state hospitals across the country or, if they have unusual skills, conduct research at the Mayo Clinic. Foreigners with specialized skills have always been recruited for top-ranked jobs here, be they Enrico Caruso to sing Verdi, Wernher Von Braun to design rockets, Canadians to play hockey, or, more recently, Dominicans to play short stop.

Fourth, the United States has a history of welcoming persecuted refugees, a history strongly tied to our fight against Communism after World War II. In the Depression decade and during World War II, the United States turned away Jews fleeing Germany, but after the war Congress enacted numerous special measures allowing refugees, first from Europe and then later from Asia, to enter without regard to the ordinary restrictions. In 1948, for example, the Displaced Persons Act admitted almost 500,000 refugees from Eastern Europe, refugees who never would have qualified for regular admission. For several decades, Congress frequently passed special laws solving the persecution problems of specific groups. Then, in 1980, they tried to systematize this by adopting the United Nation's definition of who was a refugee and by calling for the Attorney General and Congress to agree annually on a number of refugees and asylees. This has not worked out as expected since Congress resumed passing special immigration acts for refugees such as those from Cuba. The political stability of the United States and our great tolerance for religious, ethnic, and linguistic minorities have made this country attractive to many people who are persecuted in their homelands. Internal strife in Iran, El Salvador, and dozens of other countries, along with the continuing Communist rule in Cuba, helps to explain why these countries are high on the list of sending nations. (For a history of refugee legislation, see Jasso and Rosenzweig 1990, chap. 9.)

Immigration Today

The impact of these four developments is portrayed in figure 5-1, which reports the number legally admitted with the prerogative to become citizens every year since 1940. From miniscule numbers during World War II, immigration rose to the level called for in the 1952 McCarran-Walter law, just under 300,000 each year, but after 1968

Figure 5-1. Immigrants Admitted for Permanent Residence: 1940 to 1994

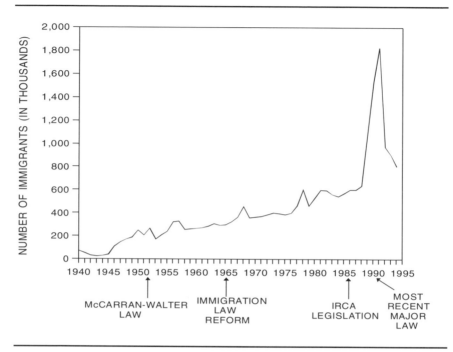

SOURCE: U.S. Immigration and Naturalization Service, 1994, *Statistical Yearbook of the Immigration and Naturalization Service, 1993*, table 1; 1995, *INS Fact Book.*

the number increased rapidly, peaking at 1.8 million in 1991. The numbers in recent years are far beyond those envisioned when the immigration laws were reformed and deserve an explanation, especially the dramatic spike in 1990–91. In the early 1980s, it became apparent that many immigrants were coming to the United States without appropriate papers, either to escape violence and tyranny or because job prospects were much better here. In 1986, Congress attempted to reassert its control over the nation's borders by passing the Immigration Reform and Control Act (IRCA)—a law radically different from earlier legislation. Although it had many provisions generally making it easier to immigrate legally, it was a carrot-and-stick measure. Illegal migrants provided low-cost labor for many employers and filled important technical positions for others. Reflecting the need for such workers, the carrot component of IRCA said that persons who

had lived in the United States since January 1, 1982, without appropriate documents could legalize their status and eventually become
citizens. The large numbers shown in figure 5-1 for 1990 and 1991
result from several million former illegals utilizing that option of the
1986 law. The stick component of IRCA were sanctions, including jail
terms, upon employers convicted of knowingly hiring illegals. Additionally, Congress appropriated more funds to secure the borders, especially the porous one with Mexico.

One might think that immigration laws specify a maximum number of persons who can enter in a year. That was not the case in the
past; the majority came under provisions that were not covered by
numerical limits. Let's take a look at the admission rationales for the
800,000 who legally entered in 1994 with the possibility of becoming
U.S. citizens after living here five years. These are shown in figure
5-2. More than one-quarter of them were quota immigrants sponsored

Figure 5-2.   Status of Immigrants Admitted for Permanent Residence:
1994

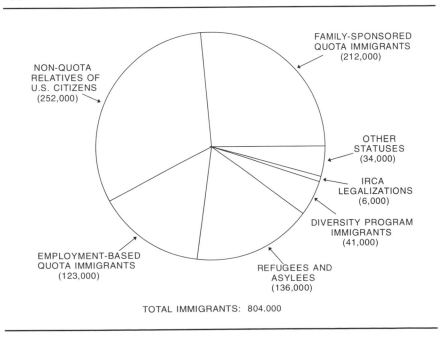

TOTAL IMMIGRANTS: 804.000

SOURCE: U.S. Immigration and Naturalization Service, 1995, *INS Fact Book*.

by U.S. citizens for reasons of family reunification. Much more than one-quarter were non-quota relatives of citizens, such as children and spouses. A smaller proportion of immigrants—about one in eight—came because they had an employment skill deemed in short supply in this country.

If an American citizen living abroad marries or becomes a parent, he or she is ordinarily allowed to bring his or her spouse and children into the United States. Similarly, foreigners residing here who marry citizens are ordinarily eligible for citizenship themselves, subject to restrictions laid out in the 1986 Marriage Fraud Act. Thus it is difficult to write a law specifying an exact number of immigrants. These are legal immigrants who were not, in the past, subject to any numerical control. This has been the most common type of immigration. In addition, a substantial fraction of current immigrants—about one in eight—satisfy the criteria to be refugees or asylees. Their claims of probable political persecution must be approved by the Attorney General and by the Immigration and Naturalization Services (INS). Refugees and asylees are also exempt from numerical caps written into immigration laws.

Many special laws reflect the foreign activities of our government and bring small or modest numbers to the United States who are also exempt from numerical limits. This is a long list, so a couple of examples will illustrate this practice. In 1979, Congress allowed up to 15,000 former employees of the Panama Canal Company to enter along with their spouses and children. In 1987, Congress allowed Amerasian children who were fathered by U.S. citizens in Vietnam to immigrate along with their spouses, children, and parents, even if these children had not had recent contacts with their American fathers. Previously, Congress had allowed children fathered by U.S. troops in Korea to enter along with their immediate kin. (For a listing of recent legislation of this nature, see U.S. Immigration and Naturalization Service 1996, appendix 1; Tienda and Liang 1994, table 13.1.)

Immigration laws are extremely complex so it is challenging to describe the status of people living here. You might think that there are only three groups: citizens, persons on the road to citizenship, and illegals, but it is much more complicated. The many different groups include:

1. Persons born in the fifty states. They became citizens at birth.
2. Persons born in Puerto Rico, Guam, the Virgin Islands, and a few other U.S. dependencies. They also became citizens at birth.

3. Persons born abroad to an American parent or parents. They became eligible for citizenship at birth but ordinarily have to file documents before their eighteenth birthdays.
4. Foreign-born persons who entered legally and successfully went through the process to become citizens, a process that ordinarily takes five years.
5. Immigrants who entered legally and became resident aliens. These people have the right to live in the United States for their entire lives and have all the privileges of citizenship except voting and office holding. They are eligible to become citizens but have not done so and, under current law, are under no pressure to become citizens. Many of these individuals are "green card holders"; that is, they have the right to work in the United States but are not currently citizens.
6. Visitors, students, business people, certain employees, and the like who entered the United States legally but are not eligible to become permanent aliens or citizens. Some of these people change their immigration status and seek citizenship, but others live here legally for long periods.
7. Persons who have been granted refugee status in the United States. Some of them are eligible to apply for citizenship, but others entered legally or illegally and are permitted to stay and work while their claims about persecution in their home country are adjudicated.
8. Persons illegally in the United States, including those who waded across the Rio Grande or walked across from Canada, as well as students, travelers, and business executives who overstayed their visas. Although illegally in the country, some—or many—may be eligible for permanent resident status or citizenship under provisions of current laws.

In this chapter, the terms *immigrant* and *foreign-born* refer to those born abroad and enumerated in the census, but we exclude those born in U.S. dependencies and those born abroad to U.S. citizens. Those people were citizens at birth or were eligible for citizenship at birth.

Continuing Efforts to Control the Flow of Immigrants

The 1986 Immigration Reform and Control Act was only four years old when Congress enacted a new, more comprehensive law. This one sought to limit immigration to about 700,000 each year and, compared to earlier legislation, gave greater priority to the needs of employers by reserving 140,000 slots for those whose job skills are in short supply here. Reflecting our commitment to diversity, the new law reserves 55,000 admissions each year for countries previously underrepresented in immigration flows, a procedure that will stimulate more migration from Africa and the Near East. The law also increased the numbers allowed to enter annually to work here without the prerogative of becoming citizens (U.S. Immigration and Naturalization Service 1996, appendix 1; Chiswick and Sullivan 1995, p. 221).

Very many foreigners enter the United States every year. While upwards of a million are admitted by the INS to become either permanent residents or citizens, more than twenty-one million are admitted for temporary stays in the United States. About 80 percent of these are tourists, about three million come each year to conduct business temporarily, and about 400,000 are students, some of them bringing spouses and children. Most of these visitors return home, but some stay for prolonged periods, while others may become eligible for citizenship by amassing job skills or marrying Americans (U.S. Immigration and Naturalization Service 1996, table 39).

Canadian citizens may visit the United States for up to six months without a visa; Mexican citizens are limited to visits of seventy-two hours. And the 1986 U.S./Canada Free Trade Act facilitated the entry of Canadian business people, allowing them to work here for long periods while retaining Canadian citizenship. The many border crossers from our two neighboring countries (about 316 million in 1993) may remain here for long spans and eventually become citizens (U.S. Immigration and Naturalization Service 1994, table 75). It is difficult to keep track of these flows and easy to see why laws and regulations cannot completely control the borders.

What about illegal residents of the United States? There is no way to obtain a precise estimate, but procedures of the Census Bureau and the INS give specific information about the two components of this group: "visa overstayers" and "entries without inspection" (EWIs), border crossers who did not go through INS checkpoints (Warren 1990, 1994; Clark et al. 1994, chap. 2). The demographic procedures show that between 1988 and 1992 there were annual net additions of 300,000 undocumented immigrants. Legal immigration in this span—including those admitted by IRCA amnesty provisions—averaged almost one million per year, implying that the current volume of undocumented or illegal immigration is at least 30 percent of legal immigration.

Immigration now makes up a major component of the nation's population growth. The population increases by almost four million each year, with net immigration making up almost one-third of that increase. This is a large fraction, but during the first two decades of this century almost one-half of population growth was due to immigration (Rumbaut 1996, table 1).

Two sources provide information about the size and characteristics of immigration flows. The INS counts people who enter this country through checkpoints such as those in airports, at bridges, or at our three international tunnels. If a person intends to become a permanent resident or citizen, INS collects information about their origin, immigration status, education, marital status, and occupational skills.

The census counts all residents of the United States regardless of their citizenship or their legal status. Since these numbers determine Congressional representation, one might think that the enumeration should be restricted to citizens, but federal courts ruled that all residents should be counted except short-term visitors from abroad and diplomats (Conk 1987; *FAIR* v. *Klutznick* 1980). The census asks about place of birth, citizenship, and date of arrival, if born abroad.

This chapter relies upon census data to portray immigration. One might ask if that is adequate. You might expect that undocumented residents would avoid filing out census forms, fearing that the Census Bureau would give their names and addresses to the Department of Justice even though federal laws prohibit such a sharing of information. Many efforts have been made to estimate the number of undocumented or illegal residents. Using information from the INS about arrivals, departures, and legal immigrants, along with Census Bureau information about the population by country of birth and date of arrival, rigorous estimates have been made of illegal residents. (For a summary and discussion, see Clark et al. 1994). The most reasonable determination is that there were about 2.6 million such individuals here at the time of the 1990 census, about one million of them born in Mexico, about 275,000 from El Salvador, about 100,000 from Guatemala, and another 1.2 million from all the other countries. About 1 percent of the total population was here in apparent violation of immigration law. Jeffrey Passel estimates that the census of 1990 counted approximately two million of them, implying an undercount rate of 25 percent for illegals in contrast to the undercount rate of 2 percent for the total population (Passel in Clark et al. 1994, table 2.1; Edmonston and Schultze 1994, table 2.1; Massey and Singer 1995).

The 1990 census counted two million people who did not have appropriate papers, but the census omitted another 650,000 illegal residents. Our picture of the immigrant population will not be seriously distorted by relying upon census data, but when we specifically focus upon data for Mexicans, El Salvadorans, or Guatemalans, we should remember that there were large numbers of illegals omitted from the census. Unfortunately, there is no way to determine whether those missed differ from those counted in terms of education and earnings. Presumably their geographic distribution was similar to those who were counted.

Where Do Recent Immigrants Come From?

Prior to the American Revolution, most migrants to the colonies came from the British Isles, but a substantial share arrived from the Caribbean or Africa. After the slave trade tapered off, there was a century-long span from the 1740s to the 1840s in which almost all migrants came from Northern Europe. Then the failure of potato crops triggered an influx from Ireland and Scandinavia. The revolution in Germany in 1848 accelerated its outmigration. The Northern European domination of immigration continued for three more decades, but then began to wane as Southern Italians and Slavic-speakers arrived in large numbers. This was the first of the two major shifts in the origins of immigrants to the United States. The post-1880 migration was dominated by Eastern and Southern Europeans, while smaller numbers arrived from the British Isles. Canada and Mexico also sent many migrants. Figure 5-3 shows the distribution of immigrants from eight origins by date of arrival.

The few immigrants who came to the United States in the 1930s, 1940s, or 1950s came mostly from Western Europe or Canada reflecting the National Origins quotas. The 1965 law, which went into effect in mid-1968, marked a second major change in the origins of immigrants. The numbers coming from Asia, Mexico, Latin America, and the Caribbean now greatly exceed those from Europe and Canada. More than eight out of ten arriving in the 1980s and 1990s were born across the Pacific or south of the Rio Grande, a pattern that will significantly alter the demographic makeup of this nation. (For an analysis, see Passel and Edmonston 1994).

Migration patterns give us a heterogeneous population. About one-eighth of Americans have African origins because of the importing of slaves more than two centuries ago. The flow from Ireland in the late 1840s increased religious diversity, and Catholicism became the largest single faith. Flows beginning in the 1880s gave us an ethnically heterogeneous white population and stimulated even more reli-

Figure 5-3. Origins of Immigrants to the United States, by Decade: 1880 to 1990

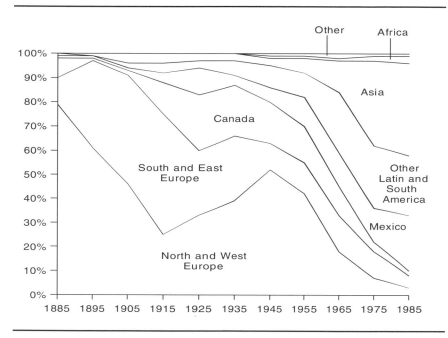

SOURCES: Bouvier and Gardner 1986; U.S. Bureau of the Census, *Census of Population and Housing: 1990*, CP-2-1, table 12.

gious diversity with the arrival of many Jews. Changes following 1968 will cause our population to become increasingly Hispanic and Asian. Indeed, within the next century the descendents of European-origin whites may become the minority, although this is far from certain, given changing patterns of identification and high rates of intermarriage—topics that we will describe in chapter 6 (U.S. Bureau of the Census 1996, table J).

Our focus is on the causes and consequences of recent immigration, so let us look at what the census of 1990 tells us about the foreign-born. Table 5-1 classifies them by their date of arrival. At the far right, information is shown about those coming before 1950, an older group averaging age 72 in 1990. Among those arriving before 1950, eleven of the fifteen leading countries-of-origin were European. Mexico, however, was the fourth leading country and two Asian nations—China and the Philippines—made the list.

Mexico tops the list of birthplaces of those arriving between 1970 and 1980—the first full decade in which nondiscriminatory laws were in operation (data shown in middle panel of table 5-1). The increasing importance of Asian migration is evident since four of the top six sending countries were across the Pacific. Italy was the only European land sending substantial numbers in the 1970s.

The top fifteen origins of immigrants in the 1980s appear to the far left of table 5-1. Once again, Mexico, the Philippines, and Vietnam dominate as birthplaces for new arrivals, but a small central American nation with a population of just five million took fourth place—El Salvador. Seven of the leading nations were Asian and another seven were Latin American. Only one of the major sending countries had a population comprising non-Hispanic whites—Russia—the sole European land on the list. A large proportion of these Russian immigrants were Jews admitted under the provisions of the 1980 Refugee Act.

Sixteen other nations sent 50,000 or more people to the United States during the 1980s. Thirteen were Asian or Latin American. Only two European countries other than Russia sent substantial numbers—Poland and England. In the 1980s, for the first time, large numbers came from Central American countries and from several South American nations: Peru, Guyana, Ecuador, and Brazil. African immigration also increased sharply in the 1980s, more than double the previous decade. Nigeria, Egypt, Ethiopia, and South Africa were the most common birthplaces among the one-quarter million Africans who came to the United States.

Where Do Recent Immigrants Live?

In the nineteenth century, Irish immigrants disembarked in Boston or New York; later in that century, Italian immigrants disembarked in those ports as well as in New Orleans. The early flow of laborers from southern China arrived in San Francisco. Although the means of transport are different, a similar pattern of geographic concentration describes current immigration. A few areas have many foreign-born residents, while many states and metropolitan areas have been hardly affected by the recent surge.

Migration to the United States—in airplanes and cars, just as in the era of ocean travel—is largely "chain" migration. A modest number of immigrants from a foreign country locate in a specific place, typically a city where they find work or, in the case of refugees, a location where their sponsors bring them. Once here, these migrants

Table 5-1. Major Countries of Origin of the Immigrant Population in 1990, by Dates of Arrival (numbers in thousands)

1980 to 1990		1970 to 1980		Pre-1950	
1. Mexico	2,161	1. Mexico	1,312	1. Canada	294
2. Philippines	431	2. Philippines	292	2. Italy	209
3. Vietnam	343	3. Vietnam	203	3. Germany	170
4. El Salvador	336	4. Korea	161	4. Mexico	161
5. Korea	298	5. India	152	5. Poland	109
6. China	288	6. Cuba	133	6. USSR	92
7. India	245	7. Jamaica	120	7. England	92
8. Cuba	187	8. China	116	8. Ireland	58
9. Dominican Republic	185	9. Canada	93	9. Austria	48
10. Taiwan	157	10. Dominican Republic	89	10. Czechoslovakia	40
11. Jamaica	155	11. El Salvador	87	11. Scotland	40
12. Guatemala	151	12. Iran	85	12. Hungary	33
13. Japan	150	13. Italy	83	13. China	28
14. Columbia	145	14. Taiwan	69	14. Philippines	28
15. USSR	132	15. Columbia	68	15. Greece	15

SOURCE: U.S. Bureau of the Census, *Census of Population and Housing: 1990*, Public Use Microdata Sample.

establish a small enclave or, if their numbers are sufficient, an ethnic neighborhood. If they are successful and if the opportunities are desirable compared to those in the homeland, they encourage their family members, friends, and relatives to come to the United States. Potential migrants—whether from Bombay or Kingston—are extremely unlikely to consult a U.S. atlas or to pursue page after page of help-wanted ads before deciding where to locate in this country. They will come to the ethnic enclave where a friend or relative has figured out how to get a job and a reasonable place to live (Massey et al. 1987; Allen and Turner 1988). This is the nature of chain migration: people leave a specific place in the sending country and locate in a specific neighborhood here because they learned about opportunities from their kin and friends who preceded them. As a result, ethnic neighborhoods are numerous and thriving but are found in just a few cities: the Korean enclave along Pico Boulevard in Los Angeles; the Russian enclave in the Brighton Beach section of Brooklyn; the Dominican neighborhood of Washington Heights in upper Manhattan; the Korean and Chinese area in Flushing, Queens; the heterogeneous Adams Morgan neighborhood just two miles north of the White House; and the Portuguese-speaking Ironbound neighborhood near downtown Newark. Another factor helping to explain the distinctive concentration of immigrants is transportation cost. Mexican and Central American immigrants find it less costly to get to San Diego or San Antonio for low-wage service sector jobs than to get to similar jobs in Duluth, Buffalo, or Detroit.

Figure 5-4 shows the foreign-born population as a proportion of the total in every state distinguishing recent arrivals from those who came earlier. Nationally, 7.9 percent of the population were immigrants—about one American in twelve. California leads the nation with immigrants accounting for almost one in four of its residents, while New York was not far behind with almost 20 percent foreign-born. New England is not often described as a place of entry for the new immigration streams, but it is, since Connecticut, Massachusetts, and Rhode Island have relatively high proportions. Not surprisingly, one of the two states closest to Asia—Hawaii—also has a high proportion of foreign-born. Florida, where Miami now serves as a port of entry for Caribbeans and Latin Americans much as New York did for Europeans a century ago, has the highest representation of immigrants in the South, but Texas—the state nearest Mexico and Central America—is not far behind. The emergence of the United States as the dominant country in the world and our involvement in both Asia and Latin America helps to explain why three other locations in the

Figure 5-4. Immigrant Population as a Percentage of State's Total Population: 1990

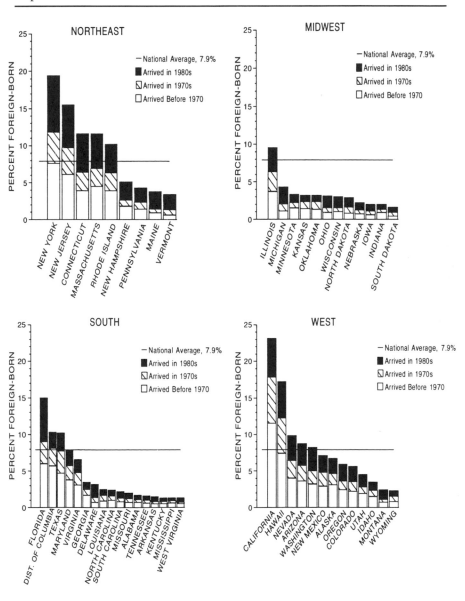

SOURCE: U.S. Bureau of the Census, *Census of Population and Housing: 1990*, Public Use Microdata Sample.

South have high proportions of foreign-born. Washington, D.C., was never a traditional center for immigration from Europe, but this changed after the war in French Indochina, and that city, along with its sprawling suburban ring, now has a high proportion of foreign-born. Only seven states had higher proportions of immigrants in 1990 than did the District of Columbia, and Maryland and Virginia rank high in immigration only because they surround the nation's capital.

Most Midwestern states have hardly been affected by the recent boom in immigration. If you exclude metropolitan Chicago, you find few recent immigrants living in the Midwest. The lack of economic opportunities in this area, resulting from the restructuring of manufacturing described in chapter 3, helps account for the miniscule numbers of new arrivals in this large region.

Almost 40 percent of the immigrants who came to the United States in the five years before 1990 went to California, and just seven states received 84 percent of recent migrants—California, New York, Florida, Texas, New Jersey, Illinois, and Massachusetts. It is understandable that calls for immigration law reform would come from those states and that California voters would be the first to enact legislation seeking to deny state-financed benefits to illegals—Proposition 187 in the fall of 1994. This law was promptly enjoined by federal courts on the grounds that the federal government, not the states, controls international boundaries. Demographic processes help explain state-to-state differences in reactions to immigration and imply that opposition to immigration will come chiefly from Florida and California.

A growing population is usually coveted by civic and political leaders since it is a strong stimulant to economic growth. Few new homes, apartments, shopping complexes, and office buildings are built in places with declining populations, and deposits in banks sink as population size contracts. It is easier for school administrators to erect new buildings and hire more teachers than it is to close empty ones and fire superfluous staff. Although most governors would probably prefer that their states attract thousands of college-educated, native-born citizens coming to work in high-tech industries, they may find immigration from abroad desirable if it wards off population decline. In five of the seven states now attracting many foreign-born individuals, immigration is doing exactly that. The information below refers to migration trends in 1985 to 1990, and compares the recent influx of foreigners to the movement of natives.

California and Florida grew rapidly, at least in the late 1980s, since

	Foreign Immigrants Arriving 1985 to 1990 (000)	Net Gain or Loss in Exchange of Native-Born Population with Other States (000)
California	1,942	+346
New York	787	−741
Florida	414	+1,100
Texas	384	−105
New Jersey	267	−154
Illinois	241	−242
Massachusetts	166	−3

they continued to attract more native-born persons from other states than they lost. On top of that, there was the high influx of international migrants. But in other leading states on the immigration list, arrivals from abroad replaced the outflow of native-born individuals, thereby stabilizing the population. Cutting off foreign immigration to these five states would lead to population loss. The District of Columbia is a clear case of international migration slowing down population decline. It lost 43,000 native-born, but attracted 19,000 immigrants from abroad. If New York, the District of Columbia, and most other states can attract more migrants from abroad, their populations may grow. (For a further examination of how international migration is making up for the net outmigration of natives in seventeen of the fifty states, see U.S. Bureau of the Census 1994a, table 2).

The chain migration process means that the geographic concentration of immigration is even more extreme when metropolises are considered. Immigrants are entering the Empire State in great numbers, but they go to New York City, not to Albany, Schenectady, or Rochester. This may be seen by looking at the large metropolitan areas shown in figure 5-5. If you wander about the streets of New York, Los Angeles, or Miami, you might assume that this nation is being invaded by foreigners and that English is becoming an endangered language. But if you wandered about the shopping malls and neighborhoods of Minneapolis, Columbus, Indianapolis, or St. Louis, you would have to make serious efforts to find someone born outside the fifty states. In 1990, there were thirty-eight metropolises with populations of one million or more. Here we are referring to those huge metropolises, some of them made up of many overlapping components. For example, the New York Consolidated Metropolitan Statistical Area (CMSA)

Figure 5-5. Foreign-Born as a Percentage of the Total Population of Metropolises of One Million or More: 1990

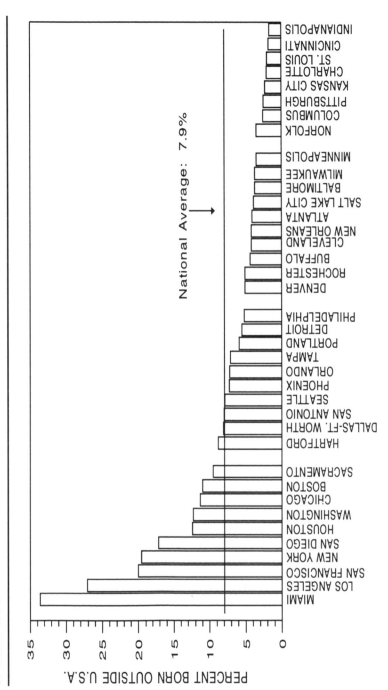

SOURCE: U.S. Bureau of the Census, *Census of Population: 1990*, Public Use Microdata Sample.

NOTE: Data refer to Metropolitan Statistical Areas or to Consolidated Metropolitan Statistical Areas.

now includes a large share of northern New Jersey as well as Long Island and a densely populated corner of Connecticut, while the Los Angeles CMSA includes a king-sized slice of southern California. Other metropolises, such as Salt Lake City and St. Louis, are more confined and stand on their own.

Metropolitan Miami leads the nation in concentration of foreign-born population: more than one-third of its population is foreign-born, while Los Angeles is the only other location with more than one-quarter foreign-born. The traditional East Coast ports of entry—New York and Boston—and one on the Pacific shores—San Francisco—have high proportions of immigrants now just as they did a century ago. Other places at the top of this list include Sacramento and three locations in Texas. Immigrants are highly concentrated, since only fourteen of these thirty-eight locations had a proportion foreign-born above the national average of 7.9 percent.

Chicago is the only Midwest metropolis now attracting substantial numbers of immigrants. Indeed, a look at this list shows that metropolitan areas in the Midwest and in the interior of the South—including rapidly growing Atlanta and Charlotte—attract few foreign-born persons. Even within the states now gaining many migrants, the foreign-born population is distinctively concentrated into a few locations. Miami leads the list of large metropolises in terms of immigration. The drive from Miami to Orlando or Tampa or Jacksonville can be accomplished in a matter of hours, but the representation of foreigners in those metropolises is far below the national average. Similarly, the proportion of foreign-born is high in metropolitan Boston, but low in Worcester, suggesting the localized nature of recent immigration. And about one resident in eight of metropolitan Washington was born abroad but, just thirty-eight miles away in Baltimore, it is fewer than one in twenty-five.

Thirty-six metropolises make up the next rank: places with populations of 500,000 to one million in 1990. Only nine of these had more than the national average of immigrants: Honolulu with its Asian immigrants; Bakersfield and Fresno in California, with their large representations of both Asians and Latin Americans; Las Vegas, where the booming tourist industry offers service-sector employment and construction jobs to immigrants from south of the border; Tucson and El Paso, close to Mexico; West Palm Beach, the Florida metropolis just north of Miami; and two older New England locations now attracting immigrants from both the Caribbean and Africa—New Bedford and Providence.

Characteristics of Recent Immigrants

Immigrants differ from the native-born population with regard to those characteristics associated with economic success or failure. But immigrants are heterogeneous: many from Mexico have no more than elementary school educations, while many from India have advanced degrees, so it is impossible to assert that immigrants are either better prepared or less well prepared to prosper in the United States. Similarly, it is impossible to conclude that immigrants bring along or lack those characteristics facilitating their assimilation into mainstream society.

Because of the dramatic changes in the origins and volume of immigrants after the reformed immigration law went into effect, most remaining sections of this chapter refer to immigrants who arrived after 1969. Since many more than one hundred different nations are now sending migrants, we sort them into sixteen groups on the basis of where they were born. Ten of these sixteen are specific countries, ranging in size from 3.5 million from Mexico to 275,000 from Jamaica. The other six are broad geographic areas, such as Africa and Eastern Europe. "Other Asia" refers to Asians from places other than the four large sending countries: China, India, Korea, and the Philippines.

Persons are classified by their birthplaces. In many cases, those arriving from a country or geographic area share the same language, religion, and culture, and they mark down the same race on the census form, but this is not always the case. Caribbean immigrants include many whose native language is English, others from Spanish-speaking islands, and some French or Creole speakers. Recent immigrants from Africa are not all black: 56 percent said they were black, 34 percent said white, 7 percent Asian Indian, and 3 percent chose some other racial identity.

The Age Distribution of Recent Immigrants

Most immigrants come to this country to find a better way to earn a living, so they have a higher proportion in the adult working ages of 25 to 54 than do native-born, non-Hispanic whites. One-half of immigrants arriving in the 1980s were these ages compared to 43 percent of native whites. These age distributions mean that, compared to natives, an unusually high proportion of migrants are working or looking for jobs. Recent immigrants from Africa are at the extreme, with more than 70 percent at ages 25 to 54.

The proportion of foreign-born at younger ages is low but not because of depressed fertility among immigrants. Indeed, immigrants have fertility patterns quite like those of native-born women, with the exception being women from Mexico who bear more children (Chiswick and Sullivan 1995, table 5-13). But children born to immigrants after their arrival in the United States are native-born. Thus, the present large volume of immigrants reverberates through the population, creating a high proportion of second-generation Americans.

Three groups—from Mexico, El Salvador, and Vietnam—include unusually high percentages of young people. The absence of a universal system of secondary schools in Mexico and Latin American encourages late teenage boys to search for jobs in the United States, so male immigrants from these countries are young, while family reunification provisions of immigration law help account for the unusual number of young Vietnamese-born persons living here.

The proportion over age 54 was high for immigrants from Cuba, Eastern Europe, China, and the Philippines. To some degree, this reflects the pre-1969 migration of people who were at younger ages when they arrived and then grew old here. But we are describing post-1969 immigrants, so we exclude those now-elderly people who arrived as displaced persons in the years following VE Day or the few surviving members of the great wave of immigration that ended in 1924. The family reunification provisions of immigrant laws now combine with the availability of Supplemental Security Income payments to stimulate a modest immigration of older parents who join their middle-age children shortly after the children become citizens (Treas and Torrecilha 1995, p. 86). Since 1972 the federal government has provided monthly payments to elderly persons who are not covered by Social Security and who have almost no assets. When that law went on the books, no one thought it would trigger more immigration. But after a legally arriving older couple lives in the United States for three years, they may be eligible for SSI payments of $669 per month if they maintain their own households, or $446 per month if they reside with their adult children. In 1995, Congress voted to terminate these payments since they believed it inappropriate to use tax dollars to finance the retirements of those who spent their lives working in another country. (For additional information about immigrants, see Rumbaut 1996.)

The Ability to Speak English

Almost all recent immigrants coming from Africa, Jamaica, Western Europe, Canada, and the Philippines speak English only or speak it very well, while the majority of migrants from Mexico and the Dominican Republic either do not speak English at all or report that they do not speak it well. Given the importance of English for employment and education in the United States and fears that the dominance of English may wane, it is important to consider linguistic ability when describing migrants.

In 1990, the census asked if a person spoke a language other than English in their homes. If they replied yes, they were told to write the name of that language, such as Chinese, Italian, or Spanish, and then go to the next question. That further inquiry asked if they spoke English very well, well, not well, or not at all. Note that it was limited to people who said they spoke a language other than English at home. Households received the enumeration form in English, but those who read Spanish and went through the form carefully found a toll-free number to call for a Spanish-language form. Census forms were printed in either English or Spanish, so a person reading neither language needed to consult someone to answer census questions.

This section is focused on recent immigrants in the prime working ages in 1990. Figure 5-6 reports the size of the groups and then describes their reported English-language abilities. Many migrants learned English in school long before they moved here or grew up in homes where only English was spoken if they came from India, Jamaica, Canada, or Britain. Others learned it in the United States, so recent immigrants at working ages overwhelmingly report that they speak English. A significant minority of those from Korea, Vietnam, and China, however, do not speak English well, and an inability to speak English describes an even larger fraction of those from the Spanish-language countries of this hemisphere.

About half of those from Cuba, the Dominican Republic, El Salvador, and Mexico said that they could not speak English well or at all. Undoubtedly, this handicaps them in their search for jobs, but they may find employment in the large Spanish-language ethnic enclaves in New York, Los Angeles, and Miami.

Most immigrants rapidly learn English. Censuses report a clear pattern of English acquisition: the longer people live in the United States, the greater the likelihood of their learning English (Jasso and Rosenzweig 1990, chap. 8). Among immigrants aged 25 to 54 arriving from El Salvador and Mexico in 1988 and 1989, 42 percent could not speak English at all. Among those who arrived from the same countries fifteen to twenty years before the 1990 census, only 11 percent could not speak English. This measures the learning of English and the selective return of those who do not learn it. Only a tiny minority

Figure 5-6. Ability of Recent Immigrants Aged 25 to 54 to Speak English: 1990[a]

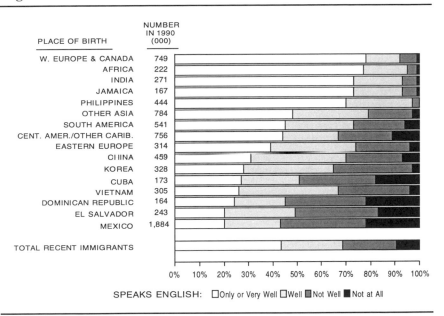

PLACE OF BIRTH	NUMBER IN 1990 (000)
W. EUROPE & CANADA	749
AFRICA	222
INDIA	271
JAMAICA	167
PHILIPPINES	444
OTHER ASIA	784
SOUTH AMERICA	541
CENT. AMER./OTHER CARIB.	756
EASTERN EUROPE	314
CHINA	459
KOREA	328
CUBA	173
VIETNAM	305
DOMINICAN REPUBLIC	164
EL SALVADOR	243
MEXICO	1,884
TOTAL RECENT IMMIGRANTS	

SPEAKS ENGLISH: ☐ Only or Very Well ☐ Well ▨ Not Well ■ Not at All

SOURCES: U.S. Bureau of the Census, Public Use Microdata Samples of 1980 and 1990 censuses.

[a] These data refer to persons arriving after 1969. China includes Hong Kong and Taiwan. Among native-born, non-Hispanic whites in this age range 98 percent spoke English only or very well.

of foreign-language immigrants live in this country for a decade or more and learn no English. Indeed, the majority of immigrants coming from Asia and Latin America in the two years before 1990 reported that they spoke English well or very well. The position of English as the national language is certainly not threatened by recent immigration. The census, of course, measures only the reported ability to speak English, not the ability to read and write it, which is now required for most high-paying jobs. (For a detailed analysis of the English-language proficiency of recent immigrants, see Stevens 1994.)

The Educational Credentials of Immigrants

Immigrants have educational attainments unlike those of natives: they are greatly overrepresented in the upper and lower tails of the educational distribution. By 1990, the majority of U.S. residents who never attended school or who dropped out before the fifth grade were born abroad. At the other extreme, about one American in five with a doctorate was an immigrant.

Figure 5-7 considers the population aged 25 to 54 in 1990 and shows immigrants as a percentage of each educational class, distinguishing recent arrivals—post-1969—from earlier ones, revealing the selectivity now involved in who migrates to the United States. We get immigrants who have virtually no formal schooling—many of them from Mexico, Central American lands, some Caribbean isles, and mainland China. Simultaneously, the growth of our sophisticated high-tech economy and the prominent status of American universities attract many foreigners who have earned M.A.s, M.D.s, or Ph.D.s.

Although immigrants are heavily represented at the extremes of

Figure 5-7. Immigrants as a Percentage of the Population Aged 25 to 54, by Educational Attainment: 1990

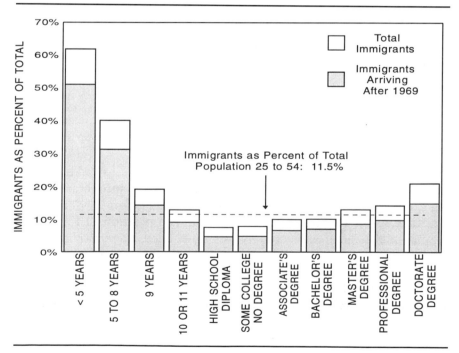

SOURCE: U.S. Bureau of the Census, *Census of Population and Housing: 1990,* Public Use Microdata Sample.

the educational distribution, an analysis would be incomplete if we stopped at this point. Educational attainment differs greatly from one group to the next. Persons moving here from India and Africa are much more extensively educated than people born in the United States, while two-thirds of those from Mexico and El Salvador spent just a few years in school, at most. These differences in schooling are large and help explain why some immigrants are much more prosperous than the native-born.

Figure 5-8 summarizes the educational attainments of recent immigrants, contrasting their attainments to those of comparable native-born non-Hispanic whites. Data are shown for both sexes. There are more male than female immigrants resulting from the search many men make for work, but for thirteen of the groups, the numbers of men and women are quite similar. Among those coming from Mexico, Africa, and "other Asia," male migrants are much more numerous than female. The unusual sex ratio among Mexicans reflects the movement of men to jobs in the United States, either before they marry or while their wives remain south of the border, a pattern similar to Italian migration around the turn of the century. Philippine migration is at the other extreme—155 women here for every 100 men—and among Koreans there are 141 women per 100 men, a finding partly accounted for by the commitment of our Armed Forces in these countries.

Migrant streams may be grouped into three types on the basis of their educational credentials. First are those from India, Africa, and the Philippines. These include many college graduates—a much higher proportion than for the native-born white population—and relatively few uneducated persons. Second are immigrant streams with high proportions of college graduates and high proportions of people with no high school training. This is especially true of Chinese immigrants, but also those from Eastern Europe and Russia and "other Asia." This "other Asia" group is diverse, with the leading sending countries being Japan, Iran, Laos, Pakistan, Cambodia, Thailand, and Lebanon, in that order. We are often reminded of the Chinese scientists who fill important positions in our society, but when the derelict freighter *Golden Venture* floundered near Coney Island in June 1993, 276 Chinese scrambled for our shores, reminding us of the Chinese at the other end of the educational distribution—uneducated, illegal Chinese immigrants destined for low-wage work in ethnic restaurants or the needlework trade. Finally, there are migration streams from Mexico, El Salvador, and the Dominican Republic with very few high school or college graduates.

Figure 5-8.   Education of Recent Immigrants Aged 25 to 54: 1990

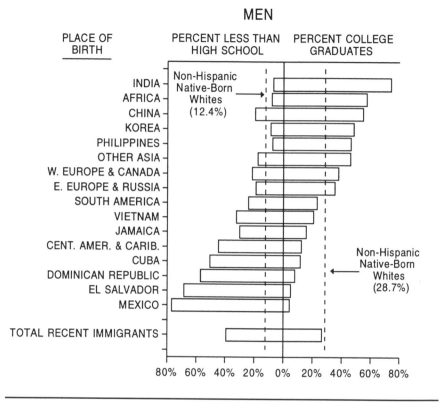

SOURCE: U.S. Bureau of the Census, *Census of Population and Housing: 1990*, Public Use Microdata Sample.

Male immigrants typically report more extensive educations than women. In two streams, those from Africa and Korea, men were much more extensively educated than women but, in the other streams, males held only a small advantage. Philippine migrants are the exception since the proportion with college degrees is much higher among women than among men. Women migrating to the United States from the Philippines are greatly overrepresented in nursing. Among Filipinas, 15 percent worked as nurses as opposed to 3 percent of employed native-born women aged 25 to 54. The new migration patterns are producing *occupational* ethnic enclaves.

Figure 5-8   (continued)

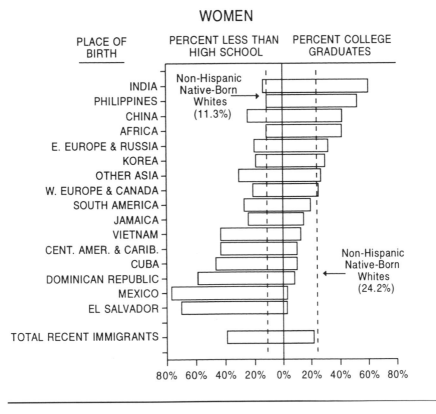

The Jobs of Immigrants

The occupations that migrants hold in the United States are closely linked to their educational attainments. I array these groups using a format similar to that for educational attainment. Figure 5-9 shows the percentage of male and female immigrants working in jobs that are toward the top and bottom of the occupational distribution. Professional and managerial occupations typically require advanced educations, but they are the most financially rewarding since they include medical professions, engineering, and high-level business administration. Jobs requiring much less education and providing modest paychecks are in the operators, fabricators, and laboring ranks.

Migrant streams may be classified but the categories are not as

Figure 5-9. Percentage of Employed Recent Immigrants Aged 25 to 54 Working in Professional or Managerial Jobs or as Operators, Fabricators, or Laborers: 1990[a]

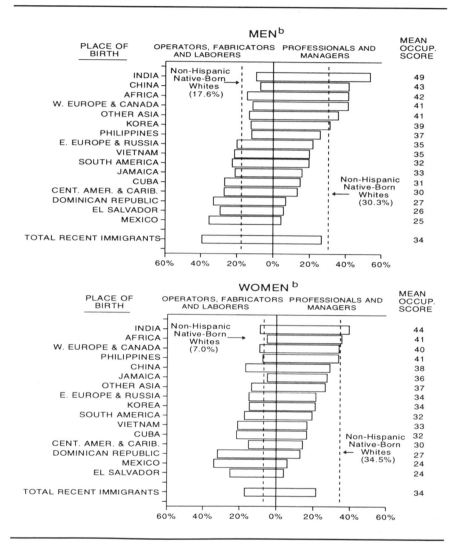

SOURCE: U.S. Bureau of the Census, *Census of Population and Housing: 1990,* Public Use Microdata Sample.

[a]Data refer to immigrants arriving after 1969 and pertain to persons employed at the time of the census.

[b]The mean occupation score for native-born non-Hispanic white men was 37; for similar women, it was 39.

succinct as they were for education. Some groups have many members working at the most prestigious jobs and few at the lower-ranking, blue-collar ones. Men from India, China, Africa, Western Europe, and Canada fit this pattern. Other streams of immigrants have lower proportions with professional and managerial jobs than the native-born, and higher proportions in lower-ranking jobs. Although about one-fifth of men coming from Eastern Europe and Russia worked as professionals or managers, this was below the mark for native-born men, and a higher proportion of men in this group worked at the low-ranking, blue-collar positions. There is an issue of licensing that helps to explain the apparent discrepancies between how groups rank with regard to education and occupation. Presumably, many extensively educated immigrants will work at jobs discrepant with their educations for some years until they qualify for licenses.

Women migrating from India are unusual in that they are over-represented in both the top ranking professional and managerial jobs and also overrepresented in the operator/fabricator/laborer category. Most of the other immigrant streams of women are tilted toward the lower-ranking jobs, with the exception of Jamaican women. Women born in the Dominican Republic, Mexico, and El Salvador are distinctive for their concentration toward the bottom of the occupational distribution.

Information is also provided about one summary index of occupational status: a mean occupational prestige score (Stevens and Cho 1985). This index assigns a numerical score to each occupation on the basis of its financial rewards and educational requirements, with high scores indicating the most desirable and rewarding jobs. Those working as professionals were assigned scores of sixty-nine while operators of assembly line machines got scores of just nineteen.

Immigrants arriving after 1969 worked at lower-ranking jobs than native whites. But in a couple of the immigration streams with many extensively educated persons, they worked at higher-status jobs, on average, than did native-born whites. This is true for men immigrating from Europe, Africa, and Asia—except for those from Vietnam. This was also the case for women from India, Africa, Western Europe, and the Philippines. At the other extreme, migrants from the Dominican Republic, El Salvador, and Mexico worked at much lower-ranking jobs than natives did. This information and that about educational attainment illustrate the distribution of immigrants across a variety of ranks in our society and suggest that it will be difficult to offer summary statements about their impact on our economy.

The Economic Status of Recent Immigrants

This indicator pertains to the economic status of recent immigrants—namely, their standing compared to the poverty line. Foreign-born persons aged 25 to 54 will often be supporting younger persons who also moved to the United States and, in some cases, may be caring for their parents who now live here. The economic measure used here concisely summarizes the standing of a group: the proportion who live in households with incomes below the poverty line and the proportion who live in households with incomes five or more times the poverty line. Figure 5-10 reports findings; because the patterns for male and female immigrants are similar, only one panel is shown. These data refer to post-1969 immigrants, some of them living with other recent immigrants and some of them married to native-born people.

Many immigrants are below the poverty line upon arrival and remain impoverished for long periods of time. Although their economic circumstances here may be favorable compared to those in Managua, Addis Ababa, or Canton, they are still poor by this nation's standards. Only two of the migration streams, from India and Western Europe/Canada, had higher proportions in the economically comfortable status than was the case for native-born whites. And there were only two migration streams in which the poverty rate was lower than for native-born whites, those from India and the Philippines. In most, there were relatively few living in comfortable economic circumstances, with many living below the poverty line.

Household size plays a role in these elevated poverty rates since households headed by the foreign-born are typically larger, often much larger, than those headed by natives, implying that they spread their earnings among more people. Those headed by Mexicans averaged 5.6 persons; by El Salvadorans, 5.2 persons; and by Chinese immigrants, 4.0 persons; compared to an average of only 3.3 for native-born, non-Hispanic whites. The chain migration process leads many migrants to provide homes for relatives and friends who come here, leading to these unusually large household sizes. (For further analysis, see Myers and Wolch 1995, pp. 283–286.)

Educational attainment also accounts for differences in poverty since migration groups toward the top of the educational ranking or the occupational ranking were also at the top of the economic line. However, there is another, less obvious factor helping to explain these differences—the length of residence in the United States. Upon arrival, many immigrants fall below the poverty line, but this proportion decreases as their length of residence increases.

Figure 5-10. Economic Status of Recent Immigrants of All Ages: 1990

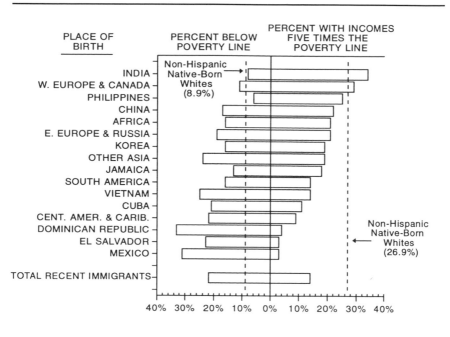

SOURCE: U.S. Bureau of the Census, *Census of Population and Housing: 1990*, Public Use Microdata Sample.

NOTES: These data refer to persons of all ages arriving after 1969.

Earnings and Hours of Employment of Recent Immigrants

For more than a century controversies have swirled about the economic status of immigrants and their place in the economy. Do immigrants provide labor to employers that native workers are unable or unwilling to supply? Are immigrants a cheap source of labor thereby lowering costs to both those who produce goods and those who buy them? Will the current high volume of immigration lead to a large economic underclass of impoverished individuals, many of them permanently dependent on welfare? And do immigrants in the labor market displace native-born workers and lower their wage rates? If so, there will be strong pressures to curtail immigration.

Numerous immigrants believe that their chances for economic success will be much greater here than in their native lands, be they physicians from India or field hands from Mexico. How do they fare in the labor market after arrival? Do their earnings fall far behind those of seemingly comparable native-born individuals or, perhaps because of their own motivation and dedication, do immigrants actually earn more than comparable natives?

Immigrants account for a disproportionately large share of the recent growth of the labor force. The total size of the labor force aged 18 to 64 grew by 19 percent between 1980 and 1990, an increase of nineteen million persons. The percentages of that total growth attributable to each of four demographic groups are shown below:

Native-born men	25%
Native-born women	51
Foreign-born men	14
Foreign-born women	10
Total growth	100%

Immigrants arriving between 1980 and 1990 made up just 4 percent of the nation's total population, but they accounted for a surprisingly large fraction of the total growth of the labor force—one-quarter—reflecting the fact that it is working age people who come here.

AN UPWARD TRAJECTORY OF EARNINGS AFTER ARRIVAL   Let's first turn to questions about the achievements of immigrants in the U.S. labor force. It is extremely unlikely that the new flow of immigration will create a large new underclass. This important issue has been investigated often: do immigrants earn as much, more, or less than ostensibly similar native-born men and women? Studies based on the censuses of 1970 and 1980 reached a consensus. Shortly after arrival in the United States, immigrants earned less, often much less, than comparable native-born workers. After immigrants lived here for some years, the gap separating their earnings from those of similar natives narrowed and, after fifteen to twenty years here, the earnings of immigrants approached those of the native-born. It is costly to be an immigrant for a dozen years or so but, after that, immigrants are not at much of a disadvantage in terms of wages. (For a thorough recent summary of such studies, see Borjas 1985, 1994; Chiswick 1978; Chiswick and Sullivan 1995; Jasso and Rosenzweig 1990, chap. 7.)

In this section, we compare the earnings and employment of immigrants to those of native whites. Because immigrants are so geographically concentrated, it is unfair to compare the economic status of all immigrants to all natives since many natives live in states and metropolises that are home to few immigrants. To make an equitable comparison, this analysis is limited to those fourteen large metropolises with a representation of foreign-born above the national average: New York, Los Angeles, Miami, Washington, Houston, and nine other locations mentioned in figure 5-11. They include two-thirds of the foreign-born population in the United States in 1990.

Figure 5-11 presents information about men and women aged 25 to 54 who worked during 1989 and contrasts the earnings of immigrants to those of native-born, non-Hispanic whites, illustrating how duration of residence in this country influences earnings. In terms of earnings, it is pretty tough to be a new arrival. Men who arrived in 1987 to 1989 earned about two-thirds as much per hour as native-born men, net of other factors influencing earnings. But immigrants who stuck around did much better. After about twenty-five years of residence, immigrants reported earning 93 percent as much as native-born whites. And, among men, parity was reached after thirty years. The differences distinguishing the earnings of the foreign-born from natives were smaller among women, but the pattern is exactly the same: the longer their duration of residence in the United States, the higher the earnings of immigrants vis-à-vis those of similar white women. After twenty years, immigrant women earned as much as native-born white women, strongly implying a process of economic assimilation. These are cross-sectional data referring to immigrants arriving in different periods, so there is no guarantee that a similar figure based on the census of 2010 or 2020 would look exactly the same. But these results match those from the earlier censuses, suggesting that immigrants, as a group, start out with earnings far below those of natives, but eventually catch up. There is no hint here that immigrants are creating an economic underclass. Indeed, those who arrive when they are young and remain here can expect to eventually earn a little more than comparable native-born whites. In terms of labor market success, the melting pot is effective since immigrants eventually do catch up with natives. (For an alternative viewpoint, see Massey 1995.)

These findings are consistent with the view that immigrants may not be extremely productive workers upon arrival, so their earnings are lower than those of comparable natives. They may have a limited knowledge of colloquial English or not know how to search effectively in the job market. Or they may be targeted for exploitation by unscrupulous employers. Furthermore, some of them undoubtedly accept jobs for which they are overqualified, or the chain migration process

Figure 5-11. Earnings of Immigrants Aged 25 to 54 by Date of Arrival, as a Percentage of Earnings of Comparable Native-Born, Non-Hispanic Whites: 1990, Metropolises with Numerous Immigrants

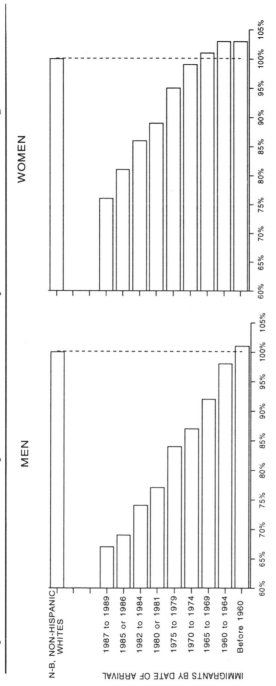

SOURCE: U.S. Bureau of the Census, Census of Population and Housing: 1990, Public Use Microdata Sample.

NOTES: This shows the earnings of immigrants aged 25 to 54 as a percentage of those of native-born, non-Hispanic whites derived from a model with the log of hourly earnings as its dependent variable, taking into account age, educational attainment, reported English language ability, citizenship, metropolis of residence, marital status, and date of arrival in the United States. Model for women also takes fertility into account. Data pertain to persons in the fourteen metropolitan areas of one million or more with proportions foreign-born above the national average who reported earnings in 1989.

Metropolises in this analysis: Boston, Chicago, Dallas, Hartford, Houston, Los Angeles, Miami, New York, Sacramento, San Antonio, San Diego, San Francisco, Seattle, and Washington.

steers them temporarily toward metropolises where they cannot utilize their skills. After a few years, immigrants become Americanized and learn how to capitalize upon their talents, so they eventually earn as much as comparable natives. Economic assimilation is also facilitated by the selective return to their native lands of immigrants whose skills are not rewarded in the United States, such as those who did not learn English, who could not obtain licenses to ply their trades, or who just found themselves falling to the bottom of the competitive U.S. labor market.

THE ECONOMIC STATUS OF IMMIGRANTS IN OUR PORTS OF ENTRY   After several decades, the earnings of immigrants equal those of similar natives. But the major impact of recent immigration has been upon those few metropolises now serving as ports of entry to millions of foreigners. What role do immigrants play in these places, and how does their employment status compare to that of natives in the same places? Are all streams of immigrants faring about equally well, or are there some that do much better than others? Does gender make a difference in the labor market outcomes of immigrants?

To answer such questions, this investigation is limited to immigrants who arrived after the reform law went into effect and who lived in the fourteen large metropolises where the representation of new arrivals was high. Two indicators of economic status are considered: hours of employment and hourly earnings. Again, I describe sixteen immigration streams (see figure 5-12.)

You might think that immigrant men would spend much more time on the job than native-born men, since many of them came here to maximize their earnings, and working long hours at a low-wage job will do that. But immigrants frequently have characteristics associated with unemployment. Furthermore, if there is overtime or extra work to be done in the factory or office, the boss will most often assign it to a employee with seniority not to a new migrant who is just learning. As figure 5-12 shows, immigrant men worked fewer hours than native-born white men. In this figure, the number of hours worked by native-born, non-Hispanic white men is equated with 100 percent. These are per capita hours of work, so all members of a group are included in this calculation. The average hours worked by recent immigrant men are shown as a percentage of the hours worked by white men. Men from Western Europe and Canada worked approximately as many hours in 1989 as did native-born white men, but in every other comparison, immigrant men, on average, worked quite a

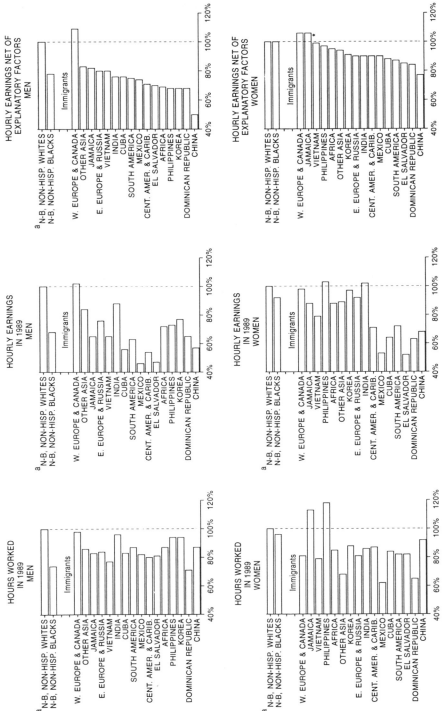

HOURS WORKED
IN 1989
MEN

HOURLY EARNINGS
IN 1989
MEN

HOURLY EARNINGS NET OF
EXPLANATORY FACTORS
MEN

HOURS WORKED
IN 1989
WOMEN

HOURLY EARNINGS
IN 1989
WOMEN

HOURLY EARNINGS NET OF
EXPLANATORY FACTORS
WOMEN

bit less than native-born white men. Interestingly, all the immigrant streams, except that of the Dominican Republic, worked more hours than native-born black men, reflecting the unusually high unemployment rates of African American men and their frequent nonparticipation in the labor force (Kasarda 1995).

The center panel reports the hourly earnings of recent immigrants as a percentage of those of native-born white men. Men from India and Western Europe/Canada earned more money for each hour on the job than did native white men, reflecting their extensive educational attainments. Men in all other immigration streams earned much less. Those coming from El Salvador and Mexico earned just one-half as much per hour of work as native-born white men. Men from China and Central American countries were close to the bottom, lagging far behind native-born white men. Seven of the immigrant streams were, on average, more extensively educated than native-born blacks and so, not surprisingly, their average earnings exceeded those of native-born blacks. (For other recent analyses of earnings of immigrants, see Borjas 1994.)

It is important to look at the actual hourly earnings of immigrants to give us the picture of how they stand relative to natives, but these

---

Figure 5-12 (opposite page).   Labor Market Characteristics of Recent Immigrants and Native-Born, Non-Hispanic Blacks and Whites in Large Metropolises with Numerous Recent Immigrants, Men and Women Aged 25 to 54: 1990

SOURCE: U.S. Bureau of the Census, *Census of Population and Housing: 1990,* Public Use Microdata Sample.

NOTES: These data refer to native-born, non-Hispanic blacks and whites and to recent immigrants living in those fourteen metropolises of one million or more with a proportion foreign-born above the national average. Recent immigrants are those who arrived after 1969. Data for hours worked refer to all persons 25 to 54. Data for hourly earnings refer to persons who worked in 1989 and reported positive earnings. Estimates of net effects shown in panel to the right result from a model with log of hourly earnings as its dependent variable and controlling for metropolis of residence, age, educational attainment, reported English language ability, marital status, citizenship, and date of arrival in the United States. Earnings model for women also controls for number of births.

[a]Mean values for native-born, non-Hispanic white men and women: Hours of work in 1990, 2,069 and 1,393; average hourly earnings, $19.51 and $13.48; log of hourly earnings, 2.75 and 2.39, respectively.

*Coefficient of net difference in hourly earnings is not significant at .01 level. Other differences are significant at .01 level.

differences come about largely because of differences in educational attainment and other characteristics determining what a person earns. The bar chart to the right in figure 5-12 compares the earnings of immigrants to native-born whites, taking into account their differences in educational attainment, reported English-language ability, age differences among the immigrant groups, their duration of residence, and the fact that they are differently distributed across the fourteen metropolitan areas. Additionally, we control for differences in labor supply by analyzing earnings per hour of work. As a result, the bars to the right in figure 5-12 illustrate differences in earnings net of those factors that account for earnings.

Only one group of immigrant men—those from Western Europe/Canada—were more effective than white men in translating their labor market characteristics into earnings. In recent years, few people in Western Europe or Canada felt economic pressure to come to the United States or left those countries because their civil liberties were compromised. There is an unusually positive selection of immigrants from these nations whose economic prosperity rivals or exceeds that of the United States. Men doing well in those countries become aware of even better opportunities in the United States or, if they work for multinational corporations, their employer assigns them here. Thus, taking their characteristics into account, they do a little better than native-born white men and much better than native-born black men in terms of converting their labor market characteristics into earnings. (For an analysis of this topic using data from both the 1980 and 1990 censuses, see Sorensen and Enchautegui 1994.)

Men in all other immigration streams fell behind white men in converting their characteristics into earnings. For Asian, Eastern European/Russian, and Jamaican men, the cost was equivalent to about 10 percent of the earnings of white men; for men from Spanish-speaking lands, it was about twice that—20 percent. This is not proof of any discrimination against immigrant workers, but some of them may be singled out for unfair treatment while others may fail to pursue opportunities for which they are qualified. The important finding is that, net of their characteristics that influence their earnings, such as education and English-language ability, immigrant men who arrived after 1969 earn less than similar native-born white men.

You might be surprised at the ranking of the Chinese on this list: the very bottom. If you have worked with engineers recently or visited a major medical center, you probably noticed the large number of Chinese scientists and doctors. How can Chinese men have such low hourly earnings and be least effective in translating their characteristics into high earnings, even less effective than native-born blacks or immigrants from the Dominican Republic?

The Chinese immigrant stream is most unusual since it includes a substantial number of highly educated men as well as others whose limited attainments rival those of immigrants from El Salvador and Mexico. Data in this figure refer to the fourteen large "ports of entry." Many of the highly educated Chinese enter the national job market and are geographically dispersed across the country. Every major university and huge hospital complex now has a substantial Chinese population. But the less-educated stream of Chinese immigrants—those who work in the needlework shops and in the kitchens of thousands of Chinese restaurants—are much more concentrated in New York, Los Angeles, or San Francisco.

Our image of the economic success of the Chinese is not all wrong, but it is influenced by those educated Chinese who have spread across the country. Specifically, the percentage of recent Chinese immigrants with college degrees was 52 percent for those living outside metropolitan Los Angeles, New York, and San Francisco, but for those living in these three cities it was only 36 percent.

Consider metropolitan New York. In 1990, more than one-third of recent Chinese immigrants aged 25 to 54 reported a ninth grade education or less compared to only 13 percent of native-born whites. Many of these minimally educated Chinese immigrants worked at low-wage jobs. About 13,000 Chinese men held service jobs in restaurants, where they averaged just over $12,000 for working full-time, year-round in 1989. A similar number of Chinese women cut cloth or operated machines in the needlework trades, where they averaged about $14,500 for full-time work. More so than other streams of current immigrants, the uneducated from China are concentrated in or trapped in a low-wage enclave economy, helping to explain why the Chinese are less effective than other immigrants in translating their characteristics into earnings.

There is little evidence of the "leap-frogging" of blacks by male immigrants. You might think that racial discrimination is so firmly entrenched in this country that when new immigrants arrive from Asia and Latin America, they are preferred by employers, causing their earnings to quickly surpass those of native blacks. To be sure, black men earned less per hour than did seven immigrant streams (see middle panel of figure 5-12), but when we take into account those many factors that explain earnings, we find that only two groups of recent male immigrants—from Western Europe/Canada and "other Asia"—translated their labor market characteristics into earnings more effectively that native-born black men. *Employed black men are not losing out to immigrants in the competition for wages in these ports of entry.*

The lower panel of figure 5-12 shows economic information about immigrant women. Gender differences are large since immigrant men and women have different characteristics producing different outcomes in the labor market. Two groups of women—from Jamaica and the Philippines—typically spent much more time at work than did native-born white *or* black women, while the other immigrant streams spent less time on the job than native-born women. Note that all but two streams of immigrant women worked fewer hours in 1989 than native African American women. In these large metropolises, Philippine and Indian women earned more per hour than native-born white women, but this is not surprising since 60 percent of these women held college diplomas. Women migrating from Mexico and El Salvador were concentrated at the low end of the educational distribution; their average hourly earnings were just half those of white women. White women earned about $13.50 for every hour on the job, immigrants from El Salvador and Mexico, just $7.00.

Most streams of male immigrants earned 10 to 20 percent less than comparable native-born white men after their characteristics were taken into account. It was pretty costly in terms of earnings to be a recent arrival from abroad if you were a man, but it made less difference in the earnings of women. There were a couple of immigrant streams where the earnings of women were unusually high or low. Women from Jamaica earned about 10 percent more than white women after controlling for their characteristics. This was not the result of Jamaican women being overrepresented in the high-wage metropolitan New York area, since the model factors in places of residence. Nor was it the result of the exceptionally long hours Jamaican women work, since we are looking at hourly earnings. Rather, women immigrating from that Caribbean isle were more effective than other immigrants and more effective than native-born women in converting their characteristics into high wages. Once again, the Chinese were at the bottom, reflecting their concentration in an ethnic economy that provides low wages.

Among women, there is also little evidence of any immigrant "leap frogging" over native-born blacks. Indeed, once their labor market characteristics were taken into account, native-born black women in these metropolises earned just as much as similar native-born white women. As we will see in the next chapter, the black-white difference in earnings is large and persistent among men but, by 1980, African American women earned as much as similar white women.

What makes Jamaican women so successful? After all, 99 percent of them marked down black as their race, a characteristic you might think would handicap them in the competition for higher earnings. They are much overrepresented in metropolitan New York, and there they differ greatly from the other streams of immigrant women in their jobs. They are concentrated in the administrative support occupations—the secretarial and clerical jobs. Apparently many Jamaican women come to the United States with excellent English-language skills, the skills that allow them to get good office jobs and then move up the ladder, not to the top managerial ranks, but to higher-paying positions in the office. And, unlike women recently arriving from China, they are not working in a low-wage enclave economy.

What Jobs Do Recent Immigrants Fill?

Examining the jobs of immigrants lets us appreciate the economic significance of this migration. Those who arrived since 1969 are greatly overrepresented in the lower-paying, blue-collar, and service jobs, are quite well represented in many science and engineering professions, but are notable by their absence from civil service jobs and those requiring state licenses.

To describe these patterns, we consider once again the fourteen large metropolises with an overrepresentation of immigrants and look at the jobs held by employed persons aged 25 to 54. Recent immigrants filled 20 percent of total jobs held by men aged 25 to 54 and 16 percent of those held by women. But such immigrants are much more numerous in these places than across the entire nation, where new arrivals constituted only 8 percent of employed men and 6 percent of employed women.

Employed persons wrote a job title or a phrase on the census form describing what he or she did while at work, and the Census Bureau coded these into five hundred occupational categories. In these immigration centers, there were 221 occupations that employed at least ten thousand men in 1990 and 166 such occupations for women. Considering these occupations, table 5-2 shows the ten with the greatest representations of recent immigrants and the ten where immigrants were most scarce.

Table 5-2. Occupations in Which Recent Immigrants Are Overrepresented or Underrepresented, Large Metropolises with Numerous Immigrants: 1990

Employed Men			Employed Women		
Occupation	Percent Recent Immigrants	Number Employed (000)	Occupation	Percent Recent Immigrants	Number Employed (000)
Overrepresented			Overrepresented		
Sewing machine operators	77%	22	Sewing machine operators	73%	108
Waiters' assistants	73	27	Dressmakers	55	19
Miscellaneous food preparation jobs	63	47	Farm workers	51	11
Farm workers	60	32	Maids	49	95
Cooks	57	99	Laundering machine operators	49	21
Precious stone workers	53	14	Graders and sorters	49	11
Parking lot attendants	52	12	Packaging machine operators	48	27
Electrical equipment assemblers	50	23	Pressing machine operators	47	13
Waiters	48	65	Electrical equipment assemblers	45	52
Bakers	47	24	Machine operators, not elsewhere classified	45	27

Underrepresented			Underrepresented		
Firefighters	1%	67	Nonfarm animal caretakers	2%	10
Police supervisors	1	16	Police officers	2	22
Police officers	1	151	Bus drivers	2	44
Sheriffs and bailiffs	2	21	Special education teachers	3	11
Lawyers	2	218	Speech therapists	3	18
Telephone line installers	3	12	Stenographers	3	19
Technical writers	4	13	Dispatchers	3	21
Airline pilots	4	30	Dental hygienists	3	19
Electrical power installers	4	21	Authors	3	21
Correctional institution officers	4	25	Secondary school teachers	3	81

SOURCE: U.S. Bureau of the Census, *Census of Population and Housing: 1990*, Public Use Microdata Sample.
NOTES: This information refers to the fourteen metropolises of one million or more that had a proportion foreign-born above the national average in 1990. Recent immigrants are those arriving since 1969. Data refer to employed persons aged 25 to 54 and show recent immigrants as a percentage of total employment in each occupation.

The upper panel lists those occupations now being filled in great numbers by immigrants. They are primarily jobs that few native-born Americans want since they bring neither a generous paycheck nor any social status. About 70 percent of the men employed as waiters' assistants, formerly called busboys, or doing unskilled food preparation in kitchens are immigrants. The importance of recent Latin American and Asian immigration for the garment industries in New York, Los Angeles, and Miami is clearly indicated—three-quarters of the sewing machine operators migrated to the United States in the last twenty years. The list for women, more so than that for men, suggests an occupational niche increasingly occupied by immigrants—unskilled machine operators. Indeed, in the centers of immigration, recent arrivals make up 30–45 percent of the personnel operating the machines that slice, paint, shape, fold, and package the consumer goods we buy every day. These are, for the most part, nonunion jobs requiring few skills, very little training, no knowledge of English, offering little pay and few fringe benefits. They should be distinguished from the much more highly skilled, blue-collar jobs now classified as the precision production and crafts occupations in which recent immigrants are not nearly so numerous (Mahler 1995, chap. 5).

It is easy to see how these occupational niches go hand-in-hand with the chain migration process. If an employer successfully uses low-wage immigrants to clean clothes, sort and package food products, sew new dresses, or help put shingles on roofs in Miami, New York, San Antonio, or Los Angeles, he will likely ask his workers to recommend others, a "help wanted" bulletin that might instantly be communicated to Port Au Prince, San Luis Potosi, or Santo Domingo, but one that would never appear in the *New York Times* or *Miami Herald.* Chapter 3 described the downward trends in male wages and the decline in good blue-collar industrial jobs. Quite likely, native-born men know about the good jobs their fathers and uncles had and expect to hold jobs just as good or even better, so they are reluctant to clear off tables, grade fruits, or work as short-order cooks. But immigrants from poor countries have no such expectations, so they fill these important but low-paying occupational niches.

One highly skilled job stands out on the list of occupations dominated by immigrant men: more than one-half of those who cut and set precious stones for the jewelry industry are recent immigrants. This is a niche dominated by a specialized flow from Europe: about five thousand men in New York City in 1990 reported that they plied this highly skilled craft. Four out of five were foreign-born and two-thirds of them reported they spoke Spanish or Yiddish in their homes.

Occupations with relatively few recent immigrants are listed in the lower panel of table 5-2. They include jobs that require an extensive knowledge of colloquial spoken and written English, such as stenographer, dispatcher, technical writer, and author. Many of them involve employment by city and state agencies, including the job of animal tender in municipal zoos. Presumably, civil service agencies give preference to long-term residents of their areas and enforce the regulations about the employment of noncitizens more strictly than private employers, so few recent immigrants fight fires, arrest misdemeanants, keep order in courtrooms, or teach in elementary and secondary schools.

Are jobs in science, medicine, and engineering now dominated by recent immigrants from Asia? Although Asians seem to be very numerous among those training for these professions, immigrants did not dominate these fields in 1990. Recent immigrants are well represented in these good jobs, but not overrepresented.

Entrepreneurial Activity

We often assume that many immigrants come to the United States, work diligently, and, after a few years, establish their own businesses. No matter where we live, we are within a few minutes' drive of a Chinese restaurant, and in many cities, both big and small, we visit retail shops and service establishments run by Koreans. If we hail cabs in New York or Washington, we are likely to speak to a newcomer. John Kasarda (1995) argues that one reason for the economic success of Asian immigrants is their ability to tap kin networks for those financial resources needed to acquire existing businesses or start new ones (see also Sanders and Nee 1995).

While it is true that many immigrants run their own firms, a note of caution is in order. Only one stream of recent immigrants—Koreans—were overrepresented among the ranks of the self-employed. Several other streams, including those from Western Europe/Canada and those from the diverse array of "other Asia" countries, rival native-born whites in self-employment. Figure 5-13 refers to the fourteen large metropolitan areas with many recent immigrants and provides information about entrepreneurship. The census allows us to identify the self-employed by their types of income in 1989. This figure reports the percentage who said their only income was from self-employment, as well as the percentage who said they got both self-employment income and wages from a salaried job. If a woman works in an office five days each week but runs her own hair salon in the

Figure 5-13. Self-Employment for Natives and Recent Immigrants Aged 25 to 54 for Large Metropolises with Many Migrants: 1990

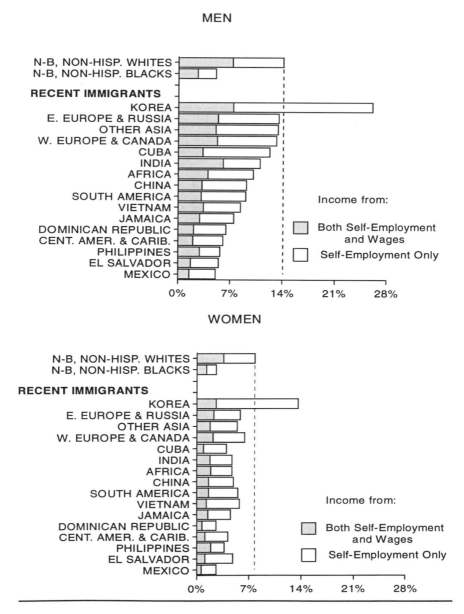

SOURCE: U.S. Bureau of the Census, *Census of Population and Housing: 1990*, Public Use Microdata Sample.

NOTE: This figure shows the percentage of recent immigrants reporting only self-employment earnings in 1989 or reporting both self-employment income and wage and salary earnings.

evenings and on Saturdays, she should report wages from her salaried job as well as self-employment income from her business.

Koreans are distinctive in that more than one-quarter of the men and one-sixth of the women reported self-employment income—more than twice the proportion self-employed among native-born, non-Hispanic whites. But the image of immigrants being vastly overrepresented among the self-employed is wrong, since most of the immigrant streams from Asia and Latin America have relatively low proportions earning their living by running their own businesses. Eight percent of Chinese men were self-employed, in contrast with 14 percent of white men. Within the broad geographic groups, there were substantial differences. Filipinos were the least likely Asians to be working for themselves; Lebanese immigrants the most likely. Cuban men ran their own businesses much more frequently than did men from Mexico or El Salvador.

Few native-born black men work for themselves. All streams of recent male immigrants had higher percentages of self-employed than native blacks. (For a discussion of the causes and implications of this, see Bates 1993; Kasarda 1995.) Black entrepreneurs must overcome formidable hurdles that limit their opportunities. They often face challenges securing capital from banks or lenders. And if they open retail stores or service establishments in largely black neighborhoods, they will be serving a clientele whose incomes are 40 percent below the national average. Thus far, black entrepreneurs have yet to find and capitalize upon a retail product as popular outside their own ethnic community as Chinese food. Those traditional stereotypes that picture blacks as less competent than whites and may also lead some whites, Latinos, and Asians to be wary of black proprietors.

The Chinese are greatly overrepresented among the ranks of restaurant owners. About three-quarters of 1 percent of the adult population identified themselves as Chinese in the census, but 6 percent of individuals who own restaurants were Chinese. This is not, however, a good way to amass the riches of Croesus. Chinese restaurant owners who worked full-time in 1989 reported average net self-employment incomes of only $9,200, 25 percent less than white restaurant owners.

The Impact of Immigrants Upon the Employment and Earnings of Natives

During the 1980s, the native-born labor force with a high school education or less fell from fifty-five million to forty-eight million, reflecting the shift toward greater educational attainment and the retirement of older workers who had less schooling. But three million immigrants who arrived in the 1980s had high school educations or less. Isn't it obvious that this high volume of immigration depresses employment opportunities and lowers wages for native-born Americans who lack college training? Wouldn't wages rise if we immediately terminated the flow of immigration? Can't we blame the high level of immigration for the declining wages reported in chapter 3?

Because of the importance of immigration, this issue receives a great deal of attention. While there are still disagreements about the details, *there is consensus that the effects of immigration on the employment prospects and wages of natives are modest.* Summarizing several dozen studies based upon the 1970 and 1980 censuses, Michael Fix and Jeffrey Passel (1994, p. 49) conclude that if immigrants as a share of the labor force in a metropolis went up from 10 percent at one census date to 20 percent at the next, the labor force participation rate of natives would drop only 1 percent, net of all other factors influencing employment. These studies agree ". . . that immigration has a weak effect on the employment of natives" (Borjas 1994, p. 1698). One dramatic finding is stressed repeatedly. Between the spring and fall of 1980, Miami's labor force increased by 7 percent as the Mariel boatlift brought 125,000 Cubans to the United States. The 1980 to 1985 trend in wages and employment in Miami was almost exactly the same as in Atlanta, Houston, and Los Angeles: similar cities, but with no spike in immigration (Card 1990). The arrival of upwards of one hundred thousand potential workers in just a few months did not drive down wages or increase unemployment in Miami.

This seems counterintuitive. How can the presence of many immigrants not depress employment opportunities and lower wages for natives? The economists who model these processes report that four factors explain this puzzle. First, immigration is concentrated in metropolises that are growing rapidly, most of them in the South and Southwest. Booming population and economic growth in these places create thousands of jobs each year, and a fraction are filled by immigrants. Migrants, to a large degree, are fitting into occupational slots created by economic and demographic growth.

Second, the presence of immigrants in a metropolis may permit industries to thrive there, industries that might otherwise move offshore. Muller and Espenshade (1985) convincingly argue that the presence of Mexican workers in metropolitan Los Angeles in the 1970s sustained low-skill manufacturing industries there. Presumably, these firms would have closed, automated their production, or moved to Mexico had there not been a source of low-wage labor in Los Angeles. Manufacturing jobs, and the many front-office and sales jobs that accompany them, were saved or created for natives by the presence of numerous immigrants. In recent years, the garment industry has prospered in New York, Los Angeles, and Miami largely because immigrants from China and the Caribbean are willing to work long hours for small paychecks, producing the costly dresses and suits that highly educated women need as they pursue careers. There is a job-creation element of immigration, one that offsets the potential displacement of native-born workers. And it is clear that quite a few new arrivals set up their own businesses, thereby hiring workers. Many ethnic-enclave firms serve the specific needs of immigrants now living in the United States, such as restaurants, newspapers, banks, and real estate brokers catering to the Korean or Chinese communities in New York and Los Angeles and similar businesses for Cubans in Miami. The influx from abroad revitalizes old and declining areas of central cities by stimulating employment in them (Winnick 1990). It also may attract "deep pocket" entrepreneurs. With an eye toward takeover of Hong Kong by the mainland Chinese, federal immigration law was changed in the 1980s to ease the admission of financially well-endowed aliens who would bring capital to the United States and create new businesses here.

Third, many immigrants fill jobs that native-born Americans are reluctant to accept—for example, the stoop labor traditionally needed in agriculture. Indeed, the *braceros* program was created almost fifty years ago to allow growers in the Southwest to hire low-cost Mexican gang labor. While the demand for such labor has declined, immigrants continue to fill numerous labor market niches that Americans avoid. For example, as women increasingly devote themselves to full-time jobs, the need for nannies grows. Few native-born women look forward to jobs as full-time housekeepers and childcare workers living in the homes of prosperous couples. With dual-career married women now running for office and seeking appointments to high federal positions, we are reminded that immigrants are willing to accept jobs as nannies without benefit of Social Security. The census of 1990 counted over one hundred thousand recent immigrant women working as domestic servants or childcare workers (Wrigley 1995).

Immigrants are also overrepresented in the upper tail of the educational distribution. More than one-quarter of the growth of the labor force with master's degrees or more in the 1980s was accounted for by immigration. But this is the segment of the labor force with improving employment prospects and rising wages. Organizations of scientists, engineers, physicians, and nurses are not protesting our liberal immigration laws, even though these occupational ranks are increasingly filled by aliens.

There may be a fourth reason: employers may prefer illegals to citizens. Recent immigrants may, perhaps, be easily exploited and are unlikely to file suits about violations of minimum wage laws, Occupational Safety and Health Administration regulations, or laws mandating extra pay for overtime. Employers may find that non-English-speaking illegals are the most docile and dependent workers for low-skill work. The 1986 IRCA legislation makes it a violation of federal law to hire undocumented workers, but few entrepreneurs have been punished and none put in a federal jail for violating it.

Studies of the economic effects of immigration most often report that the earnings of native-born workers are not reduced because of the presence of newcomers, but this is not an easy topic to investigate, even with the extensive data from the census. If you compare the earnings of natives in places with many immigrants, such as New York and San Francisco, to those of natives living in metropolises with almost no immigrants, such as Nashville and New Orleans, you find that natives earn much more where there are numerous immigrants. But it is erroneous to conclude that the presence of immigrants leads to higher wages for native-born workers, a deduction you might casually draw from a first glance at the facts. Rather, wage rates overall are much higher in New York than in Nashville. Recent immigrants, for the most part, are overrepresented in high-wage metropolises, including Boston, New York, Los Angeles, San Francisco, and Washington, and underrepresented in those many low-wage metropolises in the interior South. Determining the effects of immigration upon the earnings of the native-born demands a focus upon specific locations. Summarizing studies done through the 1980s, Fix and Passel (1994, p. 49) report: "Immigration has no discernable effect on wages overall. . . . Wage growth and decline appear to be unrelated to immigration—a finding that holds for both unskilled and skilled workers." They cite numerous studies of specific cities or special industries that found that immigrants did not displace native workers because immigrants worked at lower-skilled jobs, because employers preferred immigrants to natives, or because the industry would not exist in this country without the low-wage labor that new migrants supply (Enchuategui 1995; Tienda and Liang 1994).

There is, however, evidence to the contrary. Some studies find that immigration has a negative impact upon employment opportunities and earnings of natives. Investigations of the construction industry in New York, Houston, and Miami report that immigrants displaced natives in the low-skilled jobs (Grenier et al. 1992), and in parts of the nation, immigrants have been deliberately recruited for undesirable jobs, such as killing, plucking, quartering, and packaging chickens or killing swine, apparently displacing natives (Bach and Brill 1991). There are few authoritative studies of the indirect effects that immigration may be having upon the employment and earnings of natives by influencing internal migration. Native-born individuals with high school educations or less may remain in the Midwest rather than move to the South or Southwest since they believe that they will have to compete with immigrants there, thus increasing the labor supply in places like Detroit and St. Louis, leading to somewhat lower wages in those cities (Frey 1995, p. 287). A study using 1980 census data reported that large centers of immigration were attracting fewer native internal migrants and losing more natives than would be expected on the basis of their characteristics (White and Hunter 1993).

It is still too early to summarize what the census of 1990 reveals about the effects of immigration on the wages of native-born workers. At this point, there are indications that the optimistic findings from the census of 1980 may need to be tempered. A new approach emerged to address this issue. That is, the earnings gap between workers with college educations and workers with high school diplomas or less has widened throughout the country, as the demand for skilled labor has increased much more rapidly than that for unskilled. Across the entire country, immigration may have accounted for 5 to 10 percent of the increasing gap between the earnings of those with college educations and those with high school educations. However, in those few metropolises with very substantial immigration in the 1980s, the college/high school wage gap increased more than expected, implying that the presence of numerous immigrants lowered the earnings of workers living there who lacked college training. In Miami and Los Angeles, for example, more than one-third of the increasing gap between the earnings of college- and high school–educated workers was attributable to the increased representation of immigrants in the labor force; in New York, Washington, and San Francisco, about one-quarter of the increasing earnings gap was attributable to immigration (Jaeger 1995, table 8). It is important to make sure these findings are understood. The gap in earnings increased as much in Cleveland as in Miami and as much in Detroit as in Los Angeles, reflecting the national trend. But the economies of Miami and Los Angeles were expanding, while those of Cleveland and Detroit were not. As a consequence of their sustained economic and population growth, there was an increasing need for labor in places such as Los Angeles and Miami. Had there been no immigration, it seems likely that the wages of low-skilled native workers would have fallen less rapidly and the gap between those at the top and bottom of the earnings distribution would not have widened so much. Among the fifty largest metropolises, there were twelve in which immigration in the 1980s accounted for 10 percent or more of the increasing gap in earnings by educational attainment among natives. All were immigration centers: Chicago, Dallas, Houston, Los Angeles, Miami, New York, Providence, San Antonio, San Diego, San Francisco, Washington, and West Palm Beach.

Conclusion

Early in this century more than a million immigrants arrived each year, primarily from Eastern and Southern Europe, and concern about this rapid change in the nation's ethnic composition led to the closing of ports in the 1920s. Fortunately, with the civil rights revolution, we moved beyond Social Darwinism and so we no longer believe that skin pigmentation, national origin, or religion determine whether an immigrant will make a contribution to this country or become a burden. Our recognition of the civil rights of racial minorities in the 1960s led Congress to open our doors, and the immigration laws were rewritten, which led to the unexpected arrival of millions from Asia and Latin America. Burgeoning population growth in many countries, the restructuring of employment here, and our continued willingness to accept some of those persecuted in their home countries has driven up immigration to levels approaching those of the first two decades of this century. Each year in the 1990s, there may be a net addition of 1.2 million immigrants, perhaps 900,000 who enter with INS approval and 300,000 without legal standing.

Undoubtedly, some will raise the old cry that today's immigrants bring deficient cultures to the United States, will never be assimilated, and will harm the country (Brimelow 1995). But this will not be the major source of opposition. Economic issues may be the key when Congress debates how to fix the immigration issue. A high proportion of newcomers go to just a few states—and within these states to a few metropolises—thereby imposing burdens on the taxpayers living there. Approximately 80 percent of those arriving between 1985 and 1990 went to California, New York, Florida, Texas, New Jersey, Illinois, and Massachusetts, in that order. While immigrants pay local taxes, they also use state services and their children attend local schools.

The costs that foreigners impose have always been a crucial issue, and so the earliest Supreme Court decisions about immigration dealt with nineteenth century efforts in New York City and Boston to impose head taxes on immigrants, taxes specifically used to support newcomers who became paupers (*Passenger Cases* 1849; *Henderson* v. *Mayor of New York* 1876). It is not surprising to find a lengthy history of state laws denying benefits to aliens, such as the right to vote, to practice certain occupations, or to send their children to public schools. While federal courts struck down some of these, they let others stand, such as laws prohibiting aliens from owning land. The civil rights movement changed this. In a 1971 decision, the Supreme Court ruled that alienage, like race, was a suspect classification when it came to determining who would or would not benefit from state programs (*Graham* v. *Richardson* 1971). Shortly thereafter, federal courts struck state laws that restricted opportunities for aliens, although some remain, such as those requiring citizenship for voting and occupational licenses. In a further extension of civil rights, the Supreme Court in 1982 ruled that the Fourteenth Amendment prevented states from denying education to students who themselves were illegal immigrants (*Plyler* v. *Doe* 1982). And then, in 1986, Congress made it mandatory for states to provide emergency medical care—but only emergency medical care—to indigent aliens, including illegals under the federal-state Medicaid program. It should be stressed that all persons born here—even the offspring of illegals—are citizens since the United States grants citizenship on a *jus soli* basis.

Opposition to immigration will come from those states and cities whose budgets are greatly impacted by the high volume of recent immigration. There will be efforts to restrict governmental spending to either all aliens—as in the case of Supplemental Security Income—or to illegal aliens. Several studies have investigated the financial consequences of undocumented immigration, especially to the seven states currently most affected. There were approximately three million illegals in those states in 1992 who paid an estimated $1.9 billion annually in state sales taxes, state and local property taxes, and state income taxes (Clark et al. 1994). The investigators considered the three most expensive state programs used by illegal aliens: the costs of emergency medical care, public schools, and prisons. These charges came to about $4 billion, implying that illegals imposed a burden of $2 billion upon taxpayers in these seven states. Although $2 billion is a very large sum and gives a clear indication of the substantial cost illegals place on local governments, the total expenditures of the governments in these seven states in 1992 was approximately $245 billion, so the termination of all undocumented immigrants would produce only a very modest reduction in state spending. (For a discussion of the conflicting claims about whether recent immigrants pay much more or much less in taxes than they use in services, see Borjas 1994.)

Immigrants fill many important niches in the labor market. They are overrepresented in the upper and lower tails of the educational distribution and therefore most numerous in low-paying jobs and in high-tech occupations. Undoubtedly, there will be an array of convincing studies in the 1990s showing that some specific groups of natives in the great centers of migration had their employment opportunities cut off and their wages depressed by immigration. But there will be other convincing studies stressing the contributions that immigrants are making to the economy, including an acknowledgment that low-skill industries now remain in the United States because of immigration.

If there were a strong union movement defending the interests of low-skill workers, or if federal transfer programs were drastically reduced—that is, if there were sharp cuts in Social Security benefits to the elderly, major reductions in the Supplemental Security Income paid to the disabled and in the AFDC payments to mothers of young children—more natives would probably compete for the low-wage jobs now filled by immigrants. In such a case, sharper cries for closing our borders might be heard. Population growth and changes in our lifestyles help to create more low-skill jobs, and these positions will be desirable ones for millions of citizens of less-developed countries around the world.

The 1986 Immigration Reform and Control Act imposed employer sanctions to curb immigration, but they were not effective. In the political climate of the 1990s, it is difficult to imagine that Congress will establish a large new bureaucracy to process the paperwork of foreigners who seek to work here, or to root out and then punish the thousands of homemakers and small business proprietors who now hire workers without fully documenting their legal status.

At the other end of the educational distribution, it is probable that American employers and foreign firms with operations in the United

States will want to bring talented personnel to work here, be they scientists from India, arbitrageurs from Japan, or diamond cutters from Holland. It is difficult to imagine the United States adopting an immigration law that would prevent the employment of such persons since they contribute much to our economic growth. As American firms become more international in their marketing, they will undoubtedly lobby for liberal immigration laws.

Our dedication to civil liberties means that there will be opposition to some of the measures that might make it difficult for legal immigrants to overstay their welcome or for illegals to move around the United States. To be sure, strengthening the border patrols will make it more challenging to walk or swim across the borders from Canada or Mexico, but it may be nearly impossible to totally seal the long borders. The idea of a Berlin Wall is repugnant to most. Similarly, there will be little support for a federal law insisting that all of us carry an internal passport subject to examination by local police.

Those analyzing social and economic trends in the 1960s failed to see how increased immigration would reshape our larger states and metropolises and make the United States a much more diverse country. Perhaps, there will be a slow down in immigration, but the present combination of American values, labor needs, and demographic pressures suggests that more than a million persons will enter each year in the foreseeable future.

Chapter 6

Racial Issues Thirty Years After the Civil Rights Decade

Favorable economic trends during and after World War II created the modern middle class. But they benefited whites much more than blacks. Never in our history has there been a time when the majority of blacks were members of the middle economic class.

The popularity of General Colin Powell as a candidate for president; the verdict in the O. J. Simpson trial and reactions to it; the Million Man March on Washington on October 25, 1995: All of these occurred simultaneously and remind us of the different ways in which skin color continues to be a divisive issue in American life. From one perspective, there is progress: an African American was briefly considered as the leading candidate for the nation's highest office. From another, the situation in 1995 seems remarkably similar to that of the 1830s when deTocqueville (1969 [1838], chap. 10) observed that blacks and whites were naturally distinct and hostile races sharing the same soil but separated by insurmountable barriers and following separate destinies. This chapter has two aims: first, to describe long-run changes in the social and economic status of blacks and link them to the large-scale trends reshaping America; second, to analyze the status of the array of racial groups now well represented in this country thanks to changes in immigration laws.

Did the civil rights revolution make any difference in the lives of Americans—both black and white? The optimist will point to the tremendous progress of blacks. In 1964, just three blacks sat in Congress; when the 104th Congress took their seats in 1995, forty blacks served. Among blacks who were the parents of the baby boomers, those born from the mid-1920s through the mid-1930s, just 45 percent completed high school educations, far below the 72 percent figure for their white age mates (U.S. Bureau of the Census 1991b, table 2). Among blacks from Generation X, those born in the decade just after the Civil Rights Act, 75 percent completed high school, not so far below the 83 percent among whites (U.S. Bureau of the Census

1994b, table A-5). In 1968, when the last major civil rights bill of the 1960s, the Fair Housing Law, was enacted, only 5 percent of black households had incomes of $50,000 or more. By 1993, 15 percent of black households were that prosperous (amounts in constant dollars; U.S. Bureau of the Census 1995a, table D-1).

An equally valid perspective emphasizes persistent black-white gaps. Since the time of the Korean War, the unemployment rate of black men has been at least double that of white men, suggesting that neither encompassing civil rights laws nor economic growth closed that racial gap (Council of Economic Advisors 1996, table B-39). From the 1940s through the early 1970s, the poverty rate of blacks fell more rapidly than that of whites but, for the last two decades, no improvements have occurred. And about 31 percent of the black population, in contrast to about 11 percent of whites, live in impoverished households (U.S. Bureau of the Census 1995a, table D-4). When the median income of black families is compared to the median income of white families, we again find two decades of stagnation. Since the early 1970s, African American families have consistently reported incomes that are about 58 percent those of white families. From this perspective, the beneficial results of the civil rights decade seem meager, so miniscule that you almost need a microscope to detect them.

Race: How Should the Population Be Classified?

How we think about race and the terms we use to classify population have changed profoundly in the last half-century. At the time of the civil rights revolution we assumed that most Americans could readily be categorized as either black or white. But now the meaning of race, how people should be classified, and which terms should be used are under contention. This debate about racial categories and who belongs where will create extraordinary headlines when the Census Bureau announces its decisions about the nouns to be listed on the census questionnaire for 2000.

It is not that race is a new issue. At all points in our history, race had a clearly understood meaning, but that meaning has changed over time. In the mid- to late-nineteenth century, race referred not only to blacks but to what we now think of as national origin groups, such as Germans or Slavs. With the increasing popularity of Social Darwinism toward the end of the last century, race referred to groups of people who were biologically similar because of their ancestry and breeding.

Racial characteristics were assumed to be "in the blood," an idea that strongly influenced census-taking in that era. Supposedly, people could be sifted into fine-grained groups by their physical characteristics, characteristics that were obvious to the eye. In 1890, enumerators were told to distinguish octoroons, quadroons, and mulattos from blacks, and in 1910, a special form for Indian reservations asked enumerators to report what fraction of blood was Indian, white, or black (U.S. Bureau of the Census 1918, p. 207; 1972, p. 136).

Discussions of race in 1960 focused almost exclusively upon blacks and whites. Restrictive immigration laws dating from 1870 had kept the Asian population small—about one million out of a total count of 179 million. There were just over one-half million American Indians, many of them in rural areas of sparsely populated western states, and no census question in 1960 identified the Spanish-origin population. The civil rights movement and the Congressional deliberations that led to the civil rights laws of the 1960s focused on equal opportunities for African Americans and seldom addressed the civil rights claims of other minority groups.

The social meaning of race today is different. First, as we have seen, the civil rights revolution led to changes in immigration laws that produced massive demographic changes—increases in the population from lands that had previously sent few immigrants, including Asia, Central America, Iraq, Iran, and Arabic-speaking nations. In 1960, there had been consensus about how to classify blacks and whites, but the presence of the new immigrants raised questions about whether they should be fitted into one of the old racial categories or put into new categories of their own.

Second, demographic procedures fundamentally affect our knowledge of racial groups. Through 1960, an enumerator visited every household to gather information. Thus, racial data depended upon how people were classified by the census-takers. Since 1970, race has been self-reported: each person writes down his or her own racial identity. "Race" for our federal statistical system today means whatever a person chooses. The rapid growth of the American Indian population is a dramatic example of this change. Matthew Snipp (1989, p. 72) estimates that 60 percent of the increase of American Indians in the 1970s was due to a shift in self-enumeration (also see Harris 1994).

Third, the Spanish-origin population is now often treated as if it were a racial group, thereby challenging old classification schemes. In the late 1970s, leaders of the Hispanic community recognized that the

Voting Rights Act of 1965 protected the political interests of blacks. They sought to capitalize upon this law but knew that Hispanics would have to be separately identified and then accorded the civil rights prerogatives of a racial minority. Their important victory came in 1969. Responding to pressures from Hispanic advocates, President Nixon ordered that a special question be added to the census of 1970, allowing Spanish-origin persons to identify themselves as Hispanic regardless of their race, a directive issued after several million census forms had been printed without this separate Spanish question. This established a precedent such that, in 1977, the Office of Management and Budget mandated that all federal statistical agencies gather data about Hispanics as well as about race. For purposes of politics and litigation, this raised "Hispanic" to the status of a racial category (Choldin 1986).

Because they are distinct questions, those who identify themselves as Spanish in their origin may also identify with a race. In 1990, 57 percent of those who said their origin was Spanish selected one of the fourteen specific racial categories listed on the census form, but 43 percent did not identify with any listed race (U.S. Bureau of the Census 1993c). Presumably, they think that their Spanish identity supplants the traditional racial categories. (For further analysis see U.S. Bureau of Labor Statistics 1995.)

The concept of race is also being challenged by increasing intermarriage. A high proportion of American Indians have traditionally married whites. In recent decades, the intermarriage of Asians and whites has become common, while black-white intermarriage is also on the rise, implying that a growing fraction of forthcoming generations may not easily identify with one race. In 1990, 4 percent of children under age 18 living with two parents had parents who identified with different races (Harrison and Bennett 1995, table 4.4).

Added to these issues now confounding the classification of our population is the lack of consensus about which title should be used for each of the broad groups we often think of as races. In preparation for the next enumeration, the Census Bureau, in 1995, asked the occupants of sixty thousand households to identify themselves by race. Subsequently, they were asked in the same interview which term they preferred for their own group. Table 6-1 presents the findings.

Consensus was greatest among whites since five-eighths of that group preferred the term referring to their skin color and, among Hispanics, the label "Hispanic" was much more popular than "Latino" or "Spanish." There was less agreement among those who identified

Table 6-1.   Groups by Own Preference for Ethnic or Racial Title: 1995

White Respondents		Black Respondents	
Total	100%	Total	100%
White	62	Black	45
Caucasian	17	African American	28
European-American	2	Afro-American	12
Some other term	2	Negro	3
No preference	17	Some other term	3
		No preference	9
Hispanic Respondents		American Indian Respondents	
Total	100%	Total	100%
Hispanic	58	American Indian	50
Latino	12	Native American	37
Spanish origin	12	Alaska Native	4
Some other term	8	Some other term	3
No preference	10	No preference	6

SOURCE: U.S. Bureau of Labor Statistics, 1995, "A CPS Supplement for Testing Methods of Collecting Racial and Ethnic Information: May 1995" (October).

themselves as blacks or American Indians. Black was the preferred term, but a substantial minority selected African American or Afro-American, while a few chose the formerly popular labels: Negro and colored. American Indian was the most popular name among Indians, but more than one-third selected Native American. These variations in preferences imply continued conflict about the procedures and names we use to sort our increasingly diverse population.

Figure 6-1 describes the changing racial composition of the population. In 1940, the proportion black sank to its lowest level since the early eighteenth century when only one American in ten was African in origin. This changed only a little by 1960, the last date when a description of the country might have focused primarily upon whites and blacks. The pie for 1993 shows the large Hispanic population—about one American in ten—and the rapid growth of Asians. Figures for these later years separately identify Hispanics and exclude them from other racial categories. Shortly after 2000, the Hispanic population is projected to exceed the black population in size. As indicated by the projection for 2020, the non-Hispanic white population will continue to decline as a proportion of the total—falling from about

Figure 6-1. Population of the United States by Race: 1940 to 1995 and Projection for 2020

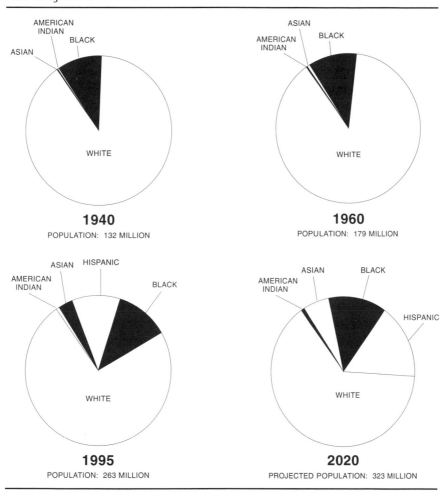

SOURCES: U.S. Bureau of the Census, *Sixteenth Census of the United States: Population: 1940,* Vol. II, table 4; *Census of Population: 1960,* Vol. 1, Part 1, table 44; *Current Population Reports,* series P-25, no. 1104 (November 1993).

NOTES: Hispanics not separately identified before census of 1970. Data for racial groups in 1993 and 2020 refer to non-Hispanics.

90 percent of the total in 1940 to 64 percent in 2020 (U.S. Bureau of the Census 1996, table J).

This chapter describes racial differences and trends with a focus upon recent changes. Since this is no longer a black-white nation, several major groups will be compared: whites, blacks, American Indians, Hispanics, and Asians. Almost all whites, blacks, and American Indians were born in the United States, but this is not the case for Hispanics or Asians. Among these groups, the native- and foreign-born differ in many important ways so, whenever the data permit, their characteristics are shown separately.

Table 6-2 provides information about the size of these groups in 1990 and their growth in the 1980s. Native-born, non-Hispanic whites made up just under three-quarters of the population, but this was a slow-growing group in the 1980s. The most rapidly increasing groups were Asians (both immigrants and native-born) and Hispanic immigrants. As this table shows, Asian immigrants are almost twice as numerous as native-born Asians. The extraordinary growth of the native-born Asian population is not an error. Rather, Asian immigrants are overwhelmingly young adults, and many of them become parents shortly after arrival, but their children are born here—hence, a doubling of the native-born Asian population in the 1980s. Throughout this analysis, the small Aleut and Eskimo populations are included with American Indians, while Pacific Islanders are included with the heterogeneous Asian population. For the most part, this analysis does not describe the foreign-born white population, an older group declining rapidly in size due to deaths of those who arrived decades ago. Foreign-born blacks are numerous in the New York area where more than one-quarter of African Americans are immigrants, but throughout the rest of the country the black population was almost exclusively native-born.

Demographic Characteristics of Racial Groups

The economic standing of a racial group is affected by its characteristics, especially its age structure and its distribution of families by type. Because of recent immigration, racial groups differ in age structure, strongly influencing educational attainment, earnings, and poverty.

Population pyramids in figure 6-2 show the age distributions of the groups. Native-born whites are oldest, having the thinnest pyramid: one in seven is at retirement age and their median age is 35 years. At the other extreme, the majority of native-born Asians and native-born Hispanics are under age 18. These are the numerous children of recent immigrants. In these groups, only one in twenty-five is

Table 6-2.   Racial/Ethnic Composition of the United States, by Nativity: 1980 to 1990

	Population in 1990 (000)	Percent Distribution of Total Population in 1990	Percent Change 1980–90
White			
Native-born	181,996	73.3%	+6%
Foreign-born	6,207	2.5	−11
Black			
Native-born	27,925	11.3	+10
Foreign-born	1,215	0.5	+65
Asian and Pacific Islander			
Native-born	2,522	1.0	+77
Foreign-born	4,489	1.8	+111
American Indian, Aleut, and Eskimo			
Native-born	1,856	0.7	+30
Foreign-born	29	<0.1	+4
Hispanic			
Native-born	13,905	5.6	+33
Foreign-born	7,722	3.1	+82
Total Population	248,124	100.0%	+9%

SOURCE: U.S. Bureau of the Census, *Census of Population and Housing: 1980 and 1990,* Public Use Microdata Samples.

NOTES: Data for whites, blacks, Asians, and American Indians exclude Hispanics. Data do not separately show the approximately 250,000 persons in each census year who were in the non-Hispanic other races category.

at retirement age. Note that the pyramids for foreign-born Hispanics and Asians are fat in the middle. Immigrants typically come to the United States to find employment or to pursue their educations, so among them, there are neither many children nor many elderly. Unless otherwise noted, data in this chapter for whites, blacks, Asians, and American Indians refer to non-Hispanics.

Figure 6-2. Distribution of the Total Population by Age for Racial Groups and Median Ages: 1990[a]

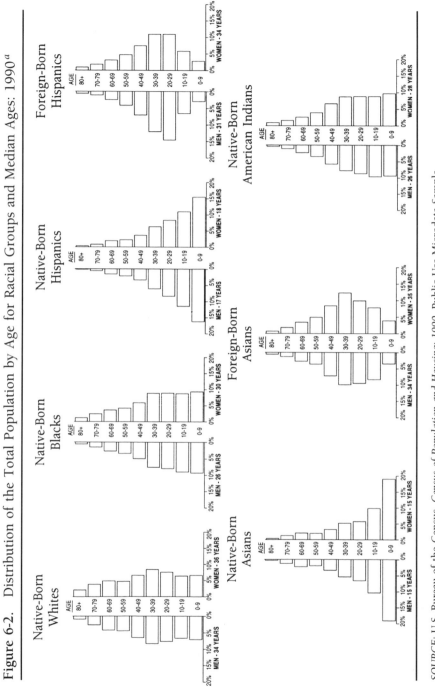

SOURCE: U.S. Bureau of the Census, *Census of Population and Housing: 1990*, Public Use Microdata Sample.

NOTE: Median ages are shown for each group.

[a]Data refer to the non-Hispanic white, black, Asian, and American Indian populations.

Households and Marital Status

Substantial differences distinguish the living arrangements of these racial groups. Husband-wife households are most common among
whites and foreign-born Hispanics, while families headed by women
are most common among blacks.

Figure 6-3 classifies households into seven types. Two types are
very common and account for three-quarters of all households—husband-wife households and families headed by a woman who has no
husband. These household data are influenced by current migration.
In particular, the proportion of households headed by a man with no
wife is unusually high among immigrants, reflecting the pattern for
male kin to live together shortly after arrival in the United States.
Many of these men, after gaining some economic security, will cease
living with their relatives and will marry or bring their wives here,
thereby shifting into husband-wife households. The proportion of

Figure 6-3.   Households, by Type and Race/Ethnicity of Head: 1990 [a]

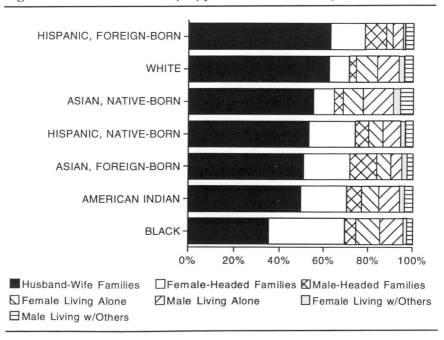

SOURCE: U.S. Bureau of the Census, *Census of Population and Housing: 1990*, Public Use
Microdata Sample.

[a] These data refer to households headed by persons aged 18 to 64 in 1990.

men and women living alone is unusually high among native-born Asians—a result of their high rates of postgraduate education: Asians living alone while enrolled in universities. Blacks differed from all the other racial groups in their dearth of husband-wife households and their large proportion of female-headed families, factors linked to their elevated rates of poverty. *The marital statuses and family living arrangements of blacks now differ substantially not only from those of whites but also from those of other minorities and immigrants.*

Chapter 4 described the trend toward delayed marriage and increased divorce, changes distinguishing baby boomers from their parents. Figure 6-4 summarizes one component of that trend by describing the marital status of the late baby boom cohort in 1990, persons aged 25 to 34. Almost all of the people in this age group who had married or divorced did so during the 1980s.

Among both men and women, blacks and native-born Asians stand out for their very delayed marriages, but the reasons differ. Proportionally more Asians than blacks defer marriage to attend school. In 1990, 20 percent of unmarried native-born Asians in the late baby boom cohort were enrolled in a college or university, but among blacks this was only 12 percent.

The percentage of adults in husband-wife households was unusually high among foreign-born Hispanics and among foreign-born Asian women, reflecting the family reunification provisions of immigration laws. In addition, some of these foreign-born Asian women had married native-born white men who were with the U.S. military.

Marital interruption, indicated by the percent currently divorced or separated from their spouses, was most common among American Indians, but relatively rare among Asians. Foreign-born individuals were much less likely to be divorced or separated than were the native-born, again reflecting current immigration laws.

Fertility

Racial groups differ substantially in their timing and amount of fertility. Several indexes of recent childbearing are shown in table 6-3, which refers to women of the late baby boom cohort in 1990. Since these women were, on average, age 30, they had completed a substantial fraction of their total childbearing, but how much depends upon trends in the birth rates during the 1990s. The upper panel refers to women who reported they were currently married or had been married in the past and then shows the percent childless, the percent with two or more children, and the average number of children born per

Figure 6-4. Marital Status of Late Baby Boom Cohort, by Race: 1990[a]

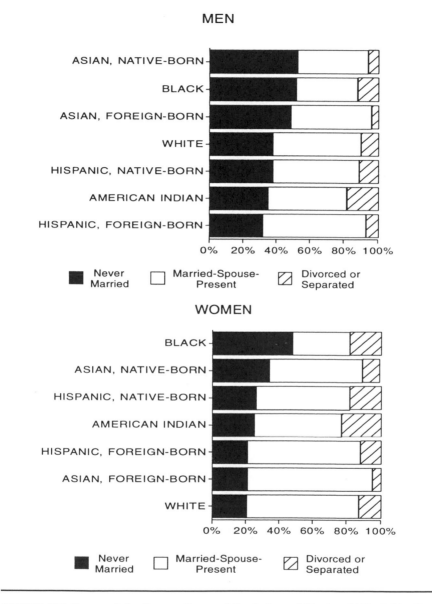

MEN

ASIAN, NATIVE-BORN
BLACK
ASIAN, FOREIGN-BORN
WHITE
HISPANIC, NATIVE-BORN
AMERICAN INDIAN
HISPANIC, FOREIGN-BORN

0%　20%　40%　60%　80%　100%

■ Never Married　□ Married-Spouse-Present　▨ Divorced or Separated

WOMEN

BLACK
ASIAN, NATIVE-BORN
HISPANIC, NATIVE-BORN
AMERICAN INDIAN
HISPANIC, FOREIGN-BORN
ASIAN, FOREIGN-BORN
WHITE

0%　20%　40%　60%　80%　100%

■ Never Married　□ Married-Spouse-Present　▨ Divorced or Separated

SOURCE: U.S. Bureau of the Census, *Census of Population and Housing: 1990,* Public Use Microdata Sample.

[a] These data refer to persons aged 25 to 34 in 1990. The small proportion of young people reporting widowed as their marital status was included with the divorced or separated.

Table 6-3. Fertility of Late Baby Boom Women Aged 25 to 34: 1990

	White	Black	American Indian	Asian Native-Born	Asian Foreign-Born	Hispanic Native-Born	Hispanic Foreign-Born
Ever-Married Women							
Childless	24%	15%	13%	34%	29%	16%	12%
2 or more children	51	60	67	38	42	62	66
Average number of children	1.5	1.8	2.2	1.3	1.4	2.0	2.1
Never-Married Women							
Childless	87%	40%	48%	90%	93%	58%	53%
2 or more children	5	37	30	5	3	25	28
Average number of children	0.2	1.3	1.1	0.2	0.1	0.9	1.0

SOURCE: U.S. Bureau of the Census, *Census of Population and Housing: 1990*, Public Use Microdata Sample.

woman. Hispanic women, both native- and foreign-born, and American Indian women were distinctive for their high fertility and averaged more than two children by age 30, while Asian women were distinctive for their delayed childbearing. The percent childless was about three times as great for native-born Asian women as for foreign-born Hispanics. Married white and married black women had more children than Asian women, but fewer than Hispanics.

Racial differences in childbearing among women who never married are shown in the lower panel. They are substantial, reflecting both cultural values and economic opportunities. Relatively few never-married Asian or white women reported that they had become mothers: only about one in ten did so by age 30. But childbearing before marriage occurred commonly among blacks and American Indians and was more frequent among Hispanics than among whites. A majority of never-married black and American Indian women and just under one-half of Hispanic women at ages 25 to 34 reported that they had children. More than one-quarter of these unmarried women had two or more children. At the other extreme, foreign-born Asian women had very low rates of nonmarital fertility.

Shown below are total fertility rates for 1993. These are the numbers of children a woman would bear in her lifetime if the birth rates of 1993 were to remain unchanged. No distinction was made between the childbearing of native- and foreign-born women (U.S. National Center for Health Statistics 1995a).

Total Fertility Rates, by Race: 1993

Race	Lifetime Births per Woman
Hispanic	3.02
Non-Hispanic Black	2.43
American Indian	2.14
Asian	1.94
Non-Hispanic White	1.76

For a population to obtain zero growth, the total fertility rate, in the long run, must average about 2.15 births per woman. The birth rates of 1993 imply relatively slow growth or eventual declines for Asians, non-Hispanic whites, and American Indians, moderate growth for blacks, but very rapid growth for Hispanics, since the typical woman would average more than three children. Although fertility is a major component of the eventual growth or decline of any population, in the short run the rapid influx of youthful migrants from Latin American and Asia ensures a high growth rate for these populations. These birth rates also reveal that the fertility of two minority groups—Asians and American Indians—are quite close to those of non-Hispanic whites, but black and Hispanic women in the 1990s continue to bear substantially more children than white women. Taking age structure into account, the birth rate of blacks is about 38 percent higher than that of whites, while that of Hispanics is 72 percent greater.

The Living Arrangements of Young Children

Racial differences in marriage and childbearing have major implications for the living arrangements and prosperity of young children. White and native-born Asian children were most likely to live in two-parent families, while black and American Indian children were more likely to live in families headed by a woman who did not have a husband—the result of frequent childbearing by unmarried women in these groups. This is illustrated in figure 6-5 with information pertaining to children under age 18 in 1990. More than 80 percent of white children and 85 percent of native-born Asian children lived in households with both parents, but among blacks the figure was about 40 percent. Indeed, blacks are distinguished from other races since they are the only group in which more children live with mother-only families than with two-parent families. White and native-born Asian children have an advantage over other children since a high proportion of them live with two parents. They are therefore more economically secure and are more likely to get help from two parents as they make that perilous journey from the teen to adult years. (See chapter 4 and McLanahan and Sandefur 1994 for a discussion of how type of family of origin influences children.)

Living in a family headed by a man was most common among foreign-born children. These men are immigrants who are raising their own or their relatives' children in the United States. Presumably, a spouse will join them after their economic status improves or they will return to a spouse living elsewhere.

Mortality

One of the most persistent racial differences involves death rates. For a century, statisticians and analysts of race have commented about the

Figure 6-5.   Living Arrangements of Children Under Age 18: 1990

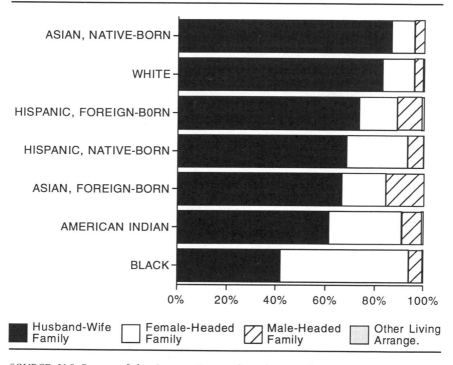

| | Husband-Wife Family | | Female-Headed Family | | Male-Headed Family | | Other Living Arrange. |

SOURCE: U.S. Bureau of the Census, *Census of Population and Housing: 1990*, Public Use Microdata Sample.

unusually high mortality of blacks in the United States (DuBois 1899, p. 150). In the age of Social Darwinism, this was attributed to biological inferiority (Hoffman 1896) but, more recently, the elevated death rates are seen as the consequence of differences in socioeconomic status, in lifestyle, in access to medical services, and in exposure to health risks (U.S. Department of Health and Human Services 1985). Because of widespread interest in this crucial indicator of racial disparity, we examine trends over time, but when doing that we are restricted to blacks and whites. The rapid immigration of Asians and Hispanics now permits the calculation of mortality rates for other races, but there is a major challenge. Death certificates are not filled out by the person dying, but rather by hospital personnel or funeral directors. With some frequency, these people mark white for the race of a decedent who previously classified himself or herself as Asian or American Indian on the self-enumerating census (U.S. National Center for Health Statistics 1995c, p. 69). This misreporting of race on death certificates may substantially lower death rates for Asians and American Indians.

Figure 6-6 shows trends in the most frequently used index of mortality conditions: the total number of years a person could expect to live if they experienced the death rates of a given year. Since women live, on average, seven years longer than men, data are shown separately for the sexes.

Examining the top panel, we see that the life span of men increased from the end of the Depression through the mid-1950s and then, for a period of about fifteen years, there were no further improvements. After this pause, the life span resumed its upward march. Indeed, more than five years were added after 1970 to the life expectancy of white men and, by the early 1990s, they could expect to live more than seventy-three years, the highest life span ever recorded for men in this country. Mortality rates for black men also fell after 1970, but this trend came to its end in the mid-1980s. For a decade now, death rates have been falling slowly for older black men but rising among young men aged 15 to 34, an increase attributable to more deaths by violence and AIDS. The net outcome is a decade-long stagnation in the life span of African American men while that of white men rose 1.5 years.

The gray area in figure 6-6 shows the black-white gap and presents pessimistic news. We will see a similarly pessimistic pattern in many of the upcoming figures comparing recent trends in the status of blacks and whites. With regard to the length of life, there is little evidence of any improvement for African Americans vis-à-vis whites in the last quarter-century.

The actual gap in life span of men was at a minimum around 1960 and widened thereafter, especially in the 1980s. It is not so much that death rates for black men went up, but rather that death rates for white men fell moderately. White men have a life span eight years longer than black men, just about the same gap as in 1950.

Between 1940 and 1970, racial change was much the same among women as among men: mortality rates fell for both races but slightly faster among black women, leading to a modest diminution of the black-white gap. But the racial gap among women closed very little in the last twenty years. Unlike the situation among black men, the death rates of black women fell in the 1980s, and their life span reached a record high of 74.1 years in 1994. For white women, there was also a record high: 79.6 years.

The death rate most closely examined as the key index of the na-

Figure 6-6. Expectation of Life at Birth for Blacks and Whites: 1940 to 1994

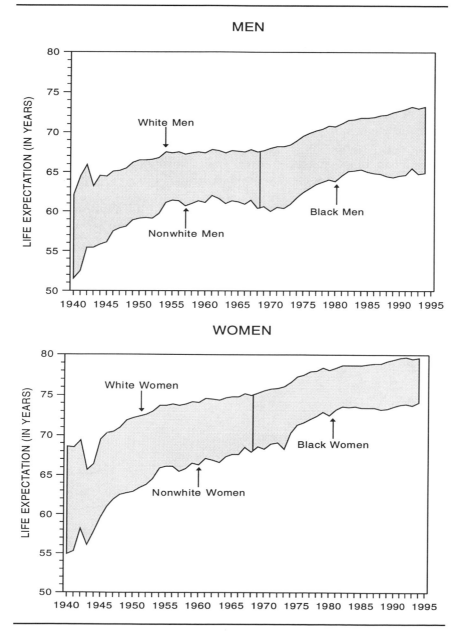

SOURCES: U.S. National Center for Health Statistics, *Vital Statistics of the United States, 1980,* Vol. II, Part A, table 6.5; *Monthly Vital Statistics Report,* Vol. 43, No. 13, table 7.

NOTE: Data for years prior to 1970 refer to nonwhites and whites.

tion's health is the infant mortality rate, or deaths of infants under age 1 per 1,000 births occurring in a year. Many recent public health efforts have been directed toward reducing infant mortality, and new developments in neonatal care allow the healthy survival of infants who would have died shortly after birth just a score of years ago. In addition, the educational attainment of both black and white mothers has steadily risen. These changes reduced mortality and so the infant death rate has steadily declined (see figure 6-7). By the early 1990s, record low proportions of black and white babies were dying before their first birthdays. But the black-white gap in infant mortality was just as large in the early 1990s as it had been in the early 1970s. Although the death rates are much lower, black infants continue to die during their first year of life at a rate more than double that of white babies.

Figure 6-7. Infant Mortality Rates for Black and Whites: 1940 to 1992

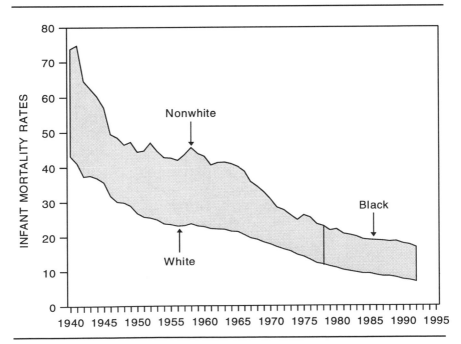

SOURCES: U.S. National Center for Health Statistics, 1984, *Vital Statistics of the United States: 1980, Vol. II Mortality,* Part A, table 2-1; *Monthly Vital Statistics Reports,* Vol. 43, No. 6 (Supplement) (December 8, 1994), table 24.

NOTE: Data for years prior to 1975 refer to nonwhites. Data for years prior to 1980 refer to imputed race of child. Data for later years refer to reported race of mother.

What about the mortality rates of other races in the United States? Innovative calculations at the National Center for Health Statistics reveal that blacks have death rates much higher than those of whites; American Indians have death rates close to those of whites; while Asians have the lowest death rates. The numbers shown below compare death rates in 1992 adjusted for differences in age composition. Mortality rates of whites are indexed at 100 percent, but no distinction is made between the native- and foreign-born (U.S. National Center for Health Statistics 1995c, table 1). Nor is it possible to accurately ascertain death rates for the heterogeneous Hispanic population. The rates below should be interpreted cautiously since the person indicating the race on the death record did not identify the person's race in the census.

Controlling for age, the risk of dying for blacks in 1992 was about 60 percent greater than for whites, while the risk of mortality for Asians was about 40 percent less than for whites. There are great racial disparities in mortality in the United States: age-standardized death rates of blacks are three times those of Asians.

Relative Death Rates, by Race: 1992

	Men	Women
Blacks	165%	158%
Whites	100	100
American Indians	93	95
Asians	59	61

How does the life span in the United States compare to other nations? Despite the investment of a large share of our gross domestic product in healthcare, the United States has rather high death rates compared to similarly developed economies. The expectation of life at birth and the infant mortality rate are summary indicators. Table 6-4 shows these measures for an array of countries using 1991 data. Because whites and blacks differ so greatly in their mortality rates, we distinguish these races in the United States.

Death rates are low in the United States compared to those in Eastern Europe, Russia, and developing countries throughout the world, but they are higher than in the prosperous Western European countries, Canada, and the developed countries of Asia. The life span

Table 6-4.   Expectation of Life at Birth and Infant Mortality Rates, United States and Fourteen Countries: 1991

	Expectation of Life at Birth (years)	Infant Mortality Rate (deaths per 1,000 births)
Japan	79.2	4.4
Switzerland	79.1	4.7
Italy	78.1	6.0
Sweden	77.8	5.9
France	77.8	6.1
Canada	77.5	7.2
Australia	77.0	7.9
United Kingdom	76.5	7.2
United States: Whites	76.3	7.3
Cuba	75.6	11.9
China-Taiwan	74.6	5.9
Jamaica	73.6	18.3
Poland	72.9	12.4
Mexico	72.2	29.3
Russia (former Soviet Union)	69.8	22.7
United States: Blacks	69.3	17.6

SOURCES: U.S. National Center for Health Statistics, 1993, *Monthly Vital Statistics Reports,* Vol. 42, No. 2 (Supplement) (August 31, 1993); U.S. Bureau of the Census, 1992, *Statistical Abstract of the United States: 1992,* table 1361.

in Japan is about three years longer than for whites in the United States; in Scandinavia and several Western European countries, it is more than one year longer. The infant mortality rate of whites in the United States compares favorably to those of some Western European nations, but it is higher than those for Japan and Taiwan. Mortality rates for blacks in the United States are much higher than those found in most economically developed countries.

Educational Attainment and School Enrollment

The restructuring of the economy places great emphasis upon educational attainment and the acquisition of those specialized skills now highly valued by employers. In the 1980s, the only major groups to experience real improvements in earnings were those with college educations (see table 3-4).

Changes in educational attainment are determined by many factors. On the supply side, numerous decisions by governments and private organizations influence how easy or how difficult it is for young persons to complete high school or get a college degree. A major story of the first half of this century was the spread of secondary schools across the nation (Duncan 1968). Only one American in six reaching their twenties in 1910 completed high school; that figure is above 80 percent today (Folger and Nam 1967, table V-5; Mare 1995, fig. 4.8). This remarkable increase resulted from the investments that states made in the development of high schools, by population movement to cities where high schools were common, and by the construction of roads in rural areas allowing farm children to easily get to secondary schools.

After World War II, the federal and state governments began investing heavily in postsecondary schools. The G.I. Bill, with the government paying college tuition, was one boost. And then the Russian's launching Sputnik in 1957 prompted more investments in higher education. Many new state colleges were created, and existing ones were expanded or upgraded from normal schools to full-fledged universities. At the same time, a system of community colleges was established, one that now extends to almost all counties and allows high school graduates to continue their schooling even if they did not complete college preparatory sequences. But in the 1980s, college costs went up much faster than inflation, making it more difficult for many students to get advanced degrees and encumbering many college graduates with substantial debt. Between 1980 and 1993, the cost of tuition, room, and board went up 37 percent faster than inflation at public colleges; 62 percent faster at private ones (U.S. Department of Education 1995, table 306).

Differences among racial groups in their attainments result in part from decisions made about the supply of education. Some racial or ethnic groups have had more access to education than others. Until 1954, the Constitution mandated equal if separate schools for black children, but schools for African Americans in the South were by no means equal. One of the unforeseen consequences of the litigation efforts to racially integrate schools after World War II was a school-building boom in the South as states sought to comply with the *Plessy* v. *Ferguson* (1896) ruling. Northern states never had Jim Crow laws, but their public schools may have been quite inhospitable to those children of Southern and Eastern European immigrants who arrived around the turn of the century (Perlmann 1988). The efforts in San Francisco to segregate Japanese children from whites in 1907 (Takaki 1989) and the rapid emergence of the segregation of black children in northern public schools after World War I strongly implies that school board policies in the North and West determined which groups would get what types and what amounts of education. Often it was the racial minorities who lost out in these allocations.

While the civil rights movement of the 1960s focused upon equal opportunities for blacks, it set the stage for subsequent decisions that broadened educational opportunities for other minorities. Sixteen years after *Brown*, the Supreme Court declared that the de jure segregation of Mexican students from whites in Texas was unconstitutional (*Cisneros v. Corpus Christi Independent School District* 1970) and then, in a decision that had great impact for the children of newly arriving immigrants, the Supreme Court unanimously ruled it a violation of civil rights to offer English-only instruction if students do not understand English (*Lau v. Nichols* 1974). Immigrants arriving from Italy, Poland, or Russia at the turn of the century had to learn English on their own in order to attend public school, but now, until children learn English, public schools are constitutionally obliged to teach in a language the children understand.

In addition to supply-side factors, children—and their parents— make decisions determining how many years of schooling they will complete. Characteristics of families of origin, especially the educational attainment of parents and the number of siblings, influence whether children drop out early or get advanced degrees. Type of family also has an effect since, net of other factors such as the family's income, children who grow up with two parents are more likely to finish secondary school than those raised by a single parent (Mare 1995, figure 4.14; McLanahan and Sandefur 1994, chap. 1).

Characteristics of children themselves also influence attainment. Not surprisingly, those scoring highly on tests of intellectual skills typically stay enrolled longer than those who score less well. Also, some children find it psychologically gratifying to accomplish the intellectual tasks teachers set before them and view the school milieu as pleasant and stimulating while others find schooling and all it involves extreme drudgery, akin to punishment.

What has happened to black-white differences in enrollment and attainment since the civil rights decade? Figure 6-8 shows the percentage of young people aged 18 to 24 who were high school graduates,

Figure 6-8.   Percentage of High School Graduates Aged 18 to 24, and Ratio of Black to White Graduates: 1968 to 1992 (three-year moving average)

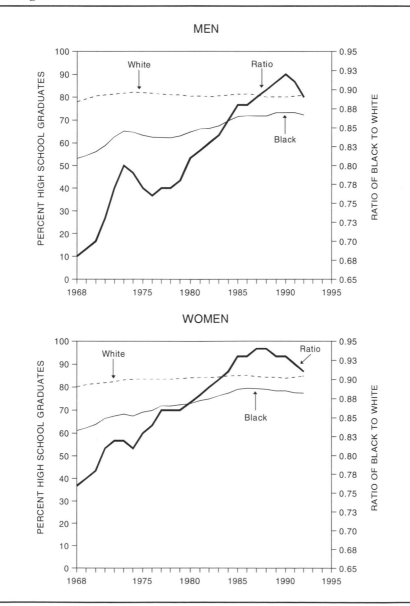

MEN

WOMEN

SOURCE: U.S. Bureau of the Census, 1994, *Current Population Reports,* Series 20, No. 479, table A4.

using information from the Census Bureau's annual October survey. This includes people who earned diplomas after twelve years of enrollment, as well as those with General Educational Development certificates (GEDs). In recent years, about one-sixth of all high school graduates obtained a GED (U.S. Department of Education 1995, tables 99 and 100). Since gender differences are important, data are shown separately for men and women. In each panel, the heavy line reports the ratio of the black proportion who graduated to that of whites.

Unlike the trend for life span and infant mortality, there are unambiguous signs of racial progress here as the black-white gap in high school attainment decreased. In the late 1960s, the number of blacks getting high school diplomas was about 70 percent that of whites, but by the early 1990s it had risen above 90 percent. Parity has not been reached, but the long-term trend toward a black-white convergence in high school education continued into the 1980s. The remaining racial gap is smaller among women than among men. It is disturbing, however, that the trend toward racial convergence did not continue into the 1990s.

Strikingly different conclusions about trends in attainment are drawn from an examination of college enrollment. Figure 6-9 reports the percentage of high school graduates aged 18 to 24 enrolled in college at the time of the October surveys. The upper panel reports that enrollment was at a record high for white men in the late 1960s when college offered an attractive alternative to military service (with its risk of a trip to Vietnam). After declining for some years, the enrollment rate of white men began to climb once again in the 1980s, but it has yet to reach the elevated levels of the Vietnam era. For young black men, there has been little fluctuation since the late 1960s. Consistently, about 30 percent of black high school graduates aged 18 to 24 were enrolled in college classes. In the early 1970s, there was almost a racial parity in college enrollment, but this did not last for long. There was no fall-off in the college enrollment of black men in the 1980s, but the enrollment rates of white men went up, leading to a larger racial gap as indicated by the declining ratio of black to white enrollment. On this important indicator, black men fell further behind white men in the 1980s.

Among women, there is a trend toward more college enrollment. Briefly, in the late 1970s, the percentage of high school graduates enrolled in college was higher for black women than for white women, but in subsequent years the enrollment rates of white women went up more rapidly, so the traditional disadvantage of blacks on this indica-

Figure 6-9. Percentage of High School Graduates Aged 18 to 24 Enrolled in College: 1968 to 1992 (three-year moving average)

SOURCE: U.S. Bureau of the Census, 1994, *Current Population Reports*, series 20, no. 479, table A4.

tor reappeared. In the early 1990s, just as in the late 1960s, the proportion of black women high school graduates attending college was 80 percent that of white women.

The trend toward a racial convergence at the high school level is the result of the many major national efforts stressing the need for such training and the many programs that local schools have established to keep those students in school who in previous decades would have dropped out, such as pregnant teenagers, those with learning disabilities, those with limited English abilities, or those charged with a crime. The patterns of college enrollment are much more difficult to understand. For a very brief period in the early 1970s, the affirmative action programs of colleges led to a situation in which the enrollment rates of young blacks and whites were similar. Because of changes in the economy and the greater economic penalty paid for dropping out early, you might expect that record high proportions of blacks and whites—and similar proportions—would now be in college classrooms, but the racial gap in college enrollment widened after 1980.

Robert Hauser and Douglas Anderson sought to determine why. Their analyses dismissed many single-factor explanations, such as declines in the income of black families, falling test scores on the part of black students, decreases in the personnel needs of the armed forces, or decreases in the intellectual skills of high school graduates. Their cautious conclusions are that the rising costs of attending college have discouraged enrollment, and that market forces drove universities to target their financial aid to middle-income students rather than to students from impoverished backgrounds. More so than potential white students, black students need extensive financial support, but both college and federal programs are now directed toward students from middle-income families. As the cost of college increases much more rapidly than inflation, colleges wish to maintain their enrollments, and the most effective way to disperse limited financial support is to spread it across many students who need modest amounts rather than to a few students who need great amounts (Hauser 1987, 1989; Hauser and Anderson 1991). Hence, changes in the cost of college and in federal support for college students may limit the enrollment of students—both black and white—who come from low-income families. High school education is usually tuition-free, and here the trend is toward racial convergence, but college entails substantial out-of-pocket costs, so there is no racial convergence (Sutterlin and Kominski 1994).

Racially, we are a much more heterogeneous country than in 1960. What about educational trends for all racial minorities? These are easy to summarize. There is a consistent ranking of groups, one that has persisted for a long time. Asians, especially native-born Asians, remain in school the longest and are most overrepresented among those getting college and professional degrees. Whites lag somewhat behind Asians but outrank blacks, American Indians, and Hispanics. Indeed, in almost all rankings, immigrant Hispanics fall at the bottom; native-born Asians at the top.

Current differences and trends throughout this century are succinctly summarized in figure 6-10. Classifying individuals by both birth cohort and race, this figure shows the percentage who completed twelve years of schooling and the percentage with bachelor's degrees. There is a trend toward much greater attainment for all groups, but Asians and whites have consistently held an advantage over other races. Among those born in the late 1960s, more than 90 percent of Asians and whites reported at least twelve years of schooling; among blacks, American Indians, and native-born Hispanics, it was about 75 percent.

Turning to information in the lower panel about those who earned those college degrees that now seem so crucial for economic success, we observe the tremendous advantage that Asians have over whites and, in turn, the advantage whites have over blacks, Indians, and Hispanics. More than 40 percent of the Asians from the late baby boom cohorts (people aged 25 to 29 in 1990) had bachelor's degrees compared to just 5 percent for American Indians. The proportion of college graduates will increase as some of the people in this birth cohort earn degrees at older ages, but the racial disparities are sure to be large when these individuals are again enumerated in the census of 2000 (at ages 35 to 39). Young Asians and whites are now making much greater investments in their educations than other groups.

In their teens and early twenties, people decide about their educations, their careers, and their families—decisions that strongly influence their lifetime social and economic status. Figure 6-11 considers the seven racial groups and focuses on men and women from Generation X, those aged 18 to 24 in 1990. They are classified into five educational categories. First, there are those without high school diplomas who are not enrolled, a group commonly called dropouts, although some of them will eventually earn GEDs. Second, there are persons without high school diplomas who are still enrolled. Most of them are termed grade-retarded, but many will eventually receive

Figure 6-10.   Percentage of Persons Completing at Least 12 Years of School or at Least a Bachelor's Degree, by Race and Year of Birth

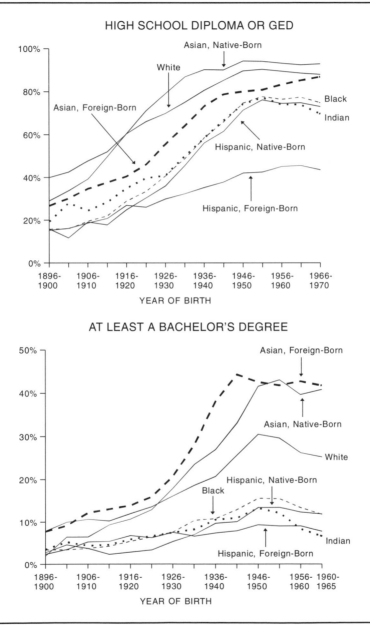

SOURCE: Mare 1995, figures 4-8 and 4-9.

Figure 6-11. Information About Attainment and Enrollment for Men and Women Aged 18 to 24, Classified by Race: 1990

SOURCE: U.S. Bureau of the Census, *Census of Population and Housing: 1990*, Public Use Microdata Sample.

diplomas. Then there are those with high school degrees, classified by whether or not they were enrolled in college in April 1990. Finally, there are those who have their bachelor's degree.

Racial differences are strikingly large. More than 60 percent of Asian men, whether born in the United States or abroad, had college degrees or were attending college. Among whites this proportion was about 55 percent. This dropped off to 30 percent for Hispanics and black women. Among American Indians and black men, less than 25 percent were either college students or college degree–holders, or, less than half the percentage among Asians. This very large difference portends equally large racial differences in earnings and occupational achievement well into the twenty-first century.

Figure 6-11 also shows an emerging gender gap in attainment, one that strongly favors women. In all seven groups, the percentage with college degrees was larger among women than among men, while men were correspondingly overrepresented in the high school dropout category. Young women are now investing more in their educations than young men are, a gender difference that may dampen the marriage rate. College-educated women will often be economically independent, perhaps making them reluctant to marry men with limited earnings prospects. This gender gap in attainment is smallest among Asians but largest among blacks (McLanahan and Casper 1995, pp. 38–42).

Employment and Earnings

President Roosevelt's Executive Order 8802 in 1941 banned racial discrimination in employment, although there were no strong enforcement mechanisms. Civil rights activists in Congress and President Truman sought to extend this temporary measure after World War II but were unsuccessful, so employers came under no federal pressure if they denied jobs to blacks. It is accurate to describe the employment situation in the early 1960s as basically a Jim Crow system. Many African Americans were employed, but they seldom worked side-by-side with whites in the same job classifications getting the same pay. The year 1964 was a true turning point, since the Civil Rights Act with its Title VII triggered developments that gradually changed employment practices as well as the nation's views about keeping blacks and women out of the better jobs. The civil rights law established the Equal Employment Opportunity Commission (EEOC), and all employers with one hundred or more workers had to report the number of minorities and women in every job classification. In 1965, President Johnson's Executive Order 11246 established the Office of Federal Contract Compliance. It rigorously enforced the requirement that firms doing business with the federal government not discriminate in employment. Indeed, their efforts were so strong that many assumed that the federal government was insisting upon specific employment quotas for minorities and later for women. In the late 1960s, the Department of Justice began litigation to show employers and unions that they would be financially penalized if they kept their staff lily-white or restricted blacks to menial jobs. Under President Nixon, the Secretary of Labor and the Attorney General proudly heralded an innovative and encompassing "Philadelphia Plan" that would bring blacks into the skilled building-trades unions through the use of quotas, thereby opening up those high-paying construction jobs traditionally reserved for white men and their sons. Federal courts upheld this procedure to overcome past discrimination (*Contractors Association of Eastern Pennsylvania* v. *Secretary of Labor* 1971). Civil rights groups were also highly successful in getting federal courts to overturn those seemingly equitable practices that had the latent effect of denying employment to blacks. For instance, in *Griggs* v. *Duke Power* (1971) the Supreme Court ruled that job candidates could be screened only on criteria directly pertinent to the specific jobs they sought, thereby outlawing the capricious or unfair use of testing. In 1972, Congress greatly strengthened the powers of the EEOC, allowing them to establish and enforce employment goals if a firm's workforce differed greatly in racial composition from that of the eligible pool of qualified workers. And successful litigation targeted at American Telephone and Telegraph, Bethlehem Steel, and U.S. Steel in the early 1970s sent the message to employers that it would be very costly if they continued with those recruitment and promotion policies that reserved the most prestigious and highest-paying jobs for white men (Rose 1994).

By the 1970s, federal laws, pressures from the EEOC, and court decisions hastened the breakdown of employment segregation on the basis of gender or race. At the same time, the racial views of whites shifted toward accepting the idea that it was unfair and even un-American to use skin color or gender as the sole criterion for determining who got a specific job, a pay raise, or a promotion. And soon enough there were reports of great success. By the mid-1970s, Freeman (1976) described a new market for college-educated black men, implying that their chances of getting good jobs and high incomes were just about as great as those of similarly educated white men, sometimes even better than those of white men.

Have we now reached a point where racial differences in employment and earnings are quite small or is the situation today much like it was several decades ago? This section briefly examines differences in employment and labor supply and then moves on to the important issue of earnings, focusing, when appropriate, upon the net effects of race as best we can measure them.

Unemployment Rates

One of the most widely used economic indicators is the unemployment rate, a number reported by newspapers every month for both blacks and whites. This indicates the percentage of men and women in the labor force who searched for a job within the last month but did not find one. It is also one of the few indicators we can trace over a long span. Here the news is quite discouraging. The black-white gap in unemployment was at least as large in 1995 as in 1970; indeed, among women it is even larger now than in the past.

Figure 6-12 refers to the average annual unemployment rate for black and white men and women aged 20 and over. At first glance, the trend lines in figure 6-12 look confusing since unemployment rates go up sharply in recessions (indicated by the shaded vertical stripes) and decline as the business cycle turns up. The heavy dark line shows the ratio of the black unemployment rate to that of whites. For both genders, there were declines in this ratio in the 1960s, a change some might attribute to the beneficial effects of the Civil Rights Act and the economic expansion of that era. But with the emergence of industrial restructuring in the next decade, the unemployment rates of African Americans went up faster than those of whites. Throughout the prosperous 1980s, black men and women had unemployment rates more than double those of whites. If unemployment is the summary indictor, there is no evidence of an improvement in the relative status of either black men or women since the civil rights revolution.

Many factors determine whether a person gets a job. Education is among the most important since the economic trends now reshaping the country provide job opportunities for highly trained persons but less rewarding opportunities for those with little schooling. Having a physical disability or being unable to speak English also dampens the likelihood that an employer will put an applicant on the payroll. Married men typically are more likely to be employed than unmarried

Figure 6-12. Unemployment Rates of White and Black Men and Women Aged 20 and Over, and Ratio of Black to White Rates: 1960 to 1995

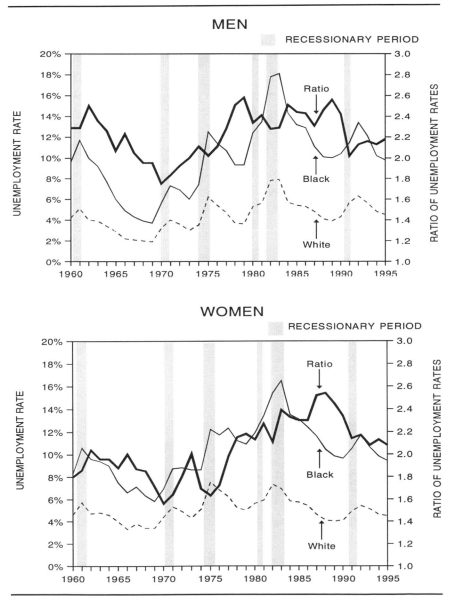

SOURCE: Council of Economic Advisors 1996, table B-41.

NOTE: Unemployment rates for years prior to 1972 refer to whites and nonwhites.

men but, among women, marital status sometimes has the opposite effect. Regional differences in unemployment persist: unemployment rates are still lower in the South than in the Midwest and Northeast. When they are taken into account, will we find that there are racial differences or will we find no net effect of race?

Figure 6-13 answers this query. Considering those aged 25 to 54 in the labor force in 1980 and 1990, we determined the odds that native-born, non-Hispanic whites were unemployed. Then we calculated the odds of unemployment for each of the six other racial groups, factoring in place of residence, educational attainment, marital status, ability to speak English well, disabilities, and—for women—their number of children. Figure 6-13 shows the odds of unemployment for each racial

Figure 6-13. Odds of Unemployment for Racial Minorities Relative to Those of Native-Born Whites, Net of Other Factors, for Labor Force Participants Aged 25 to 54: 1980 and 1990

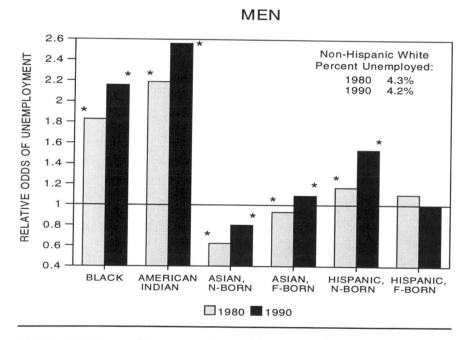

SOURCE: U.S. Bureau of the Census, *Census of Population and Housing: 1980 and 1990,* Public Use Microdata Samples.

NOTES: The bars show the net odds of unemployment for a racial group compared to those of native-born, non-Hispanic whites. These are estimated effects of race net of region, metropolitan residence, age, educational attainment, reported ability to speak group relative to the odds for whites. The top panel shows a relative odds ratio of 1.8 for black men in 1980 and 2.2 in 1990. This means that the odds of a black man being unemployed in 1980 were, net of other factors, 1.8 times those of a white man. The employment situation for black men deteriorated in that decade: the relative odds ratio went up to 2.2 in 1990. Native-born Asian men, on the other hand, were significantly less likely to be unemployed than white men. The most outstanding finding in the upper panel is the clear indication that black and American Indian men were at an unusually high risk of joblessness. Furthermore, their status vis-à-vis that of white men deteriorated in the 1980s. This deterioration also occurred among native-born Hispanic men. The cost of membership in these minority groups in terms of joblessness increased during the 1980s.

Foreign-born Hispanic men did not differ significantly from white

Figure 6-13　(continued)

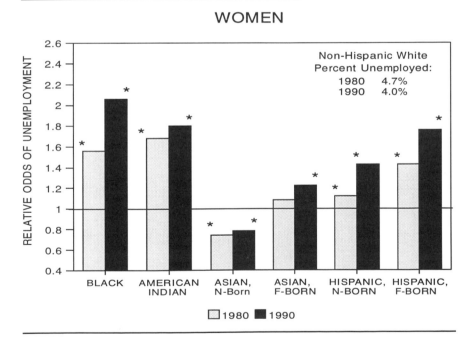

English, reported presence of a work disability, and marital status. For women, number of children ever born was also included as a control variable.

*Difference in probability of unemployment from that of native-born, non-Hispanic whites is significant at .01 level.

men at either date. This undoubtedly is the outcome of selective immigration from Mexico and Latin America of men who know that they can find jobs in the United States or return home if they have no success in the job market here. It is much easier to move from Mexico to the United States than to migrate from Asia, so the nativity effects on unemployment differ for Asians and Hispanics.

The net effects of race upon unemployment are similar for women, with the exception of Hispanic women immigrating to the United States. Native-born Asian women had the lowest rates of unemployment—significantly lower than those of whites—while black and American Indian women had the highest. Among women, as among men, racial disparities generally increased in the 1980s. In 1980, for example, the odds of unemployment for black women were 1.5 those of white women, but ten years later they went up to 2.1. This change was in the same direction for all the other racial minorities. Recall that this model takes differences in education and marital status into account. The 1980s were not good years for minorities in the U.S. labor market since all groups except Asians fell further behind native-born whites in terms of unemployment.

Hours of Employment

Unemployment rates are crucial indicators of a group's standing in the labor market. However, there is another index of labor supply—hours of employment, which is closely linked to prosperity. In many circumstances, an individual can augment his or her total earnings by working extra hours, even if it means taking a second job at a fast-food restaurant with a moderate pay rate. Do racial groups work about the same amount of time or are there great differences in labor supply?

The figures shown below report the average hours of employment in 1989 for persons aged 25 to 54 who worked for pay at some point in that year. We show the hours of work for native-born, non-Hispanic white men (2,172) and women (1,683) and then whether the other groups, on average, worked more or fewer hours. Working forty hours every week for fifty weeks generates two thousand hours of employment.

Substantial differences in hours of employment distinguish these groups, but the magnitude and direction of the difference depends upon the gender. Among men, non-Hispanic whites work the most hours, with Asian men close behind. But black, foreign-born Hispanic,

Average Hours of Employment in 1989 for Persons Aged 25 to 54
Working at Some Point in That Year

	Men	Women
Whites	2,172	1,683
Difference from Whites		
Blacks	−273	+30
American Indians	−347	−97
Native-born Asians	−66	+122
Foreign-born Asians	−126	+87
Native-born Hispanics	−206	−27
Foreign-born Hispanics	−265	−96

and American Indian men typically spend six or seven fewer hours at work each week than white men. Among women, Asians and blacks put in more time on the job than do white women. Hispanic and American Indian women are at the bottom of that list of hours of employment. Racial differences in hours of work are much smaller among women than among men.

Why do some groups work more hours than others? Many characteristics may help to account for the large discrepancies shown above. In this era of technological sophistication, the highly educated presumably have greater employment opportunities than those lacking training, and each hour they spend on the job will be much more highly rewarded. There are also group differences in marital status, number of children, and ability to speak English. If we consider the many factors influencing employment, will we find that the net racial difference in hours of work is small? Did racial differences decrease in the 1980s as we might expect if race became a less significant determinant in who gets a job?

Figure 6-14 presents information about the net impact of race upon hours of employment. For each group and for both sexes, we show the net difference in yearly hours attributable specifically to race. For example, the upper panel shows that, independent of the other factors that distinguish black men from white men, the net effect of race was a reduction of 201 hours of employment in 1989, or four hours per week. In 1979, it was 210 hours of work.

Among men, again it was costly to be a member of a minority race, least costly for Asians, and most costly for blacks and American

Indians. And the cost hardly changed in the 1980s (see also Darity, Guilkey, and Winfrey 1995).

The findings are very different among women since, in 1979, all minority women worked more hours on average than white women who had similar characteristics. In 1989, women who were black, Asian, or native-born Hispanic still spent more time on the job than white women, while American Indians were the only women falling behind whites. However, by 1989, white women had closed the gap somewhat.

It is a challenge to explain these group differences in employment.

Figure 6-14.   Difference Between Hours Worked by Racial Minorities and Native-Born, Non-Hispanic Whites Aged 25 to 54, Net of Factors Influencing Employment: 1979 and 1989

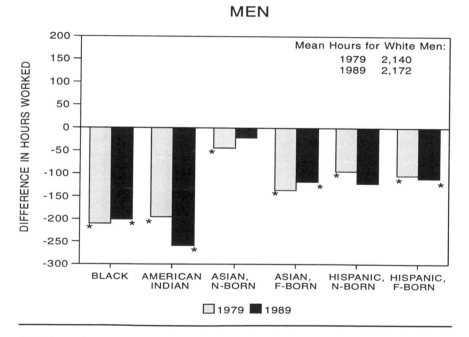

SOURCE: U.S. Bureau of the Census, *Census of Population and Housing: 1980 and 1990,* Public Use Microdata Samples.

NOTES: These data refer to persons who were employed at some point in 1979 or 1989. The bars show the net difference in hours of employment from those of native-born, non-Hispanic whites. These are estimated effects of race upon hours of employment net of

It is possible that employers still have a preference for whites, so that when extra hours are assigned or when hiring is done for part-time workers, men with white skins are chosen first. The effects of racially discriminatory practices might explain why black men work many fewer hours than white men but, if this explanation is valid, there is an important interaction with sex, since black women work more hours than do comparable white women. It is also possible that some groups are much more effectively networked into opportunities for additional hours of employment than others, perhaps through access to jobs in ethnic restaurants or in garment shops managed by members of their same ethnic group.

Figure 6-14 (continued)

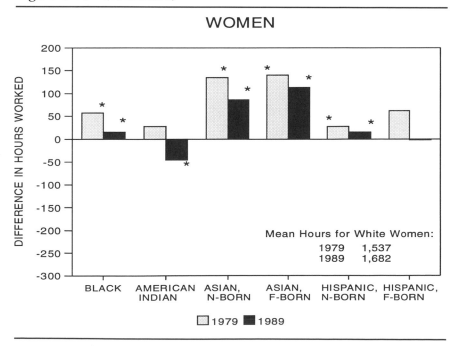

region, metropolitan residence, age, educational attainment, reported ability to speak English, reported presence of a work disability, and marital status. For women, number of children ever born was also included as a control variable.

*Difference in hours worked from those of whites is significant at the 0.01 level.

Earnings

One of the most important stories of racial change in the decades following 1940 was the increase in the earnings of black men: they moved much closer to those of white men. The definitive investigation, conducted by James Smith and Finis Welch (1986, 1989) may be summarized in just five numbers.

Census Year	Weekly Earnings of Black Men as a Percentage of Those of White Men
1940	43%
1950	55
1960	58
1970	64
1980	73

Many factors account for this progress, including the migration of blacks from the rural South to the industrialized North, the increasing willingness of employers to hire and promote blacks, and the beneficial effects of the equal employment and affirmative action policies of the 1960s. Smith and Welch attribute much of the gain to improvements in the education of black men, both the replacement of older, less educated birth cohorts with younger, more educated black men and the upgrading of schools in the South as that region began to comply first with the Supreme Court's *Plessy* ruling and later with *Brown.* (See also Margo 1990.)

What has happened recently? The trend toward a black-white convergence in earnings ceased in the mid-1970s as industrial restructuring took hold. Figure 6-15 shows the median annual earnings of black and white men and women who worked full-time from 1967 to the present. The heavy line in each panel reports the ratio of black to white earnings with the analysis restricted to full-time employees.

Earnings for men rose until the mid-1970s. A high-water mark was reached when black men earned three-quarters as much as white men. But the earnings of full-time men gradually declined after the 1970s such that, by the early 1990s, both black and white men had median earnings 10 to 15 percent less than a score of years earlier. Keep in mind that the male labor force was more extensively educated

Figure 6-15. Median Annual Earnings of Full-Time, Year-Round Black and White Workers, and Ratio of Median Earnings: 1967 to 1993

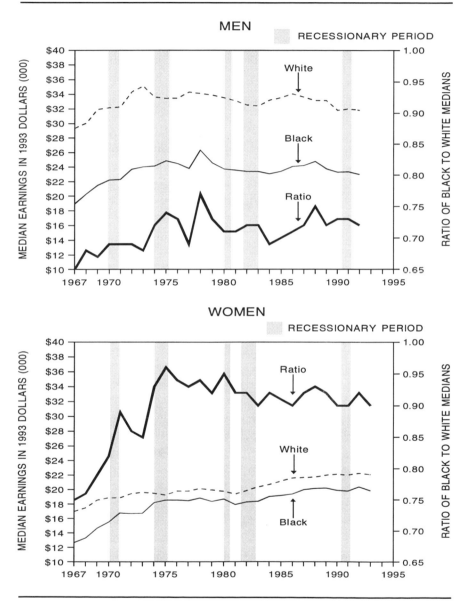

SOURCE: U.S. Bureau of the Census, 1993, *Current Population Reports,* series P-60, no. 184, table B-17.

in the 1990s than in the 1970s, so the decline in earnings is surprising and important. From the mid-1970s to the present, the median earnings of black men have been about three-quarters those of white men, and the thirty-five-year trend of earnings going up more rapidly for black men than for white men stopped.

Through the mid-1970s, the earnings of black women employed full-time also went up more rapidly than those of white women but, since then, there have been no further gains for black women vis-à-vis white women. Thus, the long-run trends are much the same as among men. Two important gender differences stand out in figure 6-15. First, the earnings of full-time women workers—both black and white—continued their long increase, reaching record-high levels in

Figure 6-16.   Earnings of Racial Minorities as Percentage of Those of Whites, Net of Characteristics: 1979 and 1989

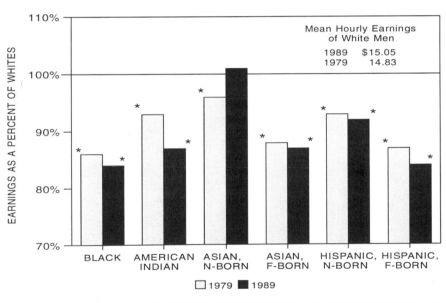

SOURCE: U.S. Bureau of the Census, *Census of Population and Housing: 1980 and 1990*, Public Use Microdata Samples.

NOTES: These bars show the effect upon earnings of membership in a racial group net of region, metropolitan residence, age, educational attainment, reported ability to speak English, reported presence of a work disability, and marital status. For women, number of children ever born was also included as a control variable. The dependent variable in these

1992. The combination of falling earnings among men and rising
earnings for women gradually narrowed the gender gap. Second, the
racial gap is much smaller among women than among men since, for
several decades, black women working full-time have earned about 92
percent as much as white women.

What about the status of other racial minorities in 1990? Are
blacks the only group to lag behind whites on this important economic indicator? Because the census includes many questions about
social and demographic characteristics, we can control for those important factors that determine whether a person's paycheck is fat or
thin, such as place of residence, education, ability to speak English,
work disability, marital status, and, for women, fertility. Taking all of

Figure 6-16   (continued)

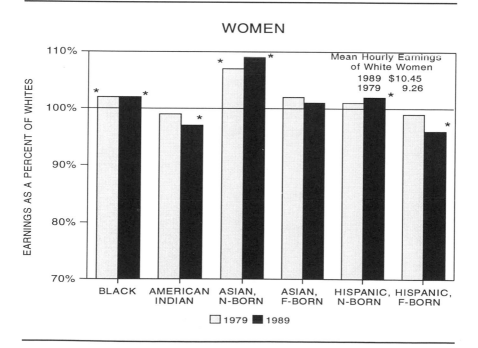

models was the log of reported hourly earnings. Data are restricted to those who worked
in the year prior to the census and reported positive earnings. Hourly earnings are shown
in 1993 dollars.

*The difference between the hourly earnings of this group and those of native-born, non-
Hispanic whites is significant at the .01 level.

these into account and controlling for racial differences in labor supply by focusing upon the hourly earnings of those who worked, figure 6-16 shows the net effects of race on earnings. It reports the earnings of each minority as a percentage of whites' earnings after all other racial differences are controlled.

Among men, it was costly to be a minority. Each minority's earnings fell behind those of white men in both years, except for native-born Asian men. Net of other factors, black and foreign-born Hispanic men earned just 84 percent as much as white men; American Indians and foreign-born Asians, 87 percent as much. Minority men are at a disadvantage in the competition for earnings, and it is not only blacks who experience this shortfall: Hispanics and American Indians do also. Furthermore, the net costs to minority men increased a bit in the 1980s since their earnings—except those of native-born Asians—fell further behind those of white men. The 1980s were not good years for minority men in terms of either unemployment or earnings. In fact, the net cost of being black, Hispanic, or American Indian increased.

But before we draw overarching conclusions about the deleterious consequences of race, we should examine the earnings of women. The census of 1990 found that once other key determinants of earnings were taken into account, black and native-born Hispanic and Asian women earned a bit more than white women. American Indian and foreign-born Hispanic women earned less, but racial differences among women were small compared to those among men.

One might think that black and Hispanic men have earnings below those of white men because of the inferior quality of the schools they attended and their lower scores on standardized achievement tests. This is possible, but such an argument cannot explain why women in these same minority groups earn as much as or more than similar white women. Black women, after all, attend the same schools as black men, yet earn as much as ostensibly similar white women.

Results in this section present the discouraging finding that the long-term trend toward a convergence in the earnings of black and white men came to an end in the 1970s, leaving black men—as well as American Indian and Hispanic men—with earnings quite below those of whites. For men, membership in those racial minorities led to a net decrease in earnings of about 15 percent. The social, economic, and political processes of the 1980s did not diminish the racial gap in earnings among men. Among women, the findings are different: by 1980, minority women from all races had earnings at least as great as those of white women, once you took into account the major factors influencing what people earn.

Prosperity and Poverty

No systematic governmental attempt to measure poverty took place until President Johnson declared his War on Poverty in 1964. Lacking any official measure, a statistician at the Social Security Administration, Molly Orshansky, priced out a minimally adequate low-cost food budget for households of different sizes, multiplied that food cost by three, and assumed that this was a poverty line. In other words, food costs should be no more than one-third of a household's expenditures. That number has been used for the last three decades with annual adjustments for inflation but with no changes for what consumers may need or what they actually buy. If a household's pre-tax cash income from all sources is less than the poverty line for a household of their size, they are impoverished. The Census Bureau developed estimates of poverty for 1959 and then, since 1966, measured it annually. This number has become a widely accepted index of the nation's welfare. By making certain assumptions and using data from earlier censuses, poverty may be estimated back to 1940.

Favorable economic trends during and after World War II created the modern middle class (see figure 3-1). But the trends benefited whites much more than blacks. Figure 6-17 shows the distribution of the white and black populations by their relationship to the poverty line since 1940. There were tremendous improvements for African Americans as the percentage of households with cash incomes of less than one-half the poverty line plunged from 71 percent at the start of World War II to 18 percent in the early 1970s. Extreme poverty was cut by three-quarters, but those beneficial economic trends extending across three decades still failed to lift the majority of blacks into the middle class. *Never in our history has there been a time when the majority of blacks were members of the middle economic class.* The majority of blacks remain poor or near poor. Figure 6-17 also suggests that statements about the continuing growth of the black middle class should be made cautiously. That population is growing, but only because the black population is growing. The economic middle class, as a proportion of the total black population, reached about 45 percent in the 1970s and has changed little in the last twenty years. One of the disturbing findings about the economic expansion of the 1980s is that it failed to substantially reduce poverty or to increase the proportionate size of the middle class among either whites or blacks (Oliver and Shapiro 1995).

The economic turmoil that followed the oil price shock of the mid-1970s brought an end to a long trend toward much lower poverty rates among both blacks and whites. Since 1973, poverty rates for both races fluctuated within a fairly narrow range. There is no consistent trend in either direction although, for both races, poverty rates went up during recessions and sank to relatively low levels during the late 1980s when the beneficial effects of that decade's economic expansion were felt. Importantly, the long-term trend toward a narrowing of the black-white gap came to its end in the mid-1970s.

Rather than focusing on poverty rates, which analyze the bottom end of the income distribution, let's look at other frequently used indicators of economic status. They are consistent with the argument

Figure 6-17.   Economic Status of the Population: 1940 to 1993

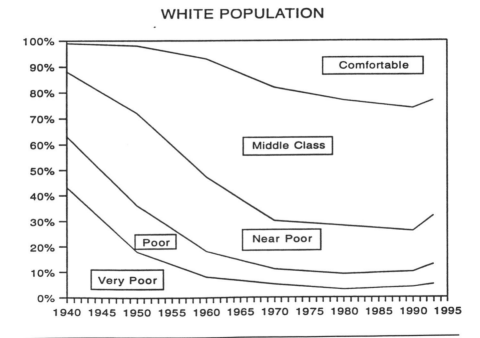

SOURCES: U.S. Bureau of the Census, Public Use Microdata Samples from the censuses of 1940 to 1980; *Current Population Survey* (March 1994).

that the forties, fifties, and sixties were decades in which blacks were gradually catching up with whites on important economic indicators, while the seventies, eighties, and nineties are decades in which blacks neither gained on nor fell further behind whites.

Figure 6-18 presents income information from 1967 to the present: the years for which we have data describing blacks and whites. If we take the income from all sources reported by blacks and divide by the number of blacks, we have per capita income. There is some good news here: per capita incomes for blacks and whites have risen. Fertility rates have fallen and labor force participation has increased among women, helping to boost per capita income even while male wages stagnate. Per capita income for blacks in the early 1990s was about 30 percent higher than twenty years earlier, but the per capita income of whites increased at just about the same rate, leaving the ratio of black to white per capita income unchanged.

Figure 6-17   (continued)

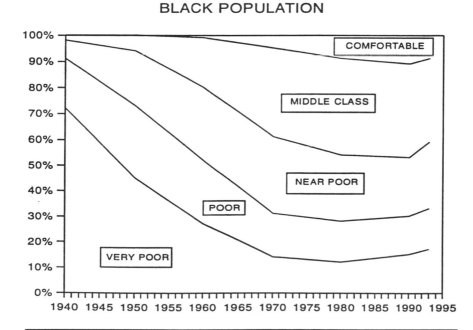

NOTES: **Very Poor:** Below 50 percent of poverty line; **Poor:** 50 to 99 percent of poverty line; **Near Poor:** 100 to 199 percent of poverty line; **Middle Class:** 200 to 499 percent of poverty line; **Comfortable:** 500 percent or more of poverty line.

Figure 6-18.   Per Capita and Median Incomes of Blacks and Whites and Ratio of Black to White Income: 1967 to 1994 (amounts in 1993 dollars)

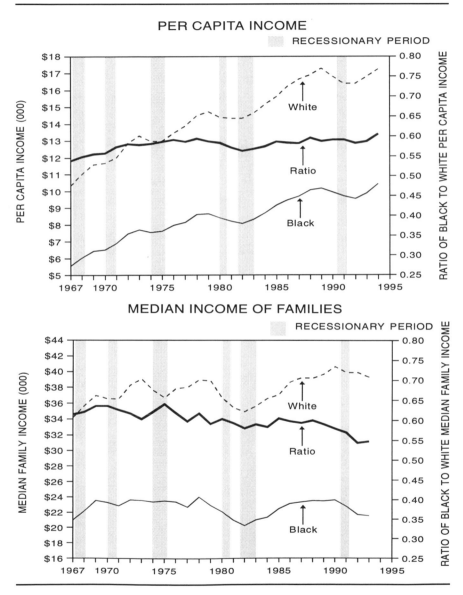

SOURCE: U.S. Bureau of the Census, 1993, *Current Population Reports,* series 60, no. 184, table B-6.

The lower panel in figure 6-18 shows trends in the median incomes of black and white families. The racial trend here is somewhat bleaker. Median incomes for families of both races reached a peak in 1973 and then stagnated for about a dozen years, but the income of white families went up more in the prosperous years of the late 1980s than did that of blacks. As a result, the ratio of black to white median incomes is lower in the early 1990s than ten or twenty years earlier. At its peak in the early 1970s, the median for black families was 64 percent that of whites; by 1994, it was down to 55 percent.

What about other racial groups in 1990? Were blacks uniquely disadvantaged? Let's consider several indicators. Household income is a widely used and very appropriate indicator. Figure 6-19 reports the average income of minority households as a percentage of that of white households in 1980 and 1990, showing information for total households and then for the two most common types—households containing husband-wife families and households consisting of families headed by women.

A familiar ranking is evident. Households headed by native-born Asians have the largest incomes while black and American Indian households are at the other extreme. As the upper panel reveals, those headed by native-born Asians had incomes about 25 percent above those of whites, while households headed by blacks or American Indians reported, on average, about 35 percent less cash income than white households. Hispanic households were just a bit more prosperous than those of blacks and Indians.

Demographic factors help to account for the high income of Asian households since many of them include husband-wife couples. Nonetheless, when we control for type, findings are similar. Asian households, especially those headed by native-born Asians, have larger incomes than white households, while blacks, Indians, and Hispanics fall very far behind whites. The higher income of Asian households is attributed to the unusual investment in education of this group and the many working hours and high earnings of Asian women. In addition, Asian households, on average, include more workers than other households.

A final indicator of the poverty or prosperity of these seven racial groups is the classification of children into five economic categories, based on the relationship of household income to the poverty line. This ranges from very poor children, those living in households with pre-tax cash incomes less than one-half the poverty line, through middle class children, those in households with incomes two to five times

Figure 6-19. Income of Minority Households as a Percentage of That of White Households: 1980 and 1990 (amounts in 1993 dollars)

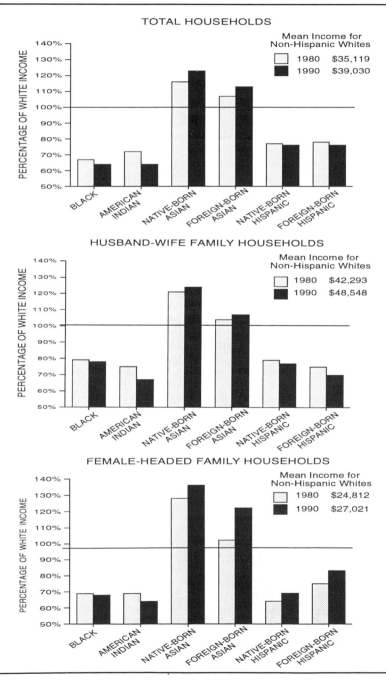

SOURCE: U.S. Bureau of the Census, *Census of Population and Housing: 1980 and 1990*, Public Use Microdata Samples.

the poverty line, to the comfortable, those with incomes five or more times the poverty line. In 1995, the poverty line for a household of four was $15,700. Figure 6-20 shows this classification.

Prosperity and poverty may be summarized succinctly. Black children in 1990 were most likely to be living in impoverished households, followed by American Indian children, and then Hispanic children born abroad. White and Asian children were less likely to be below the poverty line. At the other extreme, native-born Asian children were most likely to be in comfortable economic circumstances, even more likely than white children. To the extent that childhood economic circumstances influence adult achievements, these findings imply that black and American Indian children are disadvantaged when compared with Asian and white children.

Conclusion

Fifty years ago, blacks in much of the South could not vote, rode in the back of buses or in separate coaches on trains, and if they joined the armed forces to fight for democracy, they did so on a racially segregated basis. In the labor market, black women were generally confined to domestic service while most black men did manual labor. In all regions, blacks lived in distinct neighborhoods and most often sent their children to segregated schools. Even our professional and college sports teams operated under Jim Crow principles.

The racial attitudes and beliefs of America shifted throughout the post–World War II era, slowly at first, but then with sufficient momentum to produce a civil rights revolution in the 1960s, one that prodded Congress to enact new laws, led the Supreme Court to establish new procedures, and finally got federal administrations to uphold principles of racial equality. These, in turn, led Americans to question the many discriminatory practices that permeated our society. Changes in racial attitudes occurred for the most part on a cohort basis, so the whites who went through school during and after the civil rights revolution strongly endorsed principles of equal racial opportunity. But there is only modest white support for emphatic programs that might minimize the large remaining racial differences, such as busing to integrate schools, making sure that specific numbers of African Americans get medical degrees, or reserving job slots for blacks. Nevertheless, almost no whites today endorse racial discrimination.

An important consequence of that crucial shift in racial values was

Figure 6-20. Information About Economic Status for Children Under Age 18, by Race: 1990

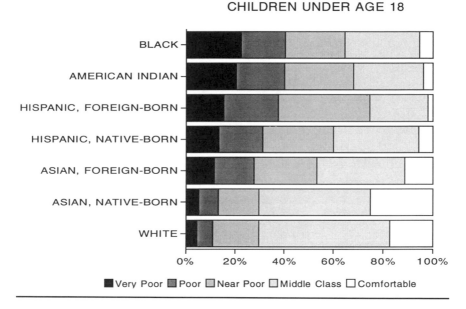

CHILDREN UNDER AGE 18

■ Very Poor ▓ Poor ▨ Near Poor ☐ Middle Class ☐ Comfortable

SOURCE: U.S. Bureau of the Census, *Census of Population and Housing: 1990,* Public Use Microdata Sample.

NOTES: **Very Poor:** Below 50 percent of poverty line; **Poor:** 50 to 99 percent of poverty line; **Near Poor:** 100 to 199 percent of poverty line; **Middle Class:** 200 to 499 percent of poverty line; **Comfortable:** 500 percent or more of poverty line. The poverty line for family of four was $12,764.

the reform of immigration policies in 1965, as Americans came to agree that country of birth, skin color, and religion should not determine who could or could not move to the United States. Because of those changes the racial composition of the nation is now in flux. Indeed, the way we think about race, the meaning of the term, and the way we define and measure racial categories are all topics of debate as the old black-white dichotomy proves inadequate for the many-hued nation we are becoming.

The first waves of Asian immigrants to arrive were either highly educated or came here to get advanced educations. The Asian and Pacific Islander population is now a diverse one, and Asian Indians, Filipinos, and Chinese differ greatly from Melanesians, Polynesians, and the hill tribes from French Indochina. Nevertheless, in the aggregate, Asians invest heavily in education, are employed for unusually long hours, do pretty well with regard to earnings, and are more likely than other racial minorities to live in prosperous husband-wife families. Among the racial minorities, native-born Asians are the most economically secure and, on many economic indicators, have already approached parity with non-Hispanic whites. Given their relatively low rates of childhood poverty, their high rates of college enrollment, and our racial attitudes strongly supporting equal opportunities, it is likely that the next generation of Asians will excel in our technologically sophisticated job market.

The Hispanic population—soon to be the largest minority—is also diverse. The educational attainment of Cubans and South Americans (now arriving in large numbers) is much greater than that of immigrants from Mexico, the Dominican Republic, or the Central American nations. On average, however, Hispanic immigrants report exceptionally low educational attainments. Given the link between the education of parents and that of their children, it is likely that a sizable fraction of Hispanic children entering the labor force in the next decades will have limited attainments, probably inferior to those of young blacks. In an economy that places great emphasis upon skills and advanced training, many Hispanics will be at a disadvantage (Bean and Tienda 1987, chap. 8).

Joel Perlmann's (1988) research points out that some European-origin groups arriving around the turn of this century—Russian Jews, for instance—caught up with native whites in education and income rapidly, while other immigrants—Italians, for instance—took longer to catch up. In another two decades, we will know how rapidly the present large wave of Latino immigrants caught up with the native white population in terms of education and economic status.

What about African Americans? Those who monitored racial trends expected a gradual or moderate diminution of black-white differences after the civil rights decade, as the attitudes of whites changed, as the Supreme Court ruled against segregation, and as the economy's expansion created millions of new jobs and educational opportunities. From the 1940s through the 1970s, that progress occurred, as black-white gaps narrowed with regard to death rates, the earnings of men and women, family incomes, and poverty. But a continuation of those favorable trends that would have brought us much closer to racial parity slowed or stopped in the mid-1970s. It is not so much that blacks have fallen further behind whites on these important indicators. They have not. But the unambiguous thirty-five-year trend toward declining black-white differences ended when the economy entered a new era in the mid-1970s.

The black population is a large and heterogeneous one. An accurate description of trends includes mention of several that indicate continuing racial progress even in the recent period. For the first time, in the 1980s the residential segregation of blacks from whites clearly declined. This did not happen in the older centers of black populations; but where there was much new housing construction, where blacks migrated in large numbers, and where they got a fair share of the better jobs, residential segregation declined. Places such as San Bernadino–Riverside, Orlando, Las Vegas, and Sacramento can be termed moderately segregated, especially when compared to Chicago, Detroit, or Cleveland (Farley and Frey 1994). The 1990 census reveals that the "chocolate city–vanilla suburbs" patterns of the Northeast and Midwest are not being duplicated in those metropolises in the West and South where much of the stock of housing was built after the Fair Housing Act went on the books. And these are the places now attracting many black internal migrants.

Younger cohorts of whites have more egalitarian racial attitudes than older individuals. Perhaps this helps to explain an increase in the proportion of black men marrying white women and black women marrying white men in the 1980s, although this still occurs infrequently. Table 6-5 describes racial intermarriage for the early and late baby boom cohorts, with the analysis restricted to the native-born to prevent any confounding effects of immigration laws. Information for the early baby boomers comes from those aged 25 to 34 in 1980, so most of those marriages took place in the 1970s while almost all of the marriages of the late baby boomers occurred during the 1980s.

Black-white intermarriage rose sharply from the 1970s to the 1980s: the percentage of black husbands marrying white wives went up from 3.8 percent in the earlier decade to 5.3 percent in the latter decade. Few black women marry white husbands, but the proportion doing so went up from 1 to 2 percent between the 1970s and 1980s. Interracial marriage is much more common among other groups. Indeed, the majority of native-born Asians and American Indians in the late baby boom cohort married persons from other racial groups. Exogamy among Asians is frequent since fewer than 20 percent of native-born Asian women selected native-born Asian men for their husbands in the 1980s.

Despite modest declines in residential segregation and increases in interracial marriages among young African Americans, black-white discrepancies on the most important indicators of economic status have been persistent for at least two decades. Why? What explains this lack of racial progress?

There are four intertwined reasons. First, as a result of slavery, the century of Jim Crow segregation that followed, and firmly rooted Social Darwinist beliefs, racial stereotypes are still invoked. Recent surveys asked samples of whites in metropolitan Detroit and Atlanta to rank their own race and blacks on numerical scales with regard to: "tends to be intelligent"; "prefers to be self-supporting rather than living off welfare"; "tends to be easy to get along with"; and "tends to speak English well." While many whites ranked both whites and blacks at the same point on these scales, the majority of whites ranked blacks below whites with regard to intelligence, saw them as preferring to live off welfare more so than whites, thought that blacks were more difficult than whites to get along with, and believed that blacks tended to speak English less well than whites (Bobo and Zubrinsky 1996; Farley et al. 1994: Table A-1; Klugel and Bobo 1993).

Many whites who support the principle of equal racial opportunity may also believe that blacks learn new skills more slowly than whites, will often be difficult to get along with, will work less diligently, and will not express themselves as clearly as whites. When whites make decisions about who they will hire, who they will live next to, which school their children will attend, where they will go for shopping or entertainment, or even who their customers will be, they may prefer whites. They may feel that it is easier, safer, and more pleasant to be living and working alongside other whites rather than with blacks. The consequences of such preferences may be particularly large in the labor market since, in the past, when a strong back was a major job qualification, beliefs about the inability of blacks to perform intellectual tasks or to speak English well were less important than in today's job market where technical skills and the ability to communicate to customers and co-workers are major criteria for getting on the payroll.

A century ago, W.E.B. DuBois (1899) described the petty insults and injuries directed at the black middle class by whites. Ten decades later, Ellis Cose (1993) and Joe Feagin and Melvin Sikes (1994) wrote about the suspicious or hostile way that whites, presumably whites who endorse equal racial opportunities, treated middle-class blacks and those aspiring to the middle class. Sometimes we are reminded of this by specific and well-documented racial incidents: six black Secret

Table 6-5. Racial Composition of Married Couples Aged 25 to 34: 1980 and 1990 (native-born population)

Race of Husband	Total	Race of Wife					Number (000)
		White	Black	Hispanic	Asian	American Indian	
White							
Early Baby Boom	1,000	973	1	15	5	6	9,392
Late Baby Boom	1,000	962	2	22	9	5	8,599
Black							
Early Baby Boom	1,000	38	944	10	5	3	851
Late Baby Boom	1,000	53	919	17	8	2	697
Hispanic							
Early Baby Boom	1,000	262	7	714	9	8	465
Late Baby Boom	1,000	332	11	640	12	4	431
Asian							
Early Baby Boom	1,000	397	22	116	397	67	22
Late Baby Boom	1,000	399	5	102	482	12	47
American Indian							
Early Baby Boom	1,000	431	9	43	16	501	95
Late Baby Boom	1,000	547	13	40	11	389	67

			Race of Husband					
Race of Wife		Total	White	Black	Hispanic	Asian	American Indian	Number (000)
White	Early Baby Boom	1,000	978	3	13	1	4	9,348
	Late Baby Boom	1,000	972	4	17	2	4	8,513
Black	Early Baby Boom	1,000	10	984	4	<1	<1	817
	Late Baby Boom	1,000	21	970	7	<1	1	661
Hispanic	Early Baby Boom	1,000	285	17	684	5	8	485
	Late Baby Boom	1,000	387	24	570	10	5	483
Asian	Early Baby Boom	1,000	715	63	61	136	23	65
	Late Baby Boom	1,000	701	50	44	198	7	114
American Indian	Early Baby Boom	1,000	499	21	34	14	432	111
	Late Baby Boom	1,000	573	17	24	8	378	69

SOURCE: U.S. Bureau of the Census, *Census of Population and Housing: 1980 and 1990*, Public Use Microdata Samples.

Service agents were denied service at a Maryland restaurant while their white colleagues were welcomed in 1993. This incident triggered two class action lawsuits, established that the Denny's chain deliberately discouraged black patronage, and led their management to a $46 million settlement with the victims of racial discrimination. One wonders how often similar racial discrimination took place but so subtly that no protest was registered or lawsuit filed.

Second, fifty years ago Gunnar Myrdal (1944, pp. 618–622) described the deleterious consequences of racial residential segregation for blacks. Not only did it deny blacks access to schools, parks, and facilities available to whites, it allowed prejudiced white officials to provide blacks with second-class services without harming their white constituents. Douglas Massey and Nancy Denton (1993) argue that continuing American apartheid is the strong backbone of the system of black-white racial stratification. I agree. Racial segregation truncates educational and employment opportunities for blacks and may generate a ghetto culture that is dysfunctional in our achievement-oriented society—the type of culture described by William Julius Wilson (1987, Chap. 2) and John Ogbu (1978). Racial residential segregation is the underlying force producing that tangle of pathology now known as the urban underclass. John Kasarda (1995) explains how the restructuring of American industries combines with residential segregation to increasingly limit economic opportunities for blacks, especially black men. Many of the sharpest decreases in blue-collar employment since the 1970s occurred in the cities with the largest black populations. The good jobs disappeared but blacks stayed behind in the city, confined their by their poverty and discrimination in the housing market.

The neighborhoods that blacks typically live in are different in their composition from those of other minority groups. Figure 6-21 shows the racial composition of the typical neighborhood of Asians, blacks, Hispanics, and whites in the 318 metropolises defined for the census of 1990. Asians live in neighborhoods where well over half the population is non-Hispanic white; Hispanics live in neighborhoods where about four out of ten residents are whites; but blacks live in neighborhoods where the white population is relatively small. If African Americans had the incomes, assets, and political clout of whites, this segregation of blacks into majority black neighborhoods might not be a problem. But white neighborhoods, with few exceptions, have better funded schools, better city services, and access to more effective political power than do most overwhelmingly black neighborhoods.

Figure 6-21. Racial Composition of Neighborhoods of Asians, Blacks, Hispanics, and Whites in 318 Metropolitan Areas: 1990

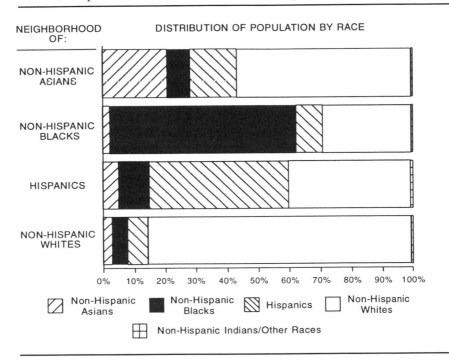

SOURCE: U.S. Bureau of the Census, *Census of Population and Housing: 1990,* Summary Tape File A.

NOTES: Using data for block groups, this figure shows the racial composition of the average neighborhood for members of each race. Data pertain to 318 metropolises as defined for the census of 1990 and are approximately weighted to reflect representation of each race. Block groups in 1990 averaged 210 occupied dwelling units.

Also observe that the potential for assimilation with a prosperous white population is much greater for Hispanics and Asians than for blacks, since they are living in the same neighborhoods as whites, often attending the same schools and churches, and presumably getting the same city services as their white neighbors.

Third, compared to whites and most other racial minorities, blacks have the family structures associated with poverty, especially childhood poverty. Senator Moynihan described the negative consequences of the high rates of family headship by black women and out-of-marriage childbearing three decades ago; an idea that William Julius Wilson stresses in his work, and one increasingly supported by empirical evidence (McLanahan and Sandefur 1994). To be sure, shifts in family structure now make white families quite like the African American families Moynihan described. The most ominous trends are the persistently high rates of poverty among black children and the increasing black-white disparity in college enrollments, trends that will likely slow the growth of the African American middle class in the next generation.

Fourth, sustained economic growth and a clear recognition of the civil rights claims of blacks may have fostered a narrowing of economic gaps before 1973. When the economy grew rapidly, when universities expanded their enrollments, when many new schools were built and new job training programs were established—often with increasingly generous funds from the federal government—it was acceptable to make sure that a discriminated-against racial minority got some share of the expanding opportunities. President Johnson set up the Office of Federal Contract Compliance to ensure that firms doing business with the government had appropriate numbers of black employees. President Nixon supported the "Philadelphia Plan" to get African American men into high-paying construction jobs. And the Supreme Court joined in this effort, even if it meant changing the traditional rules and jettisoning procedures that had been place for decades. In 1971, the Supreme Court approved the use of busing and specific racial ratios to integrate previously segregated local schools (*Swann* v. *Charlotte-Mecklenberg Board of Education* 1971). Six years later, in *Regents of the University of California* v. *Bakke* they sanctioned the use of race as one of several criteria for deciding who might be admitted to a medical school and the next year, in *Weber* (*United Steelworkers of America* v. *Weber* 1979), they upheld a very strong affirmative action/quota plan reserving job openings for black applicants even if they had less seniority than white applicants. Then *Fullilove* v. *Klutznik* (1980) upheld the law that Congress had passed designating that 10 percent of the money the federal government spent for contracting should go to minority firms.

Two developments changed the scene and slowed down or ended these programs. The first—and most important—has been those economic changes since 1973 that created greater competition for jobs and earnings, especially among those with less than college educations. Second, in the 1960s civil rights advocates could point clearly to both the nation's history of racial injustice and continuing discrimination. The success of the black civil rights movement raised the issue of whether other types of discrimination in the labor market, housing, and education should be tolerated. Thus, a women's movement successfully challenged sexual discrimination. Other racial groups made claims for special treatment or quotas even though their histories were different from that of blacks. Recognizing that many personal characteristics could be used as a basis for discrimination, advocates for those with physical limitations successfully encouraged Congress to pass the Americans with Disabilities Act in 1990. Lest there be discrimination on the basis of age, Congress passed laws prohibiting such practices and ended mandatory retirement. Although advocates for lesbians, gays, and bisexuals have been much less successful with Congress and the federal courts than other groups, they have actively claimed that they should be on the list of groups protected against possible discrimination.

The slowing of economic growth, the fundamental shift in who prospers and who falls behind in the labor market, and the explosion of claims for civil rights make it more difficult for many to support those programs of the 1960s that were designed to quickly move blacks into the economic and social mainstream. If you adopt a program to increase the number of blacks in the classroom or on the payroll, isn't there justification for a similar program for women, for Latinos, for the disabled, or for the elderly if they are underrepresented? Which civil rights claims are most valid? Should quotas be set up for all or for just some of these groups? In the 1960s, there was more understanding of the specific claims that African Americans made and an appreciation of the legitimacy of such claims. This situation is different today.

Perhaps the election of 1980 symbolizes a turning point. National surveys continue to report that almost no Americans want to deny opportunities to blacks, but affirmative action programs are in disfavor and may soon disappear. Symbolically, the appointments of Clarence Pendelton to direct the Civil Rights Commission and Clarence Thomas to head the Equal Employment Opportunity Commission were important, not that either of them opposed racial equity. However, they were not known for their fervent dedication to innovative programs that might enhance opportunities for blacks, and they helped to move the federal government away from backing such activities. And then the Supreme Court began a new examination of their decisions that had strongly supported policies designed to get more blacks into good jobs and into the best educational opportunities.

That reexamination led them to tone down such programs. In the future, they may be eliminated. Increasingly, the Supreme Court—as well as other Americans—recognized that those programs that reserved opportunities for minorities limited opportunities for whites. *Wygant* (1986), *Firefighters Local No. 1794* v. *Stotts* (1984), and *Ward's Cove Packing* (1989) put strict limits on what employers might do to overcome the discrimination that had kept blacks at the bottom of the occupational queue. *Richmond* v. *J. A. Croson Co.* (1991) and *Adarand Construction* v. *Pena* (1995) restricted those procedures setting aside a fraction of government spending for minority contractors, and *Missouri* v. *Jenkins* (1995) minimized what state authorities must do to overcome racial segregation in public schools.

The popularity of General Colin Powell, reactions to the verdict in the O. J. Simpson trial, and the Million Man March on Washington. What do these events—all occurring during the fall of 1995—tell us about race relations in the United States? They remind us how much has been achieved in recent years but also how far we still are from the color-blind society that Justice John Harlan eloquently described in his dissent in *Plessy* in 1896.

We defeated the Japanese and German dictators with Jim Crow armed forces, but racial attitudes changed shortly thereafter; and within the span of a generation, a black man rose to the nation's highest military office. When national samples of whites were first asked in 1957 whether they would vote for a well-qualified black man nominated for the presidency by their party, 63 percent said they would not. In 1994, only 10 percent of a national sample of whites said they would refuse to vote for a well-qualified black candidate nominated by their party. That's progress. In today's racial climate, a capable black may become a serious contender for the presidency.

The trial and the verdict in the Simpson litigation remind us how often we assume that a person's views are determined by their skin color. Whether it is the Simpson trial or any other high-profile trial involving whites and blacks, news stories begin with comments about the race of the defendant, the race of the prosecutor, the race of the lawyers, and the racial composition of the jury. We still believe that race determines how we evaluate most issues and which side we will take when there is controversy. The Simpson trial was significant for other reasons. We were reminded how blatant racism and hatred for blacks continue to influence at least some individuals in the criminal justice system in the 1990s. But the race of the judge—Asian—was not an important issue, telling us that the American melting pot works effectively for those racial minorities now coming to the United States in great numbers.

This chapter reports that while there is a moderate but not very economically secure African American middle class, black America would benefit greatly from:

1. The creation of millions of middle-income jobs.
2. A drastic increase in college enrollment rates so that the next generation gets a fair share of the good jobs opening up every year.
3. Many successful black entrepreneurs and capitalists.
4. More two-parent families so that more black children will grow up in economically secure homes.
5. More residential integration so that blacks will benefit from access to the same city services, public schools, job opportunities, and political influence that whites have.
6. The continued and strengthened enforcement of those laws that prohibit racial discrimination in the job and housing markets.

Will the Million Man March or other similar initiatives achieve those goals? Perhaps so, perhaps not. That answer cannot be given for some time.

Chapter 7

Americans on the Move: New Patterns of Internal Migration

Cities are locally managed growth machines. Most stakeholders in local communities benefit greatly from population growth and lose out quickly when population and paychecks—or Social Security and Medicare payments—move out. What is the best way to foster population growth and continued prosperity? Ordinarily it involves creating more jobs, and here is where the growth machines come in.

Political power and economic opportunities are now being redistributed by three types of migration. First, upwards of 1.2 million immigrants arrive from abroad each year, most of them settling in the seven states and fourteen metropolises described in chapter 5. Second, industrial restructuring and better retirement benefits accelerate migration away from the Northeast and Midwest and into the South and West. Third, within large metropolises, the outward migration of population and jobs toward edge cities continues, quite far from the old central cities. And now there is the much-delayed movement of blacks into suburban rings.

This country's history is one of both immigration from abroad and internal migration. The earliest migrants from the British Isles disembarked in five seaports—Boston, Newport, New York, Philadelphia, and Charleston—and then settled the nearby hinterlands, often using the labor of blacks imported from the Caribbean and Africa. Gradually, settlers pushed the Indians west, but before the Revolution, few Europeans crossed the Appalachians, so the British rule of reserving those remote lands for Indians remained in effect. That geographic separation did not last much longer. The Louisiana Purchase of 1803, followed by the second defeat of Britain in the War of 1812, opened the West for European Americans and their slaves. For much of the nineteenth century economic forces and the country's ideology, cleared the West of Indians, and the great expanse stretching from the Appalachians to the Pacific was settled, cultivated, and developed by migrants from the eastern part of the country. *Manifest destiny* was the label applied to this great geographic conquest. The forced removal of the five "civilized" tribes from Georgia on the "Trail of Tears" in the 1830s was one important step in the often bloody process of confining Indians to reservations—a process completed in December 1890, when the Army routed the Sioux at Wounded Knee Creek in South Dakota. But the story of our national migration is greater than the securing of lands from Indians, the Louisiana Purchase, and the military defeat of Mexico in 1848, which gave us the southwest quadrant of our country. Economic and demographic processes combined with technological developments to transform this country from thirteen Atlantic states in 1790 into a continental power a century later.

All migration trends are driven by economic and demographic processes and these, in turn, depend on technological developments. Eli Whitney's invention of the cotton gin and Robert Fulton's invention of the steamboat made the growing of cotton economically feasible throughout the South, explaining the settlement of the Gulf Coast states and accounting for their distinctive racial composition, a demographic pattern as evident in 1990 as in 1850. The meeting of railroad work crews at Promontory Point, Utah, on May 10, 1869, meant that travelers and goods could go from one coast to the other by rail. In a far-reaching strategy of economic development, the federal government's land policies after the Civil War led to an explosion of rail building, so much so that the census of 1890 marked a key turning point—the closing of the frontier. Almost all corners of the forty-eight contiguous states were settled and most people lived within less than a day's journey of a rail line linking them and the products of their farms and workshops with Boston, New Orleans, San Francisco, and all points in between. By the end of the nineteenth century, a migrant to the Northwest could travel by rail in a few days the route that Meriweather Lewis and William Clark had spent two years covering at the start of that century.

Nineteenth century migration, abetted by a high rate of natural population increase and by large-scale immigration from Europe, filled in those numerous empty and uncharted spaces on the 1800 map. Twentieth century migration is different because it occurred in an economically developed and settled nation. This migration, along with continued immigration, is reshaping the political and economic system and will reconfigure this nation's racial composition in the twenty-first century.

Historians of migration in the twentieth century will describe the shift in where people lived—in cities, not on farms or in rural ham-

lets. The census of 1920 was the first to report that the urban population outnumbered the rural. The trend to urban and suburban living
continued such that by 1990, three-quarters of the population lived in
urban areas. Between the Civil War and World War II, manufacturing
supplanted agriculture as the nation's major industrial sector. In 1900,
eleven million people worked on farms to feed a nation of seventy-
five million; by 1990, three million farm workers grew enough to feed
this nation of 260 million, as well as shipping $42 billion of farm
products overseas every year (U.S. Bureau of the Census 1995b, tables
654 and 1123).

These economic trends redistributed the population by region in
the first half of this century. The Midwestern industrial heartland and
the manufacturing metropolises of the Northeast drew migrants from
rural America, especially from the South where the boll weevil, declining world prices for cotton, and the ecological devastation of the Dust
Bowl drove millions of farm owners and sharecroppers off their lands.
This migration was the driving force behind major political changes
of this century. The liberal social and economic programs put in place
in the three decades between the Franklin Roosevelt and Lyndon
Johnson presidencies depended upon population shifts that gave the
Northeast and Midwest many electoral votes and much Congressional
representation. Joined to this was the great migration of African
Americans from the South, where they could not vote, to the Northeast and Midwest, where they could exercise their Fifteenth Amendment rights and did so, most often in support of liberal Democratic
candidates (Lemann 1991). But what industrialization gave to the
Northeast and Midwest was, toward the end of this century, taken
away by the restructuring of the economy: service employment soared
while manufacturing jobs disappeared. After 1970, the South and the
West grew much more rapidly than the Northeast and Midwest, draw-
ing migrants from those regions. When Richard Nixon won the presidency in 1968, Northeastern states cast 128 of the 535 electoral votes;
by the election of President Clinton, this was down to 118. But the
Pacific coast states saw their representation go up from 62 to 79. From
1810 through 1970, New York had a larger delegation in Congress
than any other state. New migration patterns caused California to
leapfrog over New York in 1970 and, after the census of 2000, Florida
and Texas may also have larger Congressional delegations, and more
electoral votes, than New York (U.S. Bureau of the Census 1994a,
table 1).

The story of this century's migration contains a major chapter about the shift of urban population away from older central cities and into suburbs. As Kenneth Jackson (1985) put it, we invaded and conquered a crabgrass frontier in the years after World War II, a migration much encouraged by federal policies with regard to mortgage financing and the construction of hundreds of miles of multilane expressways. Suburbanization is another of the many migration patterns that can be directly linked to specific governmental decisions, although the policies never bore the label "U.S. Government Policy to Redistribute Population Away from Central Cities." The move to the suburbs continues. In the 1980s, the most rapidly growing components of the largest metropolises were the new edge cities: those huge new office/shopping/entertainment/warehouse complexes now found toward the outer edges of metropolitan settlements but at the intersections of the interstate highways. These include King of Prussia west of Philadelphia; Buckhead/Lenox Square Mall north of Atlanta; the O'Hare Airport complex northwest of Chicago; the Auburn Hills area near Detroit; and Tysons Corners near Washington (Garreau 1991).

Immigration from abroad is also a key component of the migration story. Newcomers from Southern and Eastern Europe arrived in great numbers for the first two decades of this century, filling cities in the Northeast and Midwest, but this was followed by five decades of so little immigration that the political and economic salience of the issue disappeared. This changed in the late 1960s as immigrants found economic opportunities and civil liberties in the United States.

Why Do People Move or Stay? A Search for Explanations

What explains whether people move or stay put? What accounts for their destination once they move? Two important forces account for most internal migration—economic opportunities and the search for amenities. As businesses find their sales soaring, they ordinarily expand their workforces, and they will first employ people living nearby. But their demand for labor may exceed the local supply causing a movement of people to a location where better jobs are available. The great shift from rural America to the manufacturing metropolises of the Northeast and Midwest earlier this century was caused by the declining job opportunities in agriculture and the booming opportunities in manufacturing. Internal migration, then, equilibrates the supply of labor geographically.

This is a textbook model and the actual situation is similar in some regards, but very different in others (Greenwood 1981; Lowry 1966; Muller 1982). The migration response to shifting employment opportunities is a sluggish one. Few of us have extensive knowledge of exactly where to get the best jobs or even a clear understanding of where we will find work or be unemployed. Furthermore, even if we lose a job in one city and learn about a good one elsewhere, there are many impediments to rapid migration. Most adults have spouses and families—demographic considerations that generally retard migration. Indeed, the increasing number of dual-career families among late baby boom cohorts may dampen migration, since it is unlikely that both spouses simultaneously lose jobs in one location and find good new ones somewhere else. There are also substantial transaction costs in migrating, costs that increase with distance. Studies of migration consistently report that the volume of migration between two places is inversely related to the distance separating them (Galle and Taeuber 1966; Stouffer 1940); that is, we know more about job opportunities in our own area than at distant points, and the expenses of moving long distances are considerable. Not only must the boxes be packed and the movers hired, but it is often costly to sell a home in one location and then find a comparable home in another. At some points in the life span—just after high school or college—the constraints on moving are few, and so migration rates are highest at these ages.

What are the amenities people seek to maximize when they move? People differ profoundly in their tastes, although there is consensus about some geographic and climatic considerations. Within metropolitan areas, the post–World War II movement has been toward more spacious and newer homes—most often located toward the fringes of settled areas, where public schools and governmental services are often viewed as much better than those in the central cities. But some prefer big city living; and in the 1980s there was a modest boom in the gentrification of old central-city neighborhoods (Laska and Spain 1980).

Recent internal migration has overwhelmingly been away from the cold weather states and toward the coasts, especially along the Atlantic from the Chesapeake Bay southward, along the Gulf Coast, and along the Pacific Rim. How much of this massive migration is attributable to favorable meteorological conditions and how much to the economic boom of these places has yet to be determined.

Explanations for migration focus on "push" and "pull" factors. Supposedly, many characteristics of a person's present place of residence propel him or her to think about moving away. The rent may be too high, the job pay too little, the commute to work too long, the public schools deficient, too many immigrants or a "bad" racial composition to the neighborhood, or the city's taxes too high. Sometimes a specific event tips the balance and provokes a move—a job is abolished, a person is robbed on the street corner, an additional child makes it imperative to find a larger house, or a marriage comes to its end—so someone has to move out. That is the "push" side of the equation. Efforts to explain migration also assume that there are "pull" factors associated with the destination point chosen by the migrant. Jobs may be readily available, attractive housing might be obtained at low cost, the streets are safe, or there is warm, sunny weather all year. Those who describe migration assume that most of us keep the idea of moving in the back of our heads, and sometimes right up front. Just as the economist assumes that we are always contemplating a possible change in our employment, so too the demographer assumes that we often contemplate changes in where we live. If "push" and "pull" factors are simultaneously strong, presumably we will move. Since individuals vary greatly in how they weigh the same factors, it is impossible to account for who migrates or who stays, even when they have many good reasons to move. A dramatic change in circumstances usually leads people to move, but not always. When employers close their factories and offices, there is seldom a rush to leave, and when employers create many jobs in new locations, there is not always a rush of migrants to the area. If internal migration effectively balanced the labor market, there might be little variation from one area to another in unemployment rates. But migration does this slowly and imperfectly. Furthermore, few government policies specifically encourage labor migration since elected representatives seldom endorse programs that might cut their state's population. As a result, geographic differences in unemployment are surprisingly large. Among major metropolises in 1994, the unemployment rate ranged from a low of 3 percent in Minneapolis to a high of 9 percent in Los Angeles (U.S. Bureau of the Census 1995, table 632).

All persons in the United States are, in theory, free to move wherever they wish. In the past, states have tried to enact legislation seeking to keep out undesirable migrants from other states. California in the 1930s, for example, passed an "Okie" law—named after the leading Dust Bowl state—prohibiting anyone from bringing an indigent U.S. citizen into the state, but the Supreme Court ruled that interstate travel is a constitutional right so no state can control its own borders.

(*Edwards* v. *California* 1941). But there are many rules and laws that effectively place restrictions on migration into specific places. For example, federal courts have upheld zoning ordinances that specify minimum property values or acreage for housing units and, until the Fair Housing Act of 1968 went on the books, many suburban municipalities actively discouraged the entry of blacks, Jews, or other minorities (*Euclid* v. *Ambler Realty Co.* 1926; *Arlington Heights* v. *Metropolitan Housing Development Corp.* 1977). Presumably, those municipal practices that once kept blacks out of specific suburbs are less rigorously enforced now, although zoning regulations maintain economic segregation. Early this century more than a dozen states passed alien land laws with the intent of keeping Asians out. These laws held that no land could be purchased by an individual ineligible for U.S. citizenship; since persons born in Asia were the only group ineligible for citizenship, the laws applied to Asians.

Although the census tells us a great deal about where people live, three issues make the study of migration complicated. First, what is the time period of interest? Are we interested in people who moved recently or in those who moved at some point in their lifetime? Since 1850, censuses have asked about state or country of birth. We can consider the population of a state, county, or city and determine how many moved there from another state or foreign country. But this does not tell the story of how migration is reshaping the country. Consider Florida in 1990. We must distinguish between young, college-educated people born elsewhere who recently moved there from those nonogenarians who migrated south from Buffalo. Since 1940, censuses have asked for place of residence five years ago, allowing us to study the recent migrants coming to a place (Long 1988, chap. 1).

Second, there are questions about how much information you need about where a person lived before they moved, and where exactly they live now. At first glance, this seems easy. You ask someone where they lived five years ago and you get all the information. Assuming that people can accurately answer that question, you still have a problem classifying them. Is region of the country five years ago sufficient, or do you want their state of residence, their county of residence, or even more precise information about their city or even their street address?

Place of current residence seems obvious. People are counted at a specific location on the census day, so this is where they lived. But it is not that simple. Much to the dismay of some communities and the pleasure of others, college students are counted where their dormitories are located, even if they return home every weekend and all sum-mer—a rule adding to the populations of State College, Pennsylvania; Hanover, New Hampshire; Boulder, Colorado; and dozens of other places. Persons on military duty in the United States are counted at their base or port, but those serving abroad are attributed back to one of the fifty states. More tricky in this age of an affluent elderly popula-tion is the question of where to count those who have more than one home: a summer home in Michigan and a winter home in Palm Springs. There is no formal system of state citizenship, so people are counted where they were on the census date, but this raises constitu-tional questions. The reapportioning of Congress after the census of 1980 meant that the final seat would be allocated to either Indiana or Florida. If the snowbirds counted in Florida at the start of April had been allocated to the states where they lived most of the year, Indiana would have gotten one more representative; Florida, one less. (For a discussion of such lawsuits, see Choldin 1994, chap. 12). And after the 1990 count, Massachusetts took the matter of attributing military personnel serving overseas back to a specific state to the Supreme Court since this residency rule cost them a seat in Congress. The Supreme Court ratified the Census Bureau's practice (*Franklin* v. *Massachusetts* 1992).

Third, how far do you have to move to be a migrant? For a couple of decades after World War II, a distinction was made between mov-ers—those who went from one place of residence to another *within the same county*—and migrants—those who *crossed at least one county line* when they moved. As metropolitan areas grew to encompass many counties, this mover versus migrant distinction made less sense, and so it disappeared. A useful and convenient distinction—one used in this chapter—distinguishes:

1. International migrants: persons migrating to a place in the United States from abroad.
2. Interregional migrants: those people who lived in one of the four regions in the United States in 1985 but in a different region in 1990.
3. Interstate migrants: those who crossed at least one state line as they moved from their previous to present residence.

The nation's history of heterogeneous political divisions creates headaches for those who study migration. Moving within Rhode Is-land entails a change of no more than about sixty miles, but you can move almost two thousand miles in Alaska or one thousand miles in

Texas and never cross a state line. West of the Mississippi, moving within one metropolis is almost always a move within one state. But you can readily move a short distance within metropolitan New York, Philadelphia, or Chicago and cross a state line. And in the Washington area, you can cross several state lines and remain within the same metropolis.

Migration and the Distribution of Population by Region

When Thomas Jefferson supervised the first census, half the population lived in the Northeast, the other half in the South. The migration trends that produced the nation of the 1990s are summarized in figure 7-1. Northeastern states were centers for immigration in the nineteenth century, but they lost greatly in their exchange with other states as first the Midwest and then the West were settled. Throughout the nineteenth century, the share in the Northeast declined—from about one in two in 1790 to one in four in 1890. Industrialization and the

Figure 7-1. Distribution of the Total Population of the United States: 1790 to 1994

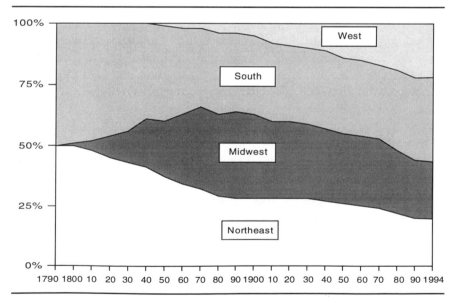

SOURCE: U.S. Bureau of the Census, 1975, *Historical Statistics of the United States: Colonial Times to 1970*, series A172-194; 1995, *Statistical Abstract of the United States: 1995*, table 30.

shift to urban living then allowed this region to hold its share of the total population for the first half of this century but, after the 1950s, it resumed its decline in relative size.

Ohio was the first state west of the Alleghenies to join the Union, doing so in 1803. The productive croplands of that area had first attracted migrants from New England. Indeed, one of the veterans' benefits provided to Revolutionary War fighters by Connecticut was land in Ohio. The population of the Midwest boomed even more after the Civil War as industries capitalized on the region's proximity to iron ore, coal, good transportation, and markets. At its peak in 1890, 36 percent of the nation's population lived in this region. Throughout the twentieth century, the Midwest has grown less rapidly than the rest of the nation. Its growth was curtailed first by drastic increases in agricultural productivity and then by industrial restructuring. Only one city in that region—Chicago—has attracted many immigrants from Asia and Latin America. Its share of the nation's population has fallen to where it was on the eve of the Civil War. Since young people move to where jobs are increasing, the population outlook for the Midwest is not bright.

For eighteen decades after the Revolution, the population of the South grew, but at a rate much lower than the national average. Southern agricultural products fared poorly on world markets in the late nineteenth century and, early this century, manufacturers located their plants in the Midwest or Northeast more often than in the South. The demographic slide for the South continued until 1970 when its share of the nation's total population had sunk to 30 percent. The drop has ended. The restructuring of employment and the growth of the service sector mean that many jobs are no longer bound to mines, deep water ports, or rail lines (Kasarda 1995, pp. 216–219). And three southern metropolises—Houston, Miami, and Washington—are now major ports of entry for immigrants, so the South grows rapidly.

In 1848, California became the first western state, starting a trend that was completed more than a century later with the admission of Hawaii. An economic boom—the gold rush—first attracted thousands of migrants to Pacific shores and allowed California to join the Union, even though it was more than one thousand miles from the nearest state. Subsequent events have been more prosaic, but the rapid growth of this region continues. When the Civil War began, just two Americans in one hundred lived in the Rockies or further west. This grew to five in one hundred at the turn of this century, but the biggest increases occurred in recent decades, the era in which jet planes and modern communication linked Pacific Rim states fully into the nation's economy and commercial ties to Asia became crucial. Growth in the West also depended upon modern cheap energy, and the massive governmental spending that made it possible to ship water from Colorado and northern California to the arid lands of Arizona and southern California. If those funds had not been appropriated, there would be a much slower transfer of political power to the West. Importantly, Los Angeles, San Francisco, and Seattle are ports of entry for huge flows of foreign immigrants. By 1990, almost one-quarter of the nation's population lived in this booming region, and by 2000 the West will have a larger population than either the Northeast or Midwest.

Moving to current trends, map 7-1 shows migration in the five years ending with the census of 1990. Arrows indicate the numbers (in thousands) of interregional migrants. This information pertains to all persons age 5 and over in 1990, both native- and foreign-born, but excludes international migration during this period.

The South was the biggest winner, gaining greatly in its exchange of migrants with the Northeast and Midwest, and held its own against the West. Numbers beneath the map indicate that the South had a population of almost eighty million in 1990 and a net interregional gain of 1.4 million in the half-decade before the census. The West gained in its exchange with every other region, but its numerical advantage and rate of net migration gain was smaller than the South's.

The Midwest and Northeast were the losers. Even though these regions are still alluring to many migrants, the numbers arriving fall far short of the numbers leaving. For every 1,000 residents of the Midwest in 1985, there was a net loss of fifteen interregional migrants; in the Northeast, the net loss was twenty-three per 1,000 causing the Northeast to be the region losing migrants most rapidly.

Migration by Age Group

If governors and mayors could secretly express their wishes about migration, they would request a substantial influx of highly educated young migrants who would pursue professional careers, buy expensive homes, obey all laws, and pay taxes dutifully. This would lead to an economic boom generating new jobs to be filled by more immigrants. Mayors might not object if there were an outmigration of poorly educated, welfare-dependent minorities so long as their leaving did not cost them any seats in Congress or the state house. Thus, this chapter focuses on the types of migrants entering or leaving an area,

Map 7-1. The Interregional Exchange of Migrants: 1985 to 1990 (in thousands)

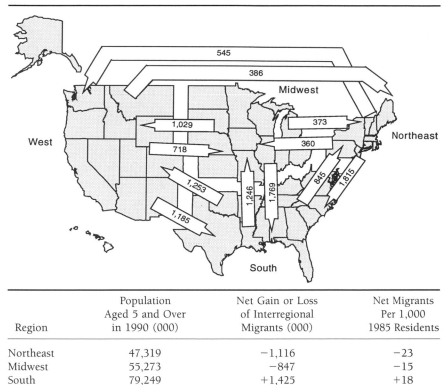

Region	Population Aged 5 and Over in 1990 (000)	Net Gain or Loss of Interregional Migrants (000)	Net Migrants Per 1,000 1985 Residents
Northeast	47,319	−1,116	−23
Midwest	55,273	−847	−15
South	79,249	+1,425	+18
West	48,604	+538	+11

SOURCE: U.S. Bureau of the Census, *Census of Population and Housing: 1990*, Public Use Microdata Sample.

as determined by three important characteristics: age, education, and race.

The late baby boomers—those aged 25 to 34 in 1990—influenced national trends by moving to the South and West. Map 7-2 shows the actual flows among the regions. As these young people completed their schooling and made decisions about marriage or families, they often moved West, causing this region to gain handsomely in its exchange with the other regions. For every 1,000 late baby boomers living in the West in 1985, there was a net gain of fifteen in the

Map 7-2. The Interregional Exchange of Migrants in the Late Baby Boom Cohort: 1985 to 1990 (in thousands)

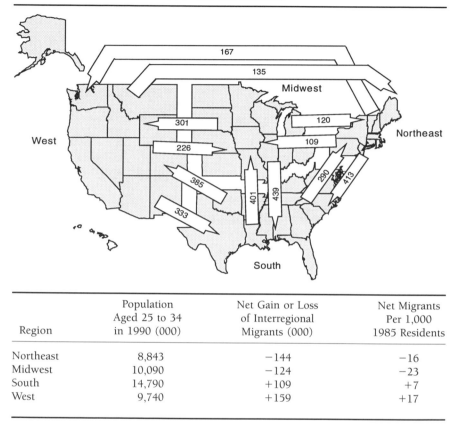

Region	Population Aged 25 to 34 in 1990 (000)	Net Gain or Loss of Interregional Migrants (000)	Net Migrants Per 1,000 1985 Residents
Northeast	8,843	−144	−16
Midwest	10,090	−124	−23
South	14,790	+109	+7
West	9,740	+159	+17

SOURCE: U.S. Bureau of the Census, *Census of Population and Housing: 1990*, Public Use Microdata Sample.

following five years. Young people are still taking the advice a New Yorker, Horace Greeley, gave more than a century ago when he recommended going West. The South also gained late baby boomers but at a much lower volume and rate. The Midwest and Northeast lost late baby boomers at a pretty high rate in their migration exchanges.

What does this mean? As individuals began their careers in the 1980s, many decided to move West or South. Although the great industrial centers of the Midwest and the financial centers in the Northeast still attract young individuals who hope to prosper there, the number leaving these places was much larger.

Quite a few areas in the South and some in the West are thriving as never before because they attract prosperous, older people who seek the amenities such places offer—sunshine, a warm climate, and low crime rates. Let's next turn to migration trends among these parents and grandparents of the baby boomers, persons aged 65 and over in 1990. Sustained economic growth in the decades following World War II, the spread of generous private pensions, and boosts in Social Security payments created an economically secure older population—a group with the time and resources to enjoy themselves as and where they wish. Jobs now constrain the movements of few people age 65 and over. As recently as 1950, 45 percent of men aged 65 and over worked, primarily because they had to support themselves and their spouses, but by 1990 this was down to just 18 percent (Treas and Torrecilha 1995, figure 2-8). When President Johnson signed the Medicare bill in 1965 and, seven years later, when Representative Wilbur Mills led the fight to index Social Security for inflation, they did not think about the demographic and economic booms they would create in Florida, Arizona, and some points in California and North Carolina.

Older persons do not have an unusually high propensity to move. It is not as if people stayed put from their thirties to their sixties and then moved at high rates when the first Social Security check arrived in their mail boxes. Figure 7-2 describes the migration by age, with each bar reporting a different age group. The twenties and thirties are peak ages for migration. About 70 percent of the late baby boom cohorts, persons aged 25 to 34 in 1990, switched their residences between 1985 and 1990, with local (intrastate) moves about four times as frequent as moves across state lines. Much of that local movement reflects changes in marital status or moving to different residences because of changes in family size. And because these people are in the early stages of parenting, migration is common for their young children. After age 30, the proportion who move steadily declines with advancing age: the proportion moving across state lines was no higher after age 55 than before. Indeed, the percentage remaining in their own homes is highest at the oldest ages. Nevertheless, as the older population increases in size and benefits from their savings and generous federal programs become available, they become an important component of those migration streams that now produce rapid growth and more political power in the South and West.

Figure 7-2. Migration Status of Persons Aged 5 and Over: 1990

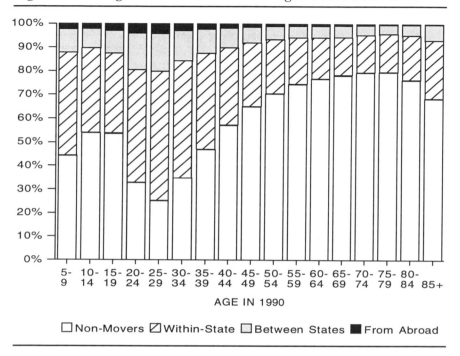

SOURCE: U.S. Bureau of the Census, *Census of Population and Housing: 1990,* Public Use Microdata Sample.

Map 7-3 reports the interregional flows of those of retirement age. The Northeast and Midwest stand out once again for their unusually heavy losses of migrants, while the South was the big winner. Older migrants bring Social Security checks, pension benefits, and, quite often, dividend and interest income with them when they retire; they seldom bring children for the public schools; and they commit few crimes. They may make use of emergency medical services, but those are paid for with federal dollars, so local communities—especially doctors, nurses, and medical technicians—prosper.

There is considerable economic selectivity in who migrates. Prosperous older people are more likely to leave the North and move South than their peers with less income. A few numbers illustrate this pattern. I considered persons aged 65 and over and compared those who remained in the Northeast and Midwest to those who moved South between 1985 and 1990. Amounts are shown in 1993 dollars.

Map 7-3. The Interregional Exchange of Migrants Aged 65 and Over in 1990: 1985 to 1990 (in thousands)

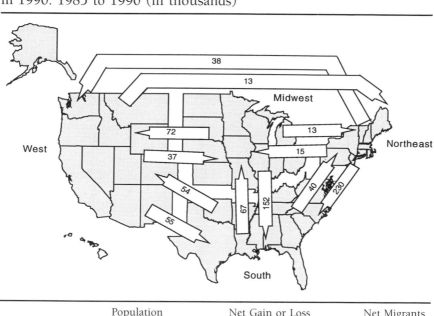

Region	Population Aged 65 and Over in 1990 (000)	Net Gain or Loss of Interregional Migrants (000)	Net Migrants Per 1,000 1985 Residents
Northeast	6,958	−217	−30
Midwest	7,709	−118	−15
South	10,690	+276	+26
West	5,724	+59	+10

SOURCE: U.S. Bureau of the Census, *Census of Population and Housing: 1990*, Public Use Microdata Sample.

Those retiring in the South in this half-decade had 20 percent more income than those who stayed in the North; furthermore, their spending power was augmented by more dollars from investments and retirement pensions. Social Security and Medicare are frequently thought of as income redistribution programs that take money from young and middle-aged workers and give it to retirees. That certainly happens. Less frequently do we think of these federal programs as strategies for redistributing money from the Midwest and Northeast to the South. These figures also point out the two sides of this migration story: the South and West generally benefit because they attract

Per Capita Income in 1989 of Persons Age 65 and Over in 1990

	Living in the Northeast or Midwest in Both 1985 and 1990	Moving from the Northeast or Midwest to the South
Per capita total income	$16,540	$19,982
Income from dividends and investments	3,968	6,156
Income from retirement programs other than Social Security	2,482	3,813

a rather prosperous older population whose income in unlikely to go down very much during a recession while the North is losing a disproportionately large number of its most financially capable older residents.

Educational Attainment and Its Link to Migration

Getting a university degree often involves student migration away from home. And completing college usually provides credentials that place the graduate in a national rather than a local job market. If the student is trained to be a mason, beautician, or bus driver, he or she is likely to seek work in his own city; but if the student earns a degree in civil engineering or secondary teaching, the job search can span the country. Thus, the likelihood of making an interstate move increases with educational attainment. Figure 7-3 shows the migration status of persons in the primary labor force years—aged 25 to 54—classified by their education.

The percentage not moving between 1985 and 1990 was highest for those with the fewest years spent in classrooms, while the percentage making local moves was about the same at all educational levels. Interstate migration, however, increased with educational attainment. Only 5 percent of those with less than high school educations crossed state lines, while among those with postcollege degrees, it was 16 percent. The educational selectivity of recent immigrants, discussed in chapter 5, is also evident since the percentage arriving from abroad was highest among those at the bottom or top of the educational distribution.

Whether the focus is upon those with advanced educations or

Figure 7-3. Migration Status of Persons Aged 25 to 54, Classified by Educational Attainment: 1990

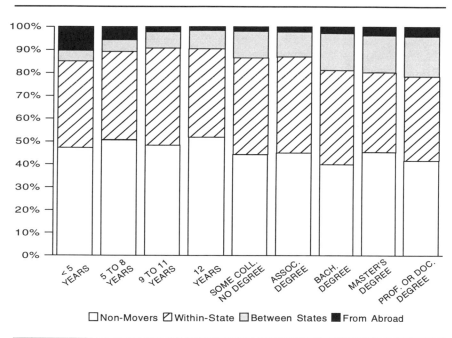

□ Non-Movers ▨ Within-State ▢ Between States ■ From Abroad

SOURCE: U.S. Bureau of the Census, *Census of Population and Housing: 1990*, Public Use Microdata Sample.

those with less than high school diplomas, the South and the West gained in the interregional exchange of migrants, while the Northeast and Midwest lost. Maps 7-4 and 7-5 refer to people aged 25 to 54 in 1990—ages when most people are employed. Map 7-4 reports the interregional exchange of college graduates and describes a loss of human capital from the North. Although the Northeast and Midwest attract many college degree–holders, they lose even more, so they are, in a sense, exporting talent. In the Northeast, the loss was seventeen college graduates per 1,000 living there in 1985; from the Midwest, an even greater loss: thirty-four per 1,000.

Map 7-5 summarizes interregional flows for those with high school diplomas or less. The Midwest and Northeast lost many migrants. The dominating exchange was between the Northeast and the

Map 7-4. The Interregional Exchange of Migrants with Complete College Educations: 1985 to 1990 (in thousands)

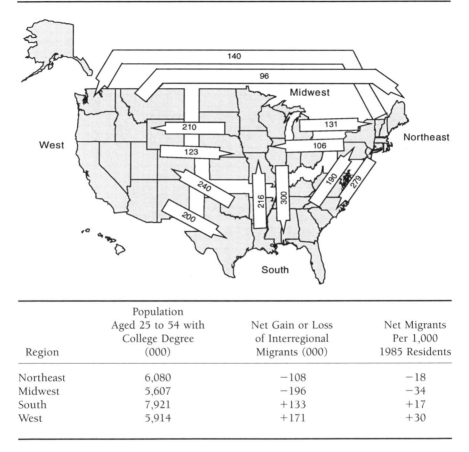

Region	Population Aged 25 to 54 with College Degree (000)	Net Gain or Loss of Interregional Migrants (000)	Net Migrants Per 1,000 1985 Residents
Northeast	6,080	−108	−18
Midwest	5,607	−196	−34
South	7,921	+133	+17
West	5,914	+171	+30

SOURCE: U.S. Bureau of the Census, *Census of Population and Housing: 1990,* Public Use Microdata Sample.

South. About three hundred thousand persons with high school diplomas or less resided in the Northeast in 1985 but lived below the Mason-Dixon line five years later. The stream going in the opposite direction included just forty-four thousand persons. In a sense, the Northeast also "gained" in this exchange since it "exported" a fraction of its least skilled labor force.

Map 7-5. The Interregional Exchange of Migrants with Less than High School Educations: 1985 to 1990 (in thousands)

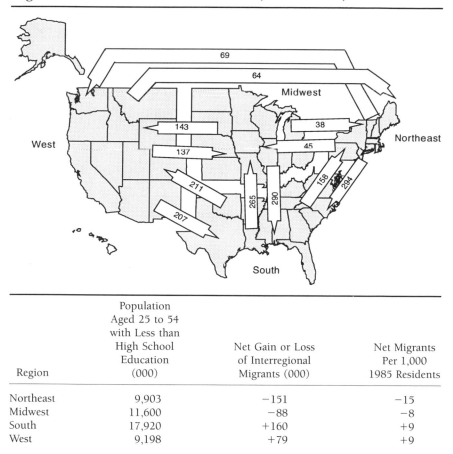

Region	Population Aged 25 to 54 with Less than High School Education (000)	Net Gain or Loss of Interregional Migrants (000)	Net Migrants Per 1,000 1985 Residents
Northeast	9,903	−151	−15
Midwest	11,600	−88	−8
South	17,920	+160	+9
West	9,198	+79	+9

SOURCE: U.S. Bureau of the Census, *Census of Population and Housing: 1990,* Public Use Microdata Sample.

Race and Its Link to Migration

Civil rights issues and national political policies have been strongly influenced by the great migration of blacks away from the South. Although small numbers left throughout the post-Emancipation era—indeed, sufficient numbers to make blacks quite visible in New York,

Philadelphia, and Boston at the turn of this century—the great movement away from the rural South did not occur until World War I, when the German navy cut the flow of Slavic and Italian immigrants. Manufacturers in the North reluctantly turned to the American South, hiring African Americans and southern whites for the first time. Decade after decade, the South sent a sizable fraction of its surplus black population North, thereby creating new racial patterns and laying the foundation for the civil rights movement of the 1960s. This migration has ended, and a new pattern of black migration was hinted at in the census of 1980 and very clearly revealed in 1990. Just like whites, blacks are moving away from the Northeast and Midwest and into the South.

Map 7-6 reports the interregional exchange of non-Hispanic blacks (aged 5 and over in 1990) between 1985 and 1990. The Northeast was the largest loser. As the map shows, blacks are returning to the South. They moved away from New York, Philadelphia, and other northern points and into Atlanta, Raleigh, and Richmond. The Midwestern black population was also depleted by net outmigration, but at a much lower rate. The era of rapid black growth along the West Coast continued through the 1980s, but in the 1990s this region will likely lose in its exchange of blacks with the South.

Map 7-7 provides information about the nation's second largest minority. The South and West have the largest Hispanic populations, many of them new arrivals in the United States or descendents of recent immigrants. You might expect there would be a dispersal away from those regions. However, Hispanics had a migration pattern similar to those of whites and blacks: the Northeast and Midwest lost in their exchanges with the South and West. We have the image of rapid Hispanic growth in the Northeast, so the migration loss for that region seems surprising. But the demographic trends summarized in these maps refer to people living in the United States in 1985. Immigration from abroad adds to the Hispanic population of New England and metropolitan New York while internal movement diminishes it since the flow of Hispanics is into the South and West.

The Effects of Age, Education, and Region on Interstate Migration: 1985 to 1990

Age, educational attainment, and race are strongly linked to migration. Do they have independent effects, or is age the dominating factor? To investigate this, we considered people who lived in the United States in

Map 7-6. The Interregional Exchange of Non-Hispanic Black Migrants: 1985 to 1990 (in thousands)

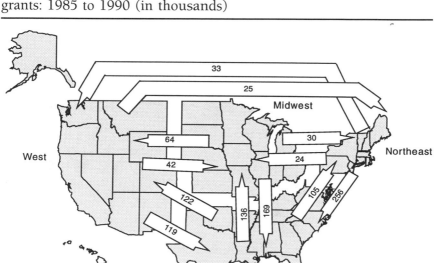

Region	Black Population Aged 5 and Over in 1990 (000)	Net Gain or Loss of Interregional Migrants (000)	Net Migrants Per 1,000 1985 Residents
Northeast	4,777	−153	−32
Midwest	5,127	−63	−12
South	14,193	+181	+13
West	2,432	+35	+14

SOURCE: U.S. Bureau of the Census, *Census of Population and Housing: 1990,* Public Use Microdata Sample.

both 1985 and 1990, distinguishing those who moved across a state border from those who did not and then determined whether age, education, and race had independent effects on the probability of moving.

Figure 7-4 shows the net impact of these characteristics on migration. The odds of moving across a state line for a specific group are compared to the odds of moving for a baseline group—25 to 34 for age, four years of high school for education, and non-Hispanic white for race.

Map 7-7. The Interregional Exchange of Hispanic Migrants: 1985 to 1990 (in thousands)

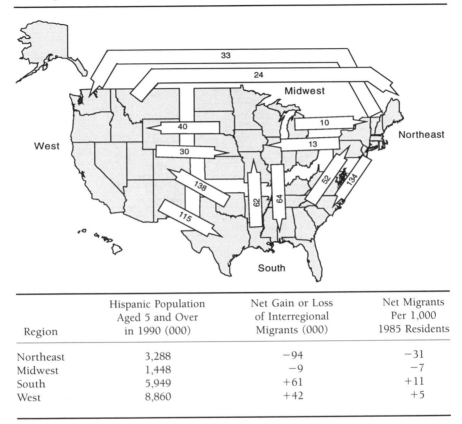

Region	Hispanic Population Aged 5 and Over in 1990 (000)	Net Gain or Loss of Interregional Migrants (000)	Net Migrants Per 1,000 1985 Residents
Northeast	3,288	−94	−31
Midwest	1,448	−9	−7
South	5,949	+61	+11
West	8,860	+42	+5

SOURCE: U.S. Bureau of the Census, *Census of Population and Housing: 1990*, Public Use Microdata Sample.

The odds of moving drop off rapidly with age. If a city or state is eager to attract a larger population, the ideal strategy is to recruit young adults, since many of them will stay once they arrive. As they get old, they are less likely to move. As figure 7-4 shows, there is no spike in the migration rate at ages of retirement. How can we equate this with the emergence of booming retirement centers in Florida and Arizona? Several processes are going on. First, if a small fraction of the older population of the North departs every year, it will produce a rapid increase in

Figure 7-4. The Net Effects of Age, Educational Attainment, and Race on Interstate Migration: 1985 to 1990[a]

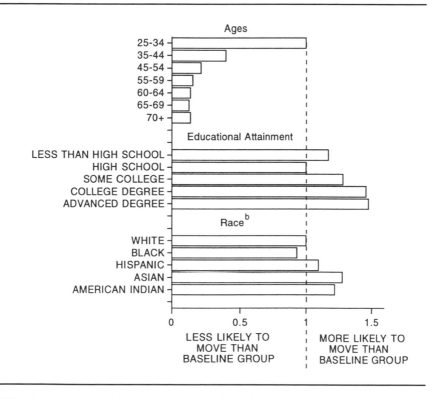

SOURCE: U.S. Bureau of the Census, *Census of Population and Housing: 1990*, Public Use Microdata Sample.

[a] This figure shows the net effect of being in a specific age group, educational category, or racial group relative to being in the baseline category: 25 to 34 for age, complete high school for education, and white for race. If the plotted value is greater than one, people in that category were more likely to move across a state line between 1985 and 1990 than those in the baseline category. The net relative odds of migration for a group are compared to the odds of migration for the baseline group.

[b] All persons reporting Spanish origin in 1990 are classified as Hispanic, regardless of race.

the population aged 65 and over in the destination points. Second, the migration of the elderly is highly targeted to specific locations, so a great share of migrants move to a few places. Finally, if the census were taken in February or March rather than early April, retirement centers would have even larger populations. The substantial number of Canadians migrating to Florida are also excluded.

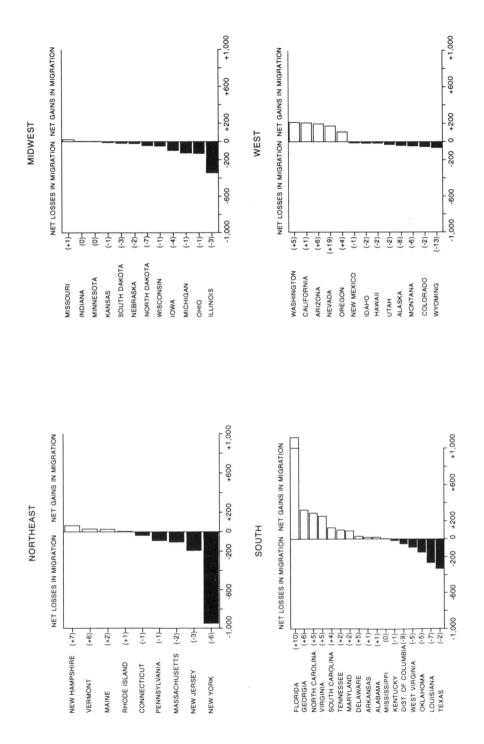

NORTHEAST

NET LOSSES IN MIGRATION   NET GAINS IN MIGRATION

NEW HAMPSHIRE (+7)
VERMONT (+6)
MAINE (+2)
RHODE ISLAND (+1)
CONNECTICUT (-1)
PENNSYLVANIA (-1)
MASSACHUSETTS (-2)
NEW JERSEY (-3)
NEW YORK (-6)

-1,000   -600   -200   0   +200   +600   +1,000

MIDWEST

NET LOSSES IN MIGRATION   NET GAINS IN MIGRATION

MISSOURI (+1)
INDIANA (0)
MINNESOTA (0)
KANSAS (-1)
SOUTH DAKOTA (-3)
NEBRASKA (-2)
NORTH DAKOTA (-7)
WISCONSIN (-1)
IOWA (-4)
MICHIGAN (-1)
OHIO (-1)
ILLINOIS (-3)

-1,000   -600   -200   0   +200   +600   +1,000

SOUTH

NET LOSSES IN MIGRATION   NET GAINS IN MIGRATION

FLORIDA (+10)
GEORGIA (+6)
NORTH CAROLINA (+5)
VIRGINIA (+5)
SOUTH CAROLINA (+4)
TENNESSEE (+2)
MARYLAND (+2)
DELAWARE (+5)
ARKANSAS (+1)
ALABAMA (+1)
MISSISSIPPI (0)
KENTUCKY (-1)
DIST. OF COLUMBIA (-9)
WEST VIRGINIA (-5)
OKLAHOMA (-5)
LOUISIANA (-7)
TEXAS (-2)

-1,000   -600   -200   0   +200   +600   +1,000

WEST

NET LOSSES IN MIGRATION   NET GAINS IN MIGRATION

WASHINGTON (+5)
CALIFORNIA (+1)
ARIZONA (+6)
NEVADA (+19)
OREGON (+4)
NEW MEXICO (-1)
IDAHO (-2)
HAWAII (-2)
UTAH (-2)
ALASKA (-8)
MONTANA (-6)
COLORADO (-2)
WYOMING (-13)

-1,000   -600   -200   0   +200   +600   +1,000

Net of age and race, education was related to the odds of moving across a state line, with increases in education beyond high school matched by rises in migration. Note that persons with less than high school educations also moved more than those with high school diplomas. High school dropouts were hard-hit by the economic restructuring of the 1980s, so much of their migration was prompted by a loss of jobs in old locations and a hope for work in destination points.

Race had a net impact also. Asians and Hispanics were more likely to move than whites, a process attributable to several factors, most importantly the movement of foreign-born Latinos and Asians—persons who entered before 1985—away from ports of arrival. Blacks were less likely than other races to move across state lines, a topic not yet well understood. One often-cited factor is the availability of more generous transfer benefits in the North: unemployment compensation and AFDC. While only a minority of African Americans receive these benefits, those who do so in the North may be reluctant to join the stream of black migrants to the South since if they move and do not find jobs they may be ineligible for the meager transfer benefits offered by southern states. If they qualify for them, they will get less. For example, the average weekly unemployment benefit in Michigan in 1993 was $215; in Mississippi, $127 (U.S. Bureau of the Census 1995b, table 603).

Winner and Loser States in the Exchange of Migrants

Internal migration is now transferring population, economic power, and political strength across regions, but these are huge expanses including up to eighteen states. States are important players in our political system. Figure 7-5 classifies them and the District of Columbia by region and shows their net gains or losses in the exchange with

Figure 7-5 (opposite page).   Net Gains or Losses in Interstate Migration: 1985 to 1990 (in thousands)

SOURCE: U.S. Bureau of the Census, *Census of Population and Housing: 1990*, Public Use Microdata Sample.

NOTE: Numbers in parentheses show the net gain or loss of interstate migrants from 1985 to 1990 per 100 residents in that state in 1985.

other states. It also reports the net migration rate per 100 persons living in specific states in 1985. Immigrants from abroad and emigrants are excluded.

Florida and New York are at the extremes. Between 1985 and 1990, the number moving into Florida was more than a million greater than the number leaving, while New York lost 950,000 more migrants than it gained. Despite this massive loss of population, New York did not lose at the highest rate. That honor went to Wyoming, an isolated state without a major metropolitan area and one damaged by the fall in energy prices. And Nevada gained migrants at an even higher rate than Florida.

Turning to regional patterns, four of the six New England states gained small numbers of migrants. The economic boom known as the "Massachusetts miracle" not only propelled Governor Dukakis into a race for the presidency in 1988 but had a beneficial effect on New Hampshire and Rhode Island. The spread of suburban growth outward from Boston crossed state boundaries, and so these neighboring states gained in the exchange of migrants.

The Midwest was the homogeneous region in terms of migration: most of the twelve states lost moderate numbers as the lure of the South and West shifted where people live. The industrial heartland—Illinois, Ohio, and Michigan—lost the greatest volume of residents, but the loss rate was highest in Iowa and North Dakota. Drops in world prices for agricultural commodities and the continued introduction of labor saving machinery on farms depleted hundreds of counties in the Great Plains, leaving them with elderly populations, since the absence of jobs forces young people to move away after high school.

Three distinct components of the South experienced very different migration trends. Atlantic Coast states from Chesapeake Bay to Key West attracted numerous migrants as they capitalized upon their geographic amenities, their relatively low labor costs, and their transportation links to domestic and foreign markets. The continued growth of Washington, as a leading international city helps explain net inmigration to Virginia and Maryland, although the District of Columbia itself lost migrants at a high rate. Despite the White House and the Capitol, Washington is a typical central city of the 1980s, losing greatly in its exchange with its suburban ring.

Other southern states fared less well with regard to migration. Their demographic trends are much like those of the Northeast and Midwest. A large swath of the South, including most of Appalachia and the old Cotton Belt, is characterized by slow population growth and outmigration. It has yet to attract modern high tech industries or prosperous retirees from New York, Chicago, and Detroit.

One of the least frequently described economic downturns of the 1980s explains the great outmigration from Louisiana, Texas, and Oklahoma. We continued to pay $1.25 each year for a gallon for gasoline throughout the 1980s, so we were unaware of the collapse of oil prices. In constant dollar amounts, they declined sharply. Being more specific, the price of crude oil, in constant dollars, more than tripled during the 1970s, making Houston the booming capital of a thriving region. If those trends had continued, Houston would have become a prominent international city. But macroeconomic trends can remove what they give, and, by 1988, producers were getting only 40 percent as much for their oil as eight years earlier. U.S. production remained about constant in amount, but every barrel was worth much less to those who pumped it out of the ground (U.S. Bureau of the Census 1995b, table 1184). Given the spectacular rise in oil prices in the 1970s, the residents of Texas, Louisiana, and Oklahoma received little sympathy from the rest of the country when energy prices plunged, but this great economic turnabout accounts for the substantial outmigration. The continuation of low energy prices benefits most of the nation, but it seriously dampens growth in this section of the South. Only one state—Wyoming—lost migrants at a higher rate than Louisiana in the late 1980s.

Figure 7-5 focuses attention upon the internal migration of persons living in the United States in 1985. But it is important to keep in mind how international migration played itself out on a state-by-state basis. Three-quarters of those who arrived in this country between 1985 and 1990 took up residence in just seven states. In four of these states—New York, Texas, New Jersey, and Illinois—international immigration offset substantial losses in the exchange of migrants with other states. New York lost 950,000 to other states, but gained 244,000 from abroad. If there had been no international migration, these states would have been much bigger demographic losers, including a loss of Congressional representation. California—but most especially Florida—were the big demographic winners in the late 1980s since they gained internal migrants and attracted many new arrivals from Latin America and Asia.

The Census Bureau collects migration data on an annual basis. Numbers from the early 1990s suggest that California is now losing in its exchange with other states—a net loss of more than one million from 1990 to 1994. Is it possible that California's politicians will take a more favorable view of immigration once they realize that newcomers from abroad are sustaining their claims for seats in Congress and for federal appropriations? (See U.S. Bureau of the Census 1994a, table 2.)

Metropolitan Migration Patterns: Why Some Areas Gain and Others Lose?

Knowing that someone moved from Ohio to Florida does not tell you much about changes in employment prospects. But if you learn that a young man with a high school diploma moved from Youngstown to Orlando in 1987, you know that he left a metropolis where employment was falling and entered one where it was booming. Presumably, some combination of warm Florida sunshine and the prospect of earning a nice living prompted this move, but the census does not question motivation.

Most stakeholders in local communities benefit greatly from population growth and lose out quickly when population and paychecks—or Social Security and Medicare payments—move out. Merchants sell more cars, clothes, refrigerators, and pet food if the local population goes up 3 or 4 percent every year. Bankers see their deposits grow and their portfolio of good loans increase if the population booms. On the downside, if the major employer shuts down, there will be outmigration, and some of those leaving will default on mortgages and car payments. Contractors and the many highly paid people who work for them are well organized and lobby effectively, since their prosperity depends directly upon the construction of new houses, shopping malls, and schools. Local governments and their numerous employees are the among the biggest local boosters since revenues for these governments increase only when homes, office buildings, and factories are added to the tax rolls year after year. In every state, public school funding depends at least in part upon enrollment, so teachers and administrators do everything possible to make sure that every school age child walks into a classroom at the start of the academic year (Logan 1987).

What is the best way to foster population growth and continued prosperity in a community? Ordinarily, it involves creating new jobs, and here is where the growth machine comes in. Financial institutions, local governmental officials, and merchants in many communities coordinate their efforts to keep the jobs they have and attract new ones—preferably high-skilled, high-paying jobs, although new low-skilled jobs are much better than factory closings and layoffs. Some areas are more capable than others of putting together the attractive packages and political clout that lure employment, be it a military base, a new automobile plant, an additional state prison, or a factory producing microchips for computers. To win a new Mercedes-Benz plant, the city of Vance and the state of Alabama provided free land, huge tax abatements, and a promise to train workers so that they would be skilled enough for this German firm. In addition, the state agreed to subsidize wages of Alabamians who built the vehicles and then promised to purchase 2,500 new Mercedes (Kasarda 1995, p. 228). More glamorous—and more controversial—have been the expenditures of taxpayers' money in Baltimore, Buffalo, Chicago, Cleveland, and a dozen other older cities to build new stadiums for their professional sports teams—a move that pleases some merchants, retains service sector jobs, and boosts downtrodden business districts, at least when there is a game in town.

Metropolises in the South and West were better able to compete for new employment than were places in the Midwest and Northeast. It is impossible to know exactly what makes a large firm locate their corporate headquarters or a major new plant in Charlotte or Raleigh rather than Detroit or Flint, but boards of directors and decision-makers may be influenced by their beliefs about the business climate in local areas, by the availability of spacious land at low cost, and by a generous supply of skilled, but low-wage, labor. Putting together large parcels of land for modern manufacturing plants or for the campuslike grounds of new corporate offices is a challenge in older metropolises of the Rustbelt. These metropolises suffer since they are often viewed as having excessively high taxes, far too many regulations, and acreage that was polluted decades ago by now-defunct firms. As regional differences in earnings attest, the Midwest and Northeast are high-wage states, some of them still retaining reputations for unionization. Quite a few new factories were built recently in the industrial heartland, including automobile assembly plants and the revolutionary mini-mills now producing steel. But these plants are much more efficient than the ones they replaced: output increased, while employment declined. It is easy to imagine that executive officers and site-visiting committees, influenced by econometric models of wage costs, taxes, and labor productivity in a location, are also strongly influenced by the climate of the Sunbelt. The golf and sailing seasons are five months longer each year in Florida and Arizona than in Massachusetts or Michigan.

Growth machines in the South and West often defeated the growth machines of the older industrial states in the fierce competition for employment. Other factors come into play in explaining where jobs were increasing or disappearing. Kasarda (1995) stresses the extensive policing and protective costs employers must pay if they locate in or near violence-prone neighborhoods. A recent study of where Japanese auto parts producers located their plants reveals that they avoided high concentrations of African Americans (Cole and Deskins 1988). After building a large green-field plant in Marysville, Ohio, Honda decided that those who lived more than thirty-five miles away could not be hired. This excluded black residents of Columbus, but permitted whites from the suburban ring to build new cars, a practice that was successfully overturned by the NAACP.

No matter how efficient it is, a local growth machine cannot thwart macroeconomic trends. Throughout the nation, employment in entertainment, healthcare, professional services, and finance boomed in the 1980s, while manufacturing jobs declined. Even if chambers of commerce and governors in the industrial states did their work competently, they swam against the tide. Given the growth of discretionary spending and the decisions that channeled billions to healthcare, Las Vegas, Nevada, and Rochester, Minnesota (the location of the Mayo Clinic), had an advantage in the competition for new jobs because of their industrial specializations, while Pittsburgh and Toledo with their World War I–era factories faced dire prospects.

Employment by Industries

The 1980s were good years for employment growth since the number of persons holding jobs went up by 19 percent, almost 2 percent each and every year. Figure 7-6 shows why every popular summary of trends in employment starts with observations about the dramatic rise in service sector jobs. Six of the seven most rapidly growing industrial categories produced services, not new cars, new homes, or new computers. And the seventh most rapidly growing sector—finance, insurance, and real estate—is also a service industry, albeit one designed to provide us with economic security and wealth.

This figure also hints at why old industrial centers grew slowly in the 1980s. Employment in durable goods manufacturing dropped by 8 percent. In nondurable manufacturing—those factories turning out food products, clothing, chemicals, and tires—the decline was 4 percent. The market for manufacturing products expanded as the population grew rapidly and per capita income went up, but it was a terrible time to hold a blue-collar factory job. Producers could lay off thousands of men and women who cut, shaped, assembled, and moved manufactured goods and still increase their output.

Figure 7-6. Percent Change in Employment, by Industry: 1980 to 1990

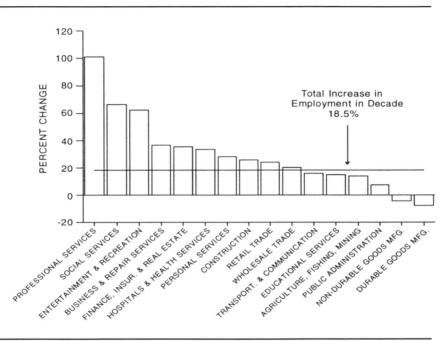

SOURCE: U.S. Bureau of the Census, *Census of Population and Housing: 1990 and 1980,* Public Use Microdata Sample.

Gains and Losses of Metropolitan Areas in the Competition for New Jobs

Whether jobs are created or lost has a great deal to do with whether people migrate into or away from a metropolis, especially those young adults who move at the highest rates. We will first describe employment changes in the major metropolises in the 1980s and then link them to migration patterns.

What do we mean when we mention geographic areas with well-known names, such as Phoenix, Orlando, and Pittsburgh? Is it just the central city bearing that name, or is it the city and its ring of contiguous suburbs or some broader geographic expanse? This is confusing since the same name is often applied to different areas. Sometimes New York means just the city with its five boroughs, while at other times the name refers to the huge, densely settled area stretching from central New Jersey through southern Connecticut.

People spread out around the locations of jobs and amenities, but our statistical systems allocate them to particular places that have legal standing because our system of government is based upon geographic entities. Since 1900, the Census Bureau has defined areas that encompass the densely settled area around a large city, but the strategies for doing so changed frequently. There is not much agreement about where the boundaries of a metropolis should be drawn, particularly when previously distinct areas grow together, such as Dallas with Fort Worth and Washington with Baltimore. Should Miami and Ft. Lauderdale be separate metropolises? You can take a train from San Francisco to San Jose. Does that mean that they are distinct metropolises?

Today, metropolitan areas include a central city—typically one city of fifty thousand or more, or two paired cities satisfying that population criterion—the county that the city is in, and all contiguous counties that are economically integrated with the county containing the central city or cities. Economic integration is the key and is indexed by commuting patterns. If an outlying county sends many workers to a central city, it is included in the metropolis. Metropolitan areas, except in New England, are defined on the basis of county lines. This is fortunate since county boundaries remain constant over time, meaning it is possible to describe changes across the decades for constant geographic areas. In New England, town lines are used for metropolises. For the census of 1990, 318 metropolitan statistical areas (MSAs) were defined, ranging in size from Los Angeles with its nine million residents to Casper, Wyoming, with just sixty-one thousand. Where the population agglomerations are the largest—greater New York or southern California, for instance—the boundaries of metropolitan areas touch. For this reason there are twenty consolidated metropolitan statistical areas (CMSAs) consisting of two to twelve component metropolises. New York was the largest CMSA, with more than eighteen million, and Providence the smallest, with just over a million. In this analysis of employment trends, we focus upon 127 metropolitan areas, or CMSAs of 250,000 or more in 1990, for which comparable data about employment could be assembled.

I began with the industrial structure of each metropolis in 1980: the number of employed persons aged 18 to 64 classified by their industry. I then asked how much employment would have increased in that metropolis if each industry had the national growth rate for jobs in that specific industry. This gives us a picture of which locations were poised for rapid growth in the 1980s and which had bleak prospects because of their unfavorable niche in the nation's economic system. We would expect rapid growth in places specializing in entertainment or professional services, such as law, medicine, and finance, but slow growth in manufacturing centers.

The column to the left in table 7-1 lists metropolises by their expected employment growth, showing the top ten and the bottom ten. Two entertainment centers head this list: Las Vegas and Reno. Because of their specialization in entertainment and services and their dearth of manufacturing jobs in 1980, they were expected to grow rapidly. Four Florida metropolises are also among the top ten, places with much service sector employment in 1980, but few manufacturing jobs. At the bottom are smaller and older manufacturing centers, including two older textile production centers in the Piedmont—Greensboro and Greenville; several steel towns—Allentown and Youngstown; and one center for the production of Buicks and Chevrolets—Flint. Even in these places, moderate growth of employment was expected. They have quite diversified economies even though their industrial base has been manufacturing, so the expected growth of employment falls in a fairly narrow range from a high of 28 percent for Las Vegas to a low of 13 percent in older manufacturing centers. There were just six places with 40 percent or more of their jobs in manufacturing in 1980: Allentown, Flint, Greensboro, Greenville, Rockford, and York. All of them made the list of slowest expected growth. These are the places where the local growth machines had to work hardest to retain jobs and population since their industrial structure was unfavorable to employment growth.

What about actual growth of employment during the 1980s? Here there is much greater variation. The ten metropolitan areas with the most rapid or the slowest growth of jobs are shown in the middle column of table 7-1. Six of the biggest winners were Florida metropolises—places that benefited both from the inmigration of retirees and the pervasive population and economic growth occurring throughout that state. Las Vegas, as expected, made the list of growing places, as did Austin, the booming capital of Texas. California's capital, Sacramento, also had spectacular job growth—twelfth on the list. In fourteen large metropolises, employment went up by more than 50 percent in the decade. All of them were located in Florida, Texas, Arizona, or California, except for Las Vegas.

The average for these large metropolises was an employment increase of 18 percent, so a place was highly unusual if it actually lost jobs, but there were eight that did. All of them were either older manufacturing places—the steel centers of Pittsburgh, Youngstown, and

Table 7-1. Metropolitan Areas Ranked by Expected and Actual Employment Growth in the 1980s

Rank	Areas Ranked by Expected Employment Growth During the 1980s		Areas Ranked by Actual Employment Change During the 1980s		Areas Ranked by Actual Change in Employment as Percentage of Expected	
			Most Rapidly Growing			
1	Las Vegas, NV	+28%	Ft. Myers, FL	+83%	Ft. Myers, FL	+340%
2	Reno, NV	+26	Orlando, FL	+76	Orlando, FL	+327
3	Sarasota, FL	+25	Daytona Beach, FL	+66	Melbourne, FL	+301
4	Ft. Myers, FL	+25	West Palm Beach, FL	+65	West Palm Beach, FL	+291
5	Washington, DC	+24	Las Vegas, NV	+65	Daytona Beach, FL	+286
6	Albuquerque, NM	+24	Melbourne, FL	+63	Phoenix, AZ	+263
7	Atlantic City, NJ	+23	Sarasota, FL	+54	Austin, TX	+259
8	Orlando, FL	+23	Austin, TX	+54	Modesto, CA	+242
9	Honolulu, HI	+23	Phoenix, AZ	+53	San Diego, CA	+242
10	Daytona Beach, FL	+23	San Diego, CA	+52	Stockton, CA	+239

		Least Rapidly Growing or Declining			
10	Lancaster, PA	+14	Toledo, OH	+2	Toledo, OH	+10
9	Youngstown, OH	+14	Canton, OH	+1	Canton, OH	+8
8	Erie, PA	+14	New Orleans, LA	−1	New Orleans, LA	−4
7	Greenville, SC	+14	Pittsburgh, PA	−2	Pittsburgh, PA	−10
6	Greensboro, NC	+14	Youngstown, OH	−2	Youngstown, OH	−14
5	Johnson City, TN	+13	Beaumont, TX	−5	Beaumont, TX	−31
4	Rockford, IL	+13	Charleston, WV	−6	Charleston, WV	−33
3	Allentown, PA	+13	Utica, NY	−7	Utica, NY	−48
2	Flint, MI	+13	Chattanooga, TN	−8	Chattanooga, TN	−57
1	York, PA	+13	Shreveport, LA	−14	Shreveport, LA	−72

SOURCE: U.S. Bureau of the Census, *Census of Population and Housing: 1990 and 1980*, Public Use Microdata Samples.

NOTES: Data refer to metropolises of 250,000 or more in 1990 using the same geographic area for 1980 and 1990. Column to the left shows the percentage increase in employment expected in a metropolis if each industrial sector in that metropolis had increased its employment at the national rate for that industrial sector in the 1980s. Center column shows actual change in employment. Column to the right shows actual change as percentage of expected change. Data refer to the employed population aged 18 to 64.

Canton—or were greatly hurt by the plunge of oil prices, as in the case of Beaumont and Shreveport. Twenty-one metropolises saw their numbers of jobs grow by less than 10 percent; sixteen were older manufacturing centers in the Midwest or were in the troubled oil patch. Declining manufacturing employment and the collapse of oil prices pretty much accounts for why some places saw the number of jobs decline or grow very slowly.

What about places that did much better or much worse than expected in the competition for jobs? The column to the right in table 7-1 ranks metropolises by how their actual increase in employment compares to their expected increase. If this number exceeds 100 percent, the metropolis gained more jobs than would be expected, on the basis of its 1980 economic structure. You might assume that growth machines in these places—the winners in the competition for jobs—worked effectively since they gained more jobs than expected. If the number in the right column is less than 100 percent, the place did not fare well in the competition to retain old jobs and win new ones. Some might think of this as a scorecard for local growth machines.

There is a familiar story here. The booming metropolises of Florida, three in California, and Phoenix did much better than expected. At the other extreme, older manufacturing places, including the chemical manufacturing center of Charleston, West Virginia, faired poorly in the competition for jobs. The center and right-hand lists are similar since metropolises joined the list of most or least rapidly growing places only if they gained or lost many more jobs than expected.

What about the very largest metropolises? They seldom appear on the lists we examined. Twenty-one metropolises had populations of two million or more in 1990. Table 7-2 provides information about these metropolises, which have traditionally been national or international centers of industry, media, and financial control. Pittsburgh alone lost jobs in the 1980s, but the growth was just 3 percent in Cleveland. In metropolitan Chicago and Detroit, jobs increased about 10 percent and in New York, 13 percent. Phoenix, Tampa, and Atlanta led with very high rates of growth. Washington also did well. Federal government employment did not grow much in the 1980s, but the continued importance of the government, more international trade, and more regulations meant a tremendous increase in those white-collar professionals who influence federal policy and federal spending. Note the contrast of two Texas cities—Houston, where jobs increased at the national rate, and booming Dallas.

The most rapidly growing metropolises stand out since they cap-

Table 7-2. Employment Change During the 1980s in Metropolises of Two Million or More

Rank	Metropolis Ranked by Job Growth in the 1980s	Actual Change in Employment 1980 to 1990	Actual Change as Percentage of Expected Change
1	Phoenix, AZ	53%	263%
2	San Diego, CA	52	242
3	Tampa, FL	50	222
4	Atlanta, GA	45	226
5	Dallas, TX	39	208
6	Washington, DC	37	155
7	Seattle, WA	35	177
8	Los Angeles, CA	32	164
9	Miami, FL	26	117
10	San Francisco, CA	25	120
11	Minneapolis, MN	25	133
12	Baltimore, MD	23	119
13	Houston, TX	18	86
14	Boston, MA	17	90
15	Philadelphia, PA	16	87
16	New York, NY	13	64
17	St. Louis, MO	12	66
18	Chicago, IL	10	55
19	Detroit, MI	9	58
20	Cleveland, OH	3	16
21	Pittsburgh, PA	−2	−10

SOURCE: U.S. Bureau of the Census, *Census of Population and Housing: 1990 and 1980,* Public Use Microdata Samples.

NOTE: Figures in right column show actual change in employment as a percentage of the change expected on the basis of that metropolis' industrial structure in 1980 and national rates of employment growth for specific industries. Data pertain to employed persons aged 18 to 64 and are based on a constant geographic area.

tured many more new jobs than expected. Their population and job growth stimulated even more inmigration and this, in turn, fostered more employment growth. This is another example of the chain migration process stimulating more growth. Phoenix, San Diego, Atlanta,

Tampa, and Dallas did best at attracting more jobs than expected on the basis of their 1980 industrial structure, and thus they were the biggest winners in the competition for new jobs. Minneapolis stands out since it was one of the few metropolises in the Midwest to gain many more jobs than expected. The Rustbelt centers, Pittsburgh and Cleveland, were least successful in the competition for jobs. Detroit, New York, and St. Louis also gained just a modest fraction of the new jobs they expected, reflecting their high land costs, their congestion, their high-wage levels, and a myriad of other factors.

Migration Trends for Metropolises: Winners and Losers

Those booming locations in Florida, California, Nevada, and Arizona that won in the competition for jobs also won in the competition for interstate migrants. Here I turn to net gains or losses in the exchange of interstate migrants during the half-decade before the census of 1990.

Table 7-3 lists metropolises that had the highest rates of migration gain or loss in the five years before the census. These data refer to people aged 5 and older in 1990 who lived in the United States in 1985—both native- and foreign-born. Florida cities and Las Vegas were winners. Ft. Pierce, a small metropolis on the Atlantic coast of Florida that just made the 250,000 cutoff, led the nation in its rate of migration gain, but Las Vegas and Ft. Myers, Florida, were not far behind. In a five-year span, they attracted migrants equal to one-quarter of their population in 1985. Orlando and Charlotte, thanks to their favorable internal migration rates, joined the ranks of the metropolises with more than one million residents. If migration trends in the 1990s are anything like those of the late 1980s, rapidly growing Las Vegas, Jacksonville, Raleigh, and Austin will become demographic millionaires by the next census.

Places losing jobs because of industrial restructuring or the fall of energy prices figure prominently on the list of net exporters of migrants, as shown toward the bottom of table 7-3. In total volume, New York led the nation: the number departing for other states was more than one million greater than the number moving in. Metropolitan New York lost 6 percent of its 1985 population in just five years in this migration exchange. On lists of losers such as these, ports of entry for the foreign-born are likely to show up. New York and Brownsville, Texas, attracted many immigrants from abroad. After living in such metropolises for a few years, many immigrants master English, learn about the U.S. job market, and then move to where

Table 7-3.   Metropolitan Areas with Highest Rates of Gain or Loss of Interstate Migrants: 1985 to 1990

Rank	Metropolis	Net Migration Rate per 100 Residents in 1985[a]	Net Number of Migrants (000) 1985 to 1990
	Highest Rates of Gain		
1	Ft. Pierce, FL	+26	+48
2	Las Vegas, NV	+24	+128
3	Ft. Myers, FL	+23	+57
4	Daytona Beach, FL	+19	+55
5	Orlando, FL	+16	+132
6	West Palm Beach, FL	+16	+107
7	Melbourne, FL	+16	+49
8	Sarasota, FL	+12	+29
9	Modesto, CA	+12	+35
10	Raleigh, NC	+11	+66
	Highest Rates of Loss		
10	Youngstown, OH	−5	−23
9	Charleston, WV	−5	−12
8	Brownsville, TX	−5	−23
7	Beaumont, TX	−6	−20
6	Flint, MI	−6	−25
5	Davenport, IW	−6	−21
4	Corpus Christi, TX	−6	−21
3	New York, NY	−6	−1,066
2	New Orleans, LA	−7	−88
1	Shreveport, LA	−8	−27

SOURCE: U.S. Bureau of the Census, *Census of Population and Housing: 1990*, Public Use Microdata Sample.

[a]The number of interstate migrants aged 5 and over in 1990 entering an area was subtracted from the number of interstate migrants leaving that area to determine net migration. The number of net migrants was divided by the metropolis's estimated 1985 population to determine net migrants per 100 persons living there in 1985. Data refer to 136 consolidated metropolitan statistical areas and metropolitan statistical areas of 250,000 or more in 1990.

economic and housing opportunities are better. This helps to explain these high outmigration rates and accounts, to some degree, for out-migration from Houston and Los Angeles.

Migration for the Age Groups

Which metropolises gained those young adults who are starting their careers? What about retirees? Which places gained them at the highest rates? Table 7-4 reports the places gaining late baby boomers, persons aged 25 to 34 in 1990, at the highest and lowest rates. These are prize catches in the competition for migrants. The list of migration destinations is a familiar one. Florida was again an obvious winner since five locations there were toward the top of the list. But two large metropolises outside the Sunshine state also attracted late baby boomers at high rates. Atlanta and Charlotte are now important desti-nation points as young people develop their careers. It is unusual to see any northern location on a list of migration winners, but Ports-mouth, New Hampshire, appears on this list, a result of its incorpora-tion into the Boston suburban ring.

Metropolises losing late baby boomers at the highest rates in-cluded several places hard hit by falling energy prices. Young adults in the 1980s moved away from New Orleans and Oklahoma City for an understandable reason—few jobs. But there is a different reason why Austin and Kileen, Texas, appear on this list. Locations with ma-jor military bases—Kileen with Fort Hood—or with universities—Austin with the University of Texas—lose a substantial fraction of their young adult population every year. They attract people aged 18 to 22 for the education and military training they offer, but after a few years these people move away. The distinctive pattern of Mormon students doing missionary work before graduating from college ex-plains why Provo, Utah, the home of Brigham Young University, leads the nation in the loss rate of late baby boomers.

What about retirees? Table 7-4 shows metropolises gaining or los-ing population aged 65 and over. It is not surprising that places in Florida and sunny Arizona lead the nation in attracting older inter-state migrants. Perhaps the only surprise is the great popularity of Las Vegas. Regardless of the demographic indicator, Las Vegas proved to be a popular destination in the late 1980s: its retiree population in-creased by one-quarter in the later half of that decade, thanks to mi-gration.

Interstate migration selects the most prosperous retirees, so the locations losing this age group at the highest rate are those that traditionally had high wage levels and good fringe benefits. These include Flint, Michigan, where the United Auto Workers emphasized retirement benefits and Binghamton, New York, where IBM was the major employer. High costs of living and fears of crime in the biggest metropolises undoubtedly encouraged many older persons to make their moves to Florida or Arizona, so New York, Los Angeles, and Chicago lead the list of places with the highest rates of outmigration. The run-up of housing prices along the coasts in the 1980s enabled many workers to complete their careers, sell their homes for lucrative capital gains, and then invest in luxurious retirement properties near Sarasota, Phoenix, or Las Vegas.

Migration of the Extensively and Minimally Educated

If you planned the economic development of a metropolis, you would try to attract employers who would recruit college graduates knowing that, after they arrived, they would create many jobs to be filled by less educated workers because they will build new homes, buy VCRs, have cars to be fixed, and will use short-order restaurants. In table 7-5, metropolises are ranked by their gain or loss of interstate migrants, classified by educational attainment. These rates refer to persons in the prime labor force ages of 25 to 54. Information to the left refers to college graduates, to the right to persons who reported high school educations or less.

Earlier this century, migration and suburbanization filled in the Atlantic coast from Boston to Philadelphia. A major story of the 1990s is the way migration is filling in the Florida coast from Miami to Jacksonville, along with a densely populated corridor reaching over to Tampa, and then stretching south along the Gulf shore to Ft. Myers. On all measures, this area proved most attractive to migrants. When the population of a metropolis goes up, there is a need for more doctors, school teachers, lawyers, and accountants; and thus these Florida metropolises, along with Las Vegas, led the nation in their rates of attracting college degree–holders. Three large metropolises, Atlanta, Charlotte, and Jacksonville, also stand out for their rates of gaining highly educated interstate migrants. Metropolises losing their educated populations at a high rate include the older industrial centers and several places where a university was the dominant employer—Madison, Baton Rouge, and Provo. They are exporting the college graduates they train.

Table 7-4. Metropolitan Areas with Highest Rates of Gain or Loss of Interstate Migrants Classified by Birth Cohorts: 1985 to 1990[a]

Late Baby Boom Cohort (age 25 to 34 in 1990)		Parents and Grandparents of the Baby Boom (age 65 and over in 1990)	
Metropolis	Net Migration Rate per 100 1985 Residents	Metropolis	Net Migration Rate per 100 1985 Residents
Highest Rates of Migration Gain			
Ft. Pierce, FL	+27	Ft. Pierce, FL	+23
Las Vegas, NV	+27	Las Vegas, NV	+23
Ft. Myers, FL	+23	Lakeland, FL	+16
Modesto, CA	+21	Ft. Myers, FL	+16
Orlando, FL	+21	Melbourne, FL	+16
Atlanta, GA	+18	West Palm Beach, FL	+15
West Palm Beach, FL	+18	Daytona Beach, FL	+13
Portsmouth, NH	+16	Sarasota, FL	+10
Charlotte, NC	+14	Tucson, AZ	+10
Daytona Beach, FL	+14	Phoenix, AZ	+9

Highest Rates of Migration Loss

New Orleans, LA	-9	Flint, MI	-3
Oklahoma City, OK	-10	Lansing, MI	-3
Honolulu, HI	-10	San Francisco, CA	-3
Austin, TX	-11	Boston, MA	-3
Kileen, TX	-11	Binghamton, NY	-3
Baton Rouge, LA	-12	Los Angeles, CA	-4
Santa Barbara, CA	-12	Washington, DC	-4
Shreveport, LA	-13	Detroit, MI	-4
Fayetteville, NC	-13	Chicago, IL	-5
Provo, UT	-28	New York, NY	-6

SOURCE: U.S. Bureau of the Census, *Census Population and Housing: 1990*, Public Use Microdata Sample.

[a]The number of interstate migrants aged 5 and over in 1990 entering an area was subtracted from the number of interstate migrants leaving that area to determine net migration. The number of net migrants was divided by the metropolis' estimated 1985 population to determine net migrants per 100 persons living there in 1985. Data refer to 136 CMSAs and MSAs of 250,000 or more in 1990.

Table 7-5. Metropolitan Areas with Highest Rates of Gain or Loss of Interstate Migrants Between 1985 and 1990 by Educational Attainment in 1990

College Graduates		High School Graduates or Less	
Metropolis	Migration Rate[a]	Metropolis	Migration Rate[a]
Highest Rates of Gain			
Ft. Pierce, FL	+41	Ft. Pierce, FL	+27
Ft. Myers, FL	+33	Las Vegas, NV	+25
West Palm Beach, FL	+26	Ft. Myers, FL	+20
Las Vegas, NV	+26	Daytona Beach, FL	+19
Sarasota, FL	+25	Melbourne, FL	+17
Orlando, FL	+18	West Palm Beach, FL	+14
Melbourne, FL	+15	Modesto, CA	+12
Atlanta, GA	+15	Lakeland, FL	+12
Jacksonville, FL	+13	Orlando, FL	+12
Daytona Beach, FL	+12	Sarasota, FL	+11
Highest Rates of Loss			
New Orleans, LA	−9	Houston, TX	−4
Binghamton, NY	−10	Denver, CO	−4
Huntington, WV	−10	Corpus Christi, TX	−4
Oklahoma City, OK	−10	San Francisco, CA	−4
Toledo, OH	−10	New Orleans, LA	−5
Lansing, MI	−11	Shreveport, LA	−5
Santa Barbara, CA	−11	New York, NY	−6
Madison, WI	−11	Honolulu, HI	−6
Baton Route, LA	−12	Fayetteville, NC	−6
Provo, UT	−29	Colorado Springs, CO	−7

SOURCE: U.S. Bureau of the Census, *Census of Population and Housing: 1990,* Public Use Microdata Sample.

[a]This shows net migrants per 100 residents in this educational category in 1985. Data pertain to persons 25 to 54 and refer to 136 CMSAs and MSAs of 250,000 or more in 1990.

Metropolises growing most rapidly simultaneously attract both college graduates and people with less education. It is no surprise that Florida locales and Las Vegas led the nation in their migration gains of people at both ends of the educational scale. If you were a high school graduate looking for a job, you would go to where the population growth is most rapid.

Metropolises losing persons with high school educations or less at a high rate include those experiencing sharp economic downturns in the 1980s, Houston and New Orleans, and places where the military was the major employer, such as Fayetteville, North Carolina, the home of Ft. Bragg.

In this era of fast-paced employment change, chambers of commerce and mayors often proclaim that their metropolises have gone through favorable metamorphoses, switching from the old-style factory production of durable goods to new high tech industries, research, and financial services. If such dramatic changes are occurring, they should show up in the migration rates we examine. If a metropolis lost its jobs in smokestack industries but gained many in research parks, there should be a substantial inmigration of the college-educated, but an outmigration of those men and women who have a strong back and a dedication to hard work, but no college credentials.

The large metropolises considered in this analysis may be classified into three types with regard to their migration patterns. First, many areas lost both the college-educated and those with much less education. This was the situation for New York, Detroit, Houston, and almost all places in the Rustbelt or Oil Patch. There is no evidence of a favorable restructuring of employment. Rather, the story is the very slow growth or loss of jobs at all levels. Pittsburgh is sometimes cited as the quintessential metropolis undergoing a beneficial industrial restructuring, but demographic evidence refutes this claim. In the last half of the 1980s, Pittsburgh lost 6 percent of the college graduates who lived there in 1985 and 2 percent of its high school–educated population—identical with trends for Buffalo and Cleveland.

Second, booming metropolises attracted both the highly educated and those with high school educations or less. Las Vegas, Sacramento, and Phoenix lead this list in the West; Tampa and Orlando in the South. Many other places attracted both types of interstate migrants, but at modest rates, a pattern found in Miami. These growing locations offer employment both to the college-educated who can sell securities and those with high school training who can plumb. Midwestern metropolises do not appear in this group.

Finally, there are the locations that had the most favorable migration exchange—a gain of the highly educated but a loss of those with little education. Four large metropolises stand for their success at this type of restructuring: Washington, San Francisco, Los Angeles, and Dallas. Employment changes made these locations attractive for college graduates who pursued careers by influencing federal policy in the nation's capital, by working in the computer industry centered in Silicon Valley just south of San Francisco, in media employment in Los Angeles, or in finance in Dallas. At the same time, their arrival, and the arrival of immigrants from abroad, may have made these locations much less appealing for people with high school degrees or less. Housing prices rose sharply, narrowing options for low-income residents while immigrants competed for the low-skill jobs, causing the outmigration of the less educated between 1985 and 1990. Two other large southern metropolises stand out for their highly favorable migration patterns—Atlanta and Charlotte. While they attracted people from both ends of the educational distribution, their rates of gain were much higher for the college-educated. Interestingly, neither of these attracted many foreign immigrants, so their economic and population growth may be stimulating an influx of workers with just high school educations to fill the many new jobs for retail clerks, truck drivers, and construction workers.

New Migration Trends by Race

Blacks are leaving the North and returning to the South, but Hispanics who move within the United States are increasingly choosing metropolises that formerly were home to few Hispanics. To understand what is happening to population distribution thus far, we ranked metros by the rate at which they gained or lost migrants. We make a slight shift here. Quite a few metropolises had tiny black or Hispanic populations in 1985, so the arrival of a hundred or so produced unusually high migration rates. A much improved picture of recent trends emerges from examining the net number of interstate black or Hispanic migrants entering or leaving a metropolis. The winners and losers in this exchange are shown in table 7-6.

Seven of the metropolises gaining the most black migrants are in the South, illustrating the new pattern of black migration. Old centers of black population—Atlanta, Dallas, Norfolk, Richmond, and Washington—are now key destination points, but Orlando also appears on the list. Soon it will be a major center for black population. The three other places—San Diego, Minneapolis, and Sacramento—point out the new dispersion of blacks across the national landscape. As the number of African American college graduates rises, many will take jobs as lawyers or engineers in traditional black centers, such as Richmond, Washington, and Atlanta, where there are many other middle-class blacks. But others will enter the national job market and get their best job offer from employers elsewhere, so they will teach, practice accounting, or develop software in Minneapolis, Sacramento, Phoenix, or Las Vegas.

The bottom panel reports places losing in the exchange of interstate migrants. While there are many discussions of urban underclass neighborhoods, few of them describe how outmigration is now sharply reducing their populations. Blacks are no longer moving into Chicago, Detroit, or New York. Quite the opposite. Metropolitan New York with a loss of 192,000 and Chicago with its loss of 70,000 had net migration declines of at least 5 percent of their 1985 black populations. The lack of good job opportunities and a constellation of urban problems involving public schools, housing, crime, and drug use help explain why migration trends for blacks in the 1980s and 1990s look nothing like those of the 1940s or 1950s.

This analysis describes the migration of people living in the United States in 1985. We might think that ports of entry for immigrants would, in any five-year period, be major losers in the exchange of interstate migrants. A person arriving from Mexico, El Salvador, or the Dominican Republic might work in their port of arrival for a few years, just as the Irish did in Boston and New York 150 years ago, but then learn that there are better jobs, safer neighborhoods, and more attractive housing in other places. Some major points of arrival for Hispanics—New York, Los Angeles, and Texas metros near the Rio Grande—appear on the list of major losers of Hispanic interstate migrants. Immigrants stay there for a while and then move on. This does not mean that Hispanic populations went down since, unlike the situation for blacks, there is a continuing major immigration of Hispanics from abroad. The list of metropolises now attracting interstate Hispanic migrants is a curious one. It includes some places near ports of arrival—Las Vegas, Phoenix, Tampa, and Orlando. The booming populations of these places create many job openings to be filled by Hispanics. But major ports of entry for Hispanic migrants are also winners on this interstate exchange. Miami stands out. Hispanics wishing to capitalize upon their skills may find unusually good opportunities there. Dade County, where Miami is located, has a population of two million. In the early 1990s, it had the distinction of becoming

Table 7-6. Metropolitan Areas with Gains or Losses of Interstate Black and Hispanic Migrants: 1985 to 1990

Rank	Blacks			Hispanics		
	Metropolis	Net Number of Migrants (000)	Net Migrants per 100 1985 Residents	Metropolis	Net Number of Migrants (000)	Net Migrants per 100 1985 Residents
	Largest Net Gains					
1	Atlanta, GA	+75	+13	Miami, FL	+48	+6
2	Norfolk, VA	+29	+9	Orlando, FL	+24	+54
3	Washington, DC	+20	+2	San Diego, CA	+20	+5
4	Raleigh, NC	+17	+12	Las Vegas, NV	+16	+34
5	Dallas, TX	+16	+3	Tampa, FL	+14	+14
6	Orlando, FL	+14	+14	Dallas, TX	+12	+3
7	Richmond, VA	+13	+6	Phoenix, AZ	+11	+4
8	San Diego, CA	+12	+10	Sacramento, CA	+11	+9
9	Minneapolis, MN	+12	+18	Modesto, CA	+10	+18
10	Sacramento, CA	+11	+14	Washington, DC	+10	+7

Largest Net Losses

1	New York, NY	−192	−6		New York, NY	−148	−6
2	Chicago, IL	−70	−5		Los Angeles, CA	−54	−1
3	Detroit, MI	−19	−2		San Francisco, CA	−24	−3
4	New Orleans, LA	−16	−4		Chicago, IL	−17	−2
5	Los Angeles, CA	−12	−1		Brownsville, TX	−11	−6
6	Cleveland, OH	−12	−3		McAllen, TX	−9	−3
7	St. Louis, MO	10	−3		El Paso, TX	−7	−2
8	San Francisco, CA	−7	−1		Houston, TX	−7	−1
9	Shreveport, LA	−5	−5		Corpus Christi, TX	−7	−4
10	Pittsburgh, PA	−5	−3		New Orleans, LA	−7	−13

SOURCE: U.S. Bureau of the Census, *Census of Population and Housing: 1990, Public Use Microdata Sample.*

the first large county with a Hispanic majority. If you feel most comfortable using Spanish to sell securities, practice law, or do therapy with your clients, metropolitan Miami is a good place to live.

Cities and Suburbs: Population Redistribution Within Metropolises

Were there new and different population distribution trends within metropolitan areas in the 1980s? Did the "chocolate city–vanilla suburbs" pattern that was sung about on soul music stations in the 1960s become more or less extreme?

The pervasive trend throughout post–World War II years was movement away from the center of the metropolis, a migration promoted by federal housing policies, by policies allowing the deduction of mortgage interest payments from taxable income, and by the willingness of taxpayers to build the expensive highways that allow easy commuting across a metropolis. These basic demographic trends continued in the 1980s, with suburban rings growing faster than central cities, just as they have done since the 1940s. A thorough discussion with provocative comments about their causes is presented by William Frey (1995).

Regional differences must be stressed when describing city and suburban growth trends since the Northeast and South are quite different. In the Northeast, central cities and the places around them were generally chartered in the eighteenth century. With urbanization, the population of central cities grew first. Indeed, in the nineteenth century big cities—New York, Philadelphia, and Pittsburgh—were formed by merging separate smaller towns we would call suburbs, but this came to an end with the turn of the twentieth century. When urban populations grew in the Northeast this century, people moved into individual municipalities surrounding the central city, each of them with their own zoning laws, their own police departments, and their own public school systems. After World War II, these suburbs competed with each other for upscale new housing and the shopping centers and office complexes that they assumed would bring prosperity through high tax revenues. The situation is much the same in the Midwest, but in that region the individual municipalities were typically chartered in the nineteenth century. Here, too, suburbanization filled in little towns incorporated generations ago. As a result, large cities, such as New York, Boston, Cleveland, Chicago, Detroit, and St. Louis, are now surrounded—and have been for a century—with hundreds of distinct incorporated places.

These rings are far from homogeneous. Some suburbs that attracted manufacturing firms around World War I or moderate- to low-income housing in the 1940s are now in more dire economic straits than central cities because they lack major shopping or office districts and their stock of housing is unattractive. State governments in the 1990s will bail out these older suburbs as they fall into bankruptcy. But there are also booming corners in the slowing growing suburban rings of the North. The suburban winners in the Northeast and Midwest have been those that captured the edge cities; that is, they attracted headquarters for high tech firms, research parks, and shopping malls oriented to the carriage trade, and have become centers for recreation/hotel/restaurant complexes. A few of the suburban communities—Foxboro near Boston, Auburn Hills near Detroit, and the Meadowlands near New York—were victorious in the competition for professional sports teams and the revenue they generate.

The political history of the South produced greatly different city-suburban patterns. Annexation laws were liberal, so farsighted central-city governments in the 1950s incorporated outlying areas that later housed their burgeoning suburban populations. When housing developments were built, central cities got credit for the population growth and cashed the checks of the taxpayers who lived there. Counties also have an importance in the South that they lack elsewhere. Southern state governments at the end of the last century often gave counties responsibility for public schools, for policing, and for the many local governmental services provided by individual suburbs in the North. This century-old decision also had an effect on present-day residential segregation. White residents of northern cities, fearing the growth of a black population, could select any one of dozens of almost all-white suburbs with their all-white public schools. This was less of an option for southern central-city residents, especially after federal courts in the 1970s mandated the thorough integration of school districts. In the South, this meant an entire county, whereas integration orders in the North applied to only one individual city or one suburb. This helps to explain why black-white residential segregation is now lower in the South than in the Northeast or Midwest (Farley and Frey 1994).

A few of the older western cities—San Francisco, Los Angeles, and Portland—are similar to those in the Midwest in being surrounded by many independent suburbs, but a more common pattern was that of extensive annexation after World War II. Around Phoenix, Las Vegas, and San Bernadino, the area that would be divided into dozens of suburbs if it were in the Northeast is now well within the corporate limits of the central city.

The implications of these decisions about governmental bound-

Table 7-7. Percent Change in Population for All Central Cities and Their Suburban Rings

Region	1960 to 1970		1970 to 1980		1980 to 1990	
	Central Cities	Suburban Rings	Central Cities	Suburban Rings	Central Cities	Suburban Rings
Northeast	+10%	+21%	−1%	+6%	+3%	+5%
Midwest	+13	+23	+3	+14	+3	+6
South	+22	+21	+22	+38	+17	+25
West	+28	+30	+23	+29	+24	+25
Total	+17	+23	+11	+20	+12	+15

SOURCE: Frey 1995, table 6.6.

aries are reported in table 7-7. Growth rates for central cities and suburban rings in the four regions are shown for the last three decades. A fixed set of locations with constant geographic boundaries was used.

In each decade, western central cities grew faster than central cities in other regions and at a rate quite close to that of their suburban rings. Migrants to these places in the 1970s and 1980s filled the land that central cities had annexed previously, and quite a few of these cities benefited from foreign immigration. But in the Northeast and Midwest, central cities grew much less rapidly than their suburban rings. For a quarter-century, there has been little population growth in these two regions: what growth there was occurred in suburbs. The pattern of growth in the South is between that of the West and the North: southern suburban rings growing more rapidly than central cities, but the city-ring disparity in population growth is much less than in the North.

Central cities in the Northeast lost population in the 1970s, but their size increased a bit in the 1980s. What explains this? Is there a return of suburbanites to the cities of this region? Most of these cities have a very old stock of housing, much of it built long before the great market crash of October 1929 initiated an eighteen-year hiatus in new home construction. Yet these central cities grew in the 1980. Why?

Many older cities—even those in the Rustbelt—have several types of neighborhood in which the population is stable or gradually increasing. There are areas centered around major universities or giant medical complexes, areas that attract students and young professionals who seek urban amenities, at least until they have children. And for the many dual-earner couples without children, these areas may be extremely desirable. Then there are older neighborhoods in every city that have retained their charm or have an unbeatable geographic advantage—for example, the Gold Coast along Lake Michigan north of Chicago's Loop, the expensive neighborhoods bordering Rock Creek Park in northwest Washington, Brooklyn Heights and Park Slope in Brooklyn, and Riverdale in the Bronx. Despite elevated taxes, a proximity to high-crime areas, and central-city governments in almost constant fiscal crisis, these neighborhoods offer attractions not to be found in the suburbs, so their population remains stable. Although the term *gentrifying* is no longer applied to old neighborhoods, in most older central cities there are a few areas that hold their own in the competition for homeseekers because of their appealing characteristics.

Finally—and this is the key to growth in the older central cities—there are neighborhoods filled with new foreign immigrants (Winnick 1990). Many of the older cities in the Northeast whose populations steadily and rapidly declined from 1950 through 1980 reported small increases in the 1980s because they attracted immigrants. New York City lost 10 percent of its population between 1970 and 1980 and, given its lack of vacant land, its elevated tax rates, and its aging infrastructure, most would have predicted a continued depopulation. But enough immigrants arrived from abroad to offset the outmigration of native-born whites and blacks, so the city grew by 4 percent. Boston, Hartford, Providence, and Springfield, Massachusetts, are other older central cities in the Northeast that went through the same demographic metamorphosis—from long-term population decline to growth in the 1980s. On the Pacific coast, Los Angeles grew by a modest 5 percent in the 1970s, but this jumped to a rate almost twice the national average in the 1980s, thanks to its ability to attract new Asians and Latinos. Even Washington saw its long-term population loss slowed by immigration. That city may once again grow in size if its leaders can convince more immigrants to settle there.

In terms of demographic change, central cities may be classified into three groups. Two types grew in the 1980s. Some were the old places that edged into growth because of a boom in immigration. And then there were cities that filled in the vast empty spaces they had fortuitously annexed decades earlier. This largely explains the extremely high growth rates of 58 percent in Las Vegas, 38 percent in Raleigh, 28 percent in Orlando, and 24 percent in Phoenix. The overall growth rate of the country was 10 percent, so these central cities exhibited an unusual demographic trend, attracting thousands of migrants.

There is a third class of central cities—those that continued their slide down the population ranks in the 1980s. Their stock of housing got older, they attracted few foreign immigrants, and they have few of the neighborhoods in which rich young professionals invest. Many of them were centers of metropolises with almost no growth of jobs. In these cities, the census reports sharp declines in the 1980s, just as in the 1960s and 1970s, for Cleveland and St. Louis, drops of 12 percent of their population; Pittsburgh down 13 percent; Detroit down 15 percent; Newark down 16 percent; and Gary, Indiana, lost about one-quarter of its population. Current economic and demographic trends imply smaller and smaller populations for such central cities.

The Suburbanization of Blacks

After the bloody racial riots of 1967, President Johnson appointed Governor Kerner of Illinois to head a commission to investigate their causes and to propose ways to prevent more black-white fighting on the streets of American cities. In a most surprising report, they stressed that racial discrimination denied blacks the social and economic opportunities available to white Americans. Pessimistically, the Kerner Commission predicted that unless drastic actions were taken our country was moving toward two separate societies—one largely white and prosperous living in suburban rings, and the other largely black and economically disadvantaged, concentrated almost exclusively within central cities (National Advisory Commission on Civil Disorders 1968). Demographic trends of the post–World War II era gave them excellent reasons for predicting such an unfavorable outcome. Blacks moved from the South to northern cities in great numbers, but once they arrived they found they were limited to the bottom end of the job ladder and that their children had to attend Jim Crow schools. Even the most prosperous blacks discovered that desirable central-city neighborhoods and suburban communities had erected insurmountable barriers keeping them out, thereby firmly maintaining the American apartheid system. Massive public housing projects built with federal dollars and with enthusiastic local support in such cities as Chicago, St. Louis, and Philadelphia encouraged segregation.

Fortunately, the Kerner Commission's prediction about geographic polarization was wrong, but wrong for reasons that they never foresaw. They did not realize that their report came out just as the migration of blacks from the South to the North was ending, since the restructuring of industry eliminated thousands of the manufacturing jobs that black men held. Nor did they know that their jeremiad appeared in the same year that immigration from abroad took off, thanks to the immigration reforms of 1965 and demographic pressures south of the Rio Grande and in Asia. Many major central cities are now very diverse because of this great foreign migration.

Figure 7-7 summarizes suburbanization trends of the 1980s (Frey 1995, figure 6-11). The panel to the right pertains to all central cities in the United States and their suburban rings. Observe the rapid growth of Asians and Hispanics in both cities and suburbs. Nevertheless, the rates are higher for the suburbs since, in most metropolises, suburbs offer the newer and nicer stock of housing and have the vacant land upon which new houses and apartments may be built.

What about African Americans? In the 1980s, for the first time,

Figure 7-7. Racial/Ethnic Composition of Central-City and Suburban Populations: 1980 and 1990

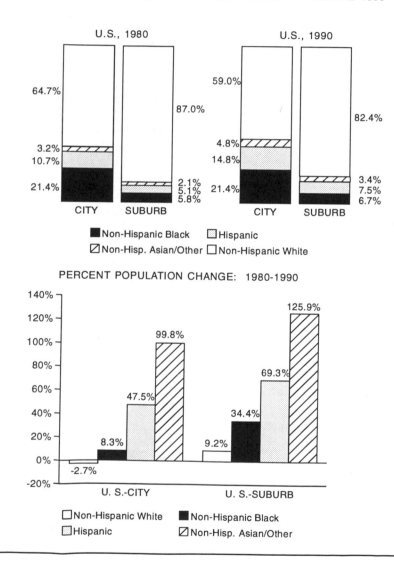

RACIAL COMPOSITION OF CITIES AND SUBURBS: 1980 AND 1990

SOURCE: Frey 1995, figure 6.11.

there was a clear trend toward black suburbanization. This black population of suburbs grew 34 percent, but just 8 percent for central cities. Several different patterns are represented by this high rate of suburban growth. In some places, central-city black neighborhoods pushed up against city limits and then crossed over them. This happened in Prince George's County, Maryland, surrounding the eastern half of Washington. In a slightly different fashion, the prosperous Detroit suburb of Southfield is now undergoing a slow shift from predominantly white to predominantly black as the African American population of that central city crosses its northern border. And the black population concentration once limited to the northern Bronx increasingly includes southern Westchester County. Residential transitions from white to black occurred more slowly in the 1980s and 1990s than in earlier decades and without the violence of former years, offering hope that real integration will persist in some of the suburbs now gaining black families.

There is a different type of black suburbanization occurring as affluent African Americans take advantage of the more liberal racial attitudes of whites and the equal housing opportunities provided, at least in theory, by the Fair Housing Law. As recently as the 1970s, many individual suburbs near the older central cities reported no black residents at all in their census counts. That is very unusual today since the census of 1990 reports that most suburbs had at least a few black, Asian, and Hispanic residents, often more than token numbers. As William Frey shows (1994 and 1995, table 6-12), regardless of the metropolis, the blacks most likely to live in the suburbs are the highly educated, implying that the migration of blacks from central cities to suburbs now resembles what occurred among whites two or three decades ago: the most prosperous central-city dwellers seek the attractive housing and presumably better schools, safer neighborhoods, and prompter city services of the suburbs.

Despite this migration, central cities and their suburban rings differ greatly in racial composition. It is still too early to put away the chocolate city–vanilla suburbs imagery. Central cities continued to see their non-Hispanic white population decline in the 1980s. Figure 7-7 shows the racial composition of central cities and suburban rings at the start and end of this decade. Whites predominate in the suburbs even though minority representation is inching up.

Looking at individual places reveals several patterns of black distributions across cities and suburbs. Some older cities are overwhelmingly black and contain almost all of the metropolitan black population, while their suburban rings house few blacks. Detroit is an extreme example of this type of city-suburban segregation, perhaps the type the Kerner Commission had in mind.

Then there are places where the suburban black population grew rapidly in the 1980s as blacks migrated into the metropolises and some central-city blacks opted for the suburbs. Some of these central cities—Washington and Atlanta are clear examples—have overwhelmingly black populations, but their rings are where black growth is now occurring rapidly. Indeed, in these two large metropolises, the majority of African Americans in the metropolis lives in the suburbs, only a minority in the central cities. By 2000, there will be a longer list of metropolitan areas where, similar to whites, the majority of blacks will be suburbanites.

A third pattern is found in older southern metropolises—New Orleans, Memphis, and Richmond—a fairly high representation of blacks in both central cities and their suburban rings. As suburbanization occurred, whites moved into a ring that already had sizable black populations, some of them farmers and others residents of older black communities that were incorporated into the suburban fringe of a big city.

The new patterns of interregional black migration mean that more will live in places that do not have extensive histories of racial polarization, places such as Sacramento, Orlando, Phoenix, Las Vegas, and Minneapolis. If you ask anyone who has lived for a couple of years in a neighborhood in metropolitan Philadelphia, Detroit, or Chicago, he or she can tell you whether it is a white area or a black area. Undoubtedly, when people look for homes or apartments, they take those popular images of racially homogeneous neighborhoods into account. But in many of the new places attracting blacks, neighborhoods are less coded by skin color. In the South and West, much of the housing stock was built in the last two decades when federal and state laws proscribed racial discrimination. The stricter enforcement of fair housing legislation and the modest growth of the black middle class also portend a gradual shift of blacks away from central cities and into suburbs.

Conclusion

Few federal policies are specifically designed to encourage internal migration. Yet numerous federal programs have that as their unintended and unforeseen consequences. When Congress funded programs to foster homeownership in the 1930s and 1940s, it did not imagine the suburban boom or sharp declines in central-city population. Representatives from central cities might not have voted for those laws if they would have known the consequences. When interstate highways were built in the Eisenhower years, the rationalization was that they would allow residents of central cities to leave speedily in case Russian bombers or missiles delivered nuclear warheads. But the highways inadvertently contributed to the creation of an urban underclass and the maintenance of racial residential segregation. Twenty-five years later, when President Reagan and Congress directed the taxpayers' dollars to the military in the 1980s, they did not do so to encourage population growth and economic prosperity around the many large military bases located in the South, but that was the outcome. When immigration laws were changed in 1965, it was certainly not done to revive population growth in older, declining central cities of the Northeast. Macroeconomic decisions were not made to bring about rapid population growth in some metropolises and declines in others. However, all of those changes had major impacts upon where people chose to live and which metropolises boomed or declined.

Why is this important? One of our important freedoms is the right to move wherever we wish anytime we wish. States have virtually no control over who moves in, nor can they limit the benefits that their taxpayers provide to long-term residents: a Supreme Court decision prevents them from imposing strong residency requirements to qualify for voting rights, professional licenses, or welfare payments (*Shapiro v. Thompson* 1969)

These trends are important for two closely related reasons. First, political power at every level is directly based upon population size. Court rulings since the *Baker v. Carr* decision of 1962 insist that each electoral district have exactly the same population size. Political representation depends upon the total number of people counted in the census, not the number of adults or the number of voters in the last election or the number of U.S. citizens. Migration trends accelerated the shift of political power to suburbs, to the South and West, and to suburban rings, thereby diminishing the clout of central cities and the North. This is as it should be in a democracy.

You might expect that the political views of individuals will be pretty much the same before and after they move. There is no reason to believe that crossing a state line or a central-city boundary will make a liberal into a conservative or vice versa. This may be the case, but the history of political institutions in an area and the characteristics of that place strongly influence what policies are favored or opposed regardless of who or how many live there.

Members of Congress from the Great Plains generally favor generous price supports for agriculture, but representatives from urban areas may oppose them because their constituents' food prices and taxes increase due to such subsidies. Representatives from Florida and Southern California will support cheap energy since low-cost air conditioning and inexpensive automobile transportation allow their populations to grow. Skyrocketing energy prices would boost the economies of Texas, Louisiana, Wyoming, Alaska, West Virginia, and all other points where coal is mined or oil pumped. Representatives from manufacturing states will, at least in the short run, favor a cheap dollar since it allows toolmakers in Cincinnati and Milwaukee to sell their products abroad and keeps assembly lines running overtime in Michigan because German and Japanese cars are then too expensive for all but the affluent. But the cheap dollar will force Honda, BMW, and Mercedes to build plants in the United States, thereby creating jobs but also competing with U.S. car companies. It is easy to imagine representatives from the urban Northeast and from a few big cities elsewhere favoring a tax on gasoline to rebuild subways or lay down new commuter rail lines, but such an expenditure of the taxpayers' money won't be supported elsewhere. While there is much concern about the environment throughout the country, Joel Garreau (1981) argues that there are two sections where these issues dominate the political scene: northern New England and the Pacific coast from San Francisco north. In these areas, if the choice were between rapid economic growth involving new factories and more airports or making compromises to protect the environment, most voters will choose the environment. Migration to such locations may be selective of people who favor such policies. The interests of suburbs are often different from those of older central cities, although major battles about these issues are played out in state legislatures rather than in Congress. In Massachusetts, New York, Michigan, and Illinois, the largest city has received special treatment from the legislature, often a flow of funds or a taxing power not granted to smaller cities. As the population moves to the suburbs, so too does political power, and thus these central cities find it more challenging to obtain the fiscal aid they need. Because of these geographic differences in politics, migration flows help to change the political agenda both nationally and at the state level.

Second, in-migration is usually a cause of more population growth and economic expansion. The assumption that migrants are costly to their destination points has been the root cause of attempts to keep migrants out, be they the efforts of Boston and New York to tax Irish immigrants in the last century or California's efforts to keep "Okies" out in the Depression. In the 1960s, it was often asserted that southern blacks were migrating to New York specifically to get generous welfare payments, and many in California now believe that the state suffers since taxpayers must educate the children of foreign immigrants and provide them with medical care if they are indigent. Although there may be situations in which migrants are costly to their destination points, this is usually not the long-run outcome.

Migrants tend to be young adults who fill a need for labor. Certainly, most employers at destination points are pleased with an increased supply of labor, often labor willing to work at lower wage rates. The migrants, in turn, pay local taxes directly in the case of sales and income taxes and indirectly in the case of property taxes and the taxes levied on their employers. In an economically developed and prospering country, population growth generates economic expansion. The job prospects of skilled and unskilled residents of Atlanta, Charlotte, and Orlando improved in the 1980s because of the rapid population growth attributable to internal migration.

For every place gaining a migrant, some other place loses. The closing of iron mines in Michigan's upper peninsula, the huge layoffs in the oil industry around Houston, and the sharp declines in employment in the nation's steel towns certainly caused hardships, not just for the men and women laid off, but for the merchants, school teachers, chiropractors, preachers, and lawyers who serviced their needs. It is not easy to close schools, hospitals, and universities in an area losing thousands of migrants each year. One of the great challenges facing the older, now declining central cities is that of maintaining an infrastructure built for a population one and one-half or two times their present sizes. Central-city Detroit went from 1.8 million in 1950 to 1.0 million in 1990, while Philadelphia fell from about 3 million to 1.6 million. St. Louis has the distinction of being the only major city whose population was just about as large shortly after the Civil War as it is now.

Federal and state policies stimulate growth in some areas and implicitly curtail it in others, thereby triggering outmigration. But little is done to minimize the problems flowing from job loss and outmigration in declining places. The current national policy assumes that local growth machines will successfully generate new jobs to replace those that disappear, or that people will vote with their feet and move to where the jobs are. Our analysis shows that this happens, but slowly and imperfectly. Young adults will leave rapidly if there are few jobs, but the migration option is much less feasible and attractive for couples with children in school, or for those with major investments in their homes, or others tied to their communities in many other ways.

Chapter 8

The Evidence About America in Decline and the Challenges of the 1990s

We are better off now than in the past. A look at the most important indicators shows we are a healthier, better educated, richer nation than we were a quarter-century ago and a nation that provides more nearly equal opportunities to a larger share of the population.

An ever-expanding array of books contends that this nation is in decline. The diverse authors of such books assert that the solid blue-collar jobs that created the middle class are disappearing, that our economic growth rate is too low, that the gap between the rich and the poor is growing too wide, that welfare has destroyed families and the work ethic, that our political parties can no longer solve national problems, that recent high levels of immigration will compromise our cultural heritage, and that the intelligence level in this country is gradually slipping lower.

But has the United States truly lost its edge? One way to answer that question is to ask another. Which would we prefer—to live in this nation as it is today or as it was a generation ago? Was the United States a more just or more prosperous society then? Was it kinder to its citizens? Did it provide a larger share of the population with equal opportunities?

America in Decline?

Most of us would forcefully reject any efforts to turn back the clock. We are better off now than in the past. *The census of 1990 reveals that the United States is not a nation in decline.* The most important indicators show that we are a healthier, better educated, richer nation than we were a quarter-century ago and a nation that provides more nearly equal opportunities to a larger share of the population. Higher standards of living, remarkable medical innovations, more government spending for health, and changes in our lifestyles (including less smoking) have added five years to the average life span since 1970 and cut the infant mortality rate in half. Babies, both white and black, were twice as likely to die before their first birthday in 1970 as in 1994.

Americans have become more educated. The percentage of adults who finished high school rose from 55 percent in 1970 to 81 percent in 1994; the percentage of people who hold college degrees doubled from 11 percent to 22 percent (U.S. Department of Education 1995, table 8). Young people are staying in school longer, too. The improved educations of their parents, sustained government spending for schools, changing demands from the labor market, and new programs developed by local schools substantially reduced the dropout rate from secondary schools. About eighty-five out of one hundred young people now obtain high school diplomas or GEDs by their late twenties. While there is much room for further improvement, most studies also show that elementary and high school students in the 1990s are scoring moderately better on tests of reading, math, and science than they did in the 1970s. College enrollment rates have gone up substantially for women and, after years of stagnation, the enrollment rates of men are slowly rising and may soon reach the high levels of the Vietnam War years.

Despite the economic travails of the 1970s, per capita income has risen steadily at a rate of 1.5 percent a year. Per capita income increased from $11,100 in 1970 to $15,800 in 1993 (in 1993 dollars). The typical American had only 70 percent as much to spend in 1970 as did the typical American in 1993.

You might ask how per capita income can increase while wages are falling, a finding repeatedly stressed in these chapters. Demographic trends and changes in labor force participation are the reason. Many more women are working; indeed, the proportion of adults aged 25 to 54 holding jobs rose from 69 percent in 1970 to 80 percent in 1995, largely because women joined the labor force. Hence, we now have a higher ratio of workers to total population. The decline in the birth rate also reduced the proportion who are too young to work. Continuing immigration has a similar effect. Most immigrants are working age adults, so this demographic process also boosts per capita income. Moreover, private and governmental income-support programs serving the older population also boost per capita income.

We seldom think about wealth holdings on a per capita or per household basis since "wealth" seems to imply a rich individual living in a huge home trading stocks and bonds. To be sure, wealth holdings are highly concentrated in the United States, but 86 percent of households own a car or truck; 71 percent have interest-bearing assets at financial institutions; 64 percent own their home; 23 percent have IRA or KEOGH accounts; and 21 percent own stocks (U.S. Bureau of the Census 1995c, table A). Trends in household wealth since 1970 also have been highly favorable. Tangible net worth—that is, owner-occupied real estate and consumer durables, but not stock and bonds—grew over 2 percent annually in constant dollar value in the 1970s and 1980s. Americans became the owners of more cars, bigger television sets, more air conditioners, and some costly things no one had in 1970: VCRs and personal computers (Committee on Ways and Means 1993, appendix L; U.S. Bureau of the Census 1995b, table 759). By the mid-1990s, more than 30 percent of households owned personal computers.

Higher per capita income helped to change the nation's tastes, especially for cars and homes. In the 1970s, economy cars—some of them small and flimsy by today's standards—still captured a share of the auto market; by the 1990s, the most popular vehicles were vans, pick-up trucks, and large sedans. In 1970, the typical new house had 1,500 square feet of floor space; by 1994, new homes were one-third larger, averaging 2,100 square feet (U.S. Bureau of the Census 1995b, table 1214). These also have been rosy years for those who invested in the stock market. Between 1970 and 1995, the value of the Dow Jones Industrial stock index (in constant dollar amounts) rose 220 percent.

Two generations ago many white Americans promoted or passively endorsed a system of black-white segregation. The civil rights revolution of the 1960s helped change the way most Americans thought about race, as they came to believe that the nation should live up to the phrase chiseled on the pediment of the Supreme Court building: "Equal Justice for All." Americans came to agree that skin color, country of origin, ethnicity, and religion should not determine who gets a job or promotion, who can buy a house or rent an apartment, or even whom one marries. Gradually, the power of the federal government switched from upholding Jim Crow laws to upholding the principle of equal racial opportunities, culminating in three authoritative federal laws in the 1960s banning racial discrimination in all areas of public life.

Changes in norms and social values often occur on a cohort basis.

Those who attended school and reached their adult years after the 1960s were taught that American principles call for equal opportunities. Consequently those generations endorse egalitarian principles more strongly than did earlier generations. There has been much more than just changes in abstract values. African Americans who have specialized skills or the educational credentials needed to succeed in the restructured economy of the 1990s face fewer barriers than did their parents or grandparents. A generation ago, most of the nation's well-known blacks were sports stars or performers. Today, the many well-known African Americans in a wide range of fields reflect our society's greater openness. We are no longer surprised to find that medical professionals, middle-level managers in business, professors, and high-level civil servants are African Americans. Our neighborhoods are more integrated than they were a generation ago, our colleges enroll more black students, and young blacks and whites are marrying each other in increasing numbers.

The civil rights revolution also effectively challenged discrimination on the basis of sex—namely, those practices that limited the occupations women could pursue, that reserved the best jobs for men, that kept the pay of women lower than that of comparable men, and that, in some states, kept women off juries and limited their property rights if they married. Our norms no longer mandate that women marry early, devote themselves exclusively to childrearing and home-making, or remain in marriages after love and affection have died.

In the last two decades, the nation's colleges and universities have been extensively feminized. In 1970, 42 percent of college students were women; in 1993, 56 percent were women. In graduate schools, the number of female students increased from 39 to 54 percent. Federal laws such as Title VII of the Civil Rights Act, and subsequent successful litigation against employers who sexually discriminate, broadened opportunities for women in the labor market.

As men and women increasingly accept the idea that women will work most of their lives, even when raising young children, women's occupational choices are coming to resemble those of their brothers. In the 1980s, the gender gap in earnings began to diminish for the first time, albeit a convergence hastened by the falling wages of men. The expansion of women's educational and employment opportunities occurred simultaneously with the increasing popularity of effective new contraceptives, and in 1973 abortion was legalized. These changes reflect new social values that gave women more control over their childbearing as well as new career opportunities.

With regard to crime, many people believe we were better off a generation ago. Today's newspapers are filled with stories of murder, rape, and gang violence. The fear of crime keeps many Americans out of major sections of our largest cities. Many think that the police have lost the battle to maintain public safety so, at least with regard to this crucial issue, we appear to be a nation in decline.

That, however, is a hasty conclusion. Two different systems measure crime. Crimes reported to and recorded by police agencies do reveal a dismal trend. They show persistently high and even increasing crime rates. The murder rate, for example, peaked about 1980 and then declined just a bit, but the risk of being murdered was higher in the early 1990s than in 1970—eleven murders per 100,000 in 1991 compared to eight per 100,000 in 1970. And reported rapes rose from 46 per 100,000 women age 12 and over in 1970 to 101 per 100,000 women in 1992.

Another, perhaps more accurate, system involves a yearly survey of a representative national sample of households. The National Crime Victimization Survey which has been conducted by the Census Bureau since 1973, asks respondents if they have been victims of violent crimes, such as rape, robbery, and assault, or property crimes, including larceny, burglary, and motor vehicle theft. Surprisingly, the surveys show a modest but consistent trend toward lower crime rates, including a drop in rape victimization. The survey finds a 35 percent decline in the larceny rate from 1973 to 1992, a decline in rape by almost as much, and a drop in robbery victimization rate by 12 percent. In 1980, for example, 3 percent of the nation's households were victimized by crime. By 1992, this was down to 2.3 percent of households (U.S. Bureau of the Census 1995b, tables 317–321).

Several factors help explain the discrepancy between the two systems of measuring crime. Although the ranks of police officers grew by 8 percent each year in the 1970s and 1980s, the total population grew by less than 2 percent annually. More police facilities, combined with an increased willingness to report crimes and the greater attention given to "new" crimes, such as spouse and child abuse, may account for some of the rise in reported crimes. In addition, the populations of state and federal prisons rose by about 7 percent every year since 1970. This growing incarceration of those convicted of crimes may partly explain the declines in criminal victimization. In sum, the recent period—especially since 1980—has been one of moderately declining crime rates.

The American Anxiety: Why?

It seems strange given the improvements in U.S. living standards that many Americans openly yearn for earlier times. Clearly, few wish to revisit the sad and—by today's standards—premature losses of young infants and older parents, or to return to an era when the population was less well educated and less affluent, or to turn our backs on the progress we have made in creating a more egalitarian and less violent society. Why then do Americans seem so discontent and uneasy with their present lot? Why have so many people concluded that our society is deteriorating, and why do so many politicians tell us that current policies will doom us?

Americans are a hopeful people, who expect the United States to be the most prosperous and most just nation in the world, providing opportunities and economic success to all. Yet we seem to be far from where we could be and where we wish to be. We do not seem to be on the road to becoming a more prosperous and equitable nation, and many people seem to be falling behind. *This is the reason for the persisting American anxiety.*

Consider recent economic trends. The United States has experienced three different periods since the end of World War II. First was an era of continued growth extending from the end of the war until the oil crisis in the early 1970s. This was followed by a decade of great economic change, which came to an end in the early 1980s. The third and current period is an era of growth, but it is quite different from the post–World War II years.

Table 8-1 provides key indicators of economic trends for these three periods. In the first period, the national product increased by an average of 2.2 percent per worker each year, leading to a much higher standard of living. From 1973 to 1982, the period Frank Levy (1987, p. 82) calls "the quiet Depression," the national product per worker stagnated. Growth resumed in the early 1980s, but since then the annual increases in the national product per worker have been half of what they were during the post–World War II boom. Table 8-1 also shows the average annual increase in the consumer price index, the average interest rate on a three-month treasury bill—a key index of the cost of borrowing money—and the unemployment rate. These indicators show that the present era of sustained economic growth is not as prosperous or favorable as the several decades that followed World War II. (For a discussion of the pervasive implications of this lower rate of economic growth, see Madrick 1995.)

Table 8-1.   Economic Indicators for Three Periods

	Average Annual Rates		
	Post–World War II Boom 1947 to 1972	The Quiet Depression 1973 to 1982	Post-1980 Expansion 1983 to 1994
Growth of goods and services[a]	+3.6%	+2.0%	+2.8%
Growth of goods and services per worker[a]	+2.2	+0.1	+1.1
Change in consumer price index	+3.0	+8.8	+3.6
Interest rate on 3-month treasury bills	3.00	8.45	6.33
Unemployment rate	4.8	7.0	6.7

SOURCE: Council of Economic Advisors 1978, tables B-10 and B-28; 1995, tables B-7, B-34, B-40, B-63 and B-72.

[a] Change for 1947 to 1972 refers to gross national product; for later periods, it refers to gross domestic product.

Parents of the baby boomers and early baby boomers themselves remember those halcyon decades. Young people today—late baby boomers and Generation X—have heard about them from their parents and older relatives, but their experience is very different. Richard Easterlin (1987) convincingly argues that the aspirations we develop for our standards of living are strongly influenced by the standards of living of our parents and their own aspirations. People who entered the labor market after World War II prospered and could amass much greater wealth than their parents, who had lived through the Great Depression. Today's young adults learned their aspirations from parents who benefited for decades from a rapidly growing economy. Those who begin their careers in the 1990s may be severely disappointed with their own opportunities since they are not much improved from those of their parents.

Declining Earnings

The new economic trends generously reward many individuals, while threatening some of those who prospered in the past with poverty and unemployment. Services replaced manufacturing as the leading employment sector but, within all industrial sectors, the emphasis has been upon reducing labor costs by laying off workers and stressing technological sophistication. Employment has grown rapidly and a shortage of jobs may not be the fundamental problem. The increasingly high tech economy created marvelous opportunities for trained and imaginative individuals who could design and program computers, transplant livers or hearts, come up with ingenious financial instruments, or play sports better than anyone else. As per capita income and population rose, employment also boomed in retail trade, personal services (for example, cosmetologists and childcare workers), and entertainment and recreation. The most rapidly growing occupations, however, are those at the tail ends of the skill distribution. Many of the lower-ranked jobs require no more than a high school education and—as many immigrants from Latin America and China know—you can get some of them with little knowledge of English.

Only a minority of the labor force has the college degrees or specialized training now highly rewarded in the new American labor market. Figure 8-1 describes the two major economic trends of the recent past, smaller paychecks and increased economic inequality. The upside-down U tells the story of wages. After growing steadily for thirty years, the earnings of the typical nonsupervisory private sector worker peaked at $475 a week in the early 1970s (in constant 1993 dollars), then fell about 15 percent. The downward trend in earnings helps to explain the America-in-decline literature and to account for why young people today may feel that they will never attain the economic status of their parents. Perhaps the rebellion against taxes is the outcome of these leaner paychecks. Elected officials can hardly raise wages, but they can reduce the tax rate.

Not everybody suffered in this era of slipping wages. An abbreviated summary stresses that the earnings of men with high school educations or less fell steadily; those of men with college training or more went up through the 1980s but have been declining recently. Earnings rose for women with college training, while at lower educational levels the earnings of women declined more slowly than those of similarly educated men. The following table summarizes what has happened by comparing the earnings of people who worked full-time for the entire year in 1974, when wages were high, with those in 1993.

In this prosperous span, the only men who did not lose ground were those with postgraduate degrees. The purchasing power of men with high school diplomas—the typical attainment—fell 18 percent. Women with college degrees saw their earnings rise and, at every level, the gender gap decreased.

| | Percent Change in Real Earnings 1974 to 1993 | |
Educational Attainment	Men	Women
College, 5 years or more	No change	+28%
College, 4 years	−7	+20
College, 1 to 3 years	−14	+9
High school, 4 years	−18	+3
High school, 1 to 3 years	−26	−7
Less than 9 years	−27	−8

Changes in the early 1990s may be an aberration, but they reveal a continued downward trajectory for earnings. As Levy (1995) observes, the brief recession in 1991–92 propelled firms to downsize by eliminating mid- and late-career white-collar managers, many of them men with college degrees. Between 1989 and 1993 earnings fell at all educational attainment levels among both women and men. Efforts to contain healthcare costs and to reduce governmental expenditures may lead to smaller or fewer paychecks in the future. In 1994, 9 percent of workers were in the healthcare industry, and 15 percent worked for governmental agencies. Even one group of workers with an effective union saw their earnings diminish: the salaries of major league baseball players fell 5.8 percent between 1994 and 1995, adjusting for the strike.

What should be done about these trends in earnings? Because more people, especially women, are working longer and because of favorable demographic trends, per capita income has grown in this era of declining wages, but the effects of these adjustments cannot continue forever. Sooner or later declining wages will mean declining per capita income. Many young individuals are responding to the new realities of the labor market by staying in school longer. Therefore, a higher proportion of Generation X will have the educations associated with higher earnings. Economic theory implies that increases in the productivity of the labor force will inevitably lead to bigger paychecks, and firms have been investing in technology and streamlining their operations resulting in more output per hour worked. However, we have yet to see the benefits in the wages of workers. Reversing the downward trend in earnings will be the most important economic issue in the coming decade.

Figure 8-1. Gini Index of Income Inequality for Families and Average Weekly Wage for Private Sector, Nonagricultural Employees: 1947 to 1993 (amounts in 1993 dollars)

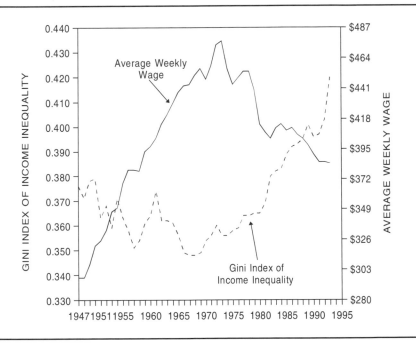

SOURCE: Council of Economic Advisors 1976, table B-28; table B-45; U.S. Bureau of the Census, 1994, *Current Population Reports*, series P-60, no. 146, table 17; no. 184, tables B-1 and B-7.

New Family Living Arrangements

This is still a society in which most children are born to married mothers and spend the majority of their youth with their two parents. However, age at first marriage has rapidly advanced to a record high, cohabitation has replaced marriage as the typical way to begin a live-in sexual relationship, proportionally more of those who eventually marry subsequently divorce, and children are increasingly born to and raised by a mother who has no husband. While there is no agreement about what caused these dramatic shifts—ones that also occurred throughout Western Europe—the most convincing explanations focus on the following issues:

- Social values concerning personal sexuality and living arrangements have changed. We no longer condemn so strongly those

who cohabit, those who bear children before marriage, or those
who live as gay or lesbian couples.
- Falling wages make it impossible for young men to marry early
  and support their families as their fathers did.
- Women are increasingly psychologically and economically independent. As McLanahan and Sandefur (1994, p. 100) put it,
  women who have their own earnings, particularly if they earn
  as much or more than their prospective mates, "can be picky
  about whom they marry, they can leave bad marriages, and they
  can bear and raise children on their own, if they wish to."

These changes give people in their twenties, and older, more options and more personal freedom. On the negative side, they also put
women and children at greater risk of poverty. In 1990, two-thirds of
the women who headed their own families with children were impoverished or near poor. We have developed no system to ensure the
economic security that the two-parent family provided in those days
when the earnings of men were higher and when wives did not have
to work to keep their families in the middle class.

Solving this issue will be a major challenge. Some will argue for a
return to the traditional family: no cohabitation, no childbearing by
single women, earlier marriage, and much less divorce. This might
happen. No one predicted the marriage and baby booms that trans-
formed this country just after World War II. A significant minority of
Generation X still endorses the ideal of the husband working while
the wife stays home raising children, but a return to such families
seems unlikely. Given our emphasis upon personal liberties, there
likely will be little support for policies that punish unwed mothers,
cohabitors, or those in same-sex unions. Federal courts are extending
to same-sex and cohabiting couples the legal prerogatives and benefits
enjoyed by married couples. And economic trends demand that both
men and women spend their lives working, regardless of their feelings
about mothers staying home with children. Furthermore, it is difficult
to know what specific policies would bring back the families of the
1960s. Governmental payments that would allow women to stay home
with their children or would ensure health care for all children—such
as those in force in prosperous European countries—are unlikely to
be enacted here.

An important turning point in social values was reached in the
1960s. If wages had continued to increase rapidly, some of the problems associated with single parenting might not be so extreme, but

earnings have been falling so there are major questions about ensuring the welfare of many children. Should government policies guarantee some minimum standard of prosperity for those women who head their own families and their children, or should they be left to their own solutions even if it means more women and children below the poverty line?

Poverty

Although there has always been much poverty in this country, it was not systematically measured, nor was it a front-page political issue until the 1960s. The economic expansion of the post-Depression era made the United States into a prosperous nation with a dominant middle class and gave hope to the possibility of eliminating poverty entirely.

When we started to measure poverty, we found that great progress had been made. Back in 1940, 40 percent of the population lived in households with incomes below the current poverty line (see figure 3-1). Poverty rates fell steadily thanks to industrialization, higher wages, and favorable governmental policies. All extrapolations of these trends implied that poverty would be virtually eliminated by the 1990s. Those who planned the War on Poverty expected to be victorious, projecting a poverty rate as low as 3 percent.

The economic shifts of the 1970s abruptly ended the decline in poverty, and although the sustained expansion of the 1980s lifted per capita income, it hardly reduced the poverty rate. In 1994, the poverty rate was 14 percent or three points higher than the minimum attained in 1973. Among children under age 18, the poverty rate was 22 percent in 1994, a substantial increase from the 14 percent impoverished in 1973. The decline in wages combined with the shift in family structure keeps the poverty rate higher than those beneficial earlier trends indicated. Is persistent poverty a national concern calling for new policies? If so, what should these policies be?

Government Policies and Spending

Economic expansion after World War II allowed state and federal governments to address many of the needs of people. In the late 1940s, federal programs successfully encouraged homeownership, helping to create the suburbs. Local governments then built roads, sewer and water systems, schools, town halls, parks, and later new colleges for the baby boomers to attend. In the 1950s, the United States fought a war in Korea without the economy on the home front slowing down, and then we built the 45,000-mile interstate highway system, perhaps the most massive construction project in the nation's history. In the early 1960s, our tax dollars funded the costly space program, and in 1969 we achieved the remarkable feat of landing Neil Armstrong on the moon. In the same decade, President Johnson and Congress initiated many new programs designed to provide better opportunities for the underprivileged. These included federal funding for local schools, the Head Start program for children from low-income families, food stamps and school lunches to eliminate hunger among the poor, and Medicaid to provide them with comprehensive health services. For the older population, Medicare was initiated to pay for costly medical bills, and Social Security checks were increased. A variety of other monumental programs began during the 1960s and early 1970s: the Model Cities programs designed to replace inner-city slums with attractive new buildings; the Low Income Energy Assistance program to provide federal funds to the poor hit hard by the escalation of fuel prices; the Supplemental Security Income program to provide income for those too infirm to work but too young for Social Security; and the Women, Infants and Children program to provide food for poor pregnant and postpartum women. During the Nixon administration, serious consideration was given to the Negative Income Tax, a plan to send federal checks to persons at the bottom of the income distribution to eliminate poverty. Congress never passed such a law but, in 1975, they enacted its cousin, the Earned Income Tax Credit, which now supplies a modest federal check to employed but low-income parents of children. Believe it or not, for a brief time in the early 1970s, the federal government's problem was how to spend an excess of cash, not how to deal with a huge deficit. President Nixon's solution was revenue sharing, a remarkably egalitarian plan distributing excess federal funds to local governments on the basis of their populations, their per capita incomes, and the taxes they levied (Katz 1989; Levitan 1973).

The development and expansion of government programs from the 1950s through the early 1970s depended upon the fortuitous concatenation of three events. First, there was great faith that the government could solve fundamental problems, increase opportunities, and raise living standards for Americans. Second, there was an effective coalition of unionized workers, politically organized white ethnics in cities, and racial minorities who elected candidates supporting their interests and put pressure on those who did not. Finally, the growing economy and growing tax revenues meant that programs could be initiated or expanded without imposing burdensome new taxes.

The situation is different in the 1990s. Few people support the idea that the government can solve our problems; now the government is seen as the problem. No effective coalition initiates new programs for the poor or effectively defends those enacted during the War on Poverty. Indeed, Congress permitted the purchasing power of the minimum wage to fall by 28 percent from the late 1970s to the mid-1990s. Demographic and economic trends constrain federal spending. Obligations to fund Social Security and Medicare combine with the aging of our population to determine federal spending. In 1994, 49 percent of the government spending went to Social Security, Medicare, and interest payments on the growing national debt. If strong resistance to higher taxes continues and if the economy continues to grow at current rates, it seems inevitable that the federal government will cut back on spending for all other programs, especially antipoverty programs initiated in the 1960s.

Racial Inequalities

Thanks to immigration, the Asian and Hispanic populations are growing rapidly. The low educational level of many immigrants will restrict their economic achievements and may limit the attainment of their children. While it is possible that an underclass of poorly educated immigrants will develop and persist for generations, such a development seems unlikely. It did not happen when the then-despised Italian, Slavic, and Jewish immigrants arrived early in the twentieth century. In today's era of widespread support for the principle of equal opportunities, we celebrate the contributions immigrants have made. Diversity is now a virtue, and the courts censure those who blatantly discriminate. Many Asian and Latinos will take advantage of America's opportunities—some of which are still denied to blacks—and assimilate.

From the 1940s through the 1960s, demographic and economic changes reduced black-white gaps in economic status as blacks left southern agriculture and filled the blue-collar ranks in the North and West. For a decade after the civil rights revolution of the 1960s, blacks continued to catch up with whites on important indicators. The trend toward convergence ended in the 1970s, and only someone with rose-tinted glasses would now argue that recent decades have been good ones for African Americans.

How much black-white inequality is acceptable? Are current levels too great? Is the poverty rate for black children, 46 percent in 1993, too high compared to the rate for white children—18 percent? Is it a matter of national concern that, in 1993, black husband-wife families had incomes only 83 percent those of similar white families? Is it important that blacks live seven fewer years than whites or that black babies are twice as likely to die before their first birthday as white infants?

Of course, it is. Yet, no currently operating economic or political trend will narrow black-white differences, either in the short or long run. The nation recognized the problems of racial injustice a generation ago and, in the spirit of that age, moved gingerly toward affirmative action. Originally, this meant that employers were encouraged to change their traditional recruitment strategies so that blacks would have more access to the better jobs. Colleges were encouraged to change recruitment strategies to admit blacks other than basketball and football stars. Gradually, affirmative action came to mean something much stronger and, around 1970 when the economy grew rapidly and when civil rights were prominent on the national agenda, all branches of government supported affirmative action programs specifically designed to produce outcomes for blacks similar to those for whites. Presidents Johnson and Nixon approved policies pressuring employers to hire specific numbers of blacks, the Supreme Court cautiously endorsed using race as a criterion for employment and college admission, and Congress set aside 10 percent of federal construction moneys for minority contractors.

Dudley Duncan (1969), whose investigations motivated a generation of scholars to measure black-white differences, argued that the race problem and the poverty problem are not the same:

> I have no doubt that the instigators of the War on Poverty thought that it could be planned in such a way as to remedy the gross discrepancies in achievement and rewards between the races. But this just does not happen as a benign fallout from conventional measures taken to enhance 'opportunity.' Until we summon up the courage to distinguish between the problems of poverty and the problems of race, we shall have to reckon with the consequences of our lack of candor.

In the late 1960s and early 1970s, the national leadership began to address the problem of race. Affirmative action intended to produce roughly equal outcomes was one strategy.

The cohort replacement process and the scarcity of high-paying jobs account for the shrinking support for affirmative action among today's electorate. Parents of the baby boom remember the drinking fountains and toilets marked "colored" or "white"; they recall the stereotypical Hollywood portrayal of blacks as jesters or household servants. They grew up with Aunt Jemima syrup on their breakfast tables and listened to Amos and Andy on their radios. And they remember Birmingham Police Chief "Bull" Connor turning his attack dogs and fire hoses on black children. Late baby boomers and Generation X learned about those events from history books and film clips, if they learned about them at all. Many younger whites have had black classmates, have seen successful black politicians on the national stage, and, if they lived near a metropolis, they probably grew up close to a city that elected a black mayor. They know that African Americans can work their way up to the top jobs, so affirmative action appears to be a needless and illegal violation of a fundamental American principle they were taught in school: skin color should not matter.

If black-white differences in the 1990s result from equitable practices and from economic processes that treat all people alike, there is no justification for affirmative action. But is that the case, or does our history of racial discrimination and prejudice continue to limit opportunities for blacks?

Some of the largest black-white differences are in the labor and housing markets. These, in turn, account for the persistent economic gaps described in chapter 6. Why does the unemployment rate remain twice as high for blacks as for whites? Joleen Kirshenman and Kathryn Neckerman (1991) interviewed Chicago-area employers who hired entry-level workers in the late 1980s. Employers, they found, recognized the principle of racial fairness and knew what the law required. Simultaneously, they believed that young white workers would be more productive and easier to get along with than young black men. Thus they invoked rules that were ostensibly fair but which gave the advantage to white applicants. Some young blacks were hired but they typically had unusually strong credentials, credentials that convinced the employers that these black men had the favorable characteristics of whites. As Neckerman and Kirshenman summarized, it was a matter of "We'd love to hire them but. . . ." These findings and a continuing series of successful law suits about employment discrimination suggest that black men may still not have equal opportunities in the job market.

Do African Americans have equal opportunities in the housing market? They are much more equal now than in the past, but the extensive audit studies sponsored by the Department of Housing and Urban Development—those that send whites and then blacks to inquire about homes and apartments advertised in newspapers—report that black homeseekers are often treated differently than similar whites. Blacks are shown fewer homes, steered more often to black or mixed neighborhoods, and provided with less information than whites. When blacks apply for mortgages, they are significantly more likely to be turned down by lenders than are whites with similar financial credentials (Munnell et al. 1992; Yinger 1995). Are opportunities really equal for blacks in the housing market or does skin color still help determine where you live?

Continuing black-white residential segregation explains why public schools in many areas are coded by color. Much progress has been accomplished in eliminating segregation in many locations. In the South, countywide school districts in Charlotte, Jacksonville, Nashville, and scores of smaller cities provide the integrated classrooms that Chief Justice Warren and his associate justices foresaw. In the larger metropolises of the Northeast and Midwest, however, black-white school segregation is the rule. White students enroll primarily in the suburban schools or private schools, leaving the central-city public schools to educate blacks and the children of recent immigrants. Has the promise of *Brown* been fulfilled?

To the extent that current and past racial discrimination and prejudice limit opportunities for blacks, the affirmative action programs developed during and after the civil rights decade are justified. But there is also a challenge to find new and better ways to provide equal opportunities to blacks. In his 1965 commencement address at Howard University, President Johnson proclaimed the civil rights accomplishments of his administration and then argued (Johnson 1964, p. 558):

> But freedom is not enough. You do not wipe away the scars of centuries by saying:
>
> "Now you are free to go where you want, do as you desire, and choose the leaders you please." . . . You do not take a person who, for years, has been hobbled by chains and liberate him, bring him up to the starting line of a race and then say, "You are free to compete with all the others," and still believe that you have been completely fair. . . . We seek not just freedom but opportunity—not just legal equity but human ability—not just equality as a right and theory but equality as a fact. . . . To this end, equal opportunity is essential, but not enough.

Gender Inequality

On one crucial economic indicator, inequality declined in the 1980s: the earnings and occupational achievements of women moved closer to those of men. Parity has not been reached and may never be attained, but the gender gap in earnings is smaller now than before (Bianchi 1995).

Two different perspectives describe these trends. The optimist stresses that only thirty-five years ago, most doors were closed to women seeking to pursue careers outside the home. Federal laws and court decisions tolerated gender discrimination, so public universities could admit only men, and employers could hire only men for the best jobs. Laws and our social norms changed in the 1960s, so late baby boom and Generation X women entered the labor force in great numbers. They also have the protection of equal opportunity legislation and benefit from successful lawsuits charging gender discrimination. They can control their own pregnancies more effectively and are under less pressure to marry early or to remain with their first husband. These normative changes and the economic shifts—the growth of jobs that require brainpower rather than brawn—may eventually bring gender equity in the labor market as well as in all spheres of public life. The next generation of women will have an asset this generation did not—mothers who worked for most of their lives.

The more pessimistic observer, while recognizing the substantial gains of women, would hesitate to compose accolades since gender differences remain large. Dramatic gains for women have not eliminated sexual disparities nor ended subtle discrimination that women face. Consider the earnings of full-time workers in 1993:

	Average Earnings of Men (000)	Average Earnings of Women (000)	Gender Gap in Earnings (000)	Percentage of Men's Earnings Earned by Women
College, 5 years or more	$58	$42	$−16	72%
College, 4 years	45	32	−13	70
College, 1 to 3 years	33	24	−9	72
High school, 4 years	28	20	−8	72
High school, 1 to 3 years	22	15	−7	70
Less than 9 years	18	14	−5	71

Is there any reason why women with four-year college educations who work full-time should earn $13,000 less per year than comparable men? Women with high school educations averaged $8,000 less per year than similar men, while women who dropped out of high school earned $7,000 less than men. Jobs at these educational levels seldom require years of seniority or extensive on-the-job training. Are these differences the outcome of gender-neutral labor market practices or could selective hiring and promotion practices account for persisting gender differences?

In 1991, Senator Robert Dole introduced the Glass Ceiling Act to study why women in the corporate world were seldom promoted to the top jobs: women made up 47 percent of the labor force but held only 3 percent of senior managerial jobs with the leading private sector firms. A commission originally chaired by Secretary of Labor Elizabeth Dole investigated. Although its primary mission was to explain why women did not fare well with the largest corporations, the commission realized that racial minorities were also absent from the peak of the hierarchy. After ordering academic studies and interviewing executives, personnel managers, and corporate recruiters, the commission concluded that minorities and women did not get the most powerful jobs because of prejudice. Decision-makers saw women and minorities as different from themselves—in gender, race, cultural backgrounds, and lifestyles. They did not belong to the same social clubs or participate in the same sports as did top executives, who happened to be white men. The Glass Ceiling Commission contended that women and minorities failed an unwritten but sternly administered test of acceptability and that even women and minorities with appropriate credentials "face a brick, opaque and thick glass ceiling that blocks their advancement to senior level decision making positions" (U.S. Federal Glass Ceiling Commission 1995, p. 9).

These ceilings may be so firmly established and so well buttressed by stereotypes about women and minorities that few changes are possible. But women increasingly are earning the credentials required for the most rewarding positions. Future generations of business executives may become more willing to accept women and minorities, so that in time the glass and brick ceilings may disappear.

Growing Economic Inequality

A decade ago debates flared about whether economic inequality had really increased. The census of 1990 and similar surveys resolve that question unambiguously: inequality increased in the 1970s and 1980s.

Figure 8-1 shows what has happened. The right-side-up U reports the Gini index of family income inequality since the end of World War II. If all families received about the same incomes, this index would approach its minimum value of zero; if a few rich families received almost all income, it would approach 1.00. From the late 1940s through 1970, the Gini index declined but then a turning point was reached. The index moved up, and by the 1990s family income inequality was greater than at any previous point in the last half-century (Karoly 1993). This phenomenon occurred because of the increasing inequality of wages and changes in family composition: more dual-earner families with high incomes, but also more single-parent families with small incomes.

No consensus exists about whether greater income inequality is good or bad. Some experts defend it, contending that it results from equitable market forces and the decisions people make either to maximize their earnings or to forgo the training and effort needed to earn large sums. Others argue that growing inequality not only disadvantages many families but moves the nation toward a larger gap between the rich and the poor.

Greater inequality shows up on most indicators linked to income or earnings. From time to time, the Federal Reserve measures the concentration of household wealth, including home equity and the value of durable goods and financial instruments. Looking at the Federal Reserve's 1983 and 1989 surveys shows that in constant dollars the median net worth of American households rose 11 percent. All would agree that is good news. Whether or not wealth holdings became more concentrated over the long run is a subject of dispute, but the numbers below help clarify the changes in the 1980s (Committee on Ways and Means 1993, pp. 1553–1554).

Household Wealth Distribution	Share of Total Net Wealth Held by Households	
	1983	1989
Bottom 90%	33%	32%
Next 9%	35	31
Top 1%	32	37
Total Households	100%	100%

More than one-third of the assets in this country are held by the top 1 percent of households and two-thirds by the richest 10 percent. Consistent with trends previously described, it is obvious that wealth became more concentrated in the 1980s.

Dowell Myers and Jennifer Wolch (1995) conducted a major investigation of polarization in housing status in the last decade. They found a modest trend toward both "mansionization" and "homelessness." They defined the "generously housed" as those households who had high incomes, devoted no more than 15 percent of their income to housing costs, and lived where there were at least three rooms for each person. The "precariously housed" had low incomes— most of them below or just above the poverty line—and spent more than one-half of their meager incomes for rent. Some of them were candidates for possible homelessness if they lost a job, if their rent jumped, or if they had a financial crisis. In the 1980s, the percentage of households generously housed increased from 6 to 7 percent while those precariously housed also rose: from 5 to 6 percent.

The United States is usually viewed as a nation of middle-class families, and we often assume that the middle class dominates numerically and politically. The middle class is certainly not in danger of extinction but, unlike the decades before 1973, it is not growing. The middle class must work longer and harder to maintain its status, and it is increasingly difficult for families to move up from poverty.

Facing the Future

Censuses are national self-portraits. The 1990 census shows that although the United States faces many challenges, it remains a land of great opportunity for most of its citizens. Much like other developed countries, we are adjusting to a new economic system and to pervasive changes in the structure of family life. The United States has endured previous painful economic shifts that increased inequality— the transition from agriculture to urban manufacturing and the travail of the Great Depression. But the nation has never before simultaneously experienced both a fundamental economic restructuring and a basic shift in family life.

Fears about decline are based upon the fact that, despite growth and change, disparities between socioeconomic classes and between blacks and whites are not decreasing. Some people and families will lose out the fight for economic success in this new era. Rather than focusing on decline, however, it is important to ask questions about persistent and increasing inequality, as well as the opportunities we provide or deny to children, women, blacks, and those who lack college diplomas. How much inequality should we tolerate? What, if anything, can be done to halt the trend toward greater inequality? How we answer these questions will determine how well we adapt to life in the twenty-first century.

References

Adarand Construction v. Pena. 1995. 115 S. Ct. 2097.

Alba, Richard. 1990. *Ethnic Identity: The Transformation of White America.* New Haven, CT.: Yale University Press.

Allen, James Paul, and Eugene James Turner. 1988. *We the People: An Atlas of America's Ethnic Diversity.* New York: Macmillan.

Archdeacon, Thomas J. 1983. *Becoming American: An Ethnic Essay.* New York: The Free Press.

Arlington Heights v. Metropolitan Housing Development Corp. 1977. 429 U.S. 252.

Asbell, Bernard. 1995. *The Pill: A Biography of the Drug That Changed the World.* New York: Random House.

Auletta, Ken. 1982. *The Underclass.* New York: Random House. (First published in *The New Yorker,* November 16, 23, and 30, 1981.)

Bach, R., and H. Brill. 1991. *Impact of IRCA on the U.S. Labor Market and Economy: Final Report to the U.S. Department of Labor.* Binghamton, NY: State University of New York: Institute for Research on Multculturalism and International Labor.

Bancroft, Gertrude. 1958. *The American Labor Force: Its Growth and Changing Composition.* New York: Wiley.

Bartlett, Donald L., and James B. Steel. 1992. *America: What Went Wrong?* Kansas City, MO: Andrews and McMeel.

Bates, Timothy Mason. 1993. *Banking on Black Enterprise: The Potential of Emerging Firms for Revitalizing Urban Economics.* Washington, D.C.: Joint Center for Political and Economic Studies.

Bean, Frank D., and Marta Tienda. 1987. *The Hispanic Population of the United States.* New York: Russell Sage Foundation.

Bianchi, Suzanne M. 1995. "Changing Economic Roles of Women and Men." In *State of the Union: America in the 1990s.* Vol. I. Edited by Reynolds Farley. New York: Russell Sage Foundation.

———. and Daphne Spain. 1986. *American Women in Transition.* New York: Russell Sage Foundation.

Blankenhorn, David. 1995. *Fatherless America: Confronting Our Most Urgent Social Problem.* New York: Basic Books.

Blau, Peter M., and Otis Dudley Duncan. 1967. *The American Occupational Structure.* New York: Wiley.

357

Bluestone, Barry, and Bennett Harrison. 1982. *The Deindustrialization of America: Plant Closing, Community Abandonment, and the Dismantling of Basic Industry.* New York: Basic Books.

Bok, Derek. 1993. *The Cost of Talent: How Executives and Professionals Are Paid and How it Affects America.* New York: The Free Press.

Borjas, George J. 1994. "The Economics of Immigration." *Journal of Economic Literature* XXXII (December): 1667–1717.

Bouvier, Leon F., and Robert W. Gardner. 1986. "Immigration to the U.S.: The Unfinished Story." *Population Bulletin* 41(4) (November).

Bowers v. Hardwick. 1986. 478 U.S. 186.

Branch, Taylor. 1988. *Parting the Waters: America in the King Years: 1954–63.* New York: Simon & Schuster.

Brimelow, Peter. 1995. *Alien Nations: Common Sense About America's Immigration Disaster.* New York: Random House.

Brown v. Board of Education of Topeka. 1954. 347 U.S. 483.

Bumpass, Larry L. 1984. "Children and Marital Disruption: A Replication and Update." *Demography* 21: 71–83.

Burt, Martha. 1992. *Over the Edge.* New York: Russell Sage Foundation.

Card, David. 1990. "The Impact of the Mariel Boatlift on the Miami Labor Market." *Industrial and Labor Relations Review* 43: 245–257.

Cherlin, Andrew. 1981. *Marriage, Divorce, Remarriage.* Cambridge, MA: Harvard University Press.

Chiswick, Barry R. 1978. "The Effect of Americanization on the Earnings of Foreign-Born Men." *Journal of Political Economy* 86:897–921.

———, and Teresa A. Sullivan. 1995. "The New Immigrants." In *State of the Union: America in the 1990s,* Vol.I. Edited by Reynolds Farley. New York: Russell Sage Foundation.

Choldin, Harvey M. 1986. "Statistics and Politics: The Hispanic Issue in the 1980 Census." *Demography* 23(3) (August): 403–418.

———. 1994. *Looking for the Last Percent: The Controversy Over Census Undercounts.* New Brunswick, NJ: Rutgers University Press.

Cisneros v. Corpus Christi Independent School District. 1970. 324 F. Suppl. 599.

Clark, Rebecca L., Jeffrey S. Passel, Wendy N. Zimmermann, and Michael E. Fix. 1994. *Fiscal Impacts of Undocumented Aliens: Selected Estimates for Seven States.* Washington, D.C.: Urban Institute Press.

Cole, Robert E., and Donald R. Deskins, Jr. 1988. "Racial Factors in Site Location and Employment Patterns of Japanese Auto Firms in America." *California Management Review* 3(1):9–22.

Conk, Margo A. 1987. "The 1980 Census in Historical Perspective." In *The Politics of Numbers.* Edited by William Alonso and Paul Starr. New York: Russell Sage Foundation.

Contractors Association of Eastern Pennsylvania v. Secretary of Labor. 1971. 442 F. 2nd 159.

Cose, Ellis. 1993. *The Rage of a Privileged Class.* New York: HarperCollins.

Council of Economic Advisors. 1976. *Economic Report of the President.* Washington, D.C.: U.S. Government Printing Office.

———. 1978. *Economic Report of the President*. Washington, D.C.: U.S. Government Printing Office.

———. 1985. *Economic Report of the President*. Washington, D.C.: U.S. Government Printing Office.

———. 1993. *Economic Report of the President*. Washington, D.C.: U.S. Government Printing Office.

———. 1994. *Economic Report of the President*. Washington, D.C.: U.S. Government Printing Office.

———. 1995. *Economic Report of the President*. Washington, D.C.: Government Printing Office.

Danziger, Sheldon, and Peter Gottschalk. 1993. *Uneven Tides: Rising Inequality in America*. New York: Russell Sage Foundation.

———. 1995. *America Unequal*. Cambridge, MA: Harvard University Press.

Darity, William, Jr., David Guilkey, and William Winfrey. 1995. "Ethnicity, Race, and Earnings." *Economics Letters* 47: 401–408.

de Tocqueville, Alexis. 1969. *Democracy in America*. New York: Doubleday (originally published in 1838).

Duberman, Martin Bauml. 1988. *Paul Robeson*. New York: Knopf.

DuBois, W.E.B. 1899. *The Philadelphia Negro*. Philadelphia: University of Pennsylvania. Series in Political Economy and Public Law, No. 14.

Dudley, Kathryn Marie. 1994. *The End of the Line: Lost Jobs, New Lives in Postindustrial America*. Chicago: University of Chicago Press.

Duncan, Beverly. 1968. "Trends in the Output and Distribution of Schooling." In *Indicators of Social Change: Concepts and Measurements*. Edited by Eleanor Bernert Sheldon and Wilbert E. Moore. New York: Russell Sage Foundation.

Duncan, Otis Dudley. 1969. "Inheritance of Poverty or Inheritance of Race." In *On Understanding Poverty*, edited by Daniel P. Moynihan. New York: Basic Books.

Duncan, Otis Dudley, David L. Featherman, and Beverly Duncan. 1972. *Socioeconomic Background and Achievement*. New York: Seminar Press.

Easterlin, Richard A. 1987. *Birth and Fortune: The Impact of Numbers on Personal Welfare*. Chicago: University of Chicago Press.

Edgerton, John. 1994. *Speak Now Against the Day: The Generation Before the Civil Rights Movement in the South*. New York: Knopf.

Edmonston, Barry and Charles Schultze (editors). 1995. *Modernizing the U.S. Census*. Washington, D.C.: National Academy Press.

Edsall, Thomas Byrne. 1984. *The New Politics of Inequality*. New York: Norton.

Edwards v. California. 1941. 314 U.S. 160.

Ehrenreich, Barbara. 1989. *Fear of Falling: The Inner Life of the Middle Class*. New York: Harper-Perennial.

Euclid v. Ambler Realty Co. 1926. 272 U.S. 365.

FAIR v. Klutznick. 1980. 486 F. Supp. 564.

Faludi, Susan. 1991. *Backlash: The Undeclared War Against American Women*. New York: Crown.

Farley, Reynolds, and William H. Frey. 1994. "Changes in the Segregation of

Whites from Blacks During the 1980s: Small Steps Toward a More Integrated Society." *American Sociological Review* 59 (1) (February): 23–45.

Farley, Reynolds, Charlotte Steeh, Maria Krysan, Tara Jackson, and Keith Reeves. 1994. "Stereotypes and Segregation: Neighborhoods in the Detroit Area." *American Journal of Sociology* 100 (3)(November): 750–780.

Feagin, Joe R., and Melvin P. Sikes. 1994. *Living with Racism: the Black Middle Class Perspective.* Boston: Beacon Press.

Featherman, David L., and Robert M. Hauser. 1978. *Opportunity and Change.* New York: Academic Press.

Firefighters Local Union No. 1794 v. Stotts. 1984. 467 U.S. 561.

Fix, Michael, and Jeffrey S. Passel. 1994. *Immigration and Immigrants: Setting the Record Straight.* Washington, D.C.: Urban Institute Press.

Folger, John K., and Charles B. Nam. 1967. *Education of the American Population.* Washington, D.C.: U.S. Government Printing Office.

Foner, Eric. 1988. *Reconstruction: America's Unfinished Revolution.* New York: Harper & Row.

Frank, Robert H., and Philip J. Cook. 1995. *The Winner Take All Society.* New York: Free Press.

Franklin v. Massachusetts 1992 112 S. Ct. 2767.

Fraser, Steven (editor). 1995. *The Bell Curve Wars: Race, Intelligence, and the Future of America.* New York: Basic Books.

Freedman, Ronald, Pascal K. Whelpton, and Arthur A. Campbell. 1959. *Family Planning, Sterility and Population Growth.* New York: McGraw-Hill.

Freeman, Richard B. 1976. *Black Elite: The New Market for Highly Educated Black Americans.* New York: McGraw-Hill.

Frey, William H. 1994. "Minority Suburbanization and Continued 'White Flight' in U.S. Metropolitan Areas: Assessing Findings from the 1990 Census." *Research in Community Sociology* 4: 15–42.

———. 1995. "The New Geography of Population Shifts." In *State of the Union: America in the 1990s,* Vol. II. Edited by Reynolds Farley. New York: Russell Sage Foundation.

Friedan, Betty. 1963. *The Feminine Mystique.* New York: Norton.

Friedman, Benjamin M. 1988. *Day of Reckoning: The Consequences of American Economic Policy.* New York: Vintage Books.

Fuguitt, Glenn V., David L. Brown, and Calvin L. Beale. 1989. *Rural and Small Town America.* New York: Russell Sage Foundation.

Fullilove v. Klutznick. 1980. 448 U.S. 448.

Galle, Omer R., and Karl E. Taeuber. 1966. "Metropolitan Migration and Intervening Opportunities." *American Sociological Review* 31(February): 655–664.

Garreau, Joel. 1981. *The Nine Nations of North America.* New York: Avon.

———. 1991. *Edge City: Life on the New Frontier.* New York: Doubleday.

Garrow, David J. 1978. *Protest at Selma: Martin Luther King, Jr., and the Voting Rights Act of 1965.* New Haven, CT: Yale University Press.

———. 1986. *Bearing the Cross: Martin Luther King, Jr., and the Southern Christian Leadership Conference.* New York: Morrow.

————. 1994. *Liberty and Sexuality: The Right to Privacy and the Making of Roe v. Wade*. New York: Macmillan.

Gittleman, Maury B. and David R. Howell. 1992. *Job Quality, Labor Market Segmentation, and Earnings Inequality: Effects of Economic Restructuring in the 1980s*. Annandale-on-Hudson, NY: Jerome Levy Economics Institute.

Glazer, Nathan, and Daniel P. Moynihan. 1963. *Beyond the Melting Pot: The Negroes, Puerto Ricans, Jews, Italians, and Irish of New York City*. Cambridge, MA: M.I.T. Press.

Goldin, Claudia, 1990. *Understanding the Gender Gap: An Economic History of American Women*. New York: Oxford University Press.

Graham v. Richardson. 1971. 403 U.S. 365.

Greeley, Andrew. 1994. Book Review, *Contemporary Sociology* 23(2):221–222.

Greenberg, Stanley B. 1995. *Middle Class Dreams: The Politics and Power of the New American Majority*. New York: Random House.

Greenwood, Michael J. 1981. *Migration and Economic Growth in the United States: National, Regional and Metropolitan Perspectives*. New York: Academic Press.

Grenier, Guillermo J., Alex Stepick, Debbie Draznin, Aileen LaBorwit, and Steve Morris. 1992. "On Machines and Bureaucracy: Controlling Ethnic Interaction in Miami's Apparel and Construction Industries." *Structuring Diversity: Ethnographic Perspectives on the New Immigration*. Edited by Louise Lamphere. Chicago: University of Chicago Press.

Griggs v. Duke Power. 1971. 401 U.S. 424.

Griswold v. Connecticut. 1965. 381 U.S. 479.

Hammer, Michael, and James Champy. 1994. *Reengineering the Corporation: A Manifesto for Business Revolution*. New York: Harper Business.

Harrison, Bennett, and Barry Bluestone. 1988. *The Great U-Turn: Corporate Restructuring and the Polarizing of America*. New York: Basic Books.

Harrison, Roderick J., and Claudette Bennett. 1995. "Racial and Ethnic Diversity." In *State of the Union: America in the 1990s*, Vol. II. Edited by Reynolds Farley. New York: Russell Sage Foundation.

Hauser, Robert M. 1987. "College Entry among Black High School Graduates: Family Income Does Not Explain the Decline." University of Wisconsin-Madison: Center for Demography and Ecology, CDE Working Paper 87-19.

————. 1989. "The Decline in College Entry among African Americans: Findings in Search of Explanations." University of Wisconsin-Madison: Center for Demography and Ecology, CDE Working Paper 90-20.

Henderson v. Mayor of New York. 1876. 92 U.S. 259.

Henshaw, Stanley K., and Jennifer Van Vort. 1994. "Abortion Services in the United States, 1991 and 1992." *Family Planning Perspectives* 26(3): 100–106.

Hernandez, Donald J. 1993. *America's Children: Resources from Family, Government, and the Economy*. New York: Russell Sage Foundation.

Herrnstein, Richard J., and Charles Murray. 1994. *The Bell Curve: Intelligence and Class Structure in American Life*. New York: The Free Press.

Hochschild, Arlie Russell. 1989. *The Second Shift: Working Parents and the Revolution at Home*. New York: Viking.

————. and Anne Machung. 1989. *The Second Shift: Inside the Two Job Marriage.* New York: Penguin.

Hofferth, Sandra L., Joan R. Kahn, and Wendy Baldwin. 1987. "Premarital Sexual Activity Among U.S. Teenage Women Over the Past Three Decades." *Family Planning Perspectives* 19(2):46–53.

Hoffman, Frederick L. 1896. *Race Traits and Tendencies of the American Negro.* Publications of the American Economic Association, Vol. II, Nos. 1, 2, and 3.

Hogan, Howard, and Gregory Robinson. 1993. "What the Census Bureau's Coverage Evaluation Programs Tell Us About Differential Undercount." *Proceedings of the Bureau of the Census 1993 Research Conference on Undercounted Ethnic Populations.* Washington, D.C.: Bureau of the Census.

Hughes, Langston. 1940. *The Big Sea.* New York: Hill & Wang.

Jackson, Kenneth T. 1985. *Crabgrass Frontier: The Suburbanization of the United States.* New York: Oxford University Press.

Jacob, Herbert. 1988. *Silent Revolution: The Transformation of Divorce Law in the United States.* Chicago: University of Chicago Press.

Jaeger, David A. 1995. "Skill Differences and the Effects of Immigrants on the Wages of Natives." Ann Arbor: University of Michigan Department of Economics and Population Studies Center.

Jaffe, A. J. 1992. *The First Immigrants from Asia: A Population History of North American Indians.* New York: Plenum.

Janus, Samuel S., and Cynthia L. Janus. 1993. *The Janus Report on Sexual Behavior.* New York: Wiley.

Jasso, Guillermina, and Mark R. Rosenzweig. 1990. *The New Chosen People: Immigrants in the United States.* New York: Russell Sage Foundation.

Jencks, Christopher. 1994. *The Homeless: Why Are They Everywhere and What We Can Do About It.* Cambridge, MA: Harvard University Press.

Karoly, Lynn A. 1993. "The Trend in Inequality among Families, Individuals, and Workers in the United States: A Twenty-five Year Perspective." In *Uneven Tides: Rising Inequality in America.* Edited by Sheldon Danziger and Peter Gottshalk. New York: Russell Sage Foundation.

Kasarda, John D. 1985. "Urban Change and Minority Opportunities." *The Urban Underclass.* Edited by Paul E. Petersen. Washington, D.C.: The Brookings Institution.

————. 1993. "Entry Level Jobs, Mobility, and Urban Minority Unemployment." *Urban Affairs Quarterly* 19:21–40.

————. 1995. "Industrial Restructuring and the Changing Location of Jobs." In *State of the Union: America in the 1990s,* Vol.I. Edited by Reynolds Farley. New York: Russell Sage Foundation.

Katz, Michael B. 1989. *The Undeserving Poor: From the War on Poverty to the War on Welfare.* New York: Pantheon.

Killingsworth, Charles C. 1968. *Jobs and Income for Negroes.* Washington, D.C.: National Manpower Policy Task Force.

Klugel, James R., and Lawrence Bobo. 1993. "Opposition to Race-Targeting: Self-Interest, Stratification Ideology or Racial Attitudes." *American Sociological Review* 58(4) (August): 443–464.

Krugman, Paul. 1994. *The Age of Diminished Expectations: U.S. Economic Policy in the 1990s.* Cambridge, MA: M.I.T. Press. (First published in 1990 by the Washington Post Company.)

Lasch, Christopher. 1979. *The Culture of Narcissism.* New York: Norton.

Laska, Shirley, and Daphne Spain (editors). 1980. *Back to the Cities: Issues in Neighborhood Renovation.* New York: Pergamon Press.

Lau v. Nichols. 1974. 414 U.S. 463.

Laumann, Edward O., John Gagnon, Robert T. Michaels, and Stuart Michaels. 1994. *The Social Organization of Sexuality: Sexual Practices in the United States.* Chicago: University of Chicago Press.

Lemann, Nicholas. 1991. *The Promised Land: The Great Black Migration and How It Changed America.* New York: Knopf.

Levitan, Sar A. 1973. *Programs in Aid of the Poor for the 1970s.* Baltimore: Johns Hopkins University Press.

Levy, Frank. 1987. *Dollars and Dreams: The Changing American Income Distribution.* New York: Russell Sage Foundation.

———. 1995. "Incomes and Income Inequality." In *State of the Union: America in the 1990s.* Vol. I. Edited by Reynolds Farley. New York: Russell Sage Foundation.

———, and Richard J. Murnane. 1992. "U.S. Earnings Levels and Earnings Inequality: A Review of Recent Trends and Proposed Explanations." *Journal of Economic Literature* 30 (September): 1333–1381.

———, and Mary C. Waters. 1988. *From Many Strands: Ethnic and Racial Groups in Contemporary America.* New York: Russell Sage Foundation.

Logan, John. 1987. *Urban Fortunes: The Political Economy of Place.* Berkeley: University of California Press.

Long, Larry. 1988. *Migration and Residential Mobility in the United States.* New York: Russell Sage Foundation.

Loving v. Virginia. 1967. 87 S, Ct. 1817.

Lowry, Ira S. 1966. *Migration and Metropolitan Growth: Two Analytic Models.* San Francisco: Chandler.

McFate, Katherine. 1995. *Poverty, Inequality, and the Future of Social Policy: Western States in the New World Order.* New York: Russell Sage Foundation.

McLanahan, Sara S., and Lynne Casper. 1995. "Growing Diversity and Inequality in the American Family." In *State of the Union: America in the 1990s.* Vol. II. Edited by Reynolds Farley. New York: Russell Sage Foundation.

McLanahan, Sara S., and Gary Sandefur. 1994. *Growing Up with a Single Parent: What Hurts, What Helps.* Cambridge, MA: Harvard University Press.

Madrick, Jeffrey. 1995. *The End of Affluence: The Causes and Consequences of America's Economic Dilemma.* New York: Random House.

Mare, Robert D. 1995. "Changes in Educational Attainment and School Enrollment." In *State of the Union: America in the 1990s.* Vol. II. Edited by Reynolds Farley. New York: Russell Sage Foundation.

Margo, Robert A. 1990. *Race and Schooling in the South: 1880–1950.* Chicago: University of Chicago Press.

Massey, Douglas S. 1995. "The New Immigration and Ethnicity in the United States." *Population and Development Review* 21 (3): 631–652.

————, Rafael Alarcon, Jorge Durand, and Humberto Gonzalez. 1987. *Return to Aztlan: The Social Process of International Migration from Western Mexico*. Berkeley: University of California Press.

Massey, Douglas S., and Nancy A. Denton. 1993. *American Apartheid: Segregation and the Making of the Underclass*. Cambridge, MA: Harvard University Press.

Massey, Douglas S., and Audrey Singer. 1995. "New Estimates of Undocumented Mexican Migration and the Probability of Apprehension." *Demography* 32: 203–213.

Mead, Lawrence M. 1986. *Beyond Entitlement: The Social Obligations of Citizenship*. New York: Basic Books.

————. 1992. *The New Politics of Poverty: The Nonworking Poor in America*. New York: Basic Books.

Michael, Robert T., John H. Gagnon, Edward O. Laumann, and Gina Kolata. 1994. *Sex in America*. New York: Warner Books.

Moore, Kristin. 1995. *Nonmarital Childbearing in the United States. Report to Congress on Out-of-Wedlock Childbearing*. U.S. National Center for Health Statistics, DHHS Pub. No. (PHS) 95-1257-1.

Mueller v. Oregon. 1908. 208 U.S. 412.

Muller, Charles F. 1982. *The Economics of Labor Migration: A Behavioral Analysis*. New York: Academic Press.

Muller, Thomas, and Thomas J. Espenshade. 1985. *The Fourth Wave: California's Newest Immigrants*. Washington, D.C.: Urban Institute Press.

Munnell, Alicia H., Lynn E. Browne, James McEneaney, and Geoffrey M. B. Tootel. 1992. "Mortgage Lending in Boston: Interpreting HMDA Data." Working Paper 92-7. Boston: Federal Reserve Bank of Boston.

Murray, Charles. 1984. *Losing Ground: American Social Policy: 1950–1980*. New York: Basic Books.

Myers, Dowell, and Jennifer R. Wolch. 1995. "The Polarization of Housing Status." In *State of the Union: America in the 1990s*, Vol. I. Edited by Reynolds Farley. New York: Russell Sage Foundation.

National Advisory Commission on Civil Disorders. 1968. *Report of the National Advisory Commission on Civil Disorders*. Washington D.C.: U.S. Government Printing Office.

Newman, Katherine S. 1988. *Falling from Grace: The Experience of Downward Mobility in the American Middle Class*. New York: Random House.

————. 1993. *Declining Fortunes: The Withering of the American Dream*. New York: Basic Books.

Norton, Arthur J., and Louisa F. Miller. 1992. "Marriage, Divorce and Remarriage in the 1990s." U.S. Bureau of the Census, *Current Population Reports*, Series P-23, No. 180 (October). Washington, D.C.: U.S. Government Printing Office.

O'Connell, Martin. 1991. "Late Expectations: Childbearing Patterns of American Women for the 1990s." U.S. Bureau of the Census, *Current Population Reports*, Series P-23, No. 176 (October). Washington, D.C.: U.S. Government Printing Office.

Ogbu, John. 1978. *Minority Education and Caste: The American System in Cross Cultural Perspective*. New York: Academic Press.

Oliver, Melvin L., and Thomas M. Shapiro. 1995. *Black Wealth/White Wealth: A New Perspective on Racial Inequality.* New York: Routledge.

Passel, Jeffrey S., and Barry Edmonston. 1994. "Immigration and Race: Recent Trends in Immigration to the United States." *Immigration and Ethnicity: the Integration of America's Newest Arrivals.* Edited by Barry Edmonston. Washington, D.C.: Urban Institute Press.

Passenger Cases. 1849. 48 U.S. 283.

Perlmann, Joel. 1988. *Ethnic Differences: Schooling and Social Structure among the Irish, Italians, Jews and Blacks in an American City: 1880–1935.* New York: Cambridge University Press.

Phillips, Kevin. 1990. *The Politics of Rich and Poor: Wealth and the American Electorate in the Reagan Aftermath.* New York: Harper Perennial.

———. 1993. *Boiling Point: Democrats, Republicans and the Decline of Middle Class Prosperity.* New York: Random House.

Plessy v. Ferguson. 1896. 163 U.S. 537.

Plyler v. Doe. 1982. 457 U.S. 202.

Presser, Harriet B. 1989. "Can We Make Time for Children? The Economy, Work Schedules, and Child Care." *Demography* 26(4): 523–561.

Preston, Samuel H. 1984. "Children and the Elderly: Divergent Paths for America's Dependents." *Demography* 21: 435–457.

Preston, Samuel H., and John McDonald. 1979. "The Incidence of Divorce within Cohorts of American Marriages Contracted Since the Civil War." *Demography* 16: 1–25.

Quadagno, Jill. 1994. *The Color of Welfare: How Racism Undermined the War on Poverty.* New York: Oxford University Press.

Regents of the University of California v. Bakke. 1978. 438 U.S. 265.

Richmond v. J. A. Croson Co. 1989. 488 U.S. 469.

Roe v. Wade. 1973. 410 U.S. 113.

Rose, David L. 1994. "Twenty Five Years Later: Where Do We Stand on Equal Employment Opportunity Law Enforcement?" *Equal Employment Opportunity: Labor Market Discrimination and Public Policy.* Edited by Paul Burstein. New York: de Gruyter.

Rossi, Peter. 1989. *Down and Out in America.* Chicago: University of Chicago Press.

Sanders, Jimy M., and Victor Nee. 1996. "Immigrant Self-Employment: The Family as Social Capital and the Value of Human Capital." *American Sociological Review* 61(2): 231–249.

Schor, Juliet B. 1991. *The Overworked American: The Unexpected Decline of Leisure.* New York: Basic Books.

Schuman, Howard, and Jacqueline Scott. 1989. "Generations and Collective Memories." *American Sociological Review* 54(3): 359–381.

Shapiro v. Thompson. 1969. 394 U.S. 618.

Smith, James P., and Finis R. Welch. 1986. *Closing the Gap: Forty Years of Economic Progress for Blacks.* Santa Monica, CA: The RAND Corporation.

———. 1989. "Black Economic Progress After Myrdal." *Journal of Economic Literature* XXVII (2)(June): 519–564.

Snipp, C. Matthew. 1989. *American Indians: The First of This Land.* New York: Russell Sage Foundation.

Sorensen, Elaine, and Maria E. Enchautegui. 1994. "Immigrant Male Earnings in the 1980s: Divergent Patterns by Race and Ethnicity." In *Immigration and Ethnicity*. Edited by Barry Edmonston and Jeffrey S. Passel. Washington, D.C.: Urban Institute Press.

Stevens, Gillian. 1994. "Immigration, Emigration, Language Acquisition, and the English Language Proficiency of Immigrants in the United States." In *Immigration and Ethnicity*. Edited by Barry Edmonston and Jeffrey S. Passel. Washington, D.C.: Urban Institute Press.

———, and Joo Hyun Cho. 1985. "Socioeconomic Indexes and the New 1980 Census Occupational Classification Scheme." *Social Science Research* 14 (June): 142–168.

Stouffer, Samuel A. 1940. "Intervening Opportunities: A Theory Relating Mobility and Distance." *American Sociological Review* V: 845–867.

Sutterlin, Rebecca, and Robert A. Kominski. 1994. "Dollars for Scholars: Postsecondary Costs and Financing: 1990–1991." U.S. Bureau of the Census, *Current Population Reports*. Series P-70, No. 39 (September). Washington, D.C.: U.S. Government Printing Office.

Swann v. Charlotte-Mecklenburg Board of Education. 1971. 402 U.S. 1.

Taeuber, Irene B., and Conrad Taeuber. 1971. *People of the United States in the Twentieth Century*. Washington, D.C.: U.S. Government Printing Office.

Takaki, Ronald. 1989. *Strangers from a Different Shore: A History of Asian Americans*. Boston: Little, Brown.

Thornton, Arland. 1985. "Changing Attitudes Toward Separation and Divorce: Causes and Consequences." *American Journal of Sociology* 90(4): 856–872.

Thurow, Lester C. 1980. *The Zero-Sum Society*. New York: Basic Books.

———. 1984. *Dangerous Currents: The State of Economics*. New York: Vintage Books.

Tienda, Marta, and Zai Liang. 1994. "Poverty and Immigration in Policy Perspective." In *Confronting Poverty: Prescriptions for Change*. Edited by Sheldon Danziger, Gary D. Sandefur, and Daniel H. Weinberg. New York: Russell Sage Foundation.

Tileston v. Ullman. 1943. 318 U.S. 44.

Treas, Judith, and Ramon Torrecilha. 1995. "The Older Population." In *State of the Union: America in the 1990s*. Vol. I. Edited by Reynolds Farley. New York: Russell Sage Foundation.

Tygiel, Jules. 1983. *Baseball's Great Experiment: Jackie Robinson and His Legacy*. New York: Oxford University Press.

U.S. Bureau of Labor Statistics. 1988. *Labor Force Statistics Derived from the Current Population Survey: 1948–87*. Washington, D.C.: U.S. Government Printing Office.

———. 1989. *Handbook of Labor Statistics*, Bulletin 2340 (August). Washington, D.C.: U.S. Government Printing Office.

———. 1995. *A CPS Supplement for Testing Methods of Collecting Racial and Ethnic Information: May 1995*. Washington, D.C.: Department of Labor.

U.S. Bureau of the Census. 1918. *Negro Population of the United States*. Washington, D.C.: U.S. Government Printing Office.

———. 1943. *Sixteenth Census of the United States: 1940: Housing,* Vol. I, Part 1. Washington, D.C.: U.S. Government Printing Office.

———. 1964. *Census of Population: 1960,* Vol. 1, Part 1. Washington, D.C.: U.S. Government Printing Office.

———. 1971. *Census of Housing: 1970,* HC(1)-A1. Washington, D.C.: U.S. Government Printing Office.

———. 1973a. *Population and Housing Inquiries in U.S. Decennial Censuses. 1790–1970.* Working Paper #39. Washington, D.C.: U.S. Government Printing Office.

———. 1973b. *Census of Population: 1970,* Vol. 1, Part 1. Washington, D.C.: U.S. Government Printing Office.

———. 1975. *Historical Statistics of the United States: Colonial Times to 1970.* Washington, D.C.: U.S. Government Printing Office.

———. 1984. *Current Population Reports.* Series P-25, No. 952 (May). Washington, D.C.: U.S. Government Printing Office.

———. 1985. *Statistical Abstract of the United States: 1984.* Washington, D.C.: U.S. Government Printing Office.

———. 1991a. *Current Population Reports,* P-60, No. 174. Washington, D.C.: U.S. Government Printing Office.

———. 1991b. *Current Population Reports,* Series P-20, No. 451. Washington, D.C.: U.S. Government Printing Office.

———. 1991c. *Current Population Reports.* Series P-60, No. 176-RD. Washington, D.C.: U.S. Government Printing Office.

———. 1993a. *Census of Population: 1990,* CP-2-1. Washington, D.C.: U.S. Government Printing Office.

———. 1993b. *Current Population Reports.* Series P-60, No. 184 (October). Washington, D.C.: U.S. Government Printing Office.

———. 1993c. *Census of Population and Housing: 1990.* Public Use Microdata Samples. Washington, D.C.: U.S. Government Printing Office.

———. 1994a. *Current Population Reports.* Series P-25, No. 1111 (March). Washington, D.C.: U.S. Government Printing Office.

———. 1994b. *Current Population Reports.* Series P-20, No. 479 (October). Washington, D.C.: U.S. Government Printing Office.

———. 1995a. *Current Population Reports.* Series P-60, No. 188 (February). Washington, D.C.: U.S. Government Printing Office.

———. 1995b. *Statistical Abstract of the United States: 1995.* Washington, D.C.: U.S. Government Printing Office.

———. 1995c. *Current Population Reports,* Series P-70, No. 47 (August).

U.S. Department of Education. 1991. *Digest of Education Statistics.* Washington, D.C.: U.S. Government Printing Office.

———. 1995. *Digest of Education Statistics: 1995.* Washington, D.C.: U.S. Government Printing Office.

U.S. Department of Health and Human Services. 1985. *Report of the Secretary's Task Force on Black and Minority Health,* Vol. I, Summary. Washington, D.C.: U.S. Government Printing Office.

U.S. Federal Glass Ceiling Commission. 1995. *Good for Business: Making Full*

Use of the Nation's Human Capital. Washington, D.C.: Glass Ceiling Commission.

U.S. Immigration and Naturalization Service. 1996. *Statistical Yearbook of the Immigration and Naturalization Service, 1994*. Washington, D.C.: U.S. Government Printing Office.

———. 1994. *Statistical Yearbook of the Immigration and Naturalization Service, 1993*. Washington, D.C.: U.S. Government Printing Office.

U.S. National Center for Health Statistics. 1993. *Monthly Vital Statistics Report*, Vol. 7, No. 7, Supplement (January 7) Washington, D.C.: U.S. Government Printing Office.

United Steelworkers of America v. Weber. 1979. 443 U.S. 193.

Vose, Clement E. 1965. *Caucasians Only: The Supreme Court, the NAACP and the Restrictive Covenant Cases*. Berkeley: University of California Press.

Wallace, Phyllis A. (editor). 1976. *Equal Employment Opportunity and the AT&T Case*. Cambridge: M.I.T. Press.

Ward's Cove Packing v. Antonio. 1989. 490 U.S. 642.

Warren, Robert. 1990. "Annual Estimates of Nonimmigrant Overstays in the United States: 1985 to 1988." In *Undocumented Migration to the United States: IRCA and the Experience of the 1980s*. Edited by Frank Bean et al. Washington, DC: Urban Institute Press.

———. 1994. "Estimates of the Unauthorized Immigrant Population Residing in the United States, by Country of Origin and State of Residence: October, 1992" Washington, DC: Immigration and Naturalization Service.

Waters, Mary. 1990. *Ethnic Options: Choosing Identities in America*. Berkeley: University of California Press.

Weitzman, Lenore J. 1987. *The Divorce Revolution*. New York: The Free Press.

Westoff, Charles F., and Norman B. Ryder. 1977. *The Contraceptive Revolution*. Princeton, NJ: Princeton University Press.

Wetzel, James R. 1995. "Labor Force, Unemployment, and Earnings." In *State of the Union: America in the 1990s*, Vol. I, *Economics Trends*. Edited by Reynolds Farley. New York: Russell Sage Foundation.

Whalen, Charles, and Barbara Whalen. 1985. *The Longest Debate: A Legislative History of the 1964 Civil Rights Act*. New York: New American Library.

White, Michael J., and Lori Hunter. 1993. "The Migratory Response of Native Born Workers to the Presence of Immigrants in the Labor Market." Rhode Island: Brown University, Population Studies and Training Center.

Whitfield, Stephen J. 1988. *A Death in the Delta: The Story of Emmett Till*. New York: The Free Press.

Wilson, William Julius. 1978. *The Declining Significance of Race: Blacks and Changing American Institutions*. Chicago: University of Chicago Press.

———. 1987. *The Truly Disadvantaged: The Inner City, the Underclass, and Public Policy*. Chicago: University of Chicago Press.

Winnick, Louis. 1990. *New People in Old Neighborhoods: The Role of New Immigrants in Rejuvenating New York's Communities*. New York: Russell Sage Foundation.

Wrigley, Julia. 1995. *Other People's Children: An Intimate Account of the Dilemmas*

Facing Middle Class Parents and the Women They Hire to Raise Their Children. New York: Basic Books.

Wygant v. Jackson Board of Education. 1986. 476 U.S. 267.

Yinger, John. 1995. *Closed Doors, Opportunities Lost: The Continuing Costs of Housing Discrimination.* New York: Russell Sage Foundation.

Zangrando, Robert L. 1980. *The NAACP Crusade Against Lynching, 1909–1950.* Philadelphia, PA: Temple University Press.

Boldface numbers refer to figures and tables.

abortion, 23, 57, 60, **61**

"Act for the Suppression of Trade in and Circulation of Obscene Literature and Articles of Immoral Use, An," 55

affirmative action, 34, 38, 268, 270

Africa, 21, 160, 162, 164, 171–73, 177, 181

African Americans. *See* blacks

age: birth rates for women by, **117**; distribution of immigrants, 172–73; internal migration by, **314–15**; percentage of full-time, year-round workers by, **42**. *See also* age at marriage

age at marriage: and "America in decline" arguments, 14; and changes in American families, 110, **111**, 117–18, 128, 140; and earnings, 99; and the 1960s, 23–24; record high, in the 1990s, 343; and the sexual revolution, 5–6, 23–24, 48–53

Age of Diminished Expectations: U.S. Economic Policy in the 1990s (Krugman), 10, 88

agriculture, 354; and economic shifts from 1973 to the present, 90, **91**, 92, **94**; and the Green Revolution, 72, 83; switch from, to manufacturing, 7, 72

Aid to Families with Dependent Children (AFDC), 119, 122, 138, 143, 206; and internal migration, 297; median monthly benefits, **139**; Murray on, 18. *See also* welfare

AIDS, 62, 224

"America in decline" arguments, 1, 8–20, **21**, 334–38

America: What Went Wrong (Bartlett and Steele), 10

American Dream, idealized, 48

American Indians, 2, 152; education of, 235, **236–37**, 238; employment/earnings data for, 242–43, 245–46, 247, **250–51**, 252; fertility data for, 220–21, **222**; living arrangements for young children among, 222, **223**; marital status of, **219**, **264–65**; mortality rates for, 222–24; poverty rates for, 257– 59

American Revolution, 22, 27, 162, 272, 281

Americans with Disabilities Act, 269

American Telephone and Telegraph (AT&T), 38, 239

Amtrak, 150

Anderson, Douglas, 234

Anderson, Marian, 29

armed forces: homosexuals in, 58; segregation in, 3–4, 30

Armstrong, Neil, 346

Asbell, Bernard, 53

Asia: cheap labor in, 13, 75; immigrants from, 21, 27, 69, 152, 162, **163**, 164, **165**, 166, 172, 190, 192, 196–97, **198**, 199. *See also* Asians; *specific countries*

Asians: and economic growth after World War II, 71; education of, 235, **236–37**, 260–61; employment/earnings data for, 242–43,

Asians (continued)
    245–46, 247, 250–51, 252; fertility
    data for, 220–21, 222; and intellec-
    tual ability, 16–17; living arrange-
    ments for young children among,
    222, 223; marital status of, 219,
    262, 264–65; and migration, 327,
    329; mortality rates for, 222–24; as
    a percentage of the total popula-
    tion, 215–16; poverty rates for,
    257–59; and racial inequalities,
    347–50. See also Asia
asylees, 155, 157–59, 164
Auletta, Ken, 17
automobile industry: and economic
    shifts from 1973 to the present, 75,
    78, 80–81, 84; and Germany, 81,
    332; and the internationalization
    of production, 75, 81; and Japan,
    8, 75, 81, 332; during the Reagan
    years, 84; and U.S. domination of
    world markets, after World War II,
    70

baby boom cohort, 5, 13–14; and atti-
    tudes about childrearing, 45, 46,
    47; and changes in American fami-
    lies, 109–10, 111, 112–13, 115–
    19, 121, 131, 136, 140; and di-
    vorce, 113; and economic growth
    after World War II, 67, 68; and
    economic growth, during the
    Reagan years, 104, 105; and gender
    inequality, 351; and the 1960s, 24,
    45–49, 54; and racial inequalities,
    349; and the sexual revolution, 48–
    49, 54
baby bust cohort. See Generation X
Baker v. Carr, 331
balance of trade, 75–76, 77
banking, 90, 91, 92, 155
Bartlett, Donald, 10
Bell Curve: Intelligence and Class Struc-
    ture in American Life, The (Herrn-
    stein and Murray), 16–17
Berlin Wall, 207

Bethlehem Steel, 239
Bible, 1
birth cohorts. See cohorts; specific co-
    horts
birth control, 5–6; abortion as a form
    of, 60–61; and fertility rates, 116;
    and Griswold v. Connecticut, 56–
    57; laws against, 55–57, 58; and
    the 1960s, 22, 49, 53–58, 60–61;
    and the sexual revolution, 49, 53–
    54; and Tileston v. Ullman, 55
birth rates: and the "birth dearth," 115–
    19; and changes in American fami-
    lies, 109, 115–19; during the De-
    pression, 53; and immigration,
    154; international comparisons for,
    141, 142–43; for married/unmar-
    ried women, 118; for racial groups,
    218, 221; and the 1960s, 24; for
    women by age, 117–18. See also
    fertility; out-of-wedlock births
black(s), 2, 347–50; earnings data for,
    71, 189, 190–93, 238–40, 241,
    242–43, 244, 245, 246–47, 248,
    249, 250–51, 252–53, 261; educa-
    tion of, 228–30, 231, 232, 233,
    234–35, 236–37, 238; employment
    data for, 238–40, 241, 242–43,
    244, 245, 246–47, 248, 249, 250–
    51, 252–53; as entrepreneurs, 199;
    fertility rates for, 220–21, 222; and
    intellectual ability, 16–17; living
    arrangements for young children
    among, 222, 223; marital status
    of, 110, 219, 262, 264–65; middle
    class, 3, 4, 20, 29–30, 253–54; mi-
    gration of, 327–30; mortality rates
    for, 222–24, 225–28, 261; non-
    Hispanic, migration of, 293; as a
    percentage of the total population,
    215–16; poverty rates for, 253,
    255, 257, 258, 259, 261; subur-
    banization of, 327–30
Blair, Izell, 30
blue-collar workers, 7, 8, 196; and
    "America in decline" arguments, 9,

17, 18, 19; and economic growth after World War II, 67–68; and economic growth during the Reagan years, 102, 105, 106; and economic shifts from 1973 to the present, 93; immigrants as, 193

Bluestone, Barry, 8–9, 17, 78, 88, 101–2

Bok, Derek, 154–55

"boomerang" children, 14

Bowers v. Hardwick, 58

braceros program, 201

Brandeis brief, 35

Brazil, 70, 164

Brigham Young University, 312

Britain, 272. See also British Isles; England

British Isles, 153, 162

Brotherhood of Sleeping Car Porters Union, 29

Brown v. Board of Education, 30, 230, 350

Bumpass, Larry L., 113

Bureau of Labor Data, 68

bus segregation, 32–34, 35

business administration, 39, 40, 41

Canada: family status in, 141; immigrants from, 154, 159–60, 162, 163, 165, 166, 173, 181–82, 187–88, 192, 197, 198, 199, 207; mortality rates in, 227, 228; poor families lifted out of poverty in, by government intervention, 142

capitalism, 10, 14

Carribbean: cheap labor in, 13; immigrants from, 162, 166, 171–73, 176, 187, 192–93

Carter, Jimmy, 83–84

Casper, Lynne, 52, 138–39, 142

Catholicism, 55–56, 151, 162

census of 1970, 138

census of 1980, 102

census of 1990, 1, 20–21, 102, 138; and "America in decline" argu-

ments, 334; and immigration, 161–62, 201

Chaney, James, 31

child care: and the gender revolution, 35, 43–48; revolutions, 122; and working wives, 134–36. See also children

children: and changes in American families, 108–50; economic status of, 119, 120, 121–22, 123, 124–28; below the poverty line, percentage of, 120; economic status of, 260; living arrangements of, racial comparisons for, 222, 223; living with one parent, 126; poor families with, lifted out of poverty by government interventions, 142. See also child care; family

China, 70, 152–53, 172–73, 176–77, 181–82, 189, 190–91, 197, 201

Christianity, 1, 22, 31, 152. See also Catholicism

civil rights movement, 3–4, 22, 208–71; and "America in decline" arguments, 11, 336–37; and Brown v. Board of Education, 30, 230, 350; and the Civil Rights Acts of 1866 and 1875, 27; and the Civil Rights Act of 1964, 4–5, 32–41, 238, 240, 337; and the Civil Rights Commission, 31, 269; and earnings, 71; and immigration laws, 152, 153, 204, 205, 207; and the 1960s, 22, 24–34; overview of, 24–34; and Plessy v. Ferguson, 28, 229, 248. See also segregation

Civil War, 27, 113, 273, 274, 281. See also Reconstruction era

Clark, William, 273

Clinton, Bill, 4, 12, 274

cohabitation, 6, 14; and changes in American families, 110–11, 112, 113–15, 125, 129, 130, 143; and childhood poverty, 125; new patterns of, 110–15 cohorts: advanced degrees earned by, listed by gender, **40**, 41; age/birth information for, **25**; and "America in decline" arguments, 13–14; attitudes about women's employment for, **47**; and changes in American families, 110, **111**; and divorce, 114–15; as key to understanding social change, 23–24; marital status of women by, **111**; percentage of full-time, year-round workers by, **42**; use of the term, 24. *See also specific cohorts*

college education: and "America in decline" arguments, 335, 337; and earnings, 106–7, 341–42, **342**, **351**, 352; and economic growth during the Reagan years, 95, **96**, 97, **98**, 99, 101, 105; and immigrants, **178–79**, 200, 203; and internal migration, **290**, **316**; rising cost of, 128. *See also* education

Columbia University, 26

Commission on the Status of Women, 38

communism, 155

computer technology, 86, 87, 106

Comstock laws, 55–56

Comstock, Anthony, 55

Connor, "Bull," 349

Constitution: Article I, 1; and birth control, 56–57; and the civil rights movement, 4, 22, 27, 274; Fifteenth Amendment, 4, 27, 274; Fourteenth Amendment, 27, 35, 205; Nineteenth Amendment, 35

construction industry, 34, 203, 270

consumer: expenditures for manufactured goods or services (1960–1994), 74; price index, 70–71, 84, 339–40

contraception. *See* birth control

Cook, Philip, 11

Cose, Ellis, 263

cost of living: and changes in American

families, 147; and economic shifts from 1973 to the present, 84

Council of Economic Advisors, 73–76, 79, 81, 84

crime, 20, 337–38

currency rates, 78, 80, 81

Darwinism, 16, 35, 152–53, 204, 223, 263

Daughters of the American Revolution (DAR), 29

Day of Reckoning: The Consequences of American Economic Policy (Friedman), 10

death rates, 21, 119, 121, 149, 154, 222–24, **225–28**

Declining Fortunes: The Withering of the American Dream (Newman), 13–14, 88

Defense Department, 31–32

defense spending, 7, 85, **149**, 331

deficit spending, 10, 21, 149

deindustrialization, 9, 102–3, 105

Deindustrialization of America, The (Bluestone and Harrison), 9

democracy, 1, 3, 32; and civil rights, 27; and immigration, 151, 153

Democratic Party, 11, 274

Denton, Nancy, 266

Department of Defense, 31–32

Department of Housing and Urban Development, 349–50

Depression, 7–8, 11, 84, 89, 354; and aspirations for standards of living, 340; birth rates during, 53; divorce rates during, 51; economic expansion after, 345; and immigration, 153, 155; incomes below the poverty standard during, **65–66**; and internal migration, 274, 277, 332; marriage rates since, **49–50**; the sexual division of labor during, 36; unemployment rate during, 8, 13, 29

Depression birth cohort, 23, 112, 115, 136

Dillingham Commission, 151, 153

Displaced Persons Act, 155

divorce, 6, 15; by birth cohort and age, 111; and changes in American families, 108–9, 113–15, 121, 125, 128–29, 131, 138, 141, 142–43; and childhood poverty, 125; divorced persons per 1,000 married-spouse persons, 52; increasing likelihood of, 113–15; international comparisons for, 141, 142–43; laws, 51; marriages ending in, 114; number of (1940–1995), 50; in the personal history of political candidates, 113; and the sexual revolution, 48–49, 51–53

Dole, Elizabeth, 352

Dole, Robert, 352

Douglass, Frederick, 22–23

DuBois, W.E.B., 23, 24–26, 28, 263

Dukakis, Michael, 298

Duncan, Dudley, 348

Earned Income Tax Credit, 346

earnings: average, 95, 100; and decisions made in adolescence/young adulthood, 99–101; declining, in the 1990s, 340–43; and economic growth during the Reagan years, 88, 89; and education, 97–99, 341–42, 342, 351, 352; and the gender gap, 337, 351; of married women, 135; of natives, impact of immigrants on, 199–204; racial comparisons for, 71, 189, 190–93, 238–40, 241, 242–43, 244, 245, 246–47, 248, 249, 250–51, 252–53; of recent immigrants, 183–85, 186, 187, 188–89, 190–93; after World War II, 71–72. See also income

Easterlin, Richard, 340

Eastern Airlines, 80

economic polarization thesis, 9–12

Economic Recovery Act, 85

Edsall, Thomas, 12

education: and "America in decline" arguments, 13–16, 21, 335, 337; assortive mating by, 16; and birth rates, 116; and Brown v. Board of Education, 30, 230, 350; and changes in American families, 116, 127–28, 135–36, 138; of children in two-parent vs. one-parent families, 127; and earnings, 97–99, 341–42, 342, 351, 352; and economic growth during the Reagan years, 95–97; and the economic trends of 1975–79, 83; and immigrants, 173, 175, 176–79, 181–82, 190, 199–203, 205–6; and income, 136; and internal migration, 289–91, 295, 316; labor force information by, 95, 96, 97; racial comparisons for, 228–30, 231, 232, 233, 234–35, 236–37, 238; rising cost of, 128; and standards of living, 13–14; of women, 5, 135–36. See also college education; high school education

Ehrenreich, Barbara, 15–17

Eisenhower, Dwight D., 31, 56, 68, 108, 330

elderly: and changes in American families, 120–21, 143–50; economic status of, 120–21, 143, 144, 145–50; poverty among, 120–21. See also retirement

elective office: blacks in, 270; women in, 44–45

employment: and changes in American families, 122–28, 137, 138–40, 141; and economic growth during the Reagan years, 93–97; and economic shifts from 1973 to the present, 73–76; and the economic status of children, 122–28; full, 21, 68–69, 137; growth, metropolitan areas ranked by, 306–7, 309; of immigrants, 154, 180, 183–93, 193–97; by industry, 92; international comparisons for, 141; of natives, impact of immigrants on,

employment (continued)
199–204; by occupation, 94; percentage of changes in, and internal migration, 303; percentage of, per capita hours worked, and average earnings (1970–1990), 100; racial comparisons for, 238–40, 241, 242–43, 244, 245, 246–47, 248, 249, 250–51, 252–53; ratio of working age to retirement age persons, 148

End of Affluence: The Causes and Consequences of America's Economic Decline, The (Madrick), 11, 88

engineering, 39, 40, 41, 90, 91, 92, 155

England, 164, 165, 166. See also Britain

English-language abilities, 173–74, 175, 185, 190, 193, 196–97

entrepreneurs: and "America in decline" arguments, 9; blacks as, 199; and economic growth during the Reagan years, 85; immigrants as, 197–99, 201

Equal Employment Opportunity Commission (EEOC), 238–39, 269

Equal Pay Act, 38

Espenshade, Thomas J., 200

eugenicists, 16

Evers, Medger, 31

exchange rates, 78

Executive Orders: Executive Order 8802, 29; Executive Order 9981, 30; Executive Order 11246, 239

extramarital sex, 58–63

Fair Housing Act (1968), 4, 277, 329

Falling from Grace: The Experience of Downward Mobility in the American Middle Class (Newman), 12–13

families: changes in, 108–50; and the economic status of the elderly, 120–21, 143–50; and the implications of the changing living arrangements of children, 119–28; international comparisons of, 141, 142, 143; and new fertility patterns, 115–19; and new patterns of marriage and cohabitation, 111–15; new structure of, in the 1990s, 343–45; number of, by type, 109; reunification of, and immigration, 158. See also single-parent families

Family Planning Services and Population Research Act, 56

Farmer, James, 31

Feagin, Joe, 263

Fear of Falling: The Inner Life of the Middle Class (Ehrenreich), 15–16

Federal Communications Commission, 38

Federal Glass Ceiling Commission, 352

Federal Home Administration, 67

Federal National Mortgage Association, 68

Federal Order (No.) 213, 36

Federal Reserve Board, 84, 353

Feminine Mystique, The (Friedan), 5, 38–39

fertility: and changes in American families, 115–19; among immigrants, 172–73; patterns, and intelligence levels, 16; racial comparisons of, 118, 220–21, 222; rates, and Social Security/Medicare trust funds, 148. See also birth rates; out-of-wedlock births

Fifteenth Amendment, 4, 27, 274

finance, 90, 91, 92, 155

FIRE industries, 90–92, 105

Fix, Michael, 200, 202

Food and Drug Administration, 53

Fourteenth Amendment, 27, 35, 205

France, 142, 143

Frank, Robert, 11

Frey, William, 329

Friedan, Betty, 5, 39

Friedman, Benjamin, 10

full employment, 21, 68–69, 137

full-time employees, 78, 88, 103; and changes in American families, 123, 125; percentage of, 42

Fullilove v. Klutznik, 268
fundamentalism, 152

Garreau, Joel, 332
GDP (gross domestic product), 67, 80,
  81, 87, 106
gender: advanced degrees listed by, **40**;
  and earnings, 72, 192, 337, 341,
  351–52, **351**; and education, 95,
  96, 97; employment by industry,
  listed by, **92**; employment by occupation, listed by, **94**; gap in earnings, 72, 337, 341, 351–52; labor
  force participation by, **42**, 76, 77,
  78, 95, 96, 97; percentage of full-
  time, year-round workers by, **42**.
  See also gender revolution; wom-
  en's employment
gender revolution, 32–63; and the Civil
  Rights Act of 1964, 4, 32–41; and
  full-time employment for women,
  39–41, **42**, **43**; and new attitudes
  about combining work and child-
  raising, 43–48. *See also* gender
Generation X cohort, 24–25, 41, 351;
  advanced degrees earned by, **40**;
  age/birth information for, **25**; and
  aspirations for specific standards
  of living, 340; and attitudes about
  childrearing, 45, **46**, **47**; and attitudes about women's employment,
  47; and changes in American families, 110, **111**, 112, 113, 140, 344;
  and declining earnings, in the
  1990s, 342; and the gender revolution, 41; and the housing market,
  145; marriage/divorce data for, 49,
  111, 113; and racial issues, 208–9,
  349; and the sexual revolution, 54,
  59, 62
genetics, 16–17
Germany: family status in, **141**; immigrants from, 162, **165**, 166; poor
  families lifted out of poverty in, by
  government intervention, **142**; and
  World War II, 4, 31–32, 67, 70

Gini index, **343**, 353
Glass Ceiling Act, 352
Glazer, Nathan, 26–27
gold standard, 80
Goldin, Claudia, 36
Goldwater, Barry, 34
Goodman, Andrew, 31
grandparents of the baby boom, 24; age/
  birth information for **25**; migration
  data for, **314–15**; percentage of
  full-time, year-round workers for,
  42, **43**
Great U-Turn, The (Bluestone and Har-
  rison), 9, 78
Greeley, Horace, 284
Greenberg, Stanley, 12
green card holders, 159
Green Revolution, 72, 83
Griggs v. Duke Power, 239
Griswold v. Connecticut, 56–57

Hamilton, Alexander, 51
Harlan, John, 270
Harrison, Bennett, 8–9, 17, 78, 88, 101–
  2
Hauser, Robert, 234
Head Start, 346
health care, 8; and economic shifts from
  1973 to the present, 90, **91**, 92–
  93, **94**; for immigrants, 205, 206;
  increased spending on, 73–75, 90,
  105
Hernandez, Donald J., 121–22
Herrnstein, Richard, 16–17
high school education, 335; and earnings, **342**, 351, 352; and economic
  growth during the Reagan years,
  95, **96**, 97, **98**, 99; and immigration, **178–79**, 200, 203; and income, 136; and internal migration,
  291, **316**; racial comparisons for,
  208, 232, **233**, 234–35, **236–37**.
  See also education
Hispanics, 71, 347–50; and education,
  261; employment/earnings data
  for, **242–43**, 245–46, **247**, **250–51**,

Hispanics *(continued)*
  252; fertility data for, **220–21**, 222;
  immigration of, 163, 172, 177,
  182, 185; internal migration of,
  294, 327, 329; marital status of,
  219, **264–65**; mortality rates for,
  222–24; poverty rates for, 257–
  59
Hitler, Adolf, 32
Hochschild, Arlie, 15, 134
homeless, 12, 20, 354
homeownership, 345; and economic
  growth, after World War II, 65, 67;
  and the middle class, 65. *See also*
  housing
homosexuality, 6, 55, 140, 344; changes
  in attitudes about, 58–63; laws
  banning, 57–58
households: distribution of, by type,
  129, **130**, 131; income data for,
  133–34, 336, **353**; living arrange-
  ments/economic status, of men and
  women aged 65 and older, **144**;
  and marital status, **217–21**, 222;
  size, for recent immigrants, 182;
  types, definition of, 129; wealth
  distribution, 336, **353**. *See also*
  marriage
housing, 7–8; and civil rights, 32–34,
  349–50; and economic growth
  after World War II, 67–68; market,
  and the economic status of the elderly, 145; rising cost of, 128; status, polarization of, 354. *See also*
  homeownership
Howard University, 350
Hughes, Langston, 26, 28

IBM (International Business Machines),
  315
illegal aliens, 157–58, 160–61, 202,
  204–5
immigrants: admitted for permanent
  residence, **156–57**; age distribution
  of, 172–73; characteristics of recent, 172–93; earnings of, 183–85;

186, 187–93; economic status of
  recent, 182, **183**; and education,
  173, 175, **176–79**, 181–82, 190,
  199–203, 205–6, 230; English-language abilities of, 173–74, **175**,
  185, 190, 193, 196–97; entrepreneurial activity among, 197–99,
  201; impact of, upon the employment and earnings of natives, 199–
  204; jobs filled by, 179–81, 193–
  97; labor market characteristics of,
  188–89; location of, in the United
  States, 164–71; number of, by
  state, **164**, **170**; occupations of,
  154–55, 179–81, 193, **194–95**,
  196–97; origin of, 162, **163**, 164,
  165; as a percentage of the total
  population, **167**, **176**; self-employment data for, **198**. *See also* immigration
immigration, 151–207; and "America
  in decline" arguments, 334, 335;
  efforts to control the flow of, 159–
  62; numerical limits on, 154; and
  population growth, 160–61; and
  racial inequalities, 347–50; today,
  155–71. *See also* immigrants
Immigration and Naturalization Service
  (INS), 158, 160, 161, 204
Immigration Reform and Control Act
  (IRCA), 156–57, 159–60, 202, 206
income: and changes in American families, 122–28, 134–36, 138–40; and
  economic growth during the
  Reagan years, 88–89, 105–6; and
  the economic status of children,
  122–28; Gini index for, **343**, **353**;
  by household type, **133–134**; of
  immigrants, 197, **198**, 199; inequality of, growing, 352–54; median household, 21; per capita, 73,
  88, 254–55, **256**, 335–36, 342–43;
  of persons age 65 and over (1990),
  288; pre-tax cash data for, 65, **66**;
  rise in, after 1982, 88; and working
  wives, 134–36. *See also* earnings

India, 165, 166, 172, 181, 183, 189, 207

industry: employment by, 92; percentage of changes in employment in, and internal migration, 303. *See also* automobile industry; manufacturing

inflation, 128, 145; and economic growth after World War II, 70–71, 78; and economic shifts from 1973 to the present, 78, 80, 82, 84–85; sindexing of Social Security for, 147, 148, 285; and interest rates, 84

intelligence tests, 16–17

interest rate(s), 70, 78; adoption of high, 83–89; and economic growth during the Reagan years, 85; and economic shifts from 1973 to the present, 80, 81; payments, percentage of government spending devoted to, 149

intermarriage, 35, 262, **264–65**

international competition, 8, 10, 70

internationalization, of markets/production, 13, 75

IQ scores, 16–17

IRAs (individual retirement accounts), 336

Ireland, 162, **165**, 166

Italy: family status in, **141**; immigrants from, 152, 154–55, 162, 164, **165**, 166, 173, 177

Jackson, Kenneth, 275

Janus Report, 61

Japan: and the automobile industry, 8, 75, 81; immigrants from, 153, 177, 207; mortality rates in, **228**; and World War II, 4, 32, 67, 70

Jefferson, Thomas, 1, 280

Jews: and immigration, 151–52, 155, 163–64; and intellectual ability, 16–17; war crimes against, 31

Jim Crow laws, 4, 26–32, 229, 238, 259, 263, 270, 336

job growth, 73, 101–4; by hourly wage rates, **103**; metropolitan areas ranked by, **306–7, 309**

Johnson, Lyndon B., 11, 32, 346; and discrimination in hiring, 348; Executive Order 11246, 239; Howard University speech (1964), 350; and the Kerner Commission, 327; and the Office of Federal Contract Compliance, 239, 268; and the Medicare bill, 285; War on Poverty initiated by, 17, 19, 56, 119, 124, 347, 348

Judeo-Christian tradition, 22, 31. *See also* Christianity; Jews

"Judgment at Nuremburg" (movie), 31

Justice Department, 32, 161

Kasarda, John, 18–19, 197, 199, 266, 301

Kennedy, John F., 23, 38, 75, 129; campaign against Nixon (1960), 68; and civil rights, 32

Kerner Commission, 327, 329

King, Martin Luther, Jr., 4, 30–31, 34, 37

Kinsey studies, 61

Kirshenman, Joleen, 349

Korea: immigrants from, 158, **165**, 166, 172, 177, 197, **198**, 199, 201; and world markets, 70

Korean War, 68, 158

Krugman, Paul, 10, 88

Ku Klux Klan Act, 27

labor: availability of cheap, outside the U.S., 13, 75; law, and *Mueller* v. *Oregon*, 35–36. *See also* labor force participation; labor market

labor force participation: gender changes in, 69, 72, 76, 77, 78; for men/women aged 25–54, educational attainment by, 95, **96**, 97

labor market: and the gender revolution, 35–37; immigrants in, 183–87, **188–89**, 190–93, 206

Lasch, Christopher, 48
late baby boom cohort: and aspirations for specific standards of living, 340; birth rates for, 116, **220**; and earnings, 99; and education, 235; and the housing market, 145; marital status of, by race, **219**
Latin America, 21, 27, 69, 152, 154–55, 161–62, **163**, 164, **165**, 166, 173, 177, 181–82, 189, 191–92, 196, 199, 204
layoffs, during the Reagan years, 105
Lazarus, Emma, 153
legal profession, 39, **40**, 41, 90, **91**, 92
Levy, Frank, 106, 339
Lewis, Meriweather, 273
life span/life expectancy, 75, 149
literacy tests, 151
Losing Ground: American Social Policy (Murray), 17–18
Louis, Joe, 29
Louisiana Purchase, 272–73
Loving v. *Virginia,* 35
Low Income Energy Assistance program, 346
lynchings, 28, 35

McCain, Franklin, 30
McCarran-Walter law, 155, **156**
McDonald, John, 113
McLanahan, Sara, 52, 126–27, 138–39, 142
McNeil, Joseph, 30
Madrick, Jeffry, 11, 88
managerial jobs, percentage of recent immigrants in, **180**
manufactured goods: consumer expenditures for, **74**; exported, minus value of imported, **74**. *See also* manufacturing
manufacturing, 8, 19, 354; and economic growth after World War II, 69, 70, 71; and economic shifts from 1973 to the present, 85–87, 90–92, 101, 104, 105; employees, index of output per hour for, **82**;

employment in the 1990s, 106; and immigration, **180**, 200–201; and the internationalization of production, 75, 81; shift away from, 73–76; shift from agriculture to, 7, 72. *See also* manufactured goods
Mariel boatlift, 200
marriage(s): bans, 35, 36; and changes in American families, 108–50; first, number of (1940–1995), **50**; and immigration, 158; interracial, 35, 262, **264–65**; and labor force participation, 77–78; and *Loving* v. *Virginia,* 35; marital status of women, by birth cohort and age, **111**; new patterns of, 110–15; racial comparisons for, **264–65**; and the sexual revolution, 48–54; ending in divorce, **114**; traditional responses to questions about, **44, 46**. *See also* age at marriage; divorce; family
Marriage Fraud Act, 158
Martin, Teresa Castro, 113
Massey, Douglas, 266
Mayo Clinic, 155
Mead, Lawrence, 18
Medicaid, 205
Medicare, 23, 147–50; bill (1965), 285; and internal migration, 287; percentage of government spending devoted to, **149**, 347
Mercedes-Benz, 301, 332
metropolitan areas, 322–26; internal migration rates for, **311**, **314–15**, 321; percent change in population of, by region, **324**; population of, immigrants as a percentage of, 169, **170**; racial/ethnic composition of, **328**; ranked by job growth, **306–7**, **309**
Mexico, 154, 157, 159, 161–62, **163**, 164, **165**, 166, 171–73, 176–77, 181, 183, 189, 191–92, 199–201, 207
Miami Herald, 196

middle class: and "America in decline" arguments, 8–10, 11–14, 15–16, 20, 334; black, 3, 4, 20, 29–30, 253–54; creation of, after World War II, 64–65; and economic growth during the Reagan years, 88; and economic shifts from 1973 to the present, 73, 88, 354; and new family living arrangements, in the 1990s, 344; and the 1960s, 23; and pre-tax cash income, 65, **66**; rise of, 7–8, 64–65, 68; and the sexual revolution, 48–49; and working wives, 134–36

Middle Class Dreams: The Politics and Power of the New American Majority (Greenberg), 12

migration, 272–333; by age/cohort, **284, 287**; and education, **289–91**, 295; gains/losses, by race, **321**; and immigration, 203; of non-Hispanic blacks, **293**; by region, **280, 283–84, 296**; status of persons aged 5 and over (1990), **286**

military: homosexuals in, 58; segregation in, 3–4, 30; spending, 7, 85, **149, 331**

Mill, John Stuart, 23

Miller, William, 84, 114

Million Man March, 208, 270, 271

Mills, Wilbur, 147, 285

minimum wage laws, 202

misery index, 85

Model Cities programs, 346

Montgomery bus segregation ordinance, 4, 30, 32

mortality rates, 21, 119, 121, 149, 154, 222–24, **225–28**

mortgage interest rates, 84

Moynihan, Daniel Patrick, 26–27, 267–68

Muller, Thomas, 200

Mueller v. *Oregon,* 35–36

Murray, Charles, 16–18, 119

Myers, Dowell, 354

Myrdal, Gunnar, 266

NAACP (National Association for the Advancement of Colored People), 3, 30–31, 38, 302

National Center for Health Data, 227

National Crime Victimization Survey, 337

National Opinion Research Center, 43–44, 112

National Origins quotas, 153, 162

National Socialist Party, 31

National Study of Family Growth, 62

Native Americans. *See* American Indians

Nazism, 31, 32

Neckerman, Kathryn, 349

Negative Income Tax, 346

Netherlands, **141, 142,** 143

Newman, Katherine, 12–14, 45, 88

New Politics of Inequality, The (Edsall), 12

New York Consolidated Metropolitan Statistical Area (CMSA), 169–71, 304

New York Times, 196

Nineteenth Amendment, 35

Nixon, Richard M., 11, 21, 274, 346, 348; abolition of the gold standard by, 80; campaign against Kennedy (1960), 68; and the Philadelphia Plan, 239, 268

Norton, Arthur J., 114

Occupational Safety and Health Administration, 202

occupations: and economic growth during the Reagan years, 93–95; employment by, **94**; of immigrants, 154–55, 179–81, 193, **194–95,** 196–97

O'Connor, Sandra Day, 41

Office of Federal Contract Compliance, 239, 268

Ogbu, John, 266

oil production, 7, 64–65, 67, 71, 78, 80, 83–84, 339

Open Housing Act, 34

Organization of Petroleum Exporting Companies (OPEC), 64, 67
Orshansky, Molly, 253
out-of-wedlock births, 116–19, 122, 125–26, 136
Overworked American: The Unexpected Decline of Leisure (Schor), 14

Pacific Islanders, **215**, 260–61
Panama Canal Company, 158
Pan American Airlines, 80
Parks, Rosa, 4, 30, 32
part-time employees, 78, **123**
Passel, Jeffrey, 161, 200, 202
Pearl Harbor, attack on (1941), 36
Pendelton, Clarence, 269
Penn Central Railroad, 80
per capita income, 73, 88, 255, **256**, 335–36, 342–43
Philadelphia Plan, 239, 268
Philippines, 163–64, **165**, 166, 172–73, 177, 178, 181
Phillips, Kevin, 11–12
Plessy v. *Ferguson*, 28, 229, 248
Poland, 164
Postal Service (United States), 55
poverty, 345–34; and "America in decline," arguments, 9–10, 12, 16–20; and changes in American families, 108, 119–28, 131, 142–50; childhood, 119–28; data by household type, **133–34**; and economic growth during the Reagan years, 88, 89; and the elderly, 143–50; and immigrants, 182–83; international comparisons for, **141**, 142, 143; percent of the population below the poverty line, **120**; and pre-tax cash income, 65, **66**; racial comparisons for, 253–54, **254–55**, 257, **258**, 259
Powell, Colin, 208, 270
premarital sex, 49, 58–63
Presser, Harriet, 15, 124
Preston, Samuel H., 113
privacy rights, 54–58

private sector employees, output per hour for, **82**
productivity: and economic shifts from 1973 to the present, 82–83, 104–7; during the Reagan years, 86–88; after World War II, 69–72
property ownership, 30. *See also* home-ownership

race, 208–71; identity, of immigrants, 172; internal migration data by, **293–95**; issues, and gender issues, difference between, 15–16, 35, 37; and minority contractors, 270. *See also* civil rights movement; specific racial groups
Randolph, A. Philip, 29
Reagan, Ronald (Reagan administration), 9–10, 84–89, 105; and the issue of divorce, 113; and military spending, 331
recession(s), 7–8; and economic shifts from 1973 to the present, 78, **79**, 80, **81–82**; of 1981–1982, 84–85, 87–89; and stagnating wages, 78, **79**
Reconstruction era, 22, 27, 31, 34, 38
Reengineering the Corporation (Hammer and Champy), 106
Reform Immigration Act of 1965, 153
refugees, 155, 157–59, 164
Regents of the University of California v. *Bakke*, 268
religion: Catholicism, 55–56, 151, 162; and immigration, 151–52, 155, 204. *See also* Christianity
Republican Party, 11–12, 32, 113
residential segregation, 28, 32–35, 349–50, 262, 266, **267**
restructuring, corporate, 13, 106
retail trade industry, **91**, 92, 105
retirement, 143–47, **148**, 149–50. *See also* elderly; Social Security
Revolutionary era, 22, 27, 162, 272, 281
Richmond, David, 30

Robeson, Paul, 26
Robinson, Jackie, 29
Rockefeller, Nelson, 113
Roe v. *Wade*, 23, 57, 60
Roosevelt, Eleanor, 29, 38
Roosevelt, Franklin D., 29, 119
Russia: immigrants from, 164, **165**, 166, 181, 190; mortality rates in, 227, **228**
Ryder, Norman, 53

Sandefur, Gary, 126–27
Sanger, Margaret, 55, 56
Scandinavia, 162
Schmelling, Max, 29
school(s): hiring of women in, 36; segregation, 30, 32–34, 35. *See also* education
Schor, Juliet, 14, 124
Schwerner, Michael, 31
segregation: on buses, 32–34, 35; residential, 28, 32–34, 35, 349–50, 262, 266, **267**; of schools, 30, 32–34, 35. *See also* Jim Crow laws
self-employment, 197, **198**, 199
Sex in America Survey, 112
sex, -role attitudes, 43, **42**, 43–45, **46–47**, 48. *See also* gender
sexual division of labor, 36, 43–48
sexuality: activity of young women in three cohorts, **62**; answers to questions about three types of, **59**; and *Bowers* v. *Hardwick*, 58; changes in attitudes about, 58–63; and changes in American families, 137, 138, 140, 343–44; and *Griswold* v. *Connecticut*, 56–57; privatization of, 54–58; and the sexual revolution, 5–6, 22, 48–54
Sikes, Melvin, 263
Simpson, O. J., 208, 270
single-parent families, 108, **109**, 110, 129, 138; international comparisons for, **141**, **142**, 143; and poverty, 119, 121–25, 127, 131, 136
slavery, 3–4, 35, 263

Slavs, 152, 154
Smith, Howard, 37, 38
Smith, James, 248
Social Darwinism, 16, 35, 152–53, 204, 223, 263
Social Security, 23, 121, 124, 253; and immigrants, 201, 206; and internal migration, 285, 286, 287; payments, increase in, 146–50, 346; payments, and poverty lines, **146**; percentage of government spending devoted to, **149**, 347; trust fund, 148
standard of living, 334–35, 340; and "America in decline" arguments, 13–14, 15; and the 1960s, 24
Steele, James, 10
steel industry, 86, 92
Stonewall Rebellion, 57–58
suburbs, 151, 322–26; blacks in, 327, **328**, 329–30; internal migration data for, **324**; population change, **328**; racial/ethnic composition of, **328**; rise of, after World War II, 65, 68
Supplemental Security Income (SSI), 18, 124, 173, 205, 346
Supreme Court: appointments to, 4; *Baker* v. *Carr*, 331; *Brown* v. *Board of Education*, 30, 230, 350; *Griswold* v. *Connecticut*, 56–57; *Loving* v. *Virginia*, 35; *Mueller* v. *Oregon*, 35–36; *Plessy* v. *Ferguson*, 28, 229, 248; *Regents of the University of California* v. *Bakke*, 268; *Roe* v. *Wade*, 23, 57, 60; *Tileston* v. *Ullman*, 55; *United Steelworkers of America* v. *Weber*, 268
Sweden, **141**, **142**, 143

Taiwan, **228**
taxation, 10, 85, 90–92; and anti-poverty programs, 346–47; and declining earnings, in the 1990s, 341; and immigration, 204–6; and migration, 325, 326, 332; for Social

taxation (continued)
Security and Medicare, 148, 149, 150
technological change, 86–87, 105–6, 154–55, 341, 343
Thomas, Clarence, 269
Tileston v. Ullman, 55
Till, Emmett, 31
Tocqueville, Alexis de, 208
trade, balance of, 75–76, 77
Treasury Department, 148
Truly Disadvantaged: The Inner City, the Underclass, and Public Policy (Wilson), 19–20
Truman, Harry S, 30, 153

underclass, 17–20, 185
unemployment, 4, 7–9, 10, 340; annual, 81, 340; during the Depression, 8, 13, 29; and economic shifts from 1973 to the present, 80, 81, 83, 88; and immigration, 187, 189; racial comparisons for, 189, 240, 241, 242–43, 244; after World War II, 68–69
unions: air traffic controller, 87; decline of, 12, 14, 87; and economic growth during the Reagan years, 102; and immigration, 154; and labor productivity, 86
United Kingdom, 141, 142
United Nations, 155
United Steelworkers of America v. Weber, 268
University of Chicago. See National Opinion Research Center
University of Pennsylvania, 24
University of Texas, 312
U.S.-Canada Free Trade Act, 160
U.S. Steel, 239

Veteran's Administration, 23, 67
Victorian age, 55
Vietnam, immigrants from, 164, 165, 166, 173, 181
Vietnam War, 68, 83

Virgin Islands, 158
Volcker, Paul, 84
voting: and Baker v. Carr, 331; blocs, and immigrants, 151; rights, 4, 27–28, 34–35, 205

wage(s): average hourly/weekly, 79, 343; and changes in American families, 119, 125, 136–37; and childhood poverty, 125; and economic growth after World War II, 69–72; and economic shifts from 1973 to the present, 73–76, 78, 79, 88, 102; and education, 136; and equal pay for women, 37–38; Gini index of, 343, 353; hourly, job growth by, 103; for immigrants, 184–87, 196, 206; of natives, impact of immigrants on, 199–204
War of 1812, 272
War on Poverty, 17, 19, 56, 119, 124, 347, 348
Warren, Earl, 350
Welch, Finis, 248
welfare, 12; and "America in decline" arguments, 17–18, 20; and changes in American families, 121, 137–40, 143; and fertility patterns, 16; and immigrants, 206. See also Aid to Families with Dependent Children (AFDC); War on Poverty
Westoff, Charles, 53
Wetzel, James, 104
white(s): education data for, 228–30, 231, 232, 233, 234–35, 236–37, 238; employment/earnings data for, 184–85, 186, 238–40, 241, 242–43, 244, 245, 246–47, 248, 249, 250–51, 252–53; fertility data for, 220–21, 222; and intellectual ability, 16–17; and intermarriage, 262, 264–65; marriage rates for, 110; mortality rates for, 222–24, 225–28; percentage of, giving the equal opportunity response to questions about racial equity, 33;

poverty data for, 253, **254**, 257, **258**, 259

white-collar workers: and "America in decline" arguments, 13; and economic shifts from 1973 to the present, 90, **91**, **94**, 106, 341; and labor productivity, 86; retirement of, 146

Wilson, William Julius, 18–20, 266

Wolch, Jennifer, 354

Women, Infants and Children program, 346

women's employment, 4–5, 134–36; attitudes about, for birth cohorts, **47**; traditional responses to questions about, **44**, **46**. *See also* gender

work ethic, 19

World War I, 28, 153, 292, 302

World War II: Defense Department research on racial attitudes during, 31–32; employment of women during, 36; marriage rates after, 49; rationing of gasoline during, 64; segregated armed forces during, 3–4. *See also* World War II cohort

World War II cohort: advanced degrees earned by, listed by gender, **40**; age/birth information for, **25**; attitudes about women's employment for, **47**; earnings data, 99, 101; marriage/divorce data for, **111**; and the 1960s, 24; percentage of full-time, year-round workers for, **42**; sexual activity of young women in, **62**

year-round workers, percentage of, **42**

Zangwill, Israel, 152